Also by Patricia Garfield, Ph.D.

Creative Dreaming

Pathway to Ecstasy: The Way of the Dream Mandala

Your Child's Dreams

Women's Bodies, Women's Dreams

Patricia Garfield, Ph.D.

Ballantine Books
New York

Library of Congress Catalog Card Number: 87-91556

ISBN: 0-345-33905-3

Cover design by James R. Harris
Photograph: Image Bank/Karl Hentz
Text design by Beth Tondreau Design/Carol Barr

Manufactured in the United States of America

First Edition: August 1988

10 9 8 7 6 5 4 3 2 1

To my godmother, Kathryn Lee,
who provided far more than my middle name.
Her vital involvement with helping others has been
a lifelong inspiration.

CONTENTS

ACKNOWLEDGMENTS

This book owes its existence to the generosity of many people; I am grateful to all of them.

In particular I wish to thank the fifty women who participated in the study. They opened their lives, their hearts, and their hidden experiences, as well as their dreams. Since their identities have been concealed by code names and minor changes made in identifying material in their dream reports, their characteristics as a group are described in detail in the appendix; they remain anonymous in the text.

Other women who were not part of the formal study liberally shared their dreams. Workshop participants, too, in various programs in America, Canada, England, and the Netherlands gave bountifully of their dream experiences. They helped me to grasp the difference between the aspects of dreams that are partially cultural and those that are integral to each woman's life.

Professionals endorsed the project with enthusiasm. I appreciate the time John Kerner, chief of gynecology at Mount Zion Hospital in San Francisco, took from his busy schedule to comment and make suggestions. Angela Wesling of the Mount Zion Medical Library, along with her staff, were energetic in their search of the literature for useful references.

Joëlle Delbourgo, editor in chief of trade paperbacks at Ballantine, encouraged the project from its early inception. Alice Fahs, my editor, provided a tactful blend of critical suggestion and support. Suzanne Gluck, my agent at International Creative Management, embraced the project with zeal. My appreciation goes out to these helpful hands.

Friends and colleagues were invaluable. Roger Broughton, of the School of Medicine at the University of Ottawa, who has maintained a steady interest in my work, was ever watchful for slips from the correct state of knowledge in sleep and dream research (although any remaining errors are my responsibility). Stephen LaBerge, of the Stanford University Sleep Clinic, shared his knowledge of the Macintosh computer, along with his expertise on sleep and lucid dreaming. Jayne Gackenbach-Snyder, current president-elect of the Association for the Study of Dreams, working at the University of Northern Iowa, cheered the project forward as well as contributing her own dream reports. Patricia Maybruck gave liberally from her expertise in the area of pregnancy dreams.

Other friends were lavish with their assistance in reading drafts of the chapters in order to offer responses and suggestions. Over lunch, on the telephone, after a movie, they gave me their thoughts and dream accounts.

Family members, likewise, were emotionally sustaining. My aunt Kathryn Lee, to whom this book is dedicated, has been a lifelong inspiration. As godmother, she was ever-giving throughout my childhood. As a social worker, she toiled unstintingly to help hundreds of others. Still vital in her eighties, she is a remarkable model of what a woman can accomplish.

My mother, Evelyn Goff, shared numerous records from her long-standing dream diary. Without her initial interest in dreams during my early teens, I would never have begun recording my dreams at age fourteen nor gone on to develop an extensive professional study of the subject.

My daughter Cheryl, now herself a mother of son Nicholas, volunteered her dreams throughout her pregnancy, bringing back the whole process of motherhood in luminous color. Other "children"—Wendy, Linda, and Steven—as well as their mates, contributed dream experiences.

As always, my husband, Zal—the guiding light in my life for the past twenty years—illuminated my plans and production. As a psychotherapist whose schedule is full-to-bursting, he still managed to find time to review an occasional chapter or lift my spirit when it drooped. He consulted me, as well, on many of his patients' dreams, helping me to comprehend the differences in dreaming between ordinary daily coping and crisis level. He provided the title for this book. He is living proof that man and woman can indeed fulfill each other.

To all these, my love and my thanks.

San Francisco
January 1988

Women's dreams are special: their dreams change as their bodies change. I have watched this transformation in my own dreams over almost forty years.

The subject of dreams has intrigued me since childhood—some of my earliest memories are of dreams. Shortly after I reached puberty at thirteen, I began recording into diaries the vivid images from my nightly adventures. At that time my mother was avidly reading the works of Sigmund Freud and Carl Jung; at the dinner table, she described their ideas regarding dreams. Curious to see whether my own dreams were messages to myself, I started to write them down and associate to the images within them. I found that, with each dream, I learned something new about my emotional responses to everyday life.

This practice of dreamwork became so rewarding that I have continued it ever since. From about age fourteen to my current age of fifty-three, I have continued to record my dreams and to contemplate the symbolism of their pictures. At first the entries in my dream journal were sporadic—only when something struck me as important was it given permanent form. There are a mere handful of dream entries for 1948; in 1949, when I turned fifteen, there are nearly one hundred dreams described and dated. For almost forty years my dream journal has been a constant companion. As I married, became a mother, divorced and remarried, I found that my dreams were a source of self-reflection and understanding. They helped support me through difficult times.

It was when I was a graduate student in the doctoral program in clinical psychology at Temple University in Philadelphia that I came to realize how unique my lifelong dream collection was. Freud himself destroyed his dream journals;[1] only a portion of Jung's dreams are publicly available—mainly from a four-year period of intense concentration on them.[2]

While my professional interest in dreams intensified, so did my dream recording. I trained myself to awaken at the end of each of the four or five dream periods throughout the night and found out how to record the dream in the dark with my eyes closed.[3] My diaries became tomes that today overspill two long shelves in my bookcase—more than thirty-six separate volumes, with many hundreds of dreams still in rough note form, not yet transcribed into the permanent binders.

Since the sheer size of the raw dream material was overwhelming, I wanted to understand better the patterns I sensed forming within this mass. Thus I began to write books. For me, to write is to discover.

The first book I wrote was *Creative Dreaming*.[4] In 1974, when it was published, the prevailing idea was that dreams are experiences occurring during sleep that only afterwards may be analyzed and worked with by professionals. Dreams were out of the province of the average dreamer; it was said that they could not be influenced by the dreamer and that dream style changed little over a lifetime. I knew this was not true.

Working with my own dreams since my teenage years had taught me much about myself. Each dreamer, I believed, could benefit from understanding his or her own dreams. As I experienced different life events, I observed my dreams changing.

With my second husband, I traveled extensively throughout Europe, the Middle East and the Far East. During these travels I was exposed to non-Western concepts of dreaming that asserted one could get ready to dream and could change one's behavior within a dream, as well as work with dreams after the fact. My dreams shifted even more. I discovered ways of becoming "conscious" during a dream; these lucid dreams allowed me, from time to time, to change dream scenarios at will. To my usual college schedule of teaching introductory and advanced psychology courses, I added an innovative course on dreaming.

These various experiences led to *Creative Dreaming*, in which I review the ways diverse cultures deal with dreams and show how each dreamer can use dreams to benefit waking life. At that time such ideas were quite new in the American culture. The fact that *Creative Dreaming* became a best-seller on the *Los Angeles Times* list, that it remains in print over a dozen years later, and has been published in eight foreign editions, including Japanese, indicates that other dreamers welcomed these ideas. I was invited to lecture on dreams throughout this country and abroad, to give dream workshops and seminars, to appear on national television shows, and to serve as a consultant on dreams for broadcasting systems, for advertising agencies, and for other professionals.

A few years later, in 1979, my second book, *Pathway to Ecstasy: The Way of the Dream Mandala*, appeared.[5] It was a result of my exploration of the imagery in my long dream journal and the relationship of these symbols to certain meditative techniques of self-development. I was able to uncover a pattern in lucid dreaming. Fifty Chinese brush paintings that I made of my dream images served as illustrations. This book found a narrower but devoted audience in the United States and abroad; it now appears in a Swiss-German translation.

Curious to understand the origins of dreaming, I spent two years interviewing children ages five to twelve about their dreams. The result was *Your Child's Dreams*, in 1984, which summarizes the most common nightmares and happy dream themes I found, gives their probable meanings, and offers guidance for coping with children's bad dreams.[6] This work has been widely used by child therapists and pediatricians, as well as by parents and teachers, and it now appears in French, Dutch, and Swiss-German versions.

The present book evolved from these previous works. I have long felt that women's dreams are distinctive. But how? The material currently available on this subject is generally based upon special populations—college students, pregnant women, divorced women, or hospitalized patients. I wanted to know what the average healthy woman's dreams were like. How does the woman past her college years dream? What dreams are characteristic of each stage of life? Much of the literature seemed limited in scope and inaccessible to the nonprofessional.

When I first picked Calvin Hall's and Robert Van de Castle's *The Content Analysis of Dreams* off the shelf in a London bookshop, I trembled with anticipation.[7] After a few hours of reading, I was bored with my favorite topic and had learned nothing that was useful to my personal dream life. True, I have used this book many times since as a reference, but it lacked the warmth, the love of dreams, the excitement of self-discovery that I knew to be part of dreaming.

Much of the literature, like this work, consists of lists of objects appearing in dreams of specialized groups. It seems to have little relevance to the normal woman who wants to understand her own dreams. Thus I undertook to examine the broad picture of women's dreams myself.

I think that women have a unique contribution to make to the study of dreams. As a woman, one who has matured to menarche, married, given birth to a daughter, nursed, raised a child, taken professional training, worked, divorced, remarried, gone through menopause, and lived to see my daughter give birth to a son, I feel I have something to say about the experience of women's dreams. These things cannot be said in the same way by a man, simply because he has not directly lived through these experiences. As a dreamer myself, in addition to being a dream expert, I have a rare knowledge about women's dreams. So, too, all women have something to contribute to our knowledge of this significant area of life.

For the purpose of this book, I interviewed fifty women in depth about their personal life and their dreams. These women represent, on the whole, a wide range of ages, from early twenties to early nineties; they come from a broad geographical area; they follow diverse religious faiths; they are predominantly upper-middle class in education and occupation; all are heterosexual in orientation.

Each woman participated in an in-depth interview about her life as a woman and was asked details about at least three dreams: her worst nightmare, her favorite dream, and her most recent dream. Overall, these dreamers are fairly representative of the white upper-middle-class American women in an urban setting (further details appear in the appendix). Thus, the conclusions described in the forthcoming chapters must be considered as especially applicable to this group and not necessarily true of all women.

Beyond the material collected from those in the formal study, additional dream descriptions were given to me in casual or unusual circumstances by women who were not study participants. A bride in her wedding gown in the midst of a crowded reception volunteered her dreams of the preceding night; a mother pushing a carriage with six-month-old twin boys in a checkout line recounted her pregnancy dreams; a clerk in a clothing shop grew teary-eyed telling a recent nightmare about her boyfriend; a television producer took time out from taping a program with me to describe her own catastrophic dream about work. Circumstances such as these did not permit formal interviewing but did provide some memorable illustrations for the book.

I hope this book will enable the average woman who is interested in her dreams to make better sense of them, to learn about herself from her dream pictures, and to recognize the special elements that characterize women's dreams. A woman needs to be aware that her dreams change with her changing body. How these changes come about, what we can do to recognize them, and what they mean in our lives—this is what we will explore in the pages to follow.

Although at times in this book I emphasize the physiological underpinnings of women's dreams, the psychological and spiritual are often present as well. This book underscores the biological aspect of dreaming, not because other aspects are unimportant but because the body images have been so overlooked. A redress for that neglect is provided here. We see, too, how the physical components of dreaming interact with our psychological needs and our spiritual or creative selves.

How to Use This Book

You may wish to read this book through once to get the overview. Although you might have less interest in elderly dreams, say, than in wedding dreams, each chapter adds elements of dreamwork that are significant tools to comprehend your own dreams.

Keeping a record of your dreams while you read, if you don't already do so, will help you get the most from this book. Set aside a special journal just for your dream entries. Each evening write a brief note about what happened that day, especially your feelings about the events. Put a notepad beside your bed before going to sleep at night. During the night, if you awaken, or in the morning, jot down key words and phrases from any dreams. When you have time during the next day, or in the evening before bed, write a description of your dreams of the previous night. (If you want to read more about keeping a dream diary, see chapter 8 in my *Creative Dreaming* or the introduction to *Dream Notebook.* [8]) You will be gathering material about your innermost self; this book will help you understand it better.

After having read *Women's Bodies, Women's Dreams* through once, I suggest you return to chapter 2 and check your dream records against the standards reported here. Finally, you may want to reread the chapters of the book that relate most directly to whatever life event or portion of the life cycle you find yourself currently experiencing.

By contrasting your written dreams with the experiences described in the text, you can get a good idea of how typical your dreams are. You will find the meanings of common dream symbols for that stage. You should finish the book with a clear sense of what kinds of dreams are characteristic of each phase of life, how yours compare, and the significance of such dreams. You should be able to tell when your dreams suggest that positive growth is going on and when emotional trouble is brewing. Value every dream, distressing or uplifting, as a night letter from the inner self that can help guide your days.

The women whose dreams and lives comprise the pages to come are real people. They wept, they laughed, they reached out in sorrow, in anger, and in joy. They moved me to sense the incredible wealth and beauty in a woman's life. May their words bring that appreciation to each reader of this book and enhance each life.

Women's Bodies, Women's Dreams

The Dreaming Woman

Women's dreams mirror the tides that move the fluids of their bodies. Just as the waters of earth swell and recede, so our dreams change over time. They show us to ourselves in one character before the onset of first menstruation; they shimmer with a different image when we become fertile woman; and when the red river runs dry, our dreams reflect yet another facet. As men and women enter retirement years, they display still different dreaming patterns. Perhaps only in our elder years are we most alike as each person confronts the inevitability of physical death and what that event might bring. We trace here the life cycle as experienced in dreams.

Dreams Echo the Life Cycle

What is a life cycle? Webster's defines it as a "series of changes in form" a person (or other organism) undergoes in developing from "its earliest stage to the recurrence of the same stage in the next generation."[1] According to this view, a woman's life cycle begins at conception and continues until she herself conceives a child. We, however, will consider the woman's life cycle to start at her birth and cease with her death.

Webster's is, of course, referring to the biological changes that occur during maturation. Theorists and writers have attempted to delineate psychological steps in human life that parallel physical development. Erik Erikson, for instance, has postulated the "eight stages of man";[2] William Shakespeare, in his comedy *As You Like It,* suggests there are seven stages to life;[3] Daniel Levinson's work,[4] popularized by Gail Sheehy in her book *Passages,* suggests about five adult stages between ages twenty and fifty;[5] Charlotte Buhler and her colleagues[6] have described five biological and five psychological phases throughout the entire life span, asserting that the psychological steps lag slightly behind the biological ones, as for instance, the youth making first important decisions about life shortly after reaching puberty.

These authors and other researchers of the life cycle rarely agree on the number of steps involved in transiting life, or on the nature of each developmental phase. In general, however, they concur that there is an overall pattern of increasing activity from birth, expanding and ascending to a wide range of skills and interests that culminates in a relatively stable period; this is followed by a phase of decreasing activity, a narrowing and decline of interests until death. Within this overall pattern are stages of instability alternating with stability. Buhler's idea that each stage is marked by "a principal change in direction, such as an important acquisition or loss" is a useful clue to the beginning of a new stage.

Women's Common Life Events. There are many ways of looking at the stages of life through which we must eventually pass. No one definitive pattern exists. However, there are certain life events common to all women; others are optional.

Born women, unless we have some malfunction that prevents it, we mature to puberty, we menstruate, we usually mate; we may or may not wed, we may or may not bear a child; we will probably work outside the home at some stage of our life; we reach menopause; we may retire; our loved ones sicken or leave us; we have strife, failures, successes, loves, hates, sorrows; assuredly we will eventually die. Some of these experiences we share with men; others are unique to our womanhood.

Women's Unique Patterns. The stages of our life cycle are not only different from men's stages, they are different from each other. In fact, there is often greater disparity within a group of women than there is between the same group of women compared with a group of men. Although, as a group, our maturational processes differ from men's, as individuals we also differ from each other.

How the individual negotiates each life event will vary. Page, a woman in my study who had her first menses at age ten, did not have the same psychological experience as Catherine, who reached menarche at age fifteen. Although their biological processes were similar, their emotional responses to it were disparate. Page, now in her seventies, said, "One thing I resent to this day is that my mother made me wear very tight bras. I think she was jealous of me with father. She didn't want me to develop." Catherine, although she was not eager to grow up, wanted to look like the other girls. Changing clothes in the locker room was agonizing because her figure was so immature.

Maggie, who married at eighteen, provided a contrast to Ann-Marie, who waited until age thirty-six to tie the knot. The majority of subjects in my study married in their twenties; some never married at all. Each had her own life pattern. Even when the outer facts of age were identical, the individual had her unique response. Of her first of three eventual marriages, Hilda commented, "I was twenty-one, going on twelve."

The woman who bears her first child at nineteen, like Babs, is different in certain respects from the one who gives birth for the first time at thirty-three, like Maggie, even though the physiological process is similar. Many women become first-time mothers even younger or older than these two. Some women, as much as they may desperately wish to become mothers, are unable to do so. Cookie, now in her late thirties, suffers acutely over being childless. "I'm a nurturing person. I have this body capable of reproducing and I can't. I want to have a child!" Some of this lovely woman's worst nightmares are about dying babies. Our experience will be different if we arrive "too early," "too late," or, like Cookie, skip a phase entirely. Waking or sleeping, each life is distinct.

Women's Crisis Points Arrive Earlier

The stages of a woman's biological cycle are measurably different from the phases of a man's physical development. In some dimensions we race ahead: women mature earlier, learn to speak earlier, reach puberty earlier. In other dimensions we lag behind: the male reaches sexual climax earlier and more often than the average female.

Most women go through a life crisis in their middle thirties. This crisis usually comes sooner for the female than the corresponding crisis for the male. By thirty-five a woman is keenly aware that she must choose among her options. The career woman often finds herself eager to have a family—before she is no longer capable of doing so. She knows full well that if she is childless and wants to have a baby, she must conceive *now*; her time has almost run out. Nina, in her late thirties, opted to take a break from her career, giving birth to a son while she could and then continuing with her profession three months later. Her dreams were full of the struggle to make this decision and the repercussions of it.

The housewife-mother may find herself yearning after the career she has never had. Having invested the bulk of her energies into homemaking, childbearing, and caretaking, she often decides she wants more out of life. Babs attended college for the first time after her two daughters were almost grown; she followed this training with an absorbing job in interior design. Ginny, who also married early, spends her evenings at a local college seeking the education she missed and has developed a mail-order business from her home. Like Babs and Ginny, the woman in her middle thirties is generally becoming more active and assertive than she was earlier in her life.

In contrast to women, the majority of men tend to experience the midlife crisis later, around age forty. Regardless of his level of career achievement, a man often feels "stale, restless, burdened and unappreciated" at forty.[7] Now is the time when he may choose another career or another wife. Men in their forties are usually slowing down; they are becoming more tender and loving than in their earlier years. As we shall see, these crises and changes reverberate in the dreams of both sexes.

Women's Sexual Peaks Develop Later

Women's sexual drives reach a peak later than men's, an unfortunate arrangement, many people say. While 92 percent of the almost six thousand men in Alfred C. Kinsey's historic study had had orgasm by fifteen years of age, only 22 percent of the nearly eight thousand females had experienced orgasm by the same age. The number of sexually experienced males at age fifteen was not equaled by the females until age twenty-nine.[8] Although the exact figures may differ today, the trend is likely to be similar: the average male is sexually active earlier than the female, and he has experienced more orgasms at a young age than the average female.

Males have a sudden surge in sexual activity the year or two before they reach adolescence (as measured by the appearance of pubic hair), about age fourteen. Their sexual activity reaches a peak at approximately age sixteen, one to two years after the onset of adolescence. Then their sexual responsiveness and activity begin to drop and continue to decline into old age.[9]

In comparison, the average American female reaches adolescence earlier (as measured by the appearance of pubic hair), at about twelve years and five months. Yet, most females have a slow, steady increase in erotic feelings and number of orgasms up to and during adolescence. Females do not reach their maximum sexual responsiveness until their mid twenties or thirties.[10] The healthy woman in her middle thirties is highly sensual, more open and responsive to sexual stimulation than ever before. Her sexual sensitivity matures much later than does the male's.

Women's Sexual Dreams Develop Later

The same pattern of difference appears in male and female dreams. Among males fifteen years old, almost 40 percent of Kinsey's sample had experienced nocturnal emissions (so-called wet dreams).[11] In comparison, only 2 percent of the females of the same age had experienced sexual dreams that proceeded to orgasm. Later on, by age forty-five, 83 percent of the males had experienced dreams with orgasm, whereas only 37 percent of the females of the same age had had dreams with orgasm. Furthermore men's erotic dreams that lead to orgasm reach a peak when they are in their late teens or twenties; for women the peak of sexual dreams with orgasm is in their forties.[12]

In general, then, men are more sexually experienced and respond with orgasm—awake or in dreams—more often and at an earlier age. Women are less sexually experienced when young, becoming more active and more orgasmic—awake or in dreams—when they are older. Dreams parallel lives.

Although we will occasionally mention characteristics of men's life cycles in contrast to women's, we will not be dealing with male-female differences throughout. Bear in mind, however, that male and female life patterns differ and so contribute to some of the conflicts in women's development.

Dreams as Life Guides

In the pages that follow, we watch the girl turn teen; we follow the adolescent to womanhood; we ponder mating, birthing, parenting, working, and divorcing; we see maturing, aging, sickening, and dying all through our dream spectacles.

What are the tasks we must face at each stage of life? What are the roadblocks to reaching these goals? How can we best fulfill our lives? Can our nighttime visions, by anticipating the inevitable changes, help us to cope more effectively? Dreams may seem as fragile and floating as silk chiffon, but they are nevertheless sturdy props for easing our way.

The Origin of Dreams

Where do our dreams originate? The source of dreaming is more than waking thoughts and experiences.

Biological Aspects

The Dream Cycle. On one level, the most fundamental, we are creatures of nature. Our dreams are part of a basic biological rhythm; in a cycle, they ebb and flow throughout our sleeping hours. Every ninety minutes or so all night, in progressively longer periods, our central nervous system undergoes an active phase.

When we first fall asleep, our brain waves slow down, our breathing becomes more regular, our heart rate lowers and becomes steady, our temperature falls, and our muscles relax. These changes continue through four stages of progressively deeper sleep.[13] After a phase of profoundly restful sleep, we gradually ascend through increasingly lighter stages until, approximately ninety minutes later, our brain waves accelerate, our breathing turns irregular, our heart rate quickens, and our temperature rises again. Despite small twitching in the lips and fingers, our large muscles lose their tone. Yet our sexual organs become aroused: males develop an erection; the female genitals engorge with blood and lubrication. Now is when rapid eye movements (REM) begin.

In the brain stem of the sleeping person, a group of nerve cells—called gigantocellular tegmental field (GTF) neurons—periodically fire. These cells are a kind of switch that turns on our dreams. Usually, these cells are inhibited by another group of neurons in the brain stem—called locus coeruleus—which act as an off switch. As the GTF cells become excited, they stimulate the lower brain—the area where emotions originate—and the visual and sensory cortex. When these specialized cells reach a peak of excitation, there is a burst of rapid eye movements. The sleeper begins to dream.[14]

On and off throughout the night this pattern continues. By the time an adult sleeper awakes, he or she has spent about 25 percent of sleep time in REM, totaling roughly ninety minutes each night. This REM time is divided into four or five distinct periods, the earliest about ten minutes in length and later ones increasing progressively to about thirty to forty-five minutes.[15]

Some scientists think this periodic activation is a sort of "self-test" to make sure all circuits are operative. Whatever the reason, our autonomic nervous system periodically revs up during sleep. These active phases—called rapid eye movement periods because of the back-and forth darting of the eyes that occurs—are associated with intense dreaming.

At first, scientists thought that all dreams occurred during REM sleep; now we know that many dreams occur during the remaining time as well.[16] The sleep time outside of REM is called non-REM. These two types of sleep, REM and non-REM, contain distinctive types of dreams. Dream reports from REM are usually dramatic, like descriptions of a horror film or a spy story; dream reports from non-REM tend to be more calm and thoughtlike, as in a documentary about a routine day. We can think of the mind as constantly busy during sleep, with dream valleys between the peaks of REM dream mountains.

Scientists suspect that we have a similar schedule of heightened fantasy that fluctuates during the daytime.[17] Some theorists think this periodic daydreaming is a switching of brain hemispheres, as if to keep both sides in working order. Regardless of the cause, people undergo a rhythmic cycle of dreamlike thought during the day as well as at night.

External Physical Sensations.   Beyond this basic dream cycle, our bodies affect our dreams in other ways. People who are sensitively tuned to their dreams often report the seemingly strange incorporation of stimuli in the environment into their ongoing dreams. The chill of a winter's night may take form as being lost in the Alps for one dreamer, or of swirling across ice in a dazzling display of skating skill for another; both dreamers have woven the strand of cold into their dream fabric, embroidering it according to their personality.

Our sensory organs pick up the cold, the heat, the noise, the odor, the breeze in our environment and place them into the dream basket. Although dreamers commonly notice the external sensations they incorporate into their dreams, they are less likely to recognize that their *internal* sensations also are a factor.

Internal Physical Sensations.   During the hurly-burly of our days, minute bodily sensations often pass unnoticed. In the quiet of our nights, however, the same sensations seem magnified manyfold. They seep into our dreams where they take on concrete form. We literally see the pitchfork thrust into the neck, an image stimulated by the sensation of a sore throat; a dream crab clutches the ankle that was wrenched during the day. At times our dreams seem to predict a forthcoming illness, a phenomenon observed by Aristotle, who called such dreams prodromal, derived from Greek words meaning "running before" (the illness).[18]

Dream pictures that emerge from illness, accident, or normal bodily processes may be obvious to the dreamer. Freud, after an evening consuming salty food, said he was certain to dream of drinking water.[19] The person whose bladder is full is likely to dream of going to the bathroom.

Other bodily processes that produce specific dream images are less familiar. For men, these sensations are often depicted in nocturnal emissions, or wet dreams. Climbing a staircase is frequently a symbol for sexual intercourse in dreams of both men and women, because the dreaming mind likens the rhythmic back-and-forth movements of coition to the movements of climbing. The nineteenth-century author Hervey de Saint-Denys describes a classic dream of this type, with a pretty woman beckoning him to follow her—first up staircases, then up a ladder, and finally up a mountain; the dream culminated in orgasm.[20]

Although males experience erection from infancy onward, it is not until puberty begins that they have emissions during their dreams. Kinsey, as mentioned above, found that more men than women reported orgasms in their dreams. Among the women who did have orgasmic dreams, the average frequency was three to four times a year; in contrast, males tended to have orgasmic dreams at least five to ten times a year, with even more during their teens.

When quite young, boys dream of erections in their symbolic language. Jean Piaget, the Swiss developmental expert, describes a child who, from the age of six, had recurrent dreams for several months about a bean that grew so long it crossed the room;[21] another told of dreaming about a balloon swelling until it was ready to burst. Piaget says he has frequently observed examples of erection dreams in boys. The majority of scientists who have studied the content of dreams have been male; perhaps this accounts for their observation of erection and emission imagery in dreams.

Few scientists have taken note of the special imagery that accompanies women's puberty. We know from recent research that women, too, undergo physiological arousal during dreaming, with increased blood flow to the vagina and lubrication of the vaginal walls.[22] We shall see how the pictures of their bodily changes contrast sharply with those of men. No swelling balloons or growing beans here.

Instead, the imagery of women's dreams varies, from puberty to menopause, according to the stage of their menstrual cycle. During ovulation, dreams of babies are common, for example, whereas during menstruation, dreams of disintegration are more frequent. As we shall see, the premenstrual bodily changes—water retention; swollen, sensitive breasts; mood swings—all have their correlates in characteristic dream pictures.

It is particularly important, I believe, for women to familiarize themselves with the dream images that are typical of each stage of their menstrual cycle. Women can become alerted to the status of their cycle. A dreamer who is finely focused on the messages conveyed by her dream images will be able to assess whether all is functioning smoothly or something has gone awry.

Sexual intercourse is a different experience for women and men. Each woman has her own reaction to her first intercourse, subsequent ones, the man involved, and the conditions of their mating. These emotions influence the type of pictures that arise in her dreams.

In the past, women tended to be ultraconservative in their romantic dreams, only sometimes engaging in sexual intercourse with a familiar partner in a familiar place. In contrast, men's dreams are characterized by a multitude of partners, often strangers in exotic settings, with little foreplay prior to sex.[23]

Studies in the past few years indicate that trend may be changing. One recent cross-cultural study found that American women dream of diverse sexual interactions with many partners, whereas women from Kenya rarely dream of sex.[24] Presumably, the American women's dreams are responding to the greater sexual freedom exercised in recent years. Since the epidemic spread of AIDS, however, I have observed the incorporation of fear of multiple sexual contacts in women's dreams. Monogamy has never seemed so compelling, awake or asleep. We are likely to see another shift in women's sexual dream patterns.

Pregnancy, the ultimate female experience, evokes dream imagery that varies in each trimester. Menopause, too, has its own distinctive dream patterns.

These physiological aspects of dreaming are discussed in chapter 3, "Growing-Up and Menstrual Dreams"; chapter 4, "Love and Sex Dreams"; chapter 6, "Pregnancy and Childbirth Dreams"; and chapter 10, "Menopausal Dreams." Of course, dreams are created from more than biological rhythms and external and internal physical sensations.

Psychological Aspects

The psychological aspect of dreaming is well known. Long before Freud was born, the peoples of biblical times, the ancient Chinese, the Egyptians, the

Greeks, and the Romans poured over their dreams for clues to guide their daily lives. Every ancient culture had its dream books that the populace used to interpret the future.

Ancient Dreamers.   Clay tablets found at Nineveh, Assyria, in the library of King Ashurbanipal, contain recorded interpretations of dreams believed to date back thousands of years, possibly to 5000 B.C.[25] A papyrus found in Thebes, Upper Egypt, and written around 1350 B.C. describes two hundred dreams, tells their meanings according to Egyptian tradition, and gives incantations for warding off the effects of bad dreams.[26] The sacred books of India, composed between 1000 and 600 B.C., describe using the dream state to gain enlightenment.[27] The Old Testament, written between approximately 1100 and 200 B.C., contains several examples of dreams, such as those of Joseph and Pharaoh; the New Testament, completed about A.D. 300, also describes prophetic dreams.[28] The grandfather of all modern dream books was written by a Greek named Artemidorus Daldianus; he gives the interpretations of many dreams from the perspective of the Greek culture in the second century A.D.[29] In the Talmud, the collection of writings from the fourth to sixth century A.D. that constitute the Jewish civil and religious laws, there is an entire chapter devoted to the meaning of dreams.[30] The Koran, sacred book of the Muslims, recorded during the seventh century A.D., describes rituals to induce good dreams and to defend oneself against bad ones.[31] Certain traditions regarding favorable and unfavorable dreams have been passed down orally among Asian families since ancient dynasties.[32]

Many of these ancient cultures, especially the Egyptians, the Greeks, and the Chinese, had special temples where people with illness or other difficulties could go to spend the night "incubating" a dream that would heal them or bring a solution to their problems from the god.[33] The idea that dreams influence and inspire our waking lives is as old as dreaming itself.

Modern Dreamers.   Childhood memories and experiences from our recent past are acted out upon the stage of our dreams, mixed with current conflicts and needs. (Some people would add experiences from past lives as well.) A woman's status at work, her ongoing relationship with her lover, her mother or significant others—all are involved in the construction of her dream house:

- The woman who has quarreled with her sweetheart may dream, as one in my study did, of an earthquake, expressing her concerns about the possible "breaking up" of her relationship.

- The woman who is getting divorced may see, as another of the women in the study did, her retaining wall collapsing, expressing the destruction of the relationship that had "supported" her.
- The woman who is exasperated with a work situation may dream, as yet another study participant did, of escaping from her colleagues on a flying mattress, expressing her wish to rise above and get away from the bickering throng.
- The woman newly in love may see herself, as one did, being offered a delicious drink by the man who was "intoxicating" to her, expressing her wish to "drink in" his love.

Our dreams speak to us, several times a night, in a metaphorical language, a symbolic code, a poetic tongue, that expresses our emotions. We can learn to speak this language fluently. The messages are there whether we read them or not.

The psychological elements in dreaming are discussed in chapter 5, "Wedding Dreams"; chapter 7, "Career Dreams"; chapter 8, "Divorce Dreams"; and chapter 9, "Parenting Dreams."

Spiritual Aspects

At yet another level, dreams are mysterious. We can understand the bodily processes appearing in dreams; we appreciate the personality factors that permeate dreams. Yet some people, especially those who have examined their dreams carefully over time, find that there emerges a level of dreaming that is not clearly explained by biological functions, the external and internal bodily sensations, or the psychological process.

This level is given different names; some people call it the creative source, others the universal unconscious or archetypal level, still others speak of it as extrasensory perception or simply the divine. However we conceive it, this level of dreaming is beyond the ordinary. We sometimes touch in our dreams a precious core that should be accepted and treasured rather than interpreted. Chapter 11, "Dreams of the Elderly"; and chapter 12, "A Woman's Life Cycle of Dreams," touch on this extraordinary aspect of dreaming. Today's woman is powerfully influenced by her spiritual dreams.

At least two and sometimes all three levels—biological, psychological, and spiritual—may operate in a single dream. Thus a dream is multileveled. Like a many-storied house, it has its foundation, its main living quarters, and its attic. Each area contributes something of value to the whole. Without any one of these parts, the dream is incomplete.

Different Bodies, Different Dreams

As women we dream differently from men. This is so, first of all, because our bodies are different. Obviously our potential for producing eggs and giving birth is unique, as is man's capacity to provide sperm. Today's scientists tell us that we diverge from men in several other ways. Geneticists find basic cell differences; biologists measure brain, bone, and organ differences; sociologists point out our different patterns of behavior in society; psychologists observe differences in how we function; educators note differences in how we are treated in classrooms; anthropologists collect differences in our cultural roles.[34]

Some of these differences may prove to be inborn. Others will be shown to be purely the result of training or culture. Still others will depend upon a complex interaction of both heredity and environment, as, for example, the menstrual period. The process of menstruation is biologically determined, yet it is influenced by a woman's nutrition, the degree to which she exercises, her emotional response to stress, and other environmental factors.

Scientists still debate whether nature or nurture has the stronger influence; whether our genes outweigh our cultural experience; whether our heredity is dominated by our environment. Sometimes it seems as though evidence favors one, then the other. We still do not have a final verdict. Assuredly, both interact.

Our heredity contributes certain potentials. Our environment causes these either to wither or to flourish and thrive. We come to life with certain "givens" aside from blond hair or blue eye color. How we are nurtured shapes, and sometimes contorts, the being we become. Malnutrition will stunt even the tallest genetic potential; child abuse shakes the sturdiest inherited serenity; the limited child will blossom in an enriched environment; the bright child given the right soil may reach full potential.

Our dreams, then, are composed from various elements: our biologically inherited characteristics, our psychologically derived experiences, and the mysterious unknown.

Women's Dreams,
Men's Dreams—
The Difference

Who Is This Dreamer?

The dreamer stretches, yawns, and comes fully awake. Drowsily clasping the notepad and pen at bedside, the figure jots down the essence of a just-finished dream. The room is dim, the hair is tousled, the nightshirt is unrevealing. Peeking over the writer's shoulder, can you tell if these are the words of a woman or of a man?

> Mother comes to me, dressed as she was when I was a
> child—young, in a long dress with a low waist and a Basque
> beret. She has a loose sweater on top, with a pale blue, rather
> gray, scarf tossed over her shoulder, and white sport shoes with
> dots—she always was an elegant woman. Her hair is graying,
> and on her face is a sweet, sweet expression—she lost that in her

long illness. I can vividly see her image and at the same time
feel her atmosphere, what she represents. I sense a real contact is
established, one that I had lost since her death . . .

Few readers would hesitate to identify the writer of this dream account
as a woman. Why? (Without reading further, you may wish to take the
short test at the end of this chapter right now, to assess how well you
recognize the differences between men's and women's dreams.)

The author of this dream description is, indeed, a woman—she is married,
fifty-five years old, and will be called Lynette. She had this dream sometime
after her mother's lingering death from cancer. As we shall see later, dreams
about deceased parents are a fairly common theme for adult women. We
shall also see what Lynette learned from this dream.

We have said that women's dreams are different from men's. We examine
here the characteristic features that make up that difference. Most adults sense
the contrast, qualities they intuitively recognize as "female," rather than
knowing them as findings of dream research. Several typical feminine
characteristics are contained in the excerpt above.

Empress of Dream Recall

First, women are superb dream recallers. Ms. Typical is far more aware of
the fleeting imagery of her nights than Mr. Typical. Throughout the centuries women have passed along the "secrets" of dream interpretation by oral
tradition. Among Greeks today there are still old women who are known
in their extended families and villages as the interpreters of dreams.[1] In other
Middle Eastern cultures as well, Iran and Turkey, the tellers of dream truths
are often female.[2] Who knows, perhaps they are the descendents of the
oracle at Delphi in Greece, or of the priestesses at the temples of Asklepios
at Pergamon in Turkey, or of the temple of Isis in Egypt?

In the hundreds of workshops and classes in dreamwork that I have led
over the years, the majority of attendees have been women. The ratio, I
would estimate, is about eight women to two men. Of course some men
are very good indeed at dream recall and some women poor at it, but, on
average, the female excels.

Many couples, I have also noticed in my nearly forty years of dream
study, consist of a high dream recaller and a low dream recaller. Usually
the good recaller is the woman. "It's incredible the dream stories my wife
tells—complete adventures! I hardly remember anything in the morning,"
is the oft-repeated comment a husband makes to me. When the rare male

happens to be the high dream recaller, his mate is customarily poor in this ability—an intriguing instance of opposites attracting.

Of course, these observations alone do not prove that the average woman remembers dreams better than the average man. The difference could simply be a result of greater cultural acceptance for women's interest in dreams. Suggestive, however, are studies showing that people who are good at dream recall tend to experience anxiety, are often introspective, and may be light sleepers.[3] Both men and women sometimes have these tendencies.

High Estrogen and High Dream Recall? Although they are not in total agreement, researchers routinely report that pregnant women—especially in the second trimester—recall their dreams even more readily than women who are not pregnant.[4] This finding is, I believe, an important clue to women's apparently superior dream recall.

There may be a relationship between the level of estrogen in a woman's body and her degree of dreaming. If so, this explanation would also account for the observation that the amount women dream, as well as their recall of dreams, fluctuates with the stage of their menstrual cycle. Researchers occasionally report that the peak of dreaming, and memory of doing so, occurs between ovulation (when estrogen is high) and the onset of menstruation (when estrogen is low).[5] Older women who take estrogen to replace their own diminished supply also sometimes report that their amount of dream recall varies during the month. Investigators studying menopause find that post-menopause women who ingest estrogen, to replace their diminished supply, dream more than those who do not take the hormone.

When researchers plot the lifelong pattern of sleeping and dreaming, they find several differences between the sexes. A team at the University of Florida Sleep Laboratories in 1974, led by Robert Williams, measured the sleep parameters of 237 normal males and females ages three to seventy-nine.[6] The amount of REM sleep declined sharply for both males and females from infancy to puberty, thereafter dropping gradually. In childhood both boys and girls spent approximately 30 percent of their sleep time in REM;[7] at puberty both sexes had about 25 percent of their sleep time in REM.[8]

For males the percentage of REM sleep reached a low point of 23 percent in their thirties; then it remained steady until their seventies, when there was another slight decline.[9] In contrast women's amount of REM did not show any perceptible drop from their twenties onward, only a very gradual decline. Thus although males dream less by their thirties, women's decline in REM is less steep with aging.

Women Have More Deep Sleep.   Deep sleep is the stage when our brain waves are most slow. In addition to making us feel rested and refreshed, it is the time when the growth hormones are released: it is the stage of sleep that allows us to recover from fatigue. Although both sexes showed less deep sleep (stage 4) in older years in the Williams' study, women continued to have more deep sleep than men, as well as more REM, until past menopause.

In their fifties women had less deep sleep than at younger years, but they continued to exceed men into the elder years. Among some elderly men, deep sleep disappeared entirely, but it remained present in about half of the elderly women. For example, in the Florida study that was headed by Williams only one out of ten of the elderly male subjects had any stage 4 sleep, whereas six out of eleven of the older women still slept deeply.[10]

In fact, in a study conducted by René Spiegel in Basel, Switzerland, in 1981, several elderly women exhibited no significant change in any part of their sleep patterns from those of younger persons.[11] Spiegel noted patterns similar to those of Williams and his colleagues: the elderly women in his study spent 14 percent less time in REM sleep than young men did, while the elderly men spent 19 percent less time in REM.[12] The older women had about twice as much deep sleep as the older men.[13] Furthermore, elderly men showed about twice the number of awakenings as elderly women did and they had more sleep problems.[14] The overall sleep of Spiegel's women was deeper, longer, and subject to fewer disturbances than that of the men. Men therefore show changes in sleep patterns as much as twenty years earlier than women; thus women are said to "sleep younger." There is still much we need to learn about the process, but it is certain that women continue to dream more and to sleep more deeply throughout their lives.[15]

These findings, along with the others mentioned above, suggest that female hormones are closely linked to women's greater amount of dreaming and hence their greater dream recall. Whatever the cause of dreaming may prove to be, it is small wonder that women are better dream recallers if they have more dreams to remember.

Dream recall, by the way, *decreases* during a period of mental illness.[16] This is especially so during severe depression, and cessation of dreaming in a person who usually recalls dreams has been associated in some cases with attempted suicide. Remembering our dreams seems to help us stay aware of how we are feeling and alerts us to get help when it is needed.

Approach to Life and Dream Recall.   Life-style also influences dream recall. One study showed that art students report more dreams than engineering students. Presumably, the art students had a heightened interest in imagery whether awake or asleep. High dream recallers seem to be more introspective and more interested in how the mind works than low recallers.[17] Another study revealed that high dream recallers are especially sensitive.[18]

For either sex, deliberate interest in dreaming is usually associated with greater dream recall. It is a memory skill that can be improved with training.

Researchers find that people who are learning new skills, such as a foreign language, dream more.[19] This fact has led to the speculation that dreaming is somehow crucial in consolidating our memories. More specifically, REM dreaming is believed to help process and store information, and perhaps stimulate the sensory system during sleep, whereas non-REM sleep is thought to ensure our physical growth, cell repair, and restoration.[20] Older people whose minds are still keen have been found to dream more than those whose abilities are waning. We have already pointed out that older women exhibit more dreaming.

Women's Long, Long Dream Tales

Along with being good recallers, women characteristically give lengthy dream descriptions. Dream reports increase in length with age for both sexes, according to researcher Robert Van de Castle,[21] but at every step girls give more extensive descriptions than boys. Using a collection of one thousand dreams from two hundred college students, half of them men and half women, he and Calvin Hall reported that, on average, the dreams from females were 8 percent longer than those from men.[22]

This difference would probably have been much greater had they not eliminated from the study any dream report longer than three hundred words. In my dream diary from the age of fourteen until the present age of fifty-three, comprising a series of volumes scanning over thirty-nine years and containing more than twenty thousand dreams, almost all the dream accounts exceed three hundred words. Although I am unusual in having recorded my dreams across such a broad span of time, I resemble most women in that my dream recall and dream descriptions are ample.

A study of children's dreams found that changes in length of report depended on the child's age. In children three to five years old, researcher David Foulkes noted that dream reports were almost equal in length; he found that the typical girl's dream report for his subjects at five years old was fourteen words long and the typical boy's dream report was thirteen words long. No description exceeded fifty words.[23]

However, by age nine to eleven, girls' dream reports were perceptibly longer (they averaged 75.5 words, whereas the boys' reports were 60.5 words). The maximum report length he obtained was 443 for girls and 249 for boys of this age. (In his study, this difference did not hold for the older children of eleven to fifteen.)[24]

Women give longer dream reports partly due to the fact that they remember more of their dreams; they also use more words. Adjectives and detailed descriptions are far more frequently employed by women in writing and speaking. (For this reason, the sample quiz at the end of the chapter has been made more difficult by presenting dream descriptions of roughly equal length.)

Women's Superior Language Skills.   The underlying cause of women's longer dream reports is probably due to their generally superior skill in language. On average, women test as more verbally fluent than men. Although men and women generally score as being equally intelligent on IQ tests, they differ in the items on which they excel.

Girls who are asked to give definitions of words, or read complicated passages and show they understand them ordinarily score higher than boys on the same task. Boys are much more likely to have reading problems; they are eight times more likely to stammer; and more males score in the very low range of IQ tests. In fact the highest IQ scores recorded at a major American testing center were obtained by girls (who scored 200 and 201 compared with an average score of 100).[25]

Men's Superior Spatial Skills.   In contrast, males tend to score higher than females on items that test the ability to visualize and manipulate objects in space—shown by their ability to quickly arrange parts into a pattern or to imagine them rearranged. Superiority of males in visual-spatial tasks is apparent from the age of eleven onward. Males are also better at mathematics from age eleven, a fact that is partially explained by the spatial reasoning involved, especially in geometry.[26]

Visual-spatial skills, suggests British psychologist John Nicholson, may have developed from hunting and from manipulating tools and weapons in evolutionary times; those who were good at it would survive and pass on these abilities genetically.[27] He cites evidence on both sides of the argument and concludes that the genetic explanation of sex difference in visual-spatial skills remains controversial. Also, recent studies have shown that one woman out of four exceeds the average man on this skill.[28]

Spatial Skills a Function of Practice? Moreover, the inferiority of women in spatial skills is most marked in countries where the woman is submissive, as in sections of India, and is nonexistent in others where women are more equal, as among the Eskimos.[29] This finding suggests that males tend to perform better than females on spatial skills because they have had more life experience practicing them.

Furthermore, researchers found that children who were coached in visual-spatial tasks (such as imagining three-dimensional figures turning in space or finding odd-shaped figures embedded in complex drawings) improved dramatically in geometry in only three weeks compared with children who had simply studied Euclid during the same time. Students at one university who were given visual-spatial tests at the beginning and end of the first year of an engineering class showed striking improvement in scores. Thus, it appears that at least part of visual-spatial skill is based on the experience a woman has in early or student life. Nicholson suggests that we institute remedial classes in visual-spatial skills for girls just as we now have remedial reading classes for boys.[30]

Keep in mind that we speak of groups of people—of averages—not of individuals. My husband's skill at language exceeds my own; at the same time I am much better than he is at visual-spatial tasks, usually an area of male supremacy, including such things as finding my way back to the car in a crowded parking lot, following a map to a place new to us, or "feeling" my way back to a place I have only been once. My guess is that my early experience manipulating the marionettes that my artist-father made for me on a three-dimensional stage gave me extra practice in visual-spatial skills.

Impact of Verbal Style. Feminists who have studied the language differences between men and women assert that women use "powerless" language in contrast to the more powerful sparse male style.[31] Their view is that women weaken their statements by overuse of description and qualifiers, such as "kind of" or "sort of," and by being overly polite. They characterize female language as "powerless, tentative, irritating, and trivial." Taste varies and so does literary style. Marcel Proust and Thomas Mann employ as many adjectives as any female writer and it does not seem to lessen their stature as classic authors.

Nevertheless, women's dream descriptions in English can sometimes be recognized in part by their use of words as well as by the length of the report. Choice of words is often characteristically female, as can be seen in the quiz at the close of this chapter.

In fact, Kenneth Colby, a psychoanalyst who studied the content of dreams in 1958, found that certain words discriminated between male and female dream reports.[32] He collected four hundred dreams of patients in psychoanalysis (two hundred from men and two hundred from women) that had appeared in psychoanalytic journals.[33] Counting hundreds of elements in the dream reports, he classified them into one of six categories.[34] He then compared the presence or absence of each item in the women's dreams to the same items in the men's dreams.

Colby found five significant differences between these male and female patients. In their dream reports, men more often mentioned, in the following order of frequency, the words

1. *travel* (in any vehicle)
2. *hit*
3. *auto*
4. *wife*

Women more often mentioned the word *husband*.

In another study of the same type, Colby compared the four hundred dreams of male and female college students (using a sample he obtained from Calvin Hall). He found that the students' dreams were longer than the patients' dreams. Their dream descriptions contained the same word differences, with the addition of two words, appearing mainly in the women students' dreams: *home* and *cry*.

Colby concluded that men and women's dreams differ in the frequency that they dream about "heterosexual mating objects," by which he meant "wife" and "husband," and the "intensified penetration of space" implied in the men's dreams about "travel" and "hitting." He saw the fact that female college students mentioned "home" and "crying" more often than men as confirmation of the same point, that is, women cry rather than hit, and stay home rather than travel. Perhaps, almost thirty years afterward, repeating this study would reveal changes in the dream role of women today. Later in this chapter we shall examine some evidence for this trend.

So far as I know, Colby's work has not been replicated, although it is a simple enough concept to apply to dream records.[35] The idea is intriguing and is consistent with Hall's findings.

In some cultures females utilize a totally separate language from men to communicate with one another. In Japanese, women usually employ a more polite speech and choose deferential verb forms in contrast to men, who tend to shorten verbs and express themselves in forceful bursts. In certain primitive tribes where females are forbidden to speak of men's activities, the women have invented a secret vocabulary to discuss weapons, war, hunting, and other male enterprises among themselves. Males of the Mazatec in Mexico use a private language of long and short whistles, corresponding to the syllables of certain words. Mazatec women do not understand this secret language.[36] Our words alone—or our whistles—sometimes betray our sex.

Differences in Brain Structure?   Scientists still disagree over whether the observed differences in verbal and visual-spatial skills are based upon differences in brain structure between the sexes, rather than being shaped by the environment.

In earlier centuries much was made of the fact that women have smaller brains, on average, than do men. From this it was inferred that women were less intelligent. I still see this false argument put forth today. In fact, brain size is proportional to body size and has absolutely nothing to do with intelligence level. The largest brain ever recorded was the brain of an idiot; the smallest brain ever measured was that of the French genius Anatole France.[37] So much for that theory.

More recently, scientist Marian Diamond at the University of California, Berkeley found that the female rat has a cerebral cortex that is thicker on the left than on the right.[38] In contrast the male rats had a cerebral cortex that was thicker on the right than on the left—differences that she thought might be related to the different verbal and visual-spatial skills.

Other researchers have cited evidence that men tend to use one side of their brain more than the other, whereas women tend to use both sides equally—allowing each sex to excel at different tasks. Some studies reported that women have more connective tissue between the hemispheres of their brains than men do, implying that they can therefore make more rapid associations between the two sides of their brains than men.

Recent research, however, challenges some of these earlier findings. Neuropsychologist Marcel Kinsbourne, reporting at a meeting of the American Association for the Advancement of Science in Chicago in 1987, claims that he found no difference between the way men and women perform on tasks that combine verbal and visual-spatial skills.[39]

Neurophysiologist Ruth Bleier of the University of Wisconsin, at the same meeting, showed slides of images of the insides of brains taken from thirty-nine men and women.[40] These measures, from a magnetic resonance imaging scanner, revealed no differences between brains of males and females. Bleier thinks that an earlier study was based on too few samples that were chosen without taking into account the age of the person or cause of death—factors that could affect the amount of connective tissue present. Other findings are likewise calling into question the former conclusions about sex differences in the brain.

Regardless of what the final word may prove to be on female-male brain similarities and contrasts, people associate different characteristics with each sex. These concepts influence their own behavior and their expectations about the opposite sex.

Drawings of Femininity and Masculinity.   When I asked a large number of workshop participants to draw their ideas of femininity and masculinity, I found a striking contrast in the drawings. Women and men alike portrayed their conceptions of the sexes differently.

Using a process first suggested by Betty Edwards in her book *Drawing on the Artist Within* (a sequel to her popular *Drawing on the Right Side of the Brain*), I asked participants to take a sheet of paper and fold it into several sections. Participants were then guided in making a drawing of several abstract qualities, such as joy, anger, femininity, depression, and peacefulness.[41] To these, I added the quality of masculinity.

You may wish to try this yourself. For example, place your pencil on a sheet or limited section of paper. Close your eyes and think back to the last time you were really angry. Remember what it was like and how it felt. Now, still holding those images, let the feelings well up from inside you and flow down your arm and out the tip of your pencil. Just let your pencil move in response to your emotion. Do not draw stereotyped designs like hearts or arrows. Let the quality of the line reflect your feeling.

Edwards found, and my collection of drawings confirms, that people tend to draw a similar type of design for each quality. Joy, for instance, is likely to be represented by rounded lines and circular motifs; anger is usually depicted by sharp, jagged lines; depression tends to be marked by lines placed low in the drawing area; femininity usually has curved or crossed lines; peacefulness is reflected in horizontal lines. Although there are individual differences, drawings tend to fall into recognizable "families."

The drawings I collected revealed that pictures of femininity closely resembled the drawings of joy, with rounded lines. Masculinity drawings more closely resembled the drawings of anger, with a sharp, harsh line quality. A similar sort of difference is replicated in people's dreams. Let's see what the researchers of dreams have caught in their nets.

Results of Research in Dream Content

Once again, keep in mind that the differences we have been discussing in women's and men's body structure and functioning are slight. So are the differences that have been measured between their dreams. We speak here of averages between groups of men and women. When women are compared with each other, there are usually greater differences between the women within the group than there are between the average woman and the average man.

Home Sweet Home: Women's Dream Settings

Investigators often report that women tend to set their dreams in familiar places.[42] Indoors, in a house or near it, is the most frequent setting, as in this example described to me by forty-year-old Jennifer:

> I am in a house made of glass, with Charlie. He is dancing
> naked. He wants me to take off my clothes and dance with him.
> I won't because it is a glass house and people would see me. I
> enjoy looking at him. He is so alive, naked. I feel so loving. I
> am sorry I haven't taken off my clothes, when I awake.

Charlie is an imaginary dream character. Jennifer's dream suggests that she is tempted to engage in some behavior that she fears would overexpose her, in the same way that the glass walls would do. Note that Jennifer uses the adjective *glass*, the adverb *naked*, and the qualifier *so*. She also refers to the concept "house" and to the human body—all characteristic of female dreamers. Although the setting is unfamiliar, it is indoors.

In contrast, men are less likely to dream of themselves in house settings;[43] they are more likely to picture themselves in unfamiliar, outdoor places, such as this dream that Len told me recently:

> I am climbing a mountain and see my father way down in the
> valley. He is calling my name and I ignore him. (I'm working
> through some problems with my father right now.)

In Len's dream language, he seems to be trying to move up in the world (the mountain) while conscious of his father's view, one that he is trying to forget. He may feel that the father-within-himself is holding him back.

Note that Len uses only one modifier—*way down*. A woman would usually elaborate the framework with more. She would also probably express the way she felt about hearing her father call her name and how it felt to ignore him, in the same way that Jennifer described her response to Charlie.

Psychoanalysts make an analogy between women's internal genitals and their inclination to indoor activity; men's erectile and projectile genitals are compared with their taste for the outdoor life. For the same reason Erik Erikson, from observations of children's play with blocks, stated that little girls build enclosures—inner space—whereas little boys build towers—outer space.[44]

Applying the concept of inner and outer space to dream content, C. B. Brenneis devised a scale to measure "ego style" in the dreams of men and women who were college students.[45] Results indicated a tendency for males to structure their dreams in terms of extension and separateness, whereas females tended to structure their dreams in terms of intimacy. Women, according to this view, confine themselves to small houses; men roam the wide-open dream ranges.

Unanswered Questions About Dream Settings. Is woman's place in the home in her dreams? Calvin Hall and Robert Van de Castle were the first to claim that it is. Their data was based upon an analysis of five hundred dreams from one hundred women and five hundred dreams from one hundred men, between the ages of eighteen and twenty-five, who were undergraduate college students in psychology classes at Case Western Reserve University and Baldwin-Wallace College. The dreams were gathered between 1947 and 1950.[46]

Examining the original data, it can be observed that the differences between male and female groups is fairly small.[47] Of the total 644 settings in the male dreams, 284 took place indoors (a proportion of .44), while 302 took place outdoors (a proportion of .46). In the female dreams with a total of 654 settings, 362 took place indoors (a proportion of .55), while 229 took place outdoors (a proportion of .35). The difference was measurable but the gap was small.

Hall and Van de Castle's data have served as a standard without question ever since it was published in their book *The Content Analysis of Dreams* in 1966. Surely there has been some change in women's dream content, reflecting the major social changes during the thirty years since the time this study began in 1947?

No, said Hall and his associates, based on a repeat of this study, carried out in 1979 and 1980.[48] This time the undergraduate college students in psychology classes were at the University of Richmond, a private, urban, coeducational institution that was judged to have students from the same socioeconomic level as Case Western Reserve in the first study. Hall reported that "there has been little change over a period of 30 years in what college students dream about."[49] Women still dream of being outdoors (a proportion of .37) less than men do (a proportion of .49). Figures for indoor settings, ambiguous settings, and no settings were not reported. Hall goes on to say that "sex difference or the lack of them in all of the content categories used in this study have remained the same in dreams collected from college students in 1950 and 1980."

However, other investigators are uncovering conflicting findings. Perhaps, as Carol Schreier Rupprecht, associate professor of comparative literature at Hamilton College, has pointed out, Hall's research has been gender-biased as well as gender-conscious.[50]

As women move more into the working world, there is some shift in this tendency to place dream action within a home. A recent study by a research team in Canada, headed by Monique Lortie-Lussier, compared the dreams of homemakers who were mothers with those of working women who were also mothers.[51]

These researchers found that changes in dream settings occur with changing roles. The dreams of the working mothers reflected more vocational settings than those of the homemaker-mothers—possibly allowing the dreamer to rehearse activities that were preoccupying her. It seems to be mainly the college-age and homebound female who tends to keep to her house in dreams and stick with well-known spots in her nighttime jaunts.

For instance, Jennifer, a professional who travels widely in her work, placed another of her dreams outdoors, followed by a vocational setting:

> I am in Hawaii to move the office. I'm unhappy. I'm driving, trying to get to the office and feeling lost. I'm on a road paralleling the coast on a cliff (it's not actually there). I see the city where I want to go, Honolulu, with tall buildings and a skyline. I am on the road to a military base.

> Finally I somehow get to the office. Everything has been removed—my books, plants, pictures, library, prints. My desk is empty. I don't have what I need to do my work. The whole office has been cleaned out. No way to do my work. I am afraid my plants will die. I can't find the boss. When I do, he is horrible, slimy, sleazy, untrustworthy, and shifty-eyed. He doesn't want to listen. I yell at him. He is impassive to my pleas.

Jennifer understood that this anxiety dream was related to her anger about not moving where she wanted to be in her office in waking life. In the first setting—outdoors in a familiar but distorted setting—she feels lost. She can see where she wants to go but has trouble getting there. She is in control (driving her own car), yet a dangerous cliff is close and she is heading toward greater restriction (the military base).

In the second scene—in a work setting that has changed—Jennifer is distraught to find she has been deprived of all that "makes life worthwhile." Her plants, she told me, were her own growth that was taken away. Her books are "what give sustenance to do my work, essential." Her pictures are "what I need to be strong. I get much beauty and pleasure from them."

The qualities of Jennifer's dream settings help her to recognize that the message of her dream relates to her feelings about work. Dramatically, they show her how alarmed, angry and deprived of valuable, essential things she currently feels. Recognizing this will help Jennifer take appropriate action in waking life.

Women who work in their daily lives also go to work in their dreams. The finding that women's dreams take place mostly in houses, as well as Erikson's concepts of inner space in the female's imagery and outer space in the male's imagery have been challenged. The bottom line seems to be that the dreamer places herself or himself in settings that are contiguous with daily life. The female attorney tries cases in her dreams; the woman runner performs marathons while she sleeps; the college-age woman whose experience is linked closely with classrooms and home will find herself in similar dream settings, whereas the professional whose work takes her to the Far East will sometimes set her dreams in Japanese hot springs or Balinese beaches.

Sheila, a well-traveled professional in her fifties, gave her dream an unfamiliar, unusual outdoor setting:

> I am with a whole group of women, jumping with parachutes
> over foreign territory. At first it looks as though we will hit
> land. Later the wind shifts and I see we are going to hit the sea.
> As we drift down, I see many small craft that will be able to
> retrieve us quickly. While we descend, we arrange ourselves
> into a rough circle and do a kind of song and dance in the air
> to try to control our descent. This raises a marvelous spirit
> among us and I think what fun it is, even though it is risky.

The air space above an unknown land is surely not a typical dream setting for a woman. Sheila's dream imagery is positive; although she is over "foreign territory" and there is some risk, the danger is small. Wherever she lands, she will have assistance. Her dream characters cooperate in a joyful pattern, easing her descent. Women sometimes select rare settings for their dream action.

The settings of dreams are not necessarily based on biology; they have, I believe, a continuity with our daily activities. The nineteenth-century female writers Jane Austen and Charlotte Brontë set their novels in drawing rooms, schools, homes, or local resorts; they were writing from their daily experience. Critics have attacked the "narrowness" of the scope of their writing without giving full recognition to the restrictions of the lives of women at the time these authors were writing.

A male like Tolstoy was free to travel extensively, engage in war, consort with women of all social levels, exchange with men of all ranks; he could write from the broader scope of his own experience. So, too, our dream lives are narrow or wide, depending upon our interaction with life.

Significance of Dream Settings. What sense can today's woman make of the controversy around dream settings and what relevance does it have for her life anyhow? Women who want to understand their dreams need not concern themselves with the ongoing debate among researchers about whether or not dream elements change over the years.

Averages mean little to the individual dreamer who wants to understand her personal dreams. To get the most information from your dream settings, think of them as stage sets for your inner dramas. Ask yourself why your dreaming mind chose to play out the scene in this particular place. Each set implies a meaning. Here are a few of the typical dream settings and their common symbolism (exact meaning will vary from dreamer to dreamer):

Dream Setting	*Common Symbolism*
Kitchen	Place where emotional nourishment is available
School	Place where one feels tested or place of learning
Bad crime area	Place where one feels in danger
Rocky area	Place where it is "hard" to move around
Shop	Place of making choices
Garden	Place of beautiful feelings

In the pages to come, we will see how dream settings help illuminate the meaning of dreams. Meanwhile, be sure to examine the characteristics of your dream settings. Are they familiar or strange? Old-fashioned or newfangled? Being torn down or expanded? Comfortable or awkward? Deteriorating or being reconstructed? Cramped or spacious? Each element adds a dimension to the symbolism of a dream setting.

"I've Grown Accustomed to Your Face": *Characters in Women's Dreams*

Results of Studies About Characters in Women's Dreams. As with settings, what we know about women's dream characters seems to depend upon when the study was made and what sample of women were examined.

The data from Hall and Van de Castle's work with college students demonstrated that women like to dream about people they know: their parents, their siblings, their mates or dates; their babies and children; their friends and foes.[52] Although men also sometimes dream of the same characters, especially their family, they are less likely to dream of familiar characters. The mention of a mother, as in Lynette's dream at the opening of this chapter, indicates a greater probability that the author of the dream is female.

In contrast, men often choose to dream of unfamiliar people, and more of groups than single individuals: these are frequently identified by their job, for example, banker, accountant, or car salesman, rather than being identified by their relationship with the dreamer.

Later studies, such as the ones conducted by Lortie-Lussier and her associates, suggest that when women move into work settings that require their dealing with more strangers on the basis of their job status, these characters make their appearance in women's dreams.[53] This is not a case of working women's dreams "becoming more like men's dreams," as some theorists have suggested. Characters in women's dreams and men's dreams mirror the areas of life each is coping with more—either directly or in fantasy—while awake.

Lortie-Lussier collected dreams from eighteen single female undergraduates who hoped later to combine motherhood with a career. She compared these dreams with those of nineteen university graduates who were already working mothers. Among the working mothers' dreams, work colleagues were featured alongside husbands and children. Only familiar characters starred in the students' dreams. Each group, it seems, was influenced by their daily contacts.

Women divide their attention into roughly equal parts between the female and male characters in their dreams. Men, in contrast, are more preoccupied with other men in dreams: twice as many men as women appear in men's dreams.[54] When I asked Van de Castle what the most striking difference between men's and women's dreams was, he asserted that it is this sex-ratio contrast, which is consistent across cultures.

We can speculate from these findings that most women have equal problems or conflicts with men and women, whereas men appear to be more concerned about their relationships with other men, especially authority figures.

However, in another study comparing the dreams of homemaker-mothers with working mothers, Lortie-Lussier and her colleagues found that more male characters appeared in the dreams of the working mothers.[55] Again, their dream content was influenced by their waking-life role.

Women register their daily activities with varying dream characters. My objection to most of the measurement scales is that they give the impression of a static picture. Women's dreams are more like an ongoing movie. They change as behavior and emotional state change. An individual woman will have characteristic trends, but the content of her dreams can shift with the blink of a night.

When the dream soup is boiled down, it reveals that women are, in general, more concerned about their emotional relationships to both sexes, whereas men are more occupied with succeeding or failing in reference to other men. Overall, women have more people in their dreams.

Significance of Dream Characters.   For the woman seeking to comprehend her own dream scenarios, it is useful to make careful note of characters that appear in her dreams. After the dreamer herself or himself, the person most dreamed about is usually the one with whom the strongest emotional bonding exists.[56]

Dreamers may ask themselves: What people do I dream about most? Why am I preoccupied with them? Do they represent themselves or a characteristic within me that I feel in need of, or one that I dislike in myself? What celebrities appear in my dreams? What quality do they represent in my dream plays? On the next page are a few short samples of common symbolism of characters in women's dreams (the precise meaning varies with the dreamer's personal associations).

Dream Character:	Common Symbolism:
Baby	A "newborn" quality of the dreamer or a special project
Husband or lover	A supportive, indifferent, or destructive aspect, depending on nature of relationship
Gardener	Someone who helps the dreamer grow

Throughout the chapters that follow, we shall see again and again how the characters in a woman's dream help her understand aspects of herself and her relationships to others. Lynette's mother, for example, in the opening dream sequence, represented for the dreamer an intuitive, sensitive part of herself that she wants to "bring to life."

The Great Nurturer: Animal Characters in Women's Dreams

In a garden near Rome stands a monumental statue-fountain known as Diana of Ephesus. She displays a multitude of breasts, each of which spout water. Viewing it one sunny afternoon, I thought how the ancients who worshiped her must have felt overwhelmed with the idea of being nourished by this goddess. Her many breasts flowing with fluid emphasized her role as nurturer.

Studies of Animals in Women's Dreams. The dreams of girls and women are filled with imagery that conveys a similar message. Mammals, according to Van de Castle, abound in the dreams of even young girls— some theorists believe that females intuitively sense at a deep level their role as milk-giving creatures.[57]

Small animals—kittens, puppies, bunnies, and so on—are very typical of women's dreams, especially during pregnancy from the second trimester onward, as we will see. In contrast, men are more likely to populate their dreamscapes with wilder, larger animals, with more birds—said to be associated with the erectile capacity of the penis—and other nonmammals.

In my 1984 study of children's dreams sixty-two girls reported roughly double the number of animals as fifty-eight boys. (However, since the girls' dreams were longer, this difference is hard to assess.) The only category in which boys had a greater number of animals than girls was dragons. No girl dreamed of a dragon, whereas six boys did so.[58]

Children as a group have more animals in their dreams than adults do. (From 28 to 60 percent of children's dreams contain animals compared with about 7 percent in adults' dreams.) The number of animals decrease as the child ages; tame animals begin to replace wild ones.[59]

Various explanations are offered for this characteristic trend of the appearance of smaller, milder animals in women's dreams. On average, women are smaller and gentler than men, as well as the makers of milk. Anthropologists estimate the size and strength of the average woman as approximately two-thirds that of the average man. Men tend to be physically larger, more muscular, and, many would say, more aggressive as well. Perhaps the dream animals reflect this condition.

Significance of Dream Animals in Women's Dreams. As with the other categories of dream content, what is important to the individual dreamer is her understanding of her own dream images.

Sonny, for example, in her late twenties, found herself puzzled by this dream:

> I am petting a friendly rat with curly, golden hair when it
> suddenly bites me. I wake up alarmed.

As we talked, it soon emerged that Sonny's boyfriend had curly hair with golden highlights in the sun. The two of them had been living together happily when they began to have a conflict about whether or not to marry. In Sonny's dream language, the "friendly rat" had turned nasty. Happily, the dilemma was solved and Sonny was married; she has developed a close and devoted relationship with her husband over the past several years.

Most dreamers have two or three favorite animals that recur in their dreams. My own, for instance, are cats and birds, whereas my husband's dream animals are usually dogs and horses. Animals often represent an instinctual part of the dreamer.

To decipher the symbolism of your own dream animals, it is helpful to ask yourself, What characteristics does this animal exhibit? How does this animal differ from other animals that are similar to it? Your answers will provide clues to the animal's presence in a particular dream. We will explore the meaning of dream animals further in the context of the specific dreams described in the following chapters.

The Sharp-Tongued Dagger:
Verbal Aggression in Women's Dreams

In general, women are more likely to resort to verbal rather than physical aggression when they are angry. Wounding with words is usually more effective for a woman than using physical strength.

Studies of Aggression in Women's Dreams.   The sting of women's aggression in dreams tends to take a similar form: a quick verbal stab or even a tongue-lashing. Male dreamers are more likely to picture men in their dreams behaving violently: chopping off heads, blowing up bodies, and slaughtering or being butchered by the enemies of the dark.

In dreams females are more likely to attack only when attacked, whereas male dreamers more often behave with unprovoked aggression. However, certain populations display different patterns of aggression. A researcher studying the dreams of 260 high school students in 1970 found, to his surprise, significantly more aggression in the females' dreams than in those of the males. Lower-class girls behaved more brutally in their dreams than their male counterparts, or than any of the middle-class students.[60]

Women dreamers usually aim aggression more at other female characters, or equally attack female and male characters. In comparison, men dreamers are mainly aggressive—in very direct ways—toward other male characters.[61] In general, there is more aggression in male dreams, and this sex difference becomes greater with age.[62]

Poor Little Matchgirl: The Victim Role in Women's Dreams.   Being the victim rather than the victor is the most common response to aggression among female dreamers. One investigatory team studying college students' dreams found that a chase scene without violence was almost unique in women's dreams. Male dreams often had male aggressors, whereas female dreams often had animal aggressors. Few victims of either sex fought back in their dreams; women were less likely to do so.[63]

In some ways female victimization in dreams parallels life events; both are subject to change. For the most part, male characters are the villains in women's dreams. The male stranger is the most common villain in dreams of both sexes.[64]

Significance of Aggression in Women's Dreams.   Individual dreamers can learn about the nature of their relationships by observing the pattern of violence in their dreams. Dreamers may ask, Am I often victimized in my dreams? Who is the villain? Are males more unfriendly to me in my dreams? Does it depend upon the man? Are females unfriendly in my dreams? Which women? Are they authority figures or colleagues? Do characters treat me differently under different dream circumstances? How do I respond? Do I defend myself? Do I resolve dream dilemmas?

In chapters to come, we will explore the meanings that aggression has to individual women in the context of their specific dreams.

Party Girl: Friendly Interactions in Women's Dreams

Studies of Friendliness in Women's Dreams.   Female dreamers seem to be more democratic than males in dispensing friendly actions: both male and female dream characters are treated in a friendly manner. "You and I were having fun in my dream last night," said one girlfriend in my study to another:

> You're dressed in a wonderful Irish tweed cape with a beret.
> We go to a special place on our way to a bird shop.

Happy, friendship-type dreams are not uncommon for women and their friends of both sexes.

"Wanna fight?" might be the motto for a man speaking to another man in his dreams. In comparison with women, men tend to be more aggressive with the male characters in their dreams, while they are more prone to treat their female characters in a friendly manner.

Several studies have reported that women exhibit more friendliness in their dreams; they also receive more friendly overtures.[65] In general, however, all dreamers have less friendly behavior in their dreams than they do aggression.

An interesting sidelight to these findings about dream aggression occurs in Van de Castle's data. He reports that the friendliness of women in their dreams varies with their menstrual cycle. Women are more friendly to other female dream characters during their periods, he says—perhaps identifying more with each other. During the remainder of the month, he found, the women in his sample were less friendly to female dream characters. Instead they tended to befriend their male dream population.

Significance of Friendliness in Women's Dreams.   Perhaps nature prompts women to feel more friendly toward men, awake or asleep, when the likelihood of conception is greater.

Whatever the cause, women may wish to observe whether their friendly dream acts change during their menstrual cycle. Also worthwhile noting is how dreamers typically relate to the men and women in their dreams. Are you always hostile or friendly to the men in your dreams? Does it depend upon the man? Do you have a consistent reaction to the females in your dreams? Do your characters typically hinder, frustrate, or cooperate with you?

The answers to these questions will give the dreamer material to assess how she or he is predisposed toward the opposite sex—in a positive or negative way. Ambivalence, most dreamers will find, exists in their dream relationships, just as in waking life.

The Romantic Interlude: Sexual Interactions in Women's Dreams

Studies of Sex in Women's Dreams. When women make love in dreams, they, more often than men, choose to do so with someone well known to them: a husband, a sweetheart, or an exciting colleague.[66] Occasionally they will select a celebrity—Paul Newman is particularly favored because of the symbolism of his name: "new man." Or, they may choose a power figure, such as the president, to become their lover in a dream. Even less seldom, women conjure up golden angels or Greek gods to raise themselves to celestial dream ecstasies. In general, however, they prefer home turf for dream romancing.

Men differ in that they seem to be most stimulated in dreams by the unknown female, the exotic stranger. Their passionate dreams soon get down to basic intercourse, with little lingering foreplay—in this, too, some will say, dreams parallel life. One study of college students found that more males had dreams of nudes than females did.[67]

We have mentioned that women, as well as men, are now known to become sexually aroused during dream periods. While dreaming, their nipples become erect, their vaginal temperature and pulse rate increase, and there is greater blood flow to the genitals. These bodily changes correspond to the penile erections long observed in males, especially on awakening from the morning dream. Even infant boys display an erect penis while dreaming—an indication that the behavior is a natural process, not a learned one.

Women, like men, also experience orgasms during dreams, although the frequency is less. Sexual mobilization of the body usually occurs regardless of whether or not the dream content is sexual; it is part of the general nervous system arousal each of us experience while we dream.

Some theorists think that sexuality in women's dreams is connected with their menstrual cycle. Unfortunately the studies that have investigated this possibility came up with contradictory findings. One research team, Ethel Swanson and David Foulkes, measured four female college students in the laboratory over forty-four nights, waking them periodically to find out what they were dreaming. The investigators reported that sexuality in dream content was highest during menstruation and also when the women reported low waking sexual desire.[68]

In another study Van de Castle asked women about their dreams. He reported more sexual dreams before ovulation than during menstruation.[69] Additional evidence is needed to determine which behavior is more characteristic.

A study done with paraplegic men and women found that several of them had orgasmic imagery in their dreams. This suggests that the experience of orgasm may be as much a function of the brain as it is of the genitals.[70] It is unclear to what extent prior experience, and therefore memory, played in these subjects' orgasmic dream responses.

Fewer Sexual Dreams in Women.   Women in general dream less about sex than men do. A study of college students found that sexual interaction appeared in only 4 percent of the women's dreams, whereas 12 percent of the men's dreams included sex.[71] In Kinsey's classical study of nearly eight thousand women, about 70 percent said they had had overtly sexual dreams sometime in their lives. Among the men, nearly 100 percent of the almost six thousand in the sample reported having erotic dreams.[72]

In chapter 1, we described how, although females mature physically at an earlier age than males, their sexual responsiveness develops later. (See the sections "Women's Sexual Peaks Develop Later" and "Women's Sexual Dreams Develop Later" for details.) It is worth repeating that it is not until females are twenty-nine years old that there is a percentage of experienced individuals that compares with that of males at age fifteen.[73]

We saw, too, how dream life seems to parallel the discrepancy of the waking-life pattern. Young men begin having nocturnal emissions with their sexual dreams at an early age. By age fifteen, nocturnal emissions occurred in dreams of about 40 percent of the males. In comparison, only 2 percent of the females had experienced erotic dreams to orgasm by age fifteen.

As they age, more women have erotic dreams to orgasm, although men still have more of them. Males have their greatest frequency of dreams with nocturnal emissions in their teens and twenties; women have the most sexual dreams with orgasm in their forties. Sex dreams seem, in part, to be a mirror of the actual experience a person has had.

Among those women who do have orgasmic dreams, they have them less often than men. The younger males reported having orgasmic dreams four to eleven times a year; the older males had them three to five times a year. One of the younger males said he had as many as twelve erotic dreams to orgasm each *week*. Women of all ages reported an average of three to four orgasmic dreams per year.

Kinsey found that a woman's sexual dreams were likely to increase under given conditions: when the dreamer's usual sexual outlet was inadequate, reduced, or eliminated; when she was widowed; when she was in prison; when her husband was away; and when she ceased ingesting certain drugs.

On the other hand sexual dreams did not usually begin until the woman had experienced sexuality in the waking state. Orgasmic dreams often started the same year that one or more of the other types of sexual activity began, such as masturbation, petting, or intercourse. There seemed to be a correlation between a high level of erotic responsiveness and the number of orgasmic dreams. Some women with high rates of orgasm in daily life also have high rates of orgasmic dreams.[74]

Content of Sexual Dreams. Heterosexual dreams were reported most often among the women in Kinsey's sample; 85 to 90 percent had such dreams. Homosexual dreams were reported by some 8 to 10 percent; dreams of sexual relations with animals were reported by about 1 percent of the women.[75]

Kinsey found that the women in his group more often mentioned sexual partners that were obscure rather than known people, in contrast to Hall and Van de Castle's finding. Sometimes the dreamer herself was participating in the sexual act; at other times she watched another dream character. Kinsey also observed that sex dreams customarily reflected experiences the dreamer had had in waking life. Dreams of intercourse were more common among those who had engaged in it; likewise, dreams of petting, rape, homosexual contact, animal contact, sadomasochistic dreams, as well as dreams of pregnancy, were more likely to be reported by women who had experienced these events.

Kinsey mentions the curious finding that a number of young men dream of women with male genitals—a phenomenon he attributes to the fact that the men who have not directly observed female genitals have difficulty visualizing them. He does not say whether females reported a similar kind of dream about men.

Significance of Sexual Intercourse in Women's Dreams.   The individual dreamer may benefit from observing romantic behavior in personal dreams. Dreamers may ask, What partner do I choose for romantic dream encounters? Is this person a stranger or is he known to me? Does he represent a genuine attraction or does he represent a quality I need? What is the nature of our contact—harsh or tender, domineering or cooperative? Do I have unusual types of sexual interactions in dreams?

Answers to such questions will guide the dreamer to better understand emotions about waking relationships. The dreamer may find that sexual intercourse in a dream symbolizes integration with a missing element more than a particular person—a need for tender treatment, a need to recontact artistic impulses, and so forth. Later on we will explore the various meanings of sexuality in the context of specific dreams.

What Women Focus on in Their Dreams

Our dreaming minds, just as in waking life, pick out the area of the ongoing activity that most piques our interest.

Color Me Fascinating.   One of the elements frequently mentioned by women that rarely arises in men's dreams is color. We know very little about color in dreams beyond this basic observation.

In one of the few studies of color in dreams, an ophthalmologist (a physician who specializes in the eye) studied the dreams of six men. These subjects recorded their dreams over five months; immediately upon awakening, or as soon as possible thereafter, they matched any dream colors they observed with samples from a color atlas.

The ophthalmologist found that only half of the dreams referred to color at all. Of the dreams that did contain color, forty-nine colors were recorded (the number of dreams was not specified by the investigator). Half of the colors mentioned were near-white or pastel. Intense colors were usually red or orange in hue. The researcher concluded that the paucity of purple, blue, or blue-green in the dreams in his study could be anatomically related to the small number of blue units in the color areas of the cortex.[76]

Would female dreams investigated in the same manner exhibit more color? I suspect they would. Females are far more aware of color in waking life as well as having been observed to speak of color in their dreams more than males do. The mention of color in Lynette's dream at the opening of this chapter is a clue to the feminine nature of its author. Notice that the colors referred to in her dream include blue—a color that was found to be extremely rare in male dreamers.

Usually the greater number of color references in female dreams is attributed to their well-known daily interest in the topic. However, it seems to me that color sensitivity may be based on biological differences between males and females.

Women's Superior Color Sense.   Women actually perceive color better than men do. In fact for the first eight months of life they see more acutely than males. Although from the age of six years, males are measured as having more acute vision, women's perception of color is less frequently impaired than males.[77] Color blindness occurs in only one out of two hundred females, whereas one out of twelve males suffers this deficiency. Small wonder that women mention color more often in their dreams if they perceive its nuances more accurately.

Of course many men have developed a fine color sense, but they are often in the art field or some other occupation where they have been exposed to special training.

Regardless of whether color awareness may be traced to genetic or environmental conditions, or a combination, dreamers can gather more information about themselves by noting the colors in their dreams. It is particularly important to observe colors that recur and in what circumstances. Do you seem to dream in black and white rather than technicolor? Do your dream colors tend to be drab and dingy? Are your dream hues vivid or garish? Luminous or ethereal? What feelings and experiences do you associate with the colors that light up your dreams?

The whole issue is a complex one, and anything we can learn about it is helpful. Intensely emotional dreams tend to be more brilliantly colored. People who are able to induce dreams in which they know they are dreaming, lucid dreams, invariably comment upon the vividness of the colors. They often speak of glowing, luminescent color, "as if lit from within," unlike any ordinary dream.

Adornment and Faces in Women's Dreams.   In addition to color, women also focus on clothing and jewelry in their dream descriptions more than the average male.[78] These objects are likely to reflect their daily interest.

Women in waking life are usually more concerned with relating to people than to things; preoccupation with the human face naturally accompanies this attitude. Females incline to speak of the hair, eyes, and features of their dream characters.[79]

Here, too, dreamers can benefit from observing the focus their dreams take. What magnetizes your attention in your dreams? What significance do these attributes or objects serve? As will become apparent, the whole dream action sometimes revolves around these "props."

Flowers in Women's Dreams. Women also have a propensity to dream about flowers. This image is thought to be a sexual referent as well as a thing of beauty—the blossom being the sexual organ of the plant, with its fragrance and form designed to attract the creature that will fertilize it.

Artist Judy Chicago's depiction of women throughout history in the form of floral plates makes use of the same analogy of female genitals and flowers. In the delightful musical *The King and I,* the king sings of the desirability of man flitting like the bee from flower to flower, ". . . but flower never goes from bee to bee to bee." Fortunately, women are not so rooted as flowers and, in their dreams and their lives, are able to move more freely.

The specific flowers that grow in dreams contain messages for the dreamer. Like the Victorian "language of love," each blossom has significance. Dreamers may ask, Why this particular flower at this particular time? What do I associate with this bloom? What have I experienced in connection with it? What qualities mark it as being different from other flowers? As we shall see, flowers are often associated in women's dreams with images of romance and sexuality.

Enclosures in Women's Dreams. Women tend to refer to household areas, especially rooms. For a large number of women these areas and the objects in them are more a part of their daily activity than they are for men. In this way dreams mirror life.

For working women household objects and areas can become symbols of obstacles or hindrances to their career. Some of these women understandably see brooms or piles of dirty laundry as extremely negative symbols in their dreams.

Rooms, we have said, are postulated to indicate something beyond daily experience. Since women's bodies enclose an internal space, inside the womb, with its entrance through the vagina, psychoanalysts have asserted that this "interior room" is represented by the rooms and houses in women's dreams. Whatever the explanation may prove to be, researchers often note that women describe more rooms in their dreams than men do.

Along this line, pregnant women report more architectural structures in their dreams than nonpregnant women do. One researcher, Patricia May-bruck, found that the buildings in the dreams of her pregnant subjects increased in size as the women's abdomens grew.[80] We explore this further in the context of specific pregnancy dreams.

Meanwhile, as we observed in reference to dream settings, it is useful for dreamers to observe the spaces in their dreams. Do your dreams take place more in one room than another? What experiences and qualities do you associate with this room? What makes it different from other rooms in the house? What takes place in these areas? Where do you have more trouble and where more pleasure?

While women are dreaming of rooms and flowers, men are busy regarding with their inner eye the tools, weapons, automobiles, and money that fill their dream spaces. These elements are thought by some theorists to be symbolic references to the male phallus and its function.

At the same time women are describing the colors and clothing, jewelry, eyes and faces, of their dream characters, men are talking about the size, the speed, and the intensity of their dream props. "A space rocket thrust off . . ." would be more typical of a man's dream account.

Feeling, Talking, Sensing, Judging— Activities in Women's Dreams

Women are infinitely more expressive of how they feel during their dreams than men are. Just as they speak more openly of feelings in everyday life, so, too, are women's dreams filled with emotion.[81]

And with words. Women describe more conversation in their dreams, and their characters tell them things: newborn babies expound truths, animals speak wisely, and inanimate objects utter comments.

In a dream that occurred as I began this book project, I was being considered as a member of an elite literary society. Several of the members stated their opinion that membership should be allowed later, not yet. A bust of Jane Austen, set on a shelf above wainscoting, spoke up on my behalf. As a founder of the organization and respected author, she was well qualified, even in statue form, to endorse my case.

Fantastic paintings, squalid tenements—the beauty or ugliness of a scene is more significant to the woman dreamer. Moral and aesthetic judgments, too, are more likely to occur in women's accounts of their dreams: "It was incredibly beautiful. . . ."; "The stranger was evil. . . ."

While women are judging, sensing beauty or lack of it, being emotional and communicating, men are occupied dreaming about success and failure—themes that dominate their side of the dream bed. We have already mentioned that they engage in more sexual adventures in their dreams than women. Sharing the same bed, a woman and her man may dream quite differently. This concept is stated succinctly in the Chinese proverb "Same bed, different dreams."[82]

Extrasensory Perception: The Psychic Side of Women's Dreams

Dream researchers find that women report more psychic dreams than men do. For example, a woman who dreams of a loved relative falling ill or dying when she has had no current physical contact with the person, or any other clue in the environment, may be experiencing extrasensory perception. Many of the women I interviewed for this study described dreams that seemed to imply psychic dimensions. Perhaps women's interest in other people tunes them in with greater sensitivity to subtle perceptions.

If you are a dreamer who experiences extrasensory perception in your dreams, you may find that keeping a record of your dreams will help you identify the difference between ordinary dreaming and predictive dreams. Notice in particular any recurring elements or themes.

Our dreams make our inner self visible. What do your dreams reveal about you? In some ways you are sure to resemble dreamers of your own sex. In other ways you are unique. The chapters to come will provide a standard against which you can compare your own dreams and will give clues to help you better understand these nightly adventures.

Following are two forms. One is a test to help sharpen your awareness of the differences that may exist between women's dreams and men's dreams. If you have already taken it, go ahead and read the *"Gender Checklist for Dream Reports."* It summarizes the differences in dreams often observed between sexes, although it is far from infallible. You may wish to use it with individual dreams to assess how accurate the current beliefs may or may not be. If you have not yet taken the *Dream Test*, you may wish to do so before examining the checklist.

While taking the test, keep in mind that some men resemble women in speech patterns. Highly fluent literary men—poets and novelists—often share women's proclivity for elaborate description. Also, homosexual men sometimes adopt speech patterns that are more feminine in style.

Gender Checklist for Dream Reports*

Characteristic	Women	Men
1. Recall	☐ better ☐ fluctuates with period	☐ poorer
2. Length	☐ longer	☐ shorter
3. Type words	☐ more adjectives ☐ may refer to husband, home, or crying	☐ few adjectives, sparse ☐ may refer to wife, auto, any vehicle, travel, or hitting
4. Setting	☐ familiar ☐ indoor	☐ unfamiliar ☐ outdoor
5. Characters	☐ equal number of males and females ☐ single characters ☐ familiar characters ☐ described by relation, e.g., mother, baby, brother	☐ males twice as often as females ☐ groups ☐ unfamiliar ☐ described by job, e.g., banker, lawyer
6. Animals	☐ mammals ☐ small creatures ☐ domesticated	☐ nonmammals ☐ large creatures ☐ wild creatures
7. Aggression	☐ equal to male or female ☐ more nonphysical	☐ mainly to males ☐ more physical

* Based on current research. Differences between male and female dreams are small. Special populations may differ. Future research may reveal changes or invalidate current findings.

Characteristic	Women	Men
8. Friendliness	☐ equal to male or female	☐ mainly to females
9. Sex	☐ more romantic flavor	☐ more basic
	☐ fewer orgasms	☐ more dream orgasms
10. Color	☐ often mentioned	☐ rarely mentioned
11. Focus	☐ clothing, jewelry	☐ cars, vehicles
	☐ eyes, face, hair	☐ money
	☐ flowers	☐ size, speed, intensity
12. Emotions	☐ often mentioned	☐ rarely mentioned
13. Sensations	☐ often	☐ rare
14. Conversation	☐ often	☐ rare
15. Judgments (moral, aesthetic)	☐ often	☐ rare
16. Themes	☐ relationships	☐ success, failure

Dream Test

....

Indicate whether these verbatim dream descriptions are from male or female dreamers:

☐ 1. I dreamt I was on an operating table. A sheet was pulled over my head and I was wheeled away. (I knew it was an omen of defeat.)

☐ 2. Dreamt that my little baby came to life again: that it had only been cold, and that we rubbed it before the fire, and it lived.

☐ 3. I dreamt I was looking in a glass when a horrible face—the face of an animal—suddenly showed over my shoulder.

☐ 4. Dreamt [a man] came into my room, his throat encircled with blood, saying, "I met [a woman] coming out of [a man's] room."

☐ 5. Dreamt many great waters fell from heaven. The first struck the earth about four miles away from me with a terrific force.

☐ 6. Dreamt of a beetle that bites like a scorpion.

☐ 7. Dreamt father was alive again and I could say all the things I had meant to say to him.

☐ 8. Dreamt I was lying in bed when [a husband and wife] entered the room. They were badly cut, with bones protruding through their skin, [the husband] weaker and leaning on [the wife]. They begged me to get up, saying that the sea was flooding the house and it was coming down. I did and looked out the terrace window fronting the sea, which rushed into the house. Then I thought I was choking [a man].

☐ 9. I dreamt I am in a house, probably mine (must have been the dining room). There are several white doves fluttering against the window. Light is coming against the window. I am very careful not to open the door, concerned they shouldn't go out of the house. I feel very happy.

☐ 10. Dreamt that I see my dead mother. In the dream I know that she is dead, but she seems young, beautiful, full of laughter. We talk and I feel very happy.

☐ **Total Correct**

Answers

1. Male, Winston Churchill, after World War II, the night before the election in which he was defeated.

2. Female. Mary Wollstonecraft Shelley, English writer and wife of the poet, two weeks after she found her baby dead on March 6, 1815.

3. Female. Virginia Woolf, English novelist, two years before she committed suicide by drowning on March 28, 1941. The dream probably relates to her fear of returning madness. She says she was sexually abused at age three by her stepbrother while looking into a mirror.

4. Male. Duncan Grant, a painter of the Bloomsbury intellectual circle. He was the lover of Vanessa Bell, Virginia Woolf's sister. The characters refer to Quentin, Vanessa's son by her husband, Clive Bell; Angelica, the daughter of Vanessa and Grant; and his former homosexual lover, Bunny, now in love with Angelica. The dream depicts Grant's jealousy of Bunny's response to Angelica.

5. Male. Albrecht Dürer, German artist-engraver. The morning of this dream he painted a picture of it and prayed that such a catastrophe would be prevented.

6. Male. D. H. Lawrence, English novelist, about men in his circle. He referred to them as "swarming selves."

7. Female. Vanessa Bell, artist, sister of Virginia Woolf. Her relationship with her father, the scholar Leslie Stephen, had been stressful.

8. Male. Percy Bysshe Shelley, English poet, two weeks before he drowned in a boating accident at age thirty, on July 8, 1822. His first wife had committed suicide by drowning on November 9, 1816. The couple referred to were houseguests at his summer villa on the Gulf of Spezia, Italy.

9. Female. Nanette, in her eighties.

10. Female. Lynette, then in her mid-thirties, about her mother who died of cancer.

Score correct: 0–5   Chance score or worse
6–8   Good at recognizing male/female dream styles
9–10   Professional level

Growing-Up and Menstrual Dreams

A huge red purse is suspended from a pole that is carried by two men, who support it between them on their shoulders. The purse is so large and heavy it requires the two to carry it. I wake up knowing that my period will start today . . .

—*Premenstrual dreamer*

Women who are sensitive to their dream imagery learn to recognize where they are in their menstrual cycle from the pictures in their dreams. If you are a woman in your menstrual years, you may find it useful to learn your own unique dream symbols for each stage of the menstrual cycle. Your time of ovulation and fertile receptivity, when your period is due, when it is about to end, and when there is a malfunction—each is represented in your dreams. Even if you are not in your menstrual years, knowing how the dreaming mind represents female genitals can expand your understanding of your dreams.

Certain symbols—such as the pocketbook in the dream quoted above—typically refer to the womb. Many objects that are shaped like a receptacle, with an opening capable of enclosing contents, may represent the womb in dreams. Other symbols—such as the two men required to support the purse—relate to the dreamer's individual circumstances. In her case, this dreamer had two lovers; between the two men in her life, her femininity hung suspended. The pole was probably the dreamer's symbol for the phallus, as elongated, oblong objects frequently are for dreamers. The heaviness of the dreamer's purse referred to the heaviness in her womb that was about to shed its accumulated monthly blood.

By learning the usual symbols for stages of the menstrual cycle in women's dreams, and by becoming aware of one's own personal symbols, a woman can gauge much of what is happening in her internal parts.

The Beginning of Womanhood: Menarche

The greatest rhythmic cycle of a woman's life is probably her span of fertility, covering a space of approximately thirty to forty years. Its onset—called menarche—is marked with emotion and accompanied by ritual. Its cessation—called menopause—may be less defined and less honored than its beginning, but it is nonetheless a dramatic marker.

Between these two milestones, woman's potential for giving birth is staked. It is now, if at all, that she is to ripen a united egg and seed, nurture it in her womb, and eventually give birth to a child. Her capacity to be uniquely female—to become a mother—is bracketed by menarche and menopause. What she chooses to make of this time, or whether she will avail herself of her biology, depends upon a multitude of factors.

We look here at how young girls experience the commencement of menstruation and how this event affects their dreams as well as their bodies. We see how, during the same time frame, they undergo an emotional struggle for independence that is also reflected in their dreams. Then we examine the established menstrual process in adult women and observe how their dreams correspond to their cycles.

Even if menarche seems to a woman like an event from her distant past, the behavioral responses she had to this key occurrence are important for her to recall to mind. From her contemporary perspective, she can better understand her attitudes toward being a female that are expressed in her dreams. She can comprehend the symbolism of menstruation as it appears in her own dreams and better assist her daughters, granddaughters, female friends, or clients in interpreting their feminine dream symbolism.

Becoming a Woman: Premenarche Changes

The orderly unfolding of changes in a young girl's body as she enters womanhood—her puberty—is understood better today than ever before.[1] As is well known, the physical pattern follows a sequence: sometime between the ages of eight and sixteen—the average menarche being between twelve and thirteen in the United States—a young girl's physique undergoes transformation. Activated by the pituitary gland at the base of her brain, her glands release sexual hormones in a complex interaction into her bloodstream.

Taller, Heavier, and Rounder. In response the girl experiences a "growth spurt." Heretofore, since she was two years old, she has been gaining height at the rate of about two inches each year; now she grows taller by as much as four inches in one year. She does not slow down again until after her first menstrual period.

Most girls reach their full adult height from one to three years after their first period, which is about two years before boys of the same age. This mismatched growth pattern makes many a teenage girl miserable. "I remember towering over my partners at Friday night dancing class. It was mortifying," reported one woman in my study. Most women in my study—for differing reasons—recalled this time of their lives with considerable discomfort.

The bones of the body are actually growing at different rates. Leg and arm bones grow more rapidly than those of the torso, giving the "all legs," coltish look to many teenagers. The lower part of the face lengthens and fills out; the hips widen. Hip breadth is the only female body measurement that exceeds those of the average male. Fat deposits accumulate on hips, buttocks, and thighs, producing a more curvaceous, womanly shape. These changes in the young girl's pelvis, of course, prepare her body to be able to accommodate and deliver a child.

Gaining weight appears to be crucial to triggering the body mechanism that brings on the first period. Researcher Rose Frisch considers the "critical weight" that activates menarche to be somewhere between 94 and 103 pounds.[2] At this weight there are enough calories stored in the body to provide energy to carry a fetus to term and breastfeed for a month, even if the girl should be poorly nourished.

The percentage of body fat to muscle is especially related to when periods begin. During the young girl's growth spurt, the composition of her body has a 5-to-1 ratio of lean to fat tissue. For her periods to start, her lean to fat ratio must be about 3 to 1. The "baby fat" that brings on menarche increases by 125 percent in two or three years.[3] Although some youngsters resent becoming plumper, it is a natural part of becoming a woman.

Girls who exercise excessively or who unduly limit their food intake, as some ballet dancers do, postpone their sexual development by maintaining bodies that have too little fat on them to stimulate the onset of menstruation. Concentration-camp victims probably lost their periods for the same reason, although one woman in the study who had survived a concentration camp told me she believes that the little food they received was medicated to eliminate sexual desire as well as menstruation.

Girls' Emotions About Altering Body Shape

Mature women in my study still remembered how uncomfortable they felt about their bodies as adolescents. These negative emotions frequently had little to do with the objective facts.

Sadly Short and Stocky.   Some women suffered because they felt too small or too plump:

> I felt chubby, too thick in the middle, and I was too short.

> I always felt thick and chunky. I was passable height, if only my knees had been higher. My knees were too low.

> By eighth grade I felt chunky and almost ungainly. My sister was svelte; I felt like an elephant.

> I always felt a little too plump—my mother talked about my being fat.

Sweetly Petite.   Other women enjoyed being shorter than average or wished for it:

> I always thought being short would be neat, to be little and feminine.

> In the South the ideal was to be petite, so I was fortunate.

Traumatically Tall and Thin.   Still other women suffered the opposite height problem:

> I've been the same height since sixth grade. It was pretty traumatic for a female. I always had crushes on the smallest boys.

> At eleven years old I was five foot six and wore a size 9 shoe. I was gigantic—the tallest kid in school. I was thrilled when I stopped growing, because my sister grew to six feet.

> I was too tall and skinny. It was a major issue between my mother and me. Our culture thinks a man should be able to have "a grab of the flesh," so it was wrong to be thin. I was a vegetarian and felt self-conscious that my family was always watching me to see if I ate enough.

> I was too skinny, too tall, and too ugly. I tried to bend over so that I would look shorter.

> I was born five foot six! I was gangly and taller than any boy in eighth or ninth grade. I felt like an ugly duckling.

> I was tall and slender, like my father's family. All my mother's family were short and round, robust with big breasts. My mother literally tied me to the chair to make me eat more.

Regally Tall.   Very few women enjoyed being taller than their class-mates:

> I liked being tall, I always liked the look of it. My father's family is tall, and among them I was only medium tall.

Pear-Shaped or Top-heavy.   Yet other women focused on the distribution of fatty tissue as the major discomfort of their changing bodies:

> I was kind of pear-shaped. I felt like two people put together; from my waist up I was one person and from my waist down I was another person. I wanted to be smaller in the hips and thighs and bigger in the breasts.

> I was heavy, but most of my weight was in my tits. I was really embarrassed.

Cute and Content.   Only a few women felt relatively happy with their body size and shape during their early adolescent years:

> Through ninth grade I felt gorgeous. I was very athletic—the head "pep girl." My body was always a great support. It was later that my self-image changed.

> I thought I was good-looking. I was very active, swam, and rode horseback.

> I was skinny and shorter than my younger sister, but it didn't bother me. I went swimming and climbing every day.

The women who felt more content about their bodies during their early teens were mostly those who were physically active. Perhaps their activity gave them greater confidence.

Differing Timetables.   Since each woman has her own internal timetable for growth, the final results are not in until mature size is reached. Some women who were content during their teens later became uncomfortable:

> I never felt real big or small. Now it's been a big issue for most of my adult life. If I'm around someone who is bigger than me, I feel young and small. If I'm with someone smaller, I feel bigger.

One of the participants, who "always thought I was tall and big and unwieldy," grew to be average height with beautifully distributed weight, yet, "Whenever I feel insecure, that's what comes to the surface again." The emotions a woman experiences about her changing body during puberty remain with her throughout life. She may look back with compassion at the foolish notions of her younger self, but, under stress, the old insecurities resurface, even though she may now be aware they are inappropriate.

Such alterations in height, in weight, and in shape begin to take place in a young girl about two years prior to her first period. They are part of the so-called secondary sex characteristics that result from her sexual hormones. Other transformations are under way.

Budding Breasts and Growing Hair.   At the same time that height, weight, and shape are shifting, pubic hairs are beginning to appear. The curly hairs that grow in the area of a woman's body where the legs come together cover a mound of flesh called the *mons veneris* (from the Latin words meaning "little hill or mount" and Venus, the goddess of love). This "hill of Venus," or "mound of love," is sometimes depicted in dreams as a forest or garden.

Researchers now classify the development of pubic hair into five stages.[4] From birth until about two years before the first menstruation, these hairs are like those on the rest of her body—soft, downy, and light colored (stage 1). Then a few dark, longer, curlier hairs appear (stage 2). They become progressively thicker (stage 3). By the time they cover most of the *mons* and the labia (outer lips of the genitals), most girls have their first menses (63 percent start at stage 4), although some start earlier and some later. By the adult stage (stage 5) the pubic hair takes the shape of an upside-down triangle.

Soon the young girl begins to grow underarm hair. The soft, dark hair under the arms does not usually appear until after the pubic hair has begun growing, or sometimes not until after the first period.

Around this same time the young girl begins developing "breast buds"; these, too, are described as undergoing five stages.[5] From infancy to about one year before her menarche, the girls' breasts are flat with only the nipples raised, much like those of boys (stage 1). When small buttonlike mounds form, the nipples enlarge, and the dark area around them—the areola—gets wider and darker, they are considered "breast buds" (stage 2). The breasts grow fuller and rounder (stage 3). When the nipple and areola form a mound that protrudes beyond the rounded breast, the majority of girls have their first periods (62 percent begin to menstruate at stage 4). At the adult stage, breasts are round and full with dark nipples and areola (stage 5).

Some girls zoom through these five stages of breast development in six months; others take six years—the average is one year. Being earlier or later in breast budding does not determine the final shape of the woman's breasts. Some women do not reach their full development until after having birthed and suckled a child.

Our culture gives much attention to the size of women's breasts. Perhaps this is why no other area of bodily change makes such an impression upon the growing girl. Many women in the study found breast development—or underdevelopment—difficult to tolerate.

In the early stages the developing girls often still went without tops in summer and found themselves teased or clutched at by "friendly" uncles or big brothers:

My uncle used to call my breasts "little buds" and grab at them when I'd be bare-topped. I used to wish I were a boy.

My older sister's boyfriend used to joke and call me "Chestnuts" when my breasts began to grow.

Now is the time for "training bras" and comparisons between girlfriends. I remember listening to two girlfriends taunting each other with being "low-slung" versus "chicken-breasted." Almost everyone in the study recalled vivid incidents about their changing bodies at adolescence.

Small and Sad.   Some of the women I interviewed described being miserable at puberty because they felt their breasts were too small:

A bunch of us decided we were destined to be flat-chested forever. We sent away for a "Guaranteed Breast Improvement" from a magazine and got back a picture of a man's hand! It was awful.

My brother called them "walnuts." Once my mother gave me a Christmas present of a "Littlest Angel" training bra. Even though I'd asked for it, I didn't want it in front of my brothers, who were home from college. They howled with laughter, and I ran to my room in tears.

Later I wore a padded bra to school and everyone made fun of me. It was so obvious because it was pointy.

I wore a padded bra and did bust exercises to no avail.

It was awful. I developed round shoulders and wore frilly blouses or overblouses that didn't show my body. It kept me from feeling sexy. I wouldn't go to the beach.

I never got any shape and was extremely sensitive about it—and am to this day. I was unmercifully teased by my brother in front of dates. He called me "No Tits" or said, "She's a carpenter's dream—flat as a board."

Small and Satisfied.   Only a very few of the women felt content to be small and wished to not be troubled with breast growth altogether:

In my country, breasts are small. I just didn't think about their size, except that older girls couldn't swim and climb as well with them. I never wore a bra until I was pregnant.

Big and Bitter.   Being larger-breasted did not solve the problem with body image. Several women suffered at puberty because they felt their breasts were too large:

> I wore a size 40 bra at age twelve—and I wasn't overweight. I looked like Mae West, twice the size of other girls. The doctors gave me all kinds of injections. The worst was that the older boys made jokes and drew nude pictures with my name. I overcompensated by being prudish and spending time in church. When I was around fourteen, I discovered some *Esquire* magazines with drawings of girls like me, and decided it was okay to have big boobs.

> My breasts were much too large. I was so ashamed I tied them flat. At that time it was the fashion to be flat-chested.

> I was far too big—bigger than any girl in school. Other kids called them "jumpers." I tried to strap them down so they wouldn't wiggle when I jumped rope.

Big and Pleased.   A few of the women enjoyed having larger breasts than the other girls, at least for a while:

> At first I liked it, because it showed I was a woman. Later I felt different from other girls and would have liked to have been smaller.

> I was on the large side. I resent to this day that my mother made me wear a very tight bra. I think she was jealous of me with father and didn't want me to develop.

> I was bigger than either of my sisters. I remember pulling up our blouses one day to compare. I was kind of proud to wear a bra. It was a badge of something.

> Oh, God, I was embarrassed because I had big tits really early, at nine or ten. Later on I realized they were the object of extreme desire and the envy of the campus.

Average but Ashamed.   Even women whose breast development felt average at menarche sometimes felt ashamed from the fact of having breasts:

I was humiliated. It came too soon. My mother was always telling me to sit up.

I used to hunch over. I was shy they were there.

I would cave in to try to hide them. My mother kept threatening, "If you don't stand up straight I'm going to get you a back brace!"

Just Right. Like Goldilocks testing the baby bear's chair, a very few women felt their size was just right:

I was perfect. I have always loved the size of my breasts. They just sit up there. I don't have to wear a bra with leotards. It's very free feeling.

They were fine. I was pretty athletic and just had to make sure they didn't get hit by a ball.

They were usual. I was too busy living to think much about it.

Whether they suffer over being too small or too large, or feel proud of, or try to hide, or simply ignore the development of their breasts, their pubic hair, or their overall shape, young women symbolize the physical sensations they are undergoing in their dreams. Adult women, too, whose hormones are fluctuating—either because they are in their menstrual years or because they are taking hormone therapy—often report dream images associated with premenstrual changes in their breasts and wombs, as we will see later.

Young Women's Dreams About Their Changing Bodies

Approaching menarche, having their first period, and establishing a rhythmic cycle, young women sense the flooding of their bloodstreams with hormones; they experience a heightened sexual awareness. During these years the young woman often dreams about her changing body.

A few samples from my dream journal at fourteen, following my menarche at thirteen, include the following:

I see blouses with Chinese collars hanging on racks in a store. I hold an aqua one up to me. It is a size 2 and I insist I can have a larger size, size 4.

There are big lawns and gardens. We are chasing or flying through crowds of people and trees.

In part the idea of wanting a larger blouse was a wish to have bigger breasts at that time; similar imagery occurs when a maiden's body is expanding. The lawns and gardens may refer to pubic-hair growth, as they often do for dreamers. The sense of rushing or flying, I have since noticed, occurs in my dreams when hormones are high.

Excerpts from other dreams when I was fourteen include the following:

I look at round jeweled pins in a department store and notice they are puffy while the one I own is flat.

I notice a bead-embroidered "falsie" laying on the floor in French class.

I notice that a popular girl in class is wearing falsies.

A man carries a box containing red jewels with salt that people taste using a whetted finger.

All the girls' mothers have their daughters' sweaters hanging on upright poles for display at school.

I go with my father to look at purses in a shop window so that he can buy one for me.

Jeweled pins—a popular style that was worn on the chest in my girlhood—were a frequent symbol of breasts for me. I was obviously concerned with the size of other girls in my class and how genuine or "false" this was. I seemed to feel that all the girls' mothers were comparing our figures—as displayed on the phallic-shaped poles—as much as we were comparing one another. In the dream of buying a purse of my own, my father seemed to approve of my becoming a woman. The box and the purse are, of course, common symbols for the vulva.

I had begun to date when I was fourteen, so the dreams of this year were full of boys and first kisses. There was dream symbolism about boy's bodies, sexual intercourse, and childbirth as well. A frequent image during the dreams of fourteen, fifteen, and sixteen years was that of fire. In retrospect the fire probably represented my own growing passion.

Dream imagery may be explicit in the dreams of the young woman of menarche age, especially today. One of the thirteen-year-olds I interviewed wept as she shared her worst nightmare—in it she had been raped. Although she was sexually inexperienced, she had been badly frightened by a group of boys at school and literally feared for her safety.

Along with modifications in stature, size and shape, breasts and hair growth, the young woman approaching menarche undergoes other shifts. Her sweat glands become more active, producing perspiration with a more adult odor. Her skin becomes oilier, often causing pimples or even acne. These, too, find their dream depictions.

For example, at fifteen I recorded this dream in my journal:

> There is a soldier who has a bullet in his cheek that he calls a
> pustule. [Shortly afterward I got a pimple on my cheek in the
> same location.]

Minute body sensations are magnified in dreams, giving the impression that certain dreams are predictive when they are actually a physical perception.

We need to know a lot more about dreams at the transition from girlhood to womanhood. Research on menarche dreams is scarce, probably because it is difficult to pinpoint its exact commencement. Let's look first at how the girl herself experiences the event.

The Big Event: The Onset of Menarche

Scientists speculate that several factors account for the timing of the first period. We have already mentioned the critical weight and lean-to-fat-tissue ratio as a trigger. These, in turn, have been influenced by the girl's general nutrition; her diet is affected by her culture and by her parents' economic ability to afford nutritious food. Social class and urban or rural environment thus affect menarche, mainly because girls from wealthier families—who often live in cities—get nutritious food and lead an easier life, whereas girls from poor families may get poor-quality food with low-fat content and are often overworked.

The girl's heredity is definitely involved; if her mother has had early menarche, the girl will tend to follow a similar pattern, as a study relating menarche in mothers and daughters showed.[6]

Climate, too, is said to play a role, although authorities disagree on how prominent this factor is. According to several studies, females in warm countries tend to begin menstruation earlier than average, whereas those in cold countries start later; those females in temperate zones reach menarche between twelve and thirteen. Other researchers find that climate has little effect on menarche. An investigator in 1869 noted that over half of the cases he studied had their first periods during September, October, or November.[7]

Modern girls are reaching menarche earlier than in previous times. Scientists observe that the age of menarche has been getting younger by four months each decade. In 1830 the first period occurred, on average, when a girl was past seventeen years of age; today in the United States it arrives between twelve and thirteen years (the average is twelve years, nine months).[8] By ten or eleven years old, the young girl's body is already changing. Higher standards of living, better diet, and improved health care are the reasons for this trend, which may soon stabilize.

Average age of menarche differs from country to country for the same reasons. In Britain the average age is reported at thirteen years one month. Among the Bundi tribe in New Guinea, girls become menstrual at an average of eighteen years, eight months; in Cuba, it is twelve years, four months.[9] In any part of the world a well-nourished girl who exercises moderately and has attained the critical weight and lean-to-fat-tissue ratio, will probably reach maturity earlier than her mates. This experience makes a profound impression on her.

Early Bloomers and Late Bloomers

In the bathroom, in the bedroom, at a meal, while playing sports or games, in class—menarche usually takes the girl by surprise. Although a girl may have warning signals as Cheryl did, she rarely recognizes them:

> I got my period one week before my thirteenth birthday. I remember, a couple of months before, I was walking down the street and got doubling-over pains. It happened two months in a row before my period came. They were cramps, but I didn't know it at the time. They passed quickly.

When a young woman reaches menarche early, it can be difficult for her. Said one, "I was embarrassed because nobody else in grade school had it. I didn't want to be first. I didn't tell any of the other girls. They usually made fun of you." Said another, "I was only the second kid in the entire grade school to get my period. I didn't know what it was!"

Others found early menarche an accomplishment: "I was young compared with my classmates. It was a very desirable achievement. I'd noticed it with my older sisters."

In one of the few studies of dream content and menstruation, researcher Robert Van de Castle asked nursing students when their first periods had begun; he also collected their current dreams.[10] Van de Castle reported that the current dreams of the women with early menarche (before age eleven in his study) had more references to time in them than the women who had late menarche (after thirteen in his study). He further found that the early bloomers' dreams contained more words that were negative.

Among those women who were late bloomers, Van de Castle reported that he found fewer dreams of sex. It is difficult to know whether these findings are valid because no other researchers have investigated the question, so far as I know.

Studies relating dream content and menarche might be better done during actual menarche rather than many years afterward. We have much to learn about the relationship between dreams and the onset of menstruation. Let's see what the women themselves said about it.

The Voices of Menarche

Ho-hum. Among the women in my study, very few were rather indifferent to their first period:

> It was just a matter of course. Nothing to it. I started bleeding and didn't know what it was. My mother just told me what to do. I was curious but nothing traumatic.

> It was not such a big deal.

> It didn't affect me too much. I was not looking forward to it.

> It just occurred. It's part of being a woman, part of life, like getting up in the morning.

A Mild Nuisance.   Some women found the first period a bit of a bother:

It was in the way. I liked playing kickball and it interfered.

It chafed when I went horseback riding.

It was most cumbersome—all the equipment was unaesthetic. I couldn't go to the beach at times.

I hated the Kotex. It seemed barbaric.

It was so messy. I didn't know what to do. I had questions but was too embarrassed to ask—how long do you wear a pad? Do you remove it when you take a bath?

My period started twice. Once I had the lead in a play and I was very nervous and had to go to the bathroom—blood was everywhere. I trusted it was my period and stuffed toilet paper in and went onstage. Six months later I got my period again, with great regularity. It was something to bother with.

I wished it wouldn't interfere with anything I did.

Shocked and Surprised.   Even in recent times, when sexual education is widespread, several women were terrified or repelled by the first bleeding that marked their menarche:

I found blood in my pants. I thought I had a deadly disease. I'm going to kill myself, throw myself in the lake. Walking to school with my sister, I told her and she explained what it was.

I was very frightened. I went to the bathroom and all of a sudden I saw some blood. I thought I was sick and told my mother.

I was too young, between fifth and sixth grade. My family had been in a car accident, my mother was still in the hospital. I thought I had internal bleeding from the accident and told my father, who was a physician.

Nobody told me anything. I woke up one morning drenched in blood. I thought I was dying.

Cheering and Celebrating. Still other women were joyous:

> It was a great feeling. I felt, "I'm growing up now. This means I can have a baby." Mom prepared me really well.

> Oh, God! I was happy because I was waiting for it. My older sister had it. It meant I was older. It made me more of an adult.

> I was very proud of myself because I was a woman. I told all my friends.

> I was happy, real excited that things were working.

> I was very happy, though physically a little shaky. "Now I'm a woman," I thought. It was reassuring and comforting.

Sometimes the source of the pleasure was the relief of being like the other girls:

> I was glad. I was late (at twelve), and all my friends had it. I was relieved to be normal.

> I was glad because most everyone had started before. I was glad to know there wasn't something wrong with me.

> I was so happy I'd arrived at this stage. I had skipped grades and wanted to be like the other girls in my class.

> I was relieved. Thank God! I was pretty late and was concerned. Now I could talk to the girls in the locker room.

Sometimes the pleasure was for other reasons:

> I was sexually abused as a child. My periods gave me power to keep from being invaded.

Embarrassment. Almost all the participants mentioned some degree of discomfort regarding their periods, even those who were proud and pleased to have them. Usual comments were:

> I felt shy.

> I was humiliated it got on my dress.

> I was mortified to find the stain on my skirt.

Several women mentioned feeling concern that their pads would show under their clothing, as well as fear the blood would seep through. "The first day I was wearing a white blouse and a very tight pink skirt. I was terrified it was going to bleed through. I was afraid the Kotex would show." "The whole topic was as taboo as sex in my family. I had to make sure my father didn't see any trace of it." Even when it was decades ago, many of the women recalled the clothing they wore, the time of day, and the exact location and details of their first bleeding.

Encumbrance.   Many of the participants mentioned the nuisance of menstrual equipment. Of course, several grew up when it was necessary to use sanitary belts and pads with safety pins. Some had used cloth napkins that were put in a bucket in the tub and had to be washed out by hand.

Those who used tampons were not free of troubles. "I forgot I already had a Tampax in and added another. I got infected and had to go to the doctor to have it removed." The recent scare with infections from superabsorbent tampons have made it necessary to use such equipment with caution.

Rites or Ridicule From Mother.   Some women felt a great deal of resentment toward their mothers over how their menarche was treated:

> I was terribly embarrassed. I told my mother not to tell my
> father. When he came home, I could hear her telling him and
> giggling as I came down the hall.
>
> I made her promise not to tell Daddy and of course that's the
> first thing she did.
>
> My mother told the whole family at the dinner table that night.

In contrast, some women felt celebrated when their menarche arrived. For example, "My mother was overwhelmed. She made a big dinner. It was a joyful occasion. She gave me more responsibility after that." In some areas of Japan, mothers still prepare a festive dish of red beans and rice when their daughters have their first menstruation. The celebration that follows assures the young woman that the changes in her body are natural and good.

Those women in my study who had some sort of traditional gesture at menarche, that they understood, felt good about it. One woman described her mother giving her the slap on the face that is part of the Jewish tradition. "I remember it vividly. It was Sunday afternoon on Mother's Day. We were at a restaurant in Chinatown. I had on a white organza dress and felt a stain on my skirt. I told Mom and she said *Mazel Tov*! (Congratulations!) and slapped me. I knew it was the thing to do. I was delighted. It was like a real initiation into womanhood. I felt like a big girl." This woman says the traditional slap probably comes from a myth that it brings the blood back to the face.[11]

One woman confided missing this kind of welcome: "My mother had no patience with anyone with cramps. There was no celebration or excitement. Later I read in a magazine about celebrating a girl's first period and I burst into tears." Obviously, this woman felt she had missed something important. Mothers can contribute to their daughters well-being by making menarche a praiseworthy event.

Occasionally, a parent turned explanations over to another child. "My mother was out of town, as she often was, when my first period came. When I woke up, I had blood on my pants. I didn't know what it was and called my dad. He said my sister would explain it and ran out of the house. My sister was really annoyed and explained you had to put this thing between your legs. 'You mean like a Band-Aid?!' She said 'Yeah.' " Needless to say, such experiences can lead to or contribute to strange misconceptions.

Confused Notions About Menstruation. I was surprised to find that women in their middle years had sometimes been so uninformed about their periods that they conceived bizarre ideas.[12]

One, for instance, recalled, "My mother had tried to explain to me, but she said, 'You bleed down there,' gesturing near my breasts. So I thought you would bleed under the breasts. I thought the blood would come out of the nipple and that you'd wear pads on the breasts."

Another told me, "I thought sanitary pads were for putting under your arms. The head of our school told me that was nonsense, adding, 'When you get older, our Blessed Mother gives girls a secret.' I still wasn't sure where the blood came from."

Still another woman described being sent to the drugstore by her mother to get "pads." She said, "I came back with notepads. I had no idea what was needed. Such things were just not discussed in my family. When a woman we knew became pregnant, the word itself was taboo. We referred to her as being 'p.g.' "

Proper and clear sexual education is still needed for our daughters.

Dreams Change During Menarche

Research on dreams of the menarche are scarce. Most studies about menstruation are focused on the process after it has been well established in adults—perhaps because it is difficult to identify exactly when an adolescent's menarche will occur.

In one of the few studies of this time bracket, investigators found that girls had "nicer" dreams before their periods began. After menarche their dream content became more aggressive and more social; characters in their dreams behaved more aggressively as well as having more social interactions. Knowing that the hormones of puberty impel more activity while awake and that mood swings are characteristic of the adolescent, this finding makes sense.[13]

Supersleepiness at Puberty. Another characteristic of puberty is sleepiness.[14] At a summer sleep camp for children held at Stanford University, the researchers found that those children who were most weary during the day were the ones who were on the verge of the hormonal changes of puberty. Parents sometimes marvel at the capacity for unbroken sleep marathons in their adolescent offspring. Teenage girls are especially prone to severe sleepiness just before and during their menstrual periods. One researcher found that the main difference between girls prior to puberty and after it was that they had more daydreams.[15] Teens who are menstrual seem to spend even more time daydreaming.

Symbolism of Menstrual Dreams in Adult Women

Sometimes adult women will dream their period is present when it is about to start. If a woman of menstrual age dreams it is her period when it is not expected, she may be wishing for it—in hopes of not being pregnant. A woman past menopausal age who dreams about her period may be wishing for some part of her younger years.

Since there is much to learn about the dreams of menarche, each young woman who observes her own experience can add to our knowledge. The woman whose cycles are well established and who is also interested in her dreams can teach us too. By observing her own dream responses, the menstrual woman can better understand the processes of her body.

Growing-Up Dreams
Declaring Independence

While primary bodily changes are under way, the adolescent woman undertakes a major life task: finding her identity. Of course, males, too, must establish their own personal identity. For young men independence often involves confronting the authority of their fathers; for young women it is more often the mother who is challenged.

From fourteen to sixteen years old is a time in which girls are usually at the height of struggle with parents, although some adolescents begin their efforts to separate from their family as early as eleven or twelve and continue active resistance until nineteen or more.

The monumental issue of teenage years—independence—becomes a dramatic theme in dream content. Several women in the study recalled dreams revolving around ambivalent feelings toward their mothers.

The Cruel Doll. During early puberty I dreamed that my favorite doll, named Mary, had become mean to me; I feared and hated her. No longer able to enjoy playing with her after this dream, I exiled her to the attic. Eventually, I came upon her again, her face crackled and her joints creaky; I discarded her entirely.

Then I did not think of the symbolism involved, that Mary was the name of the Mother of Jesus, and how I felt increasingly hostile toward my own mother as I strove to be myself, not what she wanted me to be.

The Wolf-Mother. The young woman's mother is frequently disguised in dreams, as mine was in the doll named Mary. Occasionally the costume is removed. Fiona, now in her forties, remembers being terrified as a young girl by a dream about two wolves. They menaced her and she was at their mercy. At some point in the dream:

> The creatures take off their masks. I am horrified to see that it is
> my mother and my aunt [who lived with us] underneath. It
> really frightens me.

Fiona's nightmare let her peep under the mask of her dream creatures to the authority figures they symbolized. Although she felt loving toward them while awake, her dream suggests that these women seemed to her dreaming mind to be domineering, attacking, and hurtful. She explained, "It was as though the people I loved and trusted weren't real. They didn't exist and it was always the wolves."

Dreams exaggerate. They take an emotional truth and dramatize it. Enlarged, the dream can be terrifying; the emotion it expresses is real, but not usually so life-threatening as it feels in the dream. Fiona was saying to herself in dream language, "It's as if my mother and my aunt were wolves who are hounding me." The dream picture is a metaphor.

The Vampire-Mother.   Sharp-toothed creatures in dreams usually indicate the presence of anger—in the dreamer herself or in the person the dream animal symbolizes. Lenore, too, at a young age, visualized her mother as a beast of prey. Toward the end of a frightening dream:

> I seem to wake up in my bed. My mother comes into my
> room. I am happy to see her, thinking now I'll be safe. She
> comes over to the corner of the carpet on the floor and gets
> down on her hands and knees to examine the corner. She looks
> up at me and smiles—she has fangs like a vampire! I am really
> scared. I actually wake up.

Lenore, in her thirties now, regards this nightmare as her worst. It was impossible to shake off the notion that her mother was evil and intended her harm. Lenore's mother did seem to have mixed feelings toward her daughter, an ambivalence that was sensed by the child. Although Lenore felt she loved her mother, she did not completely trust her. She felt it was "draining" to be with her, that it "sucked something out of me." Small wonder the little girl cast her mother in the part of a vampire.

The Octopus-Mother.   Helen, also in her thirties, expressed her mother's all-consuming, smothering aspect, along with her anger, in a dream she had at about ten or eleven years old:

> I am standing in the doorway of my house and some boys want
> me to come out and play—probably baseball. [I was the pitcher
> on the boys' team until I was twelve.] My mother appears from
> a stairway behind me and blocks the doorway.
>
> She turns into an octopus of the same size as herself, black, with
> a line for a mouth and eight arms, like a devouring Kali [the
> black goddess of destruction in Indian mythology]. Either I

knew or she said, "You cannot go out and play!" With one of
her arms she slapped me as hard as she could, and I fell
backward and woke up.

Helen thinks that this dream probably represented her emerging sexuality
and her mother's efforts to "block" her developing relationship with boys.
The all-embracing, smothering quality of the dream octopus made it more
difficult for Helen to relate to her mother in waking life.

Dreams in which the girl's mother is metamorphosed into an animal or
ones in which the beast is revealed to be the mother express the young girl's
fear of this powerful figure in her life and her sense of potential destructive-
ness.

Yearning to be autonomous, the girl is still nonetheless dependent upon
her mother's goodwill to provide for most of her needs. Money, clothing,
food, transportation, parties, overnight guests—such attributes of a teenage
girl's life are affected by her mother's mood and willingness to be cooperative, as well as her mother's resources. Under the best of circumstances, the
adolescent daughter and her mother will clash from time to time. Under the
worst, the tension between them is unbearable.

To become herself, the teen must separate from her parents.[16] She must
act on her own initiative and learn to make her way in the world. Her
identity is hewn by chopping herself free if she has an overwhelming,
octopus-armed mother. If this independence is not achieved, the girl may
turn into an adult who still struggles to define who she is and what her own
viewpoint is, as distinct from that of her mother. She will confuse herself
and her mother as one, rather than each being a person with their own flaws
and their own powers.

The dreams of anger toward mothers, or symbols representing them, are
part of a young woman's natural process of freeing herself from the entan-
glements of a mother who seems to engulf the girl herself. Only when the
terror of or hatred toward the mother becomes extreme is it pathological,
rather than a necessary developmental step. Sometimes resentment of the
mother is based upon more than the natural struggle for independence.

The Split Mother. The girl whose mother is literally brutal tends to have
dreams with a different sort of imagery. Coleen, for instance, whose mother
beat her as a child, recalls a remarkable dream when she was only five:

The Virgin Mary came to earth, floating in the air low enough
to grab my arm. She wanted to pull me up to heaven. . . .

Mary pulled me a little into the air. My neighbor came out and
got ahold of me from the earth and the two women struggled
over me, arguing.

Coleen explained that the neighbor woman was herself very strict, punishing
and distant, like her mother. She thinks that her dream represents the two
aspects of her own mother, the one who would sometimes lovingly care for
her, as she imagined the Virgin Mary would do, and the one who would
suddenly turn upon her to inflict pain.

The dream battle between the divine and the mortal women was eventually won by the harsh neighbor. Good and evil forces were struggling in
this girl's dreaming mind and she felt herself "torn apart" in the strife. The
Virgin Mary's attempt to draw the child into heaven suggests the girl feared
her mother might actually kill her. Happily, most young girls have a simpler
battle—to define themselves as separate beings from their parents.

Becoming an adult also involves discovering how to relate to the opposite
sex, to prepare for an occupation, to evolve a life philosophy. Each step
offers opportunities for conflict, for becoming stuck or for moving forward.
Clashes with parents are inevitable, yet to grow up, the girl must learn to
cope with life and make decisions for herself.

The Dying Mother. In contrast to a dream heightening her fear of or
anger toward her mother, some women found that their dreams improved
the relationship. Leah, for example, was in continuous conflict with her
mom when she was in her teens and felt that the limits her mother imposed
on dating, bedtime, and so forth, were intolerable. She constantly fought
against these restrictions. Then one night when Leah was about thirteen or
fourteen, she dreamed the following:

My mom is sick. Suddenly she dies. I'm really scared.

This dream had a profound effect on Leah. Now in her thirties, she recalls
it as her worst nightmare, "very powerful." For months afterward she was
exceedingly nice to her mother. "My mom didn't know what got into me."

When we dream of a loved one dying—a fairly common bad dream—
several explanations are possible. The dream may be saying.

- I wish that person were out of my way.
- The quality that person symbolizes in me is not functional now.
- I feel as though that person is seriously emotionally hurt.

Leah's tirades had probably led her to feel guilty about the impact they had on her mother. In her dream language she said, "Mom is [emotionally] injured and may desert me [die]." Having genuine love for her mother, in addition to heavy resentment, Leah was shaken by her death in the dream: "It's as if she really died. I realized how important she was to me." Thereafter, Leah's responses were modified.

Today, very much her own person, married and with her own baby daughter, Leah regards her mother as one of her best friends and enjoys spending time with her.

Beginning to Date

One aspect of forming the young girl's identity involves developing skills in relating to the opposite sex. Indeed, this is often a focus of the conflict between mother and daughter. Young girls need to master dating and social behaviors.

From quite early on, their dreams deal with these preoccupations. I have collected dreams of falling in love, of marrying, and of divorcing from girls as young as eight years old. Boyfriends, sexual attractions, and rejections abound in the dreams of the teenage girl.

Dancing With Prince Charming.   We have said that women in general tend to have more romantic dreams about love and sex. This is particularly true of the adolescent. While teenage males are having frankly sexual dreams at this time, the teenage girl's dreams tend to flow with romance. During the same time as Leah was struggling with her mother, for instance, she had one of her favorite dreams:

> I am in this very beautiful building that has a foyer with a chandelier and shiny floors. [I pass by this building on my way home from junior high school.] I am there with my true love. It is like a ballroom.
>
> We are all alone, all dressed up, dancing. There is beautiful music playing as we glide over the glossy floors.

"When I woke up, I was in heaven," Leah said. "It was a glimpse of what love and life and having a relationship could be like."

In another of her romantic dreams, Leah tells me, her "true love" was a current comedian on television. "He made me laugh and feel happy. All the kids were crazy for him. In the dream he looked beautiful, groomed, and so funny—and it was all for me! He was crazy about me."

Romantic dreams like Leah's help the young girl visualize the possibility of relating to a man as an adult woman. They hold out a promise and an ideal for a future mate—the "man of her dreams." They also offer clues to her hidden emotions in relationships.

Changing Emotional Attachments.   As a girl of sixteen I dated a boy whose last name was Green. Simultaneously I was going out with a freckled, curly-headed young man who was nicknamed Red. I knew that my affection had crystallized when I dreamed the following:

> I look out my living room window and am surprised to see
> that the leaves on the tree outside are turning from red to
> green!

Awake, I realized at once that the dream expressed a shift in my emotional attachment from the man named Red to the boy named Green. The area where I lived—my living room—served as the setting from which I observed this change. Viewing something through a window in a dream often indicates the dreamer's "viewpoint." To me, the leaves represent growth; they are the organs the tree uses to survive. Ordinarily leaves on a tree would turn from green to red. I was startled in my dream to see the opposite effect. The emotional relationship—my survival—was changing in a way I had not expected. The dream imagery made puns out of the names of my would-be sweethearts.

In addition to directly depicting the man of their dreams, teenage girls symbolize their emotional relationships, as I did with the changing leaves. In other symbolic dreams of my adolescent years I recorded images of women who wore heart-shaped hats, clusters of hearts, or a single large heart, like a crown. In retrospect, it is easy to see that these images were shorthand visual expressions of my own head's being filled with thoughts of romance and my wish for a valentine of my own. My thoughts were displayed in the form of heart-shaped headpieces. Dreamers should always pay attention to what their characters wear, since clothing and hats are meaningful messages in themselves.

We shall explore further, in chapter 4, "Love and Sex Dreams," how the young girl's dreams about this topic expand and develop.

Contemplating Life Work

Many of the young girls in my 1984 study of children's dreams depicted themselves in vocations. Usually these were good dreams that made them feel important or gave them an opportunity to make an outstanding performance.

Several of the girls pictured themselves as princesses or actresses. They often saw themselves as brides. Some, however, chose careers. Bonnie, who actually took acting lessons, frequently starred in dream films. Jan, who took singing lessons in waking life, got selected for solos in her dreams. Marta, who took dancing lessons, saw herself as a ballerina performing to great acclaim in her dreams.

Such dreams help the teenage girl visualize the possibility of a career, of being able to perform in a way that provides personal satisfaction. They may motivate her to master the skills she needs to succeed eventually in the work of her choice. Developing interests and abilities for a life's work continue, in dreams, to parallel the activities of the adolescent's days. We examine the topic of work further in chapter 7, "Career Dreams."

Thus the growing girl must gain skills on diverse fronts. Turning from girl to adult, she must adjust to the new rhythm of her changing body. She must formulate a body image she can live with and must keep pace with physical competencies to be effective in her new shape.

Furthermore, she must separate herself from her parents, especially her mother, and define who she truly is. She needs to cast her mind ahead to begin to prepare herself for the life she wants to have in the future. Studies must be undertaken that will yield the expertise she requires.

The teenage girl must also relate to a variety of young men so as to preserve her dignity and yet allow her to find a future mate who will be a reciprocal loving partner.

So much must be accomplished while the young girl's body undergoes rapid growth. These pubertal changes are generally more negative for girls than they are for boys.[17] Once her menses is well established, it will be with her for about thirty years. We look next at the process of menstruation in the adult woman and how it influences her dream content.

Being a Woman: Menstruation

Once a girl's periods begin, it takes a while for them to settle into a regular rhythm. There is often an interval of two or three months before the next menstruation. Usually a young woman has only four periods during the first year following her menarche.[18] Gradually the periods become more regular and of even length.

A woman has literally hundreds of thousands of eggs within her two ovaries. The oval-shaped ovaries of women produce the characteristic female hormone estrogen; they are situated above the pear-shaped uterus. Each month, after her period has become regular, one ovary ripens a few eggs. One of these—technically called the ovum—will fully ripen and be released. The ovaries usually alternate in producing ripe eggs. Eventually eight to nine hundred ova will ripen, although not all will be released.[19]

The young woman's early periods are not ordinarily accompanied by the release of an egg from the ovaries. Such menstrual periods (where bleeding occurs but no egg is released) are called anovulatory cycles. They may take place at any time during the woman's fertile life, but are most common during menarche and menopause.[20] Approximately one or two years following menarche the young woman has her first ovulation—the release of the ripe egg. This is the time when some adolescents experience their first menstrual pain. Among the women in my study a few claimed to be able to perceive when they were ovulating and from which ovary the egg came.

Said one, "I always get a sharp pain on one side when the ovum is released, so I can tell when I might get pregnant. I always dream about babies then." This characteristic sensation of mild cramping on one side is called middle pain (*mittelschmerz*)[21] because it comes in the middle of the cycle. It is thought to be caused by the egg breaking loose from its follicle on the ovary or, possibly, from contractions of the spaghetti-sized fallopian tube as it moves the egg along toward the womb.[22] The pain lasts a few hours and may be mistaken for acute appendicitis if it is located in the lower right-hand area of the abdomen. Most women seem unaware of its presence or else do not associate it with their cycle.

A woman's fully established menstrual cycle has a well-known pattern of seven phases (some experts suggest three, four, or five).[23] The exact length of each stage varies with the woman's body chemistry, whether or not she takes birth control pills, her exposure to males, to light, and to a host of other factors. An average sequence is reviewed here, along with brief comments on the dream imagery characteristic of each phase, as reported by various researchers.

Women's Dream Symbols for
THE MENSTRUAL CYCLE

Bodily Process   *Typical Dream Content*

Phase 1: Days one to four
MENSTRUATION

Estrogen levels are low, then begin to rise. Progesterone levels remain low. If the egg has not been fertilized by a sperm, it passes out of the womb, along with the soft, spongy womb lining. This material disintegrates and is shed as the menstrual blood. The woman's sense of smell is poorest during menses.

REM and dream recall are low. Imagery may include: the color red;[24] sinks or other receptacles overflowing with water; themes of loss, injury, dying, or destruction; references to anatomy and to enclosed spaces.[25]

Female characters are likely to be friendly to the dreamer, whereas males may be less friendly.[26] Some researchers report the most sexual and hostile dreams now.[27]

Women subject to cramping may dream of being cut in the stomach or of hospitals and operations.

One researcher found the words *alone* and *gift* mentioned more often in menstrual dreams than other phases of the cycle.[28]

....

Bodily Process	*Typical Dream Content*

....

Phase 2: Days five to eight
POSTMENSTRUAL

Estrogen levels reach first peak. The pituitary is making Follicle Stimulating Hormone (FSH). Follicles are moving to the surface of the ovary. From the end of bleeding until ovulation is called the follicular phase. Women on birth control pills sleep more overall and especially during this phase prior to ovulation.[30] The lining of the uterus starts to thicken. The woman usually feels energetic and well.

Dream images often contain outgoing activity and social contacts with males.[29]

....

Phase 3: Days nine to twelve
PREOVULATION (OR LATE POSTMENSTRUAL)

Estrogen levels are falling slightly.

Dream images may continue to show social activity with men.

....

....

| *Bodily Process* | *Typical Dream Content* |

....

Phase 4: Days thirteen to sixteen
OVULATION

Estrogen levels are low; FHS and LH (lutenizing hormone) are at a peak.

Dream images may include babies or small children.

Some researchers report dream images of eggs, jewels, and round, fragile, precious things.[31]

Among the thousands of unripe eggs in the woman's two ovaries, a few on one side develop in response to a spurt of LH from the pituitary gland. One egg wins the race, the others die off. This egg increases in size to form a small bubble or blister called the Graafian follicle. When fully developed, it bursts open and releases the mature egg. The release of the egg is ovulation; it usually occurs about fourteen days from the first day of the period. In shorter or longer cycles, ovulation occurs 14 days (plus or minus 2 days) before the next period. Thus ovulation may occur as early as day 8 (in a 22-day cycle) or as late as day 18 (in a 32-day cycle). The fringed ends of the fallopian tube reach out and grasp the ripe egg, drawing it in. The egg cell begins traveling down the four-inch fallopian tube toward the womb, moved on by tiny hairlike projections called cilia, for a journey of four to seven days.

....

Bodily Process	*Typical Dream Content*

There is a brief fall and then sharp rise in body temperature, of about one-half a degree, within twelve to twenty-four hours after ovulation.[33] This marks the time of the ovum's greatest receptivity to fertilization. The mouth of the cervix opens. The usual thin vaginal discharge changes to a thick, sticky clear mucus for about three days; sperm can more easily penetrate this "fertile" mucus. The woman's sense of smell is keenest during ovulation, perhaps the better to enjoy lovemaking.

Sexual desire may be increased and get depicted in dreams of romance or lovemaking. Male characters are usually friendly to the dreamer now, whereas female characters are likely to be less friendly.[32]

Phase 5: Days seventeen to twenty
POSTOVULATION

Estrogen is rising again and progesterone levels begin to rise. The estrogen is secreted from the ovaries.

REM and dream recall will peak now or before menses.[34] Imagery may still include babies and is often tranquil.[35]

The progesterone is being secreted from the yellow scar tissue left behind when the blister bursts—called the *corpus luteum,* or yellow body. This hormone enriches the soft, thick lining of the womb to receive an embryo in case of pregnancy; if the egg is unfertilized, it acts to break down the lining. From after ovulation until bleeding begins is known as the luteal phase. Women who are not taking birth control pills sleep more during this phase and during menses.[37]

Some researchers note that women begin to play more passive roles in their dreams after ovulation.[36]

Bodily Process	*Typical Dream Content*

Phase 6: Days twenty-one to twenty-four
EARLY PREMENSTRUAL

Estrogen reaches second peak simultaneously with the only high peak of progesterone.	REM and dream recall are lessening. Imagery may still remain peaceful and content.
Premenstrual tension sets in for those women subject to it.	

Phase 7: Days twenty-five to twenty-eight
PREMENSTRUAL

Estrogen and progesterone levels fall sharply.	REM is low. Dream imagery for women with PMS may include ripe fruit (or other symbols of the breast or womb) about to burst and water or other fluids (representing the dreamer's water retention).[39]
Premenstrual bodily changes and tension increase for those women subject to it. For unknown reasons, the fingernails and toenails grow faster now.[38]	

A woman who has two children will undergo this menstrual cycle approximately 300 times or more during her span of fertility; without children, she will have about four hundred cycles.[40] For some women it is a dreadful prospect; to others a nuisance; to still others a breeze. All women—whether or not they are aware of it—are affected by their cycles to a greater or lesser degree. Here's what's happening.

Two basic patterns of bodily discomfort are discernible: cramping and premenstrual tension (PMT or PMS). Technically the cramping pattern is known as spasmodic dysmenorrhea, which means painful menstruation from cramps; the other pattern is called congestive dysmenorrhea, which means painful menstruation from swelling caused by water retention—the PMT syndrome. Later on we will see there is a positive side to menstruation.

Menstrual Cramps (Spasmodic Dysmenorrhea)

The pain from this condition can be acute. Thought to be caused by contractions in the uterus to help expel the blood, cramping is more characteristic of the younger women and often disappears during the mid-twenties or after childbirth.[41] Some theorists think that cramps come from insufficient estrogen to mature and stretch the muscles of the womb. Another theory holds that severe cramping is caused by excessive amounts of the prostaglandins, hormones that help the uterus contract.

A woman in her seventies who participated in my study described agonizing with her menses throughout her youth:

> I suffered terribly from cramps for two or three days each month. I was so sick. My dad always made me go to school anyway, so I could have a perfect attendance record. I had to walk about three miles. My teacher would take one look at me and send me straight home.
>
> The only way I made it back was by imagining there was an Indian hiding behind each tree. I'd tell myself, "If I can just make it to the next house, I'll be okay." When I finally got home, my mother told me to lie down and gave me a sip of whiskey to revive me.
>
> The greatest joy of my old age was being over with my periods—I was quite willing to get old.

This particular woman continued to have severe discomfort after childbirth, although most women find that birthing a baby eliminates cramps. The spasmodic pains that may come every twenty minutes are similar to labor pains; they are usually worst on the first day and are sometimes incapacitating. Luckily most women who are subject to menstrual cramps find them mild to moderate.

Getting Relief From Cramps. Young women often obtain relief from cramps by lying down curled around a hot water bottle or heating pad. Aspirin is sometimes helpful; gin was the old-fashioned remedy.[42] Many women claim that masturbating or making love to orgasm brings relief because following orgasm there is less congestion at the tip of the womb and the blood flows more freely.[43] Some women find mild exercise useful; others prefer complete rest. In severe cases a dilation of the womb and curettage (scraping) of its lining (a D & C) may stretch the opening and bring relief for a time. Learning relaxation exercises and correct breathing has yielded dramatic improvement.

Dream Content in Women With Cramps.   The menstrual dreams of women who have painful cramping are likely to contain images of hospitals, operations, and injuries, such as being wounded or bitten, and red, the color of blood.

Menstrual Swelling (PMS, PMT, or Congestive Dysmenorrhea)

About 40 percent of all women experience some negative changes in the seven to ten days before their periods start.[44] These sensations and feelings may take a number of forms that are mainly a result of water retention during the last two weeks of the cycle.

The areas of discomfort in the body are different for women who suffer premenstrual tension (PMT or PMS) compared with those who have cramps. In cramping the locale is focused mainly around the lower pelvis and upper thighs. In PMT discomfort is more widespread. Water retention may cause congestion or swelling in the ankles, the fingers and wrists, the breasts, the head and face, as well as across the genitals. The woman with PMT may also have mild cramps in addition to water retention.

A large number of women gain weight between ovulation and menstruation, usually about four to seven pounds above their normal weight, although it may be more. They feel increasingly bloated and heavy during the last two weeks of their cycle. As water accumulates in the tissues, sodium is also retained, while potassium is lost. This excess water is ordinarily excreted in the urine during the first few days of the period.

Water retention—called edema—affects all of the bodily tissues but may concentrate in different areas in different women. Studies have shown that vision becomes worse during the premenstrual days in women who retain water. Contact lenses and dentures may not fit; fluid in the inner ear may cause dizziness; fluid in the skull may cause headaches; in the small tubes of the lungs, edema may trigger asthma attacks. Swelling in the hands may make the premenstrual woman feel clumsy, often causing her to drop things, or forcing her to remove her rings; edema may also cause her ankles to swell. Most women who suffer PMT complain of sore nipples and engorged breasts. Backaches and a host of other problems may arise.

The sites vary from woman to woman, with the water being attracted to cells that have been injured in the past or that are infected. Water retention symptoms are at their worst in the early morning.[45]

In addition to water retention, pimples or acne from the thick, profuse sebum that gushes forth prior to the period are common. Hair becomes lank, and skin is sometimes blotchy. Skin eruptions may appear in dream content, as in the example of my dream of a soldier with a "pustule" that was a bullet wound in his cheek. Some women report cyclic food cravings—especially of sweets—and other symptoms as they approach menstruation. One of my friends is particularly fond of white chocolate macadamia tarts at this time of month. Smoking is said to exacerbate the pain of PMT.[46]

Researchers say that while the woman who has cramps is likely to be immature in her breast development, the woman who has PMT is often maternal, with large breasts having brownish nipples; she is usually fertile and is prone to depression.

Mood Changes in Premenstrual Time.   Women who experience PMT commonly have three basic complaints: depression, irritability, and tiredness. We will see how these may stem from a lack of dreaming time. Lack of sleep may also contribute to the dark circles under the eyes that characterize many premenstrual women.

Analyst Emil Gutheil has reported a dream from a forty-five-year-old woman who still had much physical discomfort with menstruation:

> I was in the kitchen of a large apartment. I must have been
> eighteen or nineteen years old. My grandmother, who looked
> like the queen in *Alice in Wonderland* came in. I noticed that
> her eyes were circled in black and felt that mine were, too. She
> looked down upon me and said, "Poor child, you are going to
> be sick tomorrow."[47]

This dream contains the symptom of dark rings or circles under the eyes, as well as the announcement of the woman's imminent period. "Being sick" is a common expression for getting one's period. Gutheil points out that the youth of the dreamer in the dream reflects her wish to be younger, while the age of the grandmother reflects her wish to be finished with her painful periods. The pity the grandmother expresses in the dream probably relates to feelings of self-pity that are frequent in women with PMT.

Depression may range from mild feelings of "being down" to attempted suicide. One husband and wife team, both physicians, showed that more women commit suicide during their premenstrual days than at other times of the month. Other studies confirm that half of all females who attempt suicide do so in the four days before, or the first four days of, their period.[48]

Tiredness may be expressed by feeling slow and stupid, or by being in a stuporous daze. Irritability, restlessness, or agitation is hard on the family, friends, and co-workers as well as the woman herself.

British physician Katharina Dalton has made an extensive study of the menstrual cycle and its effect on women.[49] She notes that premenstrual irritability is always worse when there has been a long interval since the last meal, causing the blood sugar level to fall. Anger usually erupts during the late morning after an inadequate breakfast, or in the late afternoon after light lunches, she says. Dalton urges the woman with PMT to take regular meals every three to four hours to keep her blood sugar level high on the few days before her period.

Dalton links a vast number of problematic behaviors to PMT, including young women's misbehavior in school; assistant teachers' harsh treatment of pupils; lowering of school grades; industrial accidents (the forty-eight hours preceding the period contain the highest accident rate); trouble with the law (stemming from the woman's irritability); and crimes of violence, including child battering.

The Voices of Menstruation

Here are some of the ways women in my study described their premenstrual tension:

> The least little thing will send me up the wall in anger, or I get very sad when there is nothing to be sad or angry about.

> People get on my nerves. I get irrational, suspicious, unsure of my work. I want more space.

> I can't stand the way my boyfriend chews. Who is this person I'm living with?

> I turn into a witch before my period, screaming and carrying on. But I always seem to forget I get unreasonable about things until afterward.

> I was ready to break up with my boyfriend until I realized I was premenstrual. He seemed cruel, as though he were picking on me. Later I realized I was the one being irrational.

> I become totally paranoid.

Getting Relief From PMT.   Because stress greatly increases the discomfort of women with PMT, it is important for women with this syndrome to learn how to relax and to keep calm. If you are a person who is troubled with PMT, you might make it a general rule not to make major decisions until your period is over.

The woman who suffers from PMT may help herself by keeping a chart of her cycle or marking it on her calendar. She should note when to expect her next period. By arranging her schedule and avoiding stressful situations on premenstrual or menstrual days, she can make this time more comfortable. If movie stars and models can have a clause in their contracts forbidding filming during their premenstrual and menstrual days—because of bloatedness and puffy eyes—the average woman can surely juggle her schedule a little. Discussing her responses with family, friends, and colleagues may make them more patient when she is in discomfort.[50]

A woman with PMT should never begin a diet during her premenstrual time; she should space her food evenly throughout the day. Some experts suggest limiting fluids to four cups a day, reducing salt, and eating potassium-rich foods, such as bananas and tomatoes, as the period approaches. Nourishing foods with B vitamins are recommended. Getting extra rest in the latter half of the cycle helps, including afternoon naps when possible.[51]

Dream Content in Women With PMT.   Not surprisingly, women with PMT have frequent images of water in their dreams. I believe this is an instance of the dreaming mind sensing the presence of excess fluid in the tissues. Here, for example, are the first scenes of a dream I recorded in my journal at fifteen years old, when I had had my period for nearly two years:

> Something about boats and water at night, and not being able
> to get out of a foreign country. There is a girl and a man who
> are plotting to destroy the earth. A wire with an attached basket
> is [stretched] across a river.
>
> A sort of movie takes place. In it I see the world [from far off].
> Something buzzes around the world and it splits in half.
> Everything starts falling and spilling and crashing.
>
> A close-up shows torrents of red sand and people on individual
> hunks of earth. It turns into a red river with everything
> floating. Alan Ladd is in a canoe with his girlfriend.

The water, the torrents of red sand, the hunks of earth, the red river—such images are typical in the dreams of the woman whose body is retaining water in the tissues. The image of the world may even be a symbol for the egg that is being destroyed, "falling, spilling, and crashing" out of the young body with the red menstrual river. As a girl I was subject to passing blood clots with my period; I suspect these are reflected in the individual "hunks of earth."

Superimposed upon the more universal dream imagery are personal symbols. Alan Ladd, for instance, had starred in a romantic movie I had just seen and, although I may deplore my taste from an adult point of view, as a teenager I thought him appealing. He is surviving the catastrophe.

The dream continues:

> Suddenly the stuff settles into a town, but there is no vast water
> in this scene, just some streams. The guidance counselor looks
> very disgusted. She shakes her finger at the water and tells it
> where to go. The water settles into little puddles in the gutter.
> A shower keeps turning on and off in front of a gas station. We
> walk up the street feeling very happy. I hear toilets flushing in
> the dream—and wake up to find it happening.

In this section of the dream the guidance counselor from school is rather critically telling me where this flood should go—into the gutter. The overall symbolic theme seems to be a wish to rearrange things in "my world." Specifically the images are menstrual. After all the upheaval, there is a peaceful happiness.

For the woman who has premenstrual tension, dreaming increases. One investigator found that women who had the most severe PMT had the greatest need to dream.[52] Authorities have long been puzzled over what causes water retention and feelings of upheaval in the bodies of some females.

Basic Causes of Menstrual Pain

We have already mentioned that Dalton believes that the two types of premenstrual pain are caused by two different hormonal problems. She thinks cramping is related to an estrogen deficiency, whereas PMT is related to a progesterone deficiency.[53] Hormone therapy has been effective in bringing about balance for some women.

The fortunate few have no problem and are presumably already well balanced. Women in this category in my study made comments like the following:

> I enjoy having my period. I feel very animal-like. Everything is working, like the change of seasons.

> People enjoy suffering. If I am suffering, I figure it's my fault and I better get out of it.

Such women find it difficult to understand why others have trouble with their periods.

Another theory about the cause of PMT has recently emerged that, if proved true, has wide implications. Nora Brayshaw, a physician at the Biopsychiatry Center in Watchung, New Jersey, thinks she has pinpointed an association between PMT and the thyroid gland.[54] In an experiment with fifty-four women who complained of PMT, very sophisticated hormone tests (not the kind the general practitioner does) were run. A full 94 percent of these women had one or more indications of abnormal thyroid function.

Next, thirty-four of these women were treated with thyroid hormones. After four weeks every single woman reported complete relief of her problems. It is rare to obtain 100 percent relief, suggesting that the connection between thyroid and PMT may be strong. More follow-up studies with placebos are essential to confirm such a connection, but if they do so, it will open the path to relief for hundreds of thousands of women. Thyroid malfunction is often missed by the general practitioner. Watch for further information on this possible important relationship.

Sleeping and Dreaming Changes During the Menstrual Cycle

Dream and Sleep Time Shifts.   Although the total time that a woman sleeps may change little during her menstrual cycle, the amount that she dreams shifts considerably.

During the first two weeks of her cycle a woman's dream time is rather low. Then, following ovulation, sometime during the last two weeks of the cycle—usually late in the phase—her dreaming reaches a peak. Thus she is dreaming most when her estrogen and progesterone are at their peak. Just before and during menses, when her hormone levels fall, the woman's dream rate drops again. The changes in dream and sleep time depend in part upon the way the woman's body handles menstruation.

Researcher Ernest Hartmann found that women who have extreme premenstrual tension had the most profound changes in the amount of time they spent dreaming.[55] Their highest dream times occurred when they had symptoms of tiredness, irritability, and depression. These women were often troubled by excessive sleepiness as well. Hartmann suggests that the premenstrual hormonal changes produce an increased need to dream.

Sleeping Beauties.   Women often state that their premenstrual symptoms are worse if they cannot sleep enough; they say symptoms are improved if it is possible to sleep longer than usual. In many ways premenstrual tension resembles dream or sleep deprivation. Hartmann prescribes more sleep for women with premenstrual tension. If you are a woman with PMT syndrome, you can keep track of your periods so that you are aware of when you are premenstrual. Scheduling yourself extra time to rest during your premenstrual days may make you feel considerably more comfortable.

Women who are not troubled with premenstrual tension, in contrast, get their greatest amount of deep sleep (stages 3 and 4) in their premenstrual days.[56] Thus women without PMT are *sleeping* more during their premenstrual days, whereas women with PMT are *dreaming* more at this same time.

Dream Recall Shifts.   In a study I did examining the length of my dream descriptions over several months, published in 1973, I reported that my dream recall was greatest during the middle of the cycle or in the second half; it was lowest just prior to and during menses. This finding parallels Hartmann's measurement of the actual REM time variations during the cycle. It would seem that the quantity of dreaming, as measured in the sleep laboratory, as well as the amount of dream recall,[57] is highest when the hormones are high. Not all studies of dream content during the menstrual cycle are in agreement, however.[58]

I suspect the inconsistency in results of studies on the topic of dream variation and menstruation may be explained by an investigation in which ovulatory cycles were compared with anovulatory cycles.[59] It will be recalled that when an egg is not released from the ovum, no progesterone is secreted by the ruptured follicle (the yellow body, or *corpus luteum*). Since progesterone is linked to the woman's premenstrual bodily changes, the anovulatory cycles are not accompanied by PMT.

Researcher Adele Fekete-Mackintosh asked twenty women to tape-record their dreams for five consecutive weeks, in addition to keeping a record of their basal body temperature and completing a questionnaire before bed. Based on the basal body temperature, the women's cycles were classified as ovulatory or anovulatory. The ovulatory group had clearly higher sexual dream content and aggressive content during their premenstrual and menstrual phases. In contrast the anovulatory group had higher sexual content just prior to and at ovulation.

Researchers would be well advised to have a physical measure, such as temperature, by which to calculate ovulation rather than relying on counting back from the woman's menstrual period, as is commonly done in menstrual studies. When ovulation is not precisely pinpointed, it should be no surprise that results are inconsistent.

Length of the Menses and Dream Content

Some women find themselves finished with their periods before they have barely begun, completing the whole process in two or three days. Most women are coping with their periods for four or five days. Other women struggle through six, seven, or eight days of continuous bleeding.

Researchers have attributed various characteristics to the woman with short, average, or long menstrual periods. In a study by Van de Castle, he observed that nursing students who had brief periods had dreams with less apprehension, less anger, and less references to time than women with long periods.[60] But the women with short periods also reported more negative references in their dreams. Such findings are difficult to interpret.

The picture is further complicated by the fact that the menstrual pattern often undergoes change as the woman ages. Several women in my study described different menstrual patterns with differing life situations. And of course for dreamers who take the pill, natural periods are masked, shifting into a regular, lighter pattern.

Synchronization: Women's Menstrual Symphony

Women who spend a lot of time together tend to synchronize their menstrual cycles. This is one of the old wives' tales that has been demonstrated to be scientifically sound. Living together in a dormitory, a household, a schoolroom, or being part of a group at work—all create conditions for the women's periods to synchronize.

When my twelve-year-old daughter, Cheryl, reached her menarche, she underwent the usual preparatory stages. Still, we were both surprised when one night, feeling restless, she chose to sleep on the living room couch and awoke in a pool of blood. Had I been aware at that time of the tendency for females to menstruate in synchrony with other women in the environment, I might have been prepared—it was also my period.

Later, living in London with an older teenage daughter and a foreign student in her thirties, I was startled to become aware that we were all having our periods simultaneously. I had then never heard of menstrual synchrony and thought it merely an interesting coincidence.

Follow the Pheremone Leader.   Psychologist Martha McClintock first documented menstrual synchrony in 1970, when she studied women living together in a college dormitory.[61] After about three months of living in the same vicinity, women's cycles began to coincide with each other. Scientists wondered why; they suspected that a chemical substance in the women's body was communicated.

A recent study carried out by chemist George Preti and biologist Winnifred Cutler, at the University of Pennsylvania and the Monell Chemical Senses Center in Philadelphia, verifies menstrual synchrony and pinpoints the cause. Ten women with normal menstrual cycles were exposed to female underarm sweat. This was done by swabbing the women's upper lips with alcohol that contained "female essence" from other women. Within three months of thrice weekly swabbing on the upper lip, the women's cycles were roughly synchronized with the cycle of the donors. Women who were exposed to plain alcohol on the lip showed no difference.

Preti and Cutler found, in another study, that a body chemical called androstenol found in female underarms changes predictably during the menstrual cycle; it peaks just before ovulation. This high androstenol may subliminally communicate—by scent or contact—to other women in the environment where a particular woman is in her cycle.

Even with the deodorants and perfumes women wear, a female essence, probably a scent, is perceived by women in close environments. Scientists think the crucial ingredient is a bodily substance called a pheromone. The woman with the most effective scent, it seems, sets the pace for the group.

In still another investigation Preti and Cutler conducted a rigorous test of this concept. In this case underarm secretions from men who had worn a pad under each armpit was used. The "male essence" was then swabbed, three times a week, on the upper lip of women whose cycles were shorter or longer than average, less than 26 days or more than 33 days. By the third month of this treatment, most women's cycles were approaching the optimum 29.5 days—this is the cycle corresponding to highest fertility. A control group of women who were swabbed with plain alcohol showed no change. Neither researchers nor subjects knew which bottles contained the essence until after the experiment. Cutler concludes that male essence contains at least one pheromone that is helpful to the woman's reproductive health.

Duets in Tune.   A woman and man living harmoniously together develop a temperature pattern that is synchronous. Surprisingly the man takes the lead from the woman's rhythm. According to investigations of Margaret Henderson of Australia, men show a hormonal rise and fall that simulates that of their spouse.[62] When a woman has the characteristic mid-cycle drop and then rise in temperature at ovulation, so does the man, although his temperature does not remain as high as hers does. If the woman goes on the pill, or becomes pregnant or otherwise stops ovulating, the man's variations also cease.

We know, too, that couples who sleep in the same bed soon synchronize their brain wave patterns to a large extent. This partially explains why some devoted couples find it so hard to sleep well when their mates are absent. Dream time, too, tends to synchronize.

Is there similarity in dream content as well? Many couples report experiences in which they dreamed of similar topics. This phenomenon, sometimes referred to as dual dreaming, has yet to be investigated in depth. Perhaps the male also parallels his female partner as her dream pictures shift from phase to phase throughout her cycle, although the style of images they use will differ.

Identifying Personal Dream Symbols of Menstruation

If you are a menstrual woman who would like to understand the dream symbols for your cycle, here's how it can be done.

Dream Symbols for the Menses: Phase 1

Because there is no question whether a woman is bleeding or not, menses is a good time to look for symbols of menstruation in your dreams. Even though dreaming is less than at other times of the month, dreams are still present. If your recall appears to vanish, be patient; it will soon return.

• *Look for enclosures and receptacles—the typical symbols of the womb.*

Houses, rooms, boxes, pots, vases, sinks, and other enclosures with entrances, or containers with openings, will often symbolize your uterus. (Described more fully in the next chapter.)

One woman in my study who was menstrual dreamed:

I am back at the workroom at school [that I finished over a decade ago]. I am impressed to see how clean the wax pots and spatulas of the teacher [a demanding person] are. They are spotless. Mine are so hard to keep clean.

Her own womb was in the process of self-cleansing.

• *Notice the condition of any enclosures or receptacles—they often describe how you feel about your menstruation.*

Houses collapsing, sinks or bathtubs overflowing, and other imagery of destruction are common. Researchers Therese Benedek and Boris Rubenstein found that the most unpleasant and hostile dreams, described by women in their study, were during menses.[63]

Analyst Emil Gutheil reported the dream of a menstrual woman in her late twenties; in it she saw herself in a bathtub that suddenly filled with blood rather than water. Then she was in bed, with blood covering the linen and pillows. Next she saw a little boy covered with blood. She awoke to find that her period had started.[64]

Such imagery probably stands for the dreamer's sense of disintegration of the lining of the womb. More positive imagery comes soon.

• *Look at what is happening to any fluids—they often represent the blood.*

Water in containers, streams, rivers, and other flowing substances will often describe what is happening to your menstrual blood. In the dream described above, hot wax is used to symbolize the flow. In my dream of the red river, also described above, my symbol for the blood was moving in great torrents, a virtual flood.

Once, when I was hemorraging as a result of too much airplane travel, I dreamed of an overflowing sink with no way to stop the flooding waters. The bleeding continued for eleven days of bedrest before it ceased. At other times, dreams of draining dirty water heralded menstruation.

• *Notice references to the color red or to blood—these, too, may represent the menstrual flow.*

Hospitals, incisions, body parts, and red blood were mentioned by menstrual women in a study by Robert Van de Castle.[65]

In olden days in Japan, women traditionally wore red undergarments beneath their kimonos. The color red, in addition to being regarded as lucky in Asian cultures and being used in celebrations, was also believed to ward off menstrual pain and keep the female reproductive system functioning smoothly. This practice and these beliefs would evoke even more dreams of red at menstrual time. Do you follow any menstrual ritual? If so, look for indications of it in your menstrual dreams.

• *Notice what is happening between the characters in your dream—they often reflect your mood.*

Are the men in your menstrual dreams friendly or aggressive? Are the women characters pleasant to you or cruel? How do you act toward them? Do babies or children appear in your menstrual dreams?

Van de Castle found references to lost children in the dreams of menstrual women.[66] We have already mentioned that he noted the dreamer was more friendly to other women in her menstrual dreams than at any other time.[67] This may stem from a sense of identification with other women during menstruation.

Although Van de Castle reports more dreams of babies and small children during menses, other researchers report this imagery more during ovulation. You may find your own characteristic pattern.

Dream researchers Ethel Swanson and David Foulkes, in a recent study, reported that the sexiest dreams of the entire cycle occurred during menses.[68] Despite the fact that the women in their study said they had low sexual interest during this time, their dreams were filled with sex. Other studies have found that sex dreams are most common prior to and during ovulation.[69] Your own pattern may fit some of these findings or be unique.

• *Observe any visual puns that may symbolize your period.*

Falling off the roof, getting a little visitor, getting sick, wearing a rag—these are some of the images based on puns that may appear in dreams at the menses.

Your native language, or languages you know, determine the puns your dreaming mind creates. Anne Frank, the young Jewish woman who died in a concentration camp, mentioned her first few periods in her diary, referring to them as her "sweet secret." Advertising men in Japan liking this phrase, chose the name Anne Co. for their company manufacturing sanitary products. Japanese women thus sometimes refer to their period as "Anne's Day." A dreamer familiar with this practice might dream of a visit from a woman named Anne when her menses was due. What slang words do you employ for your period? Look for these in dreams.

• *Look for increased creativity.*

We have not yet mentioned the positive feeling some women experience during their menses. Many women say they have a surge of creativity during the days of their bleeding. One artist, for instance, tells me that she is far more original in her work during her periods. Perhaps because they tend to be inwardly focused at this time, women are more aware of fantasies.

We are accustomed to thinking about the disadvantages of the premenstrual and menstrual time. Women often speak of being "spacey" and having difficulty focusing on details.[70] The positive side of this condition is that it is easier to free-associate, to come up with new combinations of familiar things in unfamiliar ways—this is what constitutes creativity. Perhaps women's abilities at the premenstrual and menstrual times are not liabilities but powers of a different sort.

In fact in some primitive tribes the dreams of the first menstruation are regarded as being a guide for the young woman's entire life.[71] She is thought to be able to become a shaman or witch doctor only if she has developed a positive relationship with the "spirits" of her menstruation.[72]

Furthermore, a study of one hundred women found that those who were in the best mental health were the ones who had definite negative personality changes during the premenstrual and menstrual phases.[73] It may be that the negative premenstrual changes experienced by a large portion of women are hidden capacities that can be used in positive ways. By relating in constructive ways to her dream images and by using the special energy of menstrual time for creativity, the woman can transform any negative experience into positive.

Psychologist Bruno Bettelheim tells us that the tale of Sleeping Beauty is actually a story of the young woman reaching puberty.[74] The curse of the thirteenth fairy, he says, is the "curse" of menstruation. The thirteen fairies represent the thirteen lunar months, the number of the woman's menstrual periods each year. When the heroine pricks her finger, bleeds, and falls asleep, it seems traumatic. But by turning inward, by "falling asleep" as adolescence approaches, she develops and matures until she is ready to be "awakened" to sexual maturity by her lover's kiss. The curse leads to a blessing. Perhaps each menstrual period can provide the same opportunity—to turn inward, to self-reflect, to grow in understanding—and then turn outward to active life and love again.

Today's woman may find that the diffuse feelings of menstruation have a positive side, whatever direction her own creativity may take, whether she is having children or is giving birth to original ideas and products. Watch for the opportunity to think—or dream—creatively during your period.

Dream Symbols for Postmenstrual: Phase 2

Dream content begins to shift after bleeding stops:

- *Look for dreams about social activities with males.* Perhaps nature is encouraging us to find a mate.

Dreams Symbols for Preovulation and Ovulation: Phases 3 and 4

If you are a woman who has mid-cycle pain at ovulation, you will know exactly when it happens. Most women rely on changes in the normal vaginal discharge from thin to thick, or on the characteristic change of their temperature at ovulation, or on counting the days since the first day of their last period. Here are some of the typical dream clues:

- *Look for round, precious, or fragile objects—they often symbolize the ovum that is being released and starting its journey to the womb.*
  Eggs, jewelry, gemstones, and other such objects frequently appear in women's dreams at ovulation.[75]
- *Notice the behavior of your dream characters—they may impel you to relate to the opposite sex.*
  Are the men in your dreams loving and friendly during your ovulation? Are you outgoing and active in your dreams now?
  Van de Castle found more dreams of sex during preovulation and ovulation (18 percent of the dreams were sexy), as did Benedek and Rubenstein.[76] Swanson and Foulkes, in contrast, reported more sex dreams at menses.[77] Van de Castle also found that men dream characters were friendlier to the dreamer than at any other time of the cycle; he noted less dreams of misfortune.[78]
  From a biological point of view, it would make more sense for women to be responsive to men prior to and during ovulation, when the chance of impregnation is highest.

Dream Symbols for Postovulation: Phase 5

• *Look for dreams of pregnancy or nursing—they may indicate you have become pregnant. Of course, they may also be a wish fulfillment.*

One woman in my study dreamed of getting the things she needed to pack a bag to go to the hospital to have a baby, long before she discovered or even suspected that she was actually pregnant.

Dream images often become more tranquil at this stage, perhaps readying the dreamer to nourish a child.

Benedek and Rubenstein observed that women in their study had more dreams of pregnancy and nursing in this phase.[79] They noted that women's dreams became more passive and receptive, as if there were an ingathering of energy.

Dream Symbols for Premenstruation: Phases 6 and 7

• *Look for an increase of frenetic energy in your dreams—it often signals the onset of premenstrual tension.*

Confused, frightening imagery may occur at this time.

• *Look for dream indications of water retention, if you are subject to this problem.*

One woman dreamed of walking through a garden with rich, ripe pears about to burst; when she awoke, she perceived the engorged sensation in her breasts that was typical of her premenstrual time. Fruit often symbolizes the breasts in dreams; at times it may stand for the womb in its bursting ripeness.

• *Notice any references to travel or journeys—they may indicate the change about to occur in your womb.*

Studies investigating the menstrual dreams of women sometimes report contradictory and confusing findings. We have already said that the possible reason for some of these inconsistent findings may stem from the failure of investigators to distinguish between ovulatory and anovulatory cycles. In addition different researchers use different criteria to identify ovulation and the other stages of the menstrual cycle. Some researchers take vaginal samples on slides to pinpoint the stage; others merely count forward or backward from the last known period; still others use a woman's self-report. Investigators often use differing terminology as well. Male researchers may not appreciate the variations between individual women's menstrual symptoms and patterns. You will be able to learn from yourself.

If you observe and make note of your cyclic shifts, you can train yourself to recognize when your period or ovulation is approaching. You might, for instance, make a red dot or check at the top of the pages in your dream diary on the days you are menstruating. Soon your dreams may alert you before any characteristic symptom is discernible in the waking state. Remaining alert to your dream pictures can teach you about the inner rhythms of your body.

Remember that there are limitations on the research that has been done on women's menstrual dreams. You might think of the findings as a rough sketch made by someone else. Then construct your own careful drawing of the same topic.

As you observe your own dream symbols for each stage of your menstrual cycle, you will begin to observe a pattern that will help you identify the stage you are currently experiencing. You will often be able to tell whether your period will arrive the next day by the dream of the preceding night. Knowing your body through your dreams can be exceedingly useful. We turn now to recognizing the images of love and sex.

Love and Sex Dreams

A boy and a girl are walking up the road hand in hand. Suddenly a whip cracks and they separate. Standing between them is a tall masked stranger in a long black cape. He starts setting off fire crackers and cracking sparks from his whip.

—Author's dream diary, age fifteen

Falling-In-Love Dreams

In their yearning for love, young girls respond to biological urges within and cultural goals without. The virgin's dreams are filled with images like those in my youthful dream above—romantic and mysterious. Not knowing exactly what the physical expression of love is like, she is both attracted and repelled by the force of sex, as I was by the stranger who cracks his whip (symbolic of the male sexual organ) and sets off sparks (representing my awakening passion). The masked stranger is the unknown sexual encounter.

97

The virgin often views being loved as a primary goal in life. *Then* she will feel protected, then she will feel beautiful, then she will feel properly treasured. She will no longer be alone in the world—the arms of her beloved will wrap her in a cloak of bliss. In fact there are few joys in life to equal the glow of being in love.

The subject of the heroine's quest, the screen star's drama, and the songs of each generation, love gleams through adolescence like the lighthouse of safe harbor. Even in a young woman who has been abused as a child there lingers the hope that, as in the fairytale of Snow White, "one day my Prince will come" and she will be truly loved. Beginning in early grade school the best dream for many women—awake or asleep—is of being happily married.

Dreams Reflect the Dreamer's Level of Experience

Many of the inexperienced young woman's dreams of sexuality are symbolic, such as being knifed by a stranger or having her house set on fire. We will examine the way the dreaming mind works in analogies later on in this chapter.

When the virgin dreams directly about a lover, it is usually in romantic terms—the dark, mysterious stranger of Gypsy teacups, the shining prince who will sweep her off her feet. Her dream lovers kiss, hold, fondle, or actually marry her without proceeding further. In her dreams she may notice "bumps in men's trousers" without fully understanding their import. Dreams cannot reflect physical details beyond the dreamer's experience in life, although they may show the influence of the latest television heroine's dramatic escapade.

Anne Frank, only thirteen when her family went into hiding in the upper floors of a house in Amsterdam in order to escape capture by the Nazis, recorded in her diary romantic longings for the son of the other family who had taken refuge in the same space:[1]

> From early in the morning until late at night, I really do hardly anything else but think of Peter. I sleep with his image before my eyes, dream about him, and he is still looking at me when I awake. . . .
> But how and when will we finally reach each other? I don't know quite how long my common sense will keep this longing under control.

In contrast, a mature woman who has a clear idea of the process of making love is more likely to depict it explicitly in her dreams; she may dream of intercourse and orgasm in a manner unknown to virgins. She concocts, as well, dream images that symbolize her emotional responses to potential mates. She may pick up signals from her dreams long before she perceives a waking sexual attraction.

All women—experienced or not—can understand their attitudes toward love and sex better by observing their dream scenarios. Our dreams reveal our needs in graphic highlights. Let's see how.

"I'm Wishing": Dreams of Yearning for a Lover to Appear

Chased by Green Man. A woman conjures up images of "the man of my dreams" from early girlhood to old age. Kathleen, for instance, told me that when she was a teenager,

> I began having recurrent dreams that I was being chased by a man who was entirely green. The dream was frightening but I somehow thought it was symbolic.

Not long after these dreams began, Kathleen met, fell in love with, and married a man whose last name was Green. Having been his wife and the mother of his children for several decades, Kathleen thinks her marriage was foreshadowed by her repetitive dream, which ceased when she began to date him. Whether her dream was truly predictive or whether Kathleen attached her emotions about the dream to the man who seemed to fit it, is impossible to say. In either case the color green was undoubtedly important to the Irish Kathleen.

The tendency for young women to dream about future lovers is ritualized in folk customs throughout the world. In France, adolescent girls chant a rhyme to the full moon in spring. When she is ready for bed, the girl backs into it, still focusing her eyes on the moon, in order to go to sleep and dream of her beloved. A folk saying in Romania voices the same idea: "When the moon is full, you can see the face of your love." Especially if the girl wants to marry, she is to let down her hair at midnight in spring, gaze at the full moon, and make a wish to see "the one I will love forever." On retiring, she is to place her own ring under her pillow to bring a dream of her true love.

The same tradition survives in America in the practice of taking home a piece of wedding cake. Originally the cake was put under the pillow to induce dreams of the sweetheart-to-come.

Although such practices themselves are not likely to produce dreams of future mates, the belief in them can prove effective. If the woman happens to be at the stage of her menstrual cycle when the tendency for sexual dreams is high, she may find her wish for a dream lover fulfilled.

Strangely enough, although folk beliefs encourage the young woman to dream of her future mate, a dream lover who becomes too important is regarded as dangerous. Dream lovers have been linked with the devil, or an "incubus" that is said to "lie upon" the woman in her sleep and steal her soul.[2] Today we understand that sexual arousal is a natural part of dreaming and that dreams of love can help prepare the young woman for her future life as well as give expression to the romantic and sexual feelings of the experienced woman. Dream lovers have different meanings to different dreamers.

Dreams of Wanting to Change Partners

Greek God at the Door. Those women who are already mated may be restless with their choice. Edith, when she was in her thirties, had serious problems with her marriage when she began to dream of a romantic encounter:

> In my dream I am always at home when the doorbell rings. I go to answer it and find it is a Greek god. Sometimes he will take me dancing where I waltz in a full gown, whirling over the floor like in the movies, my feet not touching the floor.

Obviously Edith felt that romance was missing in her life. She yearned to be whirled away to a "divine" relationship. Her own daily existence at the time was quite drab. Although her dreams of the heavenly lover were few, they made a profound impression:

> Once he took me for a walk in the forest. We were happily sitting there when I heard a strange noise. I thought it was a bear and as I looked to see, I woke up and found that the noise was my husband snoring.

The contrast between the lover of her dreams and the reality of Edith's problematic husband was harshly underscored. In Edith's dream language she was saying, "My husband is like a bear"—to her, an unpleasant, troublesome beast.

Occasionally Edith dreamed of sexual encounters with strangers. In these she would usually engage in heavy petting to orgasm, without having intercourse. Edith, in addition to being sensitive to her body's aroused state during her dreams, was also expressing a wish for a more fulfilling partner, one who brought delight. Lovers in dreams usually reveal the dreamer's needs.

Dreams of Wishing for More in a Relationship

Many of the women in my study related dreams of an encounter with a lost lover, as well as with strangers. Although she found the passionate dream itself highly pleasurable, the dreamer was sometimes distraught when she awoke. If she had a committed relationship, she could not comprehend the reason for such a dream.

In some cases these dream lovers represent a wish for a more satisfactory relationship. Moira, for instance, in her forties, describes her twenty-some-year marriage as "atrocious." A virgin until her wedding night, she has never had any other lover than her husband. Although she has a good sexual response to him, including orgasm, Moira weeps bitterly after intercourse because she finds the marriage so devoid of other satisfactions. The couple's daily life is fraught with arguments.

Small wonder that Moira's dreams occasionally include amorous encounters with men she knows only casually. For the sake of her children she feels economically trapped in marriage with a difficult husband. Moira yearns for freedom; her sexual dreams hold forth the possibility of a different type of loving.

The Many Meanings of Dream Lovers

Lindsey found herself tormented by a dream lover. A woman in her thirties, married for a few years, she would occasionally dream of cavorting in wild delight with her first lover, a high school sweetheart. Worried about these dream orgies, she tremulously asked me what they meant. Since she is not aware of any wish to change partners, nor does she really believe that her first lover would be a good mate, her dreams may be offering compensation for some quality she feels is missing at present.

A dream lover, I find, has several possible meanings: he may be a wish for an ideal man; he may be a wish for a particular man known to the dreamer; he may express a need for sexual satisfaction; or he may represent some quality that is missing in the dreamer's current relationship. Despite Lindsey's fondness for her former sweetheart, she is quite sure he was not right for her, eliminating the possibility that she was yearning for him in particular. When I asked Lindsey what kind of person this first sweetheart was, her associations involved his warmth and tenderness—qualities that seem deficient in her current relationship. We were able to determine that she did not necessarily wish to be out of the marriage, but she did yearn for a greater expression of warmth and tenderness from her mate.

Norma, unmarried in her thirties, began having dreams of making love with an old boyfriend named Art while she was living with another boyfriend. Inquiry revealed that Art's appeal was less as a person than as a symbol. Her dream of uniting with Art was a pun on his name: Norma missed her art activities that she had been involved with before her current relationship. Such dreams—when the dreamer hears their message—give the dreamer an incentive to pursue neglected interests that have previously been fulfilling.

If you find yourself dreaming about former lovers, ask yourself the following questions:

- What were your dream lover's outstanding traits?
- Do any of these represent qualities or characteristics that you want more of today—either in a current mate or in yourself?
- If so, how can they be obtained?
- Does the dream lover resemble someone in your environment who is actually attractive to you?
- Is there a pun on the dream lover's name?
- Is his name the same as or similar to some waking-life man who appeals to you or repulses you?

Dream lovers may represent an actual person you desire, or they may be calling your attention to a current deficiency in yourself or your relationship. Knowing this, you can decide what to do about your need.

Wishing for the Ideal

Followers of Carl Jung interpret the dream lover as a projection of the masculine component within a woman—her animus. The animus is said to have both a positive and a negative aspect. In his destructive aspect he is like a ghostly lover who lures his victim away from reality by promises of bliss in another world.[3] In his constructive aspect he becomes an inner guide. When a woman "projects" this part of her psyche onto a stranger, Jungians say, it accounts for the passionate attachment women develop for a male about whom they know little in reality.

The dream lover may be someone met briefly, once or a few times, or he may be a movie star, politician, or other celebrity. A middle-aged woman who participated in one of my dream workshops had this kind of devotion to the movie actor Charlton Heston, often dreaming about him. When I asked her, "What kind of person is Charlton Heston?" she explained that he was "very spiritual." His biblical roles had apparently conveyed this notion to her. Since spirituality was something this woman hungered for in her own life, making love with this actor symbolized her wish to connect with a spiritual element.

During adolescence it is normal for a young woman to develop a "crush" or to go through a phase of hero worship. The idol she picks—be he movie hero or baseball star—embodies the qualities she most wants in her ideal mate. These are usually the very qualities she senses to be lacking in herself.

Sometimes the youngster simply wants to be the center of devoted attention. When my daughter Cheryl was thirteen, for instance, she conceived a crush on the singer Rod Stewart. His music pulsated out of her bedroom. His giant-sized image gazed down at her from the walls. Soon I was confronted with his frenzied haircut (short spikes in front and straggly locks in back) on my daughter's head. It was with mixed feelings that I saw her soon transfer her affection to accessible young men more easily within reach. These, too, were endowed in her mind with powers far beyond their age and present development.

This shift from idols to "real life" males with whom a young woman begins to have normal relationships is important. If she falls in love a time or two and begins to distinguish between impossible perfection and possible reality, she is well on the way to an eventual loving relationship with a single man in the totality of his faults and virtues.

The woman who continues to transfer her inner needs onto every appealing male, however, is disappointed over and over again, because sooner or later the man proves to be human rather than godlike. Pursuing an impossible ideal, she dooms herself to unhappy relationships as surely as if an incubus were actually pulling her to the grave.

Loving the Real

Jungian author M. Esther Harding urges women to question their responses to differing men in waking life.[4] The woman who asks herself why she is drawn to or rejects a certain male will come to understand what it is in her past life that accounts for the magnetic attraction or repulsion she feels. By continually observing herself in this way, Harding believes, a woman can make her inner compulsion conscious. Thus she will free herself to build a sound relationship with a very human mate.

Likewise a woman can question herself about the men in her dreams. If you find yourself having a rendezvous with a dream lover, ask yourself what is so appealing about him. If you have tussels with an obnoxious man in your dreams, try to define the source of your repulsion toward him. Your answers will give you clues to your current needs.

When a woman is capable of relating to a man as he is in reality, a unique blend of virtue and vice that is precious to her, she frees an inner energy. Instead of hopelessly forming internal images of a perfect dream lover, she is able to learn from her *inner* male, the one that appears in her dreams. He can become a kind of spiritual guide, a teacher, and helper in life rather than a dangerous distraction from it.

A woman who has romantic and sexual satisfaction only in her dreams may well have problems, yet dream release is better than none at all. At the least, dream lovers can bring calm and patience into a waking life that is stormy. At the most, they can bring delight and learning on many levels.

Sexual Dreams

In order to better understand her dreams of love and sex, a woman needs to be aware of (a) what is happening to her own genitals during her dreams; and (b) what women's common dream symbols for sex are, how certain images are analogous to the male and female bodies. We will see in a moment how these images become metaphors in actual dreams. First, a reminder about the ongoing physiological events while a woman is dreaming.

Sexual Arousal During Dreams

We have already pointed out that both sexes experience an arousal of their central nervous system whenever they dream. Every ninety minutes or so throughout the night, their genitals, as well, are flooded with sensation.

In a dreaming female, the clitoris becomes engorged with blood, as it does when the woman is awake and sexually aroused. Nipples become erect. The pulse in the vagina increases during the dream state, and the lubrication of the genitals is measurably greater. This swelling and moistening of the sexual organs is sometimes sensed by the dreamer, just as she would notice her condition in a waking state.

Scientists did not observe these facts about the dreaming woman until years after much data on men's sexual responses had been gathered. In 1965 researcher Charles Fisher, along with others, had proved that male erections were present during REM.[5] Since female sexual arousal is more difficult to observe than the corresponding male penile erection, and the majority of dream laboratory workers are male, this aspect of the female's response was given little attention.

Researcher Ismet Karacan and his colleagues, in 1970, reported increases in the circumference of the clitoris during REM.[6] Another investigator, in 1972, reported regular increases of about one-half a degree in the temperature of the clitoris during REM.[7] Others began to explore changes in vaginal blood flow.

In the early 1970s an instrument called the vaginal photoplethysmograph was invented that enabled researchers to more easily gauge changes in vaginal blood flow during sleep.[8] In the laboratory this instrument is inserted by the woman into her vagina prior to falling asleep, and measurements are taken throughout the night.

In Canada in 1977, one of the first studies using the vaginal photoplethysmograph with the study of dreams yielded equivocal results. All night long the investigators compared vaginal blood-volume changes in six women to changes in the blood flow to the foot. The research team observed erratic fluctuations in vaginal blood flow, most of them in REM sleep and in stage 2 sleep; blood flow to the foot scarcely changed. Therefore, although the women were exhibiting changes in vaginal blood flow during sleep, these changes were not so clear-cut as were male erections.[9]

A few years later, in the early 1980s, a team of investigators in New York headed by Charles Fisher, measuring ten women in a similar way, found definite evidence for vascular engorgement in women that was analogous to male erections during dreaming.[10] The sexual arousal responses of the women were compared during sleeping and waking. Measurements were taken during three days around the women's ovulation, because it was believed that the vaginal blood-flow effects would be enhanced at this time.[11] Subjects were asked to evoke memories of exciting sexual experiences, engage in erotic fantasy, listen to a taped description of an erotic scene, and finally to view an erotic film. After the subjects went to sleep, their sexual arousal was measured during dreaming. In addition, four subjects volunteered to masturbate in privacy while being recorded. One subject experienced an orgasm in one of her REM dreams.

All these measurements were compared. The team was able to confirm that cyclic episodes of vascular engorgement during REM appear to be equivalent to erections in men. These arousal periods occur with equal frequency (in 95 percent of the REM), although they differ in certain respects:

- Vaginal blood-flow changes were apt to appear in the first half of the REM period (in men the erections parallel the entire REM).
- The vaginal blood-flow changes in REM were shorter in duration (in men penile erections may be sustained for a total of more than two out of nine hours' sleep). There was an average of 4.4 vaginal blood-flow increases during REM. These changes lasted for a total of about 31 minutes (or 37 percent of the 84 minutes spent in REM).[12] Average duration of an individual vaginal blood-flow increase was 7.9 minutes in REM. In the male, erections during REM may continue as long as an hour.
- Vaginal blood flow changes reached maximum amplitude less often than the erections did.
- Vaginal blood-flow changes differed in distribution. As well as having blood-flow changes in REM, women had more frequent blood-flow changes than men in their non-REM periods (in about 66 percent of their non-REM).

These data confirm that women have cyclic episodes of vascular engorgement during REM that are roughly equivalent to erections in men, but differ in minor aspects, the women being more variable.

Furthermore, when sexual-arousal responses were compared under the differing conditions, it was found that they produced approximately the same degree of response.[13] Whether the woman was watching an erotic movie, masturbating, dreaming, or having an orgasm in her dream, the measurements were about the same. This suggests that vascular engorgement of the vagina is limited to a certain maximum, whether the response is in waking fantasy or in dreaming. Other researchers have since substantiated these findings that women, like men, become sexually aroused during dreams.[14]

Degree of Arousal Parallels Dream Imagery

In a later study by some members of the same team in New York over twenty-five nights, using nine of the same subjects, vaginal changes were measured and dream reports were gathered by awakening the women at various times. The dream reports showed that explicit sexual content and symbolic sexual content followed a woman's sudden increase, or a sustained rise, in her vaginal blood flow. In other words the dream reports paralleled the physical changes.

This study also showed that REM periods with large vaginal blood-flow increases have a far greater chance of being associated with sexual dreams than do REM periods with minimal blood-flow increases.[15] The investigators speculate that the great amount of sexual excitation at night during dreaming sleep may serve to reduce sexual drive during the day and help to discharge instinctual tensions. Perhaps orgasm in our dreams supplements other orgasms and thus maintains the rate of sexual release that is best for each person.[16]

Women who are able to become "lucid" in a dream, to be aware that they are dreaming during the dream, often report heightened sexual feelings. Being able to perform the activity of their choice during dreams, lucid dreamers frequently elect to make love to orgasm. These orgasms are indistinguishable from waking-life orgasms, according to measurements taken at Stanford University by Stephen LaBerge and his colleagues.[17] Perhaps, when a woman becomes lucid, the imagery of her dreams then accentuates the physical sensations already present; lucid-dream orgasms have been described by some dreamers as "soul-shattering" or "bigger than life." More of this later. Whether women are lucid in their dreams or not, whether the content of their dreams is sexual or not, their genitals undergo a cyclic activation throughout the night.

The same natural process is seen in the penile erections during REM that have been monitored in male populations, from newborn to elders in their nineties. This cyclic arousal of the penis accounts for the familiar morning erection that is part of the morning dream, lasting a half hour or so. At first scientists thought that dream content had no relationship to the penile erections. Now they understand that erections may be absent or mild when dreams are aggressive, especially if there is a threat to the dreamer's masculinity.[18] Erections that accompany provocative dreams are larger and firmer than at other times. Researchers think the brain may receive a signal about the erection that the dreaming mind weaves into an erotic dream. Instead of a sexual dream causing the erection, the erection may stimulate the dream.[19]

The sexual component of dreaming is a normal process in healthy men and women. Keeping in mind that a dreaming woman is an aroused woman, let's look at the sexual symbols in her dreams.

Female Genitals in Women's Dreams: Purses, Doors, Rings, Boxes

When women dream about their sexual organs, they usually select objects that resemble them in shape or function. These images are metaphors for the female organs, either because they have analogous shapes or because they are used in an analogous manner. The following is an outline of the table of typical dream symbols for female genitals:

Dream Image	Example
Containers with a space that can be filled	A vase
Objects enclosing a space that can be opened or closed	A room with a door
Animals or objects that are traditionally female	A ship
Feminine articles of clothing	A ring
Fruit with a cleft	A peach
Objects with a name that is a pun on a slang term	A "pussy"

The above outline will help you understand why the individual dream symbols for female genitals appear on the table. You will notice that most of the symbols on the table replicate the womb's ability to enclose menstrual blood and a fetus; the vagina's capacity to be filled with a penis; or else they resemble the vulva, or other genitals, in shape.[20] The objects selected to symbolize the breasts usually resemble them in shape (such as round fruit) or in function (such as springs), reflecting the ability of the breasts to give milk. Images appear in dreams because they resemble the object symbolized in function or in form.

We find the same principle of symbolism at work in the myths, poetry, art, popular songs and slang of each culture. When William Shakespeare, in his classic tragedy *Antony and Cleopatra,* has one character say to another, "She made great Caesar lay his sword to bed. He plough'd her and she cropp'd,"[21] the audience understood. It was not necessary to explain that Caesar had had sexual intercourse with Cleopatra and, as a result, she had given birth to a child. The plow has often been likened to the penis because of its ability to penetrate in preparation for planting the "seed." The earth has often been compared to the womb that receives the seed, nourishes it, and gives forth growing plants. Caesar's "plowing" led to Cleopatra's "cropping." We use the same symbolism in our art and literature that we use in dreams. Symbolism is part of everyday life. It is also a part of every night's dreams.

. . . .

[Women's Dream Symbols for] FEMALE GENITALS*

. . . .

Containers	*Enclosures*	*Animals*
vase, pot, urn	room with door	cat, kitten
jar, pitcher, vessel	room with window	(traditionally female)
bottle, cup	hallway	deer, doe
hole, pit	house, barn, building	cow
cave, cavern	box and cover, vault	mouse
nest	wardrobe, suitcase	mare
cage	trunk with lid	oyster, clam
sheath	bureau, drawer	shell
lock	stove, oven	
receptacle for plug		

* These images, of course, have multiple meanings, nonsexual as well as sexual.

Women's Clothing

purse, pocketbook
handbag, bag, muff
ring
glove, shoe
pocket

Fruit—Womb/ Vulva

peach (cleft)
coconut (cleft)
pear
cherry
fig

Fruit—Breasts

apples, oranges
tomatoes
melons, cantaloupes

Number—Breasts

two, matched pair

People

little girl
maid

Plants

rose, peony
other flowers
cabbage

Building Part—Breasts

balcony
porch, veranda

Geometric Shapes

circles, spheres
oval, egg
short triangle
short rectangle
square
diamond
target

Vehicles

ship, boat
automobile

Body Part

mouth, nose
eye, ear
wound

Fluids—Breast Milk

spring, fountain
well, source
liquid in jug

Bodies of Water

pond, pool, lake
well

Concrete Image of Pun or Slang Word

organ
pussy [cat]
chick, bird, doll, dish
haystack, thatch (pubic hair)

honeypot
beaver
bubbles (breasts)

Land Formations

mountains (breasts)
field

Male Genitals in Women's Dreams:
Snakes, Swords, Keys, Guns

Women often dream about the male organ in a language of sexual symbolism. Looking at the following outline, you can see that the symbols for male genitals that appear on the longer table are chosen because they usually resemble the penis in shape or function:

Dream Image	*Example*
Objects with long, slender shapes	A knife
Objects capable of penetration	A key
Objects capable of enlarging, growing, or erecting	An upright plant
Objects capable of explosion, as the penis is of ejaculation of semen	A gun
Animals with attributes resembling shape of penis	A snake
Animals traditionally considered male	A dog
Clothing articles worn by men	A tie
Fruit shaped like a penis	A banana
A projecting part of the body	A nose
Objects with names that are a slang word for male genitals	A "cock"

Women's Dream Symbols for
MALE GENITALS*

Penetrating Weapons	*Explosive Weapons*	*Men's Clothing*
knife, dagger, spear	gun, pistol, rifle	necktie, belt
sword, saber, bayonet	rocket	hat

* These images, of course, have multiple meanings, nonsexual as well as sexual. The list is not conclusive.

Slender, Oblong Objects	*Animals with Long Tails*	*People*
key, candle, screwdriver	mouse, rat, fish	dwarf
pen, pencil, brush	horse, bull, wild beast	servant
needle, syringe, hose	dog (traditionally male)	little man
pole, totem pole, mast, stick	monkey, squirrel	
pipe, cigar, cigarette	frog (long tongue, bumpy skin)	
golf club, baseball bat	bird (flying = erection)	
rope, electrical cord and plug	bee, wasp (stinger, not tail)	
tombstone, monument	elephant (trunk)	

Elongated Food	*Elongated Plant*	*Objects that Erect*
banana, cucumber, pickle	stalk, trunk, root	umbrella
hot dog, wiener, frankfurter	tall plant, tree, reed	erector set
carrot, celery	***Musical Instruments***	
lollipop, éclair, cone	flute, piccolo, violin	

Projecting Body Parts	*Numbers*	*Buildings*
tongue	one (phallus)	skyscrapers
finger, arm	three	towers, silos
nose	three-piece set (penis and two testicles)	
tooth, whiskers		

Geometric Shapes	*Concrete Images of Puns or Slang Words*	
cylinder	balls	rocks
cone, pyramid	nuts	family jewels or treasure
tall triangle	cock [rooster]	objects that prick
rectangle	organ	mail (= male)
oblong cube	cream, milk, whipped cream (semen)	
	common name: Peter, Dick, John	

The woman who is aware of the mind's tendency to select dream symbols for the phallus is able to understand her dream content better. Symbols for male genitals are metaphors for the penis's ability to penetrate and ejaculate or comparisons based on the shape of the penis or the testicles. Again the form or function determines the image chosen as a symbol. When the dream symbols for female genitals and male genitals connect, we have symbols for sexual intercourse.

Sexual Intercourse in Women's Dreams

In a woman's dreams sexual intercourse has a vast range of symbols. Which ones appear depend upon a number of factors: her past experience or lack of it; the actual nature of her sexual contacts; how the woman feels about a particular lover; what her own physical responses to her lover are; the quality of their relationship; her anticipations of the future; her own fears or conflicts between inhibition versus orgasm, between needs for closeness and needs for distance; and on puns from her waking language.

Women's dreams about sex are usually more symbolic than men's, although as mentioned earlier, there is a trend toward more open sexuality in women's dreams.

In the following outline the longer table of symbols for sexual intercourse you can see that, despite wide variation in emotional quality, the symbols resemble the sex act in function:

....

Dream Image	*Example*
Acts of attack with a weapon	A stranger shoots gun at dreamer
Acts of attack by a wild animal	A snake bites the dreamer
Acts that injure a woman	Dreamer run over by automobile
Acts of forced entry into a building	An intruder breaks into bedroom
Acts that destroy a building	A house is set on fire
Acts that construct a building	A skyscraper is erected (male arousal)
Actions of mechanical equipment	Gas pumped into tank of car
Acts of rhythmic movement	Dreamer climbs a staircase
Acts of incorporation	Dreamer eats delicious banana split
Acts of uniting opposites	A wedding ceremony takes place

....

....

Women's Dream Symbols for
SEXUAL INTERCOURSE*

....

Attack With Weapon	*Attack by Wild Animal*
man knifes dreamer	snake bites dreamer
man shoots dreamer	dog mauls dreamer

* All dreams of being attacked indicate a feeling of threat. The images above may refer to nonsexual threats or other feelings as well as sexual ones. Themes of being chased or attacked are the most common dream. The list is not conclusive.

Attack With Weapon (Cont.)

man injures with other weapon
(arrow, needle, rope, cigar, etc.)

Attack by Wild Animal (Cont.)

beast injures dreamer
(lions, tigers, bulls, rats, wasps,
etc.)

Attack by Foreigner

exotic stranger pursues dreamer
(Latin, black, white, Oriental,
etc.

Forced Entry Into Building

intruder in bedroom
burglar breaks into house
stranger breaks down door

Destruction of Building

house is bombed or explodes
house consumed by fire

Construction of Building

skyscraper erected (male arousal)
silos or towers built (male
arousal)

Destruction of Person

run over by automobile; car
crash (train, tank, bulldozer,
etc.)
earthquake crushes

Insertion

gas pumped into tank, pumping
mail into mailbox
key into lock
plowing the earth
planting seeds

Defloration

wounding, tearing, soiling,
canceling, breaking, losing
destroying

driping, gushing, or broken
pipes (functioning or
malfunctioning penis)

Incorporation of Food or Liquid

eating banana split, éclair,
lollipop
drinking milkshake through
straw

Rhythmic Activity

swinging back and forth,
seesawing
riding horse, swimming, cycling

Rhythmic Activity (Cont.)

dancing or skating or moving
(sliding, spinning, floating,
flying)
climbing staircase, etc., running
gate swinging, bell ringing

Incorporation of Food or Liquid (Cont.)

eating hot dog or other food
(ice-cream cones, mushrooms,
etc.)

Concrete Images—Puns and Slang

banging object
screwing object
balling, ball games

Uniting of Opposites

combining fire and water
combining silver and gold
wedding ceremony

....

You can see that women dream of being entered by males in ways that are injurious, mechanical, or delightful. The surrounding context of the dream, along with the emotions of the dreamer during the dream, reveal how she feels about the sexual contact. Here's how some of the women in my study experienced their sexual dreams.

Women's Symbolic Sexual Dreams

Snakes Under the Bed.   The snake has been biting Eve in her dreams ever since his legendary seduction in the Garden of Eden. Because of the snake's long, slender shape, and his bite that emits venom—corresponding to the penis and its emission of semen—young women frequently dream of snakes when they express a fear of sex as dangerous.

Dreams about snakes may begin at a tender age. Eight-year-old Hilary, for instance, reported the following to me:

> I dreamed that there were snakes under my bed and I was mad
> at my dream.

In my 1984 study of children's dreams, another girl in Hilary's age bracket reported a dream of many snakes chasing her; snakes did not appear among the dreams of boys of the same age.

Surrounded by Snakes.   Grace, in her twenties, contributed an elaborate version of the classic snake nightmare:

> I dreamed I am at the old house where I used to live in the country. I am in the kitchen looking ahead into the dining room and can see there are snakes on the floor. I go into the bedroom and find snakes on the bottom bunk and one curled on the top bunk.
>
> Then I am back in the kitchen. There are large beams across the ceiling. I can hang from them until someone comes. I am expecting Dad to come. A snake under the table says, "Now she's really scared, I'm going to get her." He comes out. I grab hold of a beam and try to stand on the snake's head. He bites my foot while I try to step on him.
>
> The scene switches to the patio. I look up and see snakes all over the roof. When I look at them, they look at me. Now I am surrounded. I can't go anywhere.

Here we see the dreamer, who is a virgin, expressing a sense of the sexual risks that surround her; the snakes are unavoidable in her living area; her house is invaded by them. She tries to fight off the talking snake, but he succeeds in biting her, suggesting that she senses the danger is close.

Note that Grace's father is viewed as the potential savior from the threat, but he does not arrive in time. In fact Grace's parents had recently separated; she continued to live with her mother. The young woman probably felt more vulnerable to sexual dangers without the presence of her father. In her dream she was overwhelmed, without escape. The overall imagery is characteristic of an inexperienced female who views sex as extremely risky.

The same theme may be represented by women in dreams of attacks by other wild animals having attributes that resemble the shape of the phallus—especially those animals with long tails, such as mice, rats, or squirrels—or those who are known for their virility, such as bulls and stallions. Bees and wasps are occasionally selected because of their penetrating stinger that emits poison, again forming an analogy for the phallus and the ejaculate.

The identical animals may also appear in positive roles because of a dreamer's individual associations. Among women who are aware of the snake's role in healing ceremonies in ancient Greece, for instance, or those who have good personal experiences with snakes, meanings other than fear of sex may be indicated.

A young woman of Greek heritage happily told me her dream of seeing a golden snake. "This means I'm going to get married," she said. Her grandmother was one of the traditional dream interpreters in her village and had taught her American granddaughter meanings of dream symbols that she accepted as true. Believing that a certain dream image has a specific meaning sometimes leads people to dream within that framework, accepting the cultural dream language as their own.

A Dog in the Grass.   An attack by a dog, an animal that is traditionally considered male, also sometimes symbolizes fear of intercourse in young women's dreams. I first noticed this in a dream of my own when I was sixteen years old:

> Our dog Corky attacks me in the yard. I am lying on the grass.
> His teeth sink through my stockings. My clothes get all messed
> up. I seem to dream this twice. Then in the dream I tell myself,
> "This is a symbol for a sexual attack or intercourse." The dream
> continues with a boy I know in a restaurant called Tasty Inn.

At the time of this dream I was totally inexperienced in sex, although I had begun to date and even kiss several boys. In fact this dog was aggressive and difficult to handle; he became wildly sexually excited when let loose from where he was chained outside. I was actually rather frightened of him.

Since I had been working with my dreams for a couple of years at the time of this one, I became semilucid within it and found myself commenting upon the ongoing action. Once I recognized the source of the fearful feeling as a fear of sex, the dream switched to an appealing boy rather than a wild dog. The Tasty Inn served as a setting for nourishment rather than a fearful encounter.

All attack dreams indicate a feeling of being threatened. Of course they may refer to nonsexual threats as well as sexual ones. A young woman often unconsciously desires sex because her body is physiologically ready for it, yet at the same time she fears the unknown experience.

Needless to say, dreams of dogs may be extremely positive.[22] Any woman who has good experiences with a dog will be likely to choose a different animal or mode to express sexual fear in her dreams, and reserve dogs for happy dreams.

The Beautiful Plants.   Women sometimes use elongated parts of plants—stalks, trunks, or roots—to symbolize the phallus in their dreams.

Jo, a recent divorcée in her thirties, was feeling happy about the prospect of sexual intercourse with some new man, as revealed in this dream:

> I am in my girlfriend's father's yard. They had just gone
> shopping to get plants to fill up the yard. There were beautiful
> plants everywhere, seven, eight, nine, ten feet high. Two were
> purple and one was a transluscent pink, eight feet high. They
> were of thin material, like Japanese rice paper, that blew in the
> breeze, or like seaweed moving in water.
>
> Interspersed with the seaweedlike part were flowers like the bud
> of nasturtium, the size of a man's hand with stamen sticking up.
> I checked the price tags that were still on. They were high, but
> I could afford them. I could get this or that, or this and that. It
> was like a litany of options for the garden enveloping you.

This dream seems to express Jo's current sense of a range of exciting new possibilities. The plants she admired were unusual, unlike any she had ever seen before, yet affordable. In part these plants may have represented new experiences Jo was undergoing in her work life. But they undoubtedly alluded to specific love and sexual alternatives, given the image of "stamen sticking up," the erect, swaying seaweedlike plants and the cylindrical shapes of the other dream plants that she drew for me. The colors and material—translucent pink and purple, of thin paper, are reminiscent of genital skin.

Shopping in dreams often represents making life choices. Depending upon the quality of the "goods," the options can be pleasant or unappealing. For this dreamer the plants were beautiful, unusual, and available. The day before Jo's dream she had dated a new man for lunch, had gone to dinner with an old admirer, and had plans to spend the following day with yet another suitor—a "litany of options" in a garden of men.

The Banana Split. Depending upon how women feel about the experience, they visualize sexual intercourse in dreams as acts of eating delicious—or repulsive—food. The food is incorporated into the mouth in a way that is analogous to the penis entering the vagina. Eating in dreams can be a metaphor for coitus, or for a romantic relationship in general.

In one of the dreams recorded in my diary when I was sixteen,

> Ginny [a girlfriend who is in love] has a good banana. I peel
> mine. Inside it is rotten and has a brown tube running through

it, so I throw it away. A bunch of kids go into a drugstore and order banana splits with cherry sauce and whipped cream. I don't think I get one.

Bananas, because of their shape, are not uncommon symbols for the phallus. The slang term *cherry*, sometimes used for the female hymen, is associated in dreams with female genitals. Likewise *cream,* a slang term for the ejaculate, may symbolize it in dreams. A banana split is an image that conjures up the combination of genitals as in sexual intercourse.

At the time of this dream, my girlfriend and I were both dating older boys. She seemed to be very happy and satisfied, whereas the boy I was dating turned out to be a liar. In my dream language he was "rotten." I had given up on him, as the dream indicates, but felt deprived not to have an enjoyable relationship—depicted as a delicious banana split with all the trimmings. Although I had not had intercourse at the time, the prospect seemed appetizing.

The Strawberry Field. Edith, who dreamed of the Greek god at her front door, had a landmark dream involving forbidden fruit. In her early thirties, she was still in her difficult marriage when she had her favorite dream:

> I wake up in a place with a beautiful spring color everywhere—green with dewdrops. All the work and problems are over. It is like being in a heaven. I walk around. There is a field, a little piece of forest, a stream. On the other side of the stream, I know there are wild strawberries.
>
> I get a container and go down the hill. I come to an electric fence. I know it could kill me. My youngest boy, then about two years old, is playing with the end of the wire. He is fine. I realize the fence is no danger to me. I go around it and get the wild strawberries.

Edith explained that the wild strawberries represented to her forbidden sexual pleasure. (I am not sure whether she had ever seen Ingmar Bergman's classic film *Wild Strawberries*, which was suffused with sexual encounters.)

She elaborated on the brilliant light yellow-green color as one of renewal and growth that lasts only two weeks or so in the spring when the trees first blossom. This particular color—sunlit grass green—I have observed in many women's powerful, positive dreams. The fence, Edith said, was, "something that keeps you out of a certain area; it restrains you. An electric one is worse in that you cannot climb over it; it can kill." The boy who made her realize the fence was not dangerous is a child she regarded as fearless. Thus, her dream language said, "The delicious experience [forbidden fruit = delicious sexuality] you wish for is available; the restraint you think exists is not lethal; you can get around it to what you want."

Edith explained, "Once I dreamed this, it seemed like something I wanted—a brand-new feeling. I always kept the possibility of the experience, of being in a place where I wasn't burdened by life." Later, life circumstances allowed Edith to obtain some of the "forbidden fruits" of sexuality. Looking back today, however, she thinks she may have overdone things, adding, "Even my favorite dream led me to things I regret."

In Edith's dream it was not the shape of the fruit so much as its succulent quality that represented sexual activity. For other women, male genitals may be symbolized by elongated foods, including fruit such as bananas, and vegetables such as cucumbers, pickles, or corn on the cob. The "hot dog," wiener, or frankfurter may also symbolize the phallus. If the woman's attitude toward sex is negative, she may find these foods repellent in her dreams; if her attitude is positive, she is more likely to find these foods tasty.

Divine Drinks or Revolting Fluid.   Beyond her anticipation about sex, the quality of the woman's amorous experience also determines whether the food or drink in her dreams is luscious. The circumstances of her actual sexual encounters are crucial.

A young virgin who was forced into a situation where she saw a young man masturbate to orgasm dreamed that night of walking through dripping sewers, an image that expressed her sense of revulsion toward the boy and the incident. Sewage was a metaphor for the undesired ejaculate.

When she was older and more experienced, the same woman dreamed of a particularly charming man offering her a delicious drink. In this case she accepted, finding the dream drink and the waking-life man sweetly appealing.

Both these dream responses to aroused men contain a typical symbol of male semen: liquid. In the first case the fluid was represented as bodily discharge that could contaminate; in the second it was depicted as an intoxicant that could be ambrosial. The attitude toward the male involved and the woman's life experience determined the difference.

Among women who have been sexually abused, dream content echoes the sordid experience. A woman in her thirties told a horrific nightmare she had the evening after having been raped and forced into oral copulation by a gang of drunken soldiers when she was seven years old:

I am drowning in white glue.

The sticky substance of this girl's dream was obviously a symbol of the semen forced into her. From this time on, the unhappy child developed severe asthma. The physical sensation of choking she had had during the brutal attack was replicated in her dream of the white glue and in her waking physical symptom. I have often noted dreams of difficulty breathing in abused women, replicating sensations experienced during the attack.[23]

The liquids we incorporate in our dreams, therefore, give important clues to our experiences and how we feel about them—whether savory or bitter. In dream language the various secretions of the body, the liquid contents, may be substituted for each other—blood, urine, pus, semen, milk, vomitus, and so on. Whitish liquids, such as milk or cream, often represent semen in women's dreams. The young woman in my study who described difficulty getting shaving cream out of a tube was expressing a passing difficulty in her sexual relationship. Dreams of drinking divine nectar tell another story.

Images of food and drink that symbolize sex may have a biological basis. An ethnologist (expert in animal behavior) has recently postulated that nature's purpose in kissing is to transfer an addictive substance that chemically bonds the partners.[24] The chemicals in the sebum of each person, he says, are transferred in the sucking action of kissing. The glands that produce sebum are clustered on the skin surface, the face, scalp, neck, nipples, sexual organs, and especially inside the lips. Recent research has shown that eagles and other birds bond through a sebum mechanism when they exchange food gifts in mating. Perhaps people become addicted to the taste of their partner. In any case the dreaming mind likens eating and drinking to the sexual act.

A woman's first experience with sex is crucial in determining how she depicts this behavior in her dreams. There is a range of typical responses, I found, and characteristic dream imagery that follows sexual intercourse.

The Voices of First Sexual Experiences

Frightened Virgins.   Each woman's initial encounter with sex is unique. For some women in my study, the first intercourse was decidedly unpleasant:

I was so afraid, I wouldn't do it for a month after I was married. It was dry and painful. I was constantly sore.

I didn't like it. I put it off for several days after our marriage. It was very painful.

It was frustrating. I think it took several trials.

It hurt.

I had excruciating pain. I could hardly walk or sit down the next day.

A few women found their first experience with sex mortifying. One in my study was particularly embarrassed by her new husband's insistence on showering together prior to sex; she had anticipated romantic contacts in the dark. Virginia Foster Durr, describing the cult of Southern womanhood and the insistence on virginity that left many women unprepared for the sexual aspect of marriage, described her aunt's two-day marriage. Returning to the home fold, the aunt said, "I'm sure my brother would never do anything like that." Another relative reverted to the single state saying, "My dear, I don't see how a lady could do it."[25]

Women who had humiliating, painful, or traumatic first intercourse were more likely to have sexual dreams with violent attacks and wounding, at least until further experience taught them differently.

Indifferent Virgins. The majority of women in my study were disappointed over their first intercourse. Typical remarks were the following:

He was totally inconsiderate. Wham-bam. I thought, "Well, this isn't much fun." I might as well have been a wall.

It was kind of boring. Not all that I hoped or expected. I had masturbated and knew what it was like to have orgasm. I felt I was standing back and observing.

It wasn't memorable. "Is that all there is?" It was the first time for both of us—very quick.

By itself it was nothing, but the whole getting married was exciting.

I was nervous. It wasn't comfortable, but it wasn't painful.

It was disappointing. Why would people be so excited about it?

So what's all the hoopla?

What's all the fuss about?

Determined Virgins.   A few of the women regarded initial intercourse as a chore to get over with:

> It was just to get the job done.

> I decided it was time to lose my virginity. It was okay.

Women in these categories were likely to dream of sexual experience as the action of mechanical gadgets or equipment. One, for instance saw her mailbox (= her genitals, her "male-box") stuffed with too much mail. In her dream language, intercourse with her first male was an automatic delivery process.

Ecstatic Virgins.   Still other women found their first sexual experience glorious:

> It was great—I was overready. I had orgasm the first time.

> It was beautiful, wonderful. A summer's night on a blanket in the backyard looking up at the stars. He was so gentle and tender.

> It was wonderful. He was very skilled, took his time with gentle foreplay for months. I had a powerful orgasm the first time.

> I didn't let him know I was a virgin. He was older and very experienced. I was transported. I remember thinking how strange it was—I had orgasm and everything—it was overwhelming. We went on for hours and hours. So this is what it's all about! The next day I could hardly walk. My legs wobbled. I was convinced that everyone who looked at me knew what I was doing all night.

Women in this category were more likely to have joyous dreams about sex—flowers and gardens, delicious foods and drinks, parties and dances at ballrooms.

Key factors in a pleasurable first experience for a woman seem to be the presence of loving feelings toward the mate, as well as an experienced and skilled man who is tender, gentle, and patient in his approach. He is virile and can sustain activity for long enough to satisfy her. The ideal first mate understands female physiology and cares enough about his partner to stimulate her to the proper state of readiness and attend to her orgasmic needs. Lucky was the woman whose initiation into sex took this form.

Many of the women who had had unpleasant first experiences grew fond of intercourse over time. As with an acquired taste, they felt deprived by its absence. When these women began to enjoy sex, their dreams reflected this change.

Passionflower: Ecstatic Sexual Dreams

"Oh, my luve is like a red, red rose . . ."[26] Poets have long celebrated the association between flowers and romantic or sexual love. The women in Victorian times said that each type of blossom carried a special message for the beloved. They called flowers the language of love. In women's dreams, too, flowers usually represent love.

At times flowers specifically refer to the female genitals. Novelists, mythmakers, and spinners of folktales have likened the woman's sexual organs to an open flower. Biologically a flower is the sexual organ of the plant, in addition to possessing the beauty and fragrance that attracts an insect to fertilize it. Oma, whose dreams are described in a later chapter, depicts her orgasm as a flower opening petal by petal. Thus when the plants of our dreams bloom and thrive, they speak of healthy loving; when they languish and die, so—for the moment—our loving falters.

Abundant Blossoms.   When Ashley fell in love with her husband-to-be, she dreamed

> I am walking in the mountains, my arms overflowing with flowers he has given me.

The woman who is happily in love often has flower-filled dreams.

Hitting the Jackpot.   Women symbolize sex in their dreams by concrete images that are puns. When Sheila, in her thirties, fell in love with a man named Jack, she dreamed:

I am gambling when suddenly I hit the jackpot. Money gushes out of the machine all over.

For Sheila, taking risks in the game of love, led to striking it rich—she won a "jackpot," her valuable Jack. There may be a double pun in the dream on the word *eJACulate*. The emphasis, however, is on the rareness of the event and the enormous return obtained. She took a chance and was "lucky."

Dreamers frequently overlook puns in the names of objects and people in their dreams. Slang words for genitals and intercourse often pass undetected. The word *organ* itself is sometimes pictured as a grand church organ or a hand organ. Beautiful music can be "played" on either one.

Female genitals may be portrayed by a "pussy" or a "chick" in American women's dreams. Their British cousins are more likely to dream of "birds," the slang term for girls in England. Words like *beaver* or *honeypot* can be given concrete form in dreams, depending upon the language of the dreamer and her exposure to the terms.

Slang Terms for Male Genitals in Dreams. Women also picture male genitals according to the slang or pun terms of the language they speak. "Balls," "nuts," "rocks," "jewels," "family treasure"—these are some of the designations for testicles that appear in American women's dreams. The penis may emerge as something that "pricks" the dreamer, a "bone," or as one of the common male names like "Peter," "Dick," or "John." The woman in a workshop who told me her dream about a giant rooster chasing and clawing her was expressing her fear of a "cock," one that was overwhelming, as was the size of the rooster. The woman who dreams of placing precious jewels into her box has a happier attitude.

Sexual intercourse is also dramatized by the use of slang phrases. The British speak of "setting fire to her haystack" to refer to intercourse; American women are more likely to refer to "balling," "banging," or "screwing." These images may appear in literal form in their dreams, for example, as a riotous ball game.

Buildings on Fire. Many women cast their dreams of sexual attraction into images of their house or other structures being on fire. In such cases the building is a metaphor for the woman's body; the fire that consumes it symbolizes the sensation of sexual arousal (as with the slang expression "feeling hot"). The fire represents sexual heat, as it did for Rose in this dream:

I look in the backyard and see the house next to the one behind ours burning furiously. I tell my youngest daughter to grab her pet rat. I get my older child and my purse and plan to leave our house in case the fire reaches us. However, I try to help wet our backyard by bringing the hose in my house and spraying it out of the second-story window. The fire is beginning to get under control because one of the firemen says that it is not necessary for me to do that.

Rose's dream continues with her walking outside and seeing houses that have been destroyed by fire, as well as someone who had just escaped being burned. Then she finds herself in another house going upstairs:

. . . and there is the man I am attracted to. He is dressed in white—in fact so was I and all the rest of the area is white. I unhesitatingly put my arms around his waist—it feels so good and warm. He responds by warm sounds and turns around and kisses me. We begin to be very warm and loving—moving slowly—he is laughing and very responsive. It is so incredibly wonderful to really let myself be so fully loving and giving. My body gradually becomes sexually excited and we are holding each other closely when I wake up.

Rose's dream had moved from the symbolic to the specific. A married woman, she regarded her attraction to another man as "dangerous," depicted by the destructive aspects of the fire in her dream and her efforts to control it. Notice that the threat of fire is near her own home, but has not yet reached it. She seems to be depicting the risks of giving in to her emotions. There are other sexual symbols—the purse, the hose—but we can only touch the highlights.

In the ending dream scene, Rose played out her anticipations of the pleasure that would result if she would permit it. It is as if her dream said, "Maybe it would be very dangerous, but on the other hand . . ." The white color represented spirituality for this dreamer, an important element in Rose's attraction to this particular man. She allowed herself to experience loving him—at least in the dream.

When tender, loving feelings are added to sexual arousal, dream imagery may take on a warm, colorful glow.

A Widow Gets Approval.   Women whose husbands are deceased often feel a need to "get permission" to become reinvolved. Minerva, in her early sixties, did not expect to fall in love again after her husband's tragic death. Much to her surprise, during her first year of widowhood, she met, dated, and fell in love with another man. The night after they first had intercourse, she dreamed:

> There is a party being given for me by a friend in my home.
> I'm sitting in a chair under the mantelpiece that has the portrait
> of my husband above it. The colors are all so beautiful—amber
> and peach. The whole atmosphere is full of warmth. It's lovely.
> My new man is upstairs looking at books in the study, when
> my husband appears. I look up and ask him, "Is it good?" He
> replies, "It's good." I awake.

Minerva, who does not usually recall her dreams, was deeply impressed by this one. "I feel as though my husband gave his approval. I laid him to rest and myself to rest," she said.

Here we see the dreamer accepting the new love relationship that is expressed for her in terms of a party, of warmth, and of lovely colors. These echo her emotional happiness and her rediscovered physical pleasure. Perhaps some part of her heart still hesitated before this dream. After it, her husband's memory was preserved—like the portrait above the mantel—but she felt a permission and approval that allowed her to participate wholeheartedly in the new relationship. She was aglow.

In sound, loving relationships, the qualities of warmth, color, and beauty are characteristic of dreams.

The Swinging Gate.   "If I were a gate, I would swing. If I were a bell, I would ring" goes the popular song. Rhythmic activities in dreams often represent zestful sexual intercourse. Sliding, skating, swinging, spinning, dancing, floating, flying—these sensuously pleasant activities stand for the steady back-and-forth movements of sexual intercourse. They may also depict the lightheaded feeling that accompanies it. Rhythmic walking, running, and climbing a staircase often appear as symbols for the mating dance.

Dancing itself is not only rhythmic in movement but also has romantic overtones, as in Edith's dream of dancing with the Greek god and in Leah's dream of gliding across the glossy floor of a ballroom with her own true love.

Orgasms in Lucid Dreams. Among the women in my study, several spoke of learning to experience orgasm years after they had begun to have sexual intercourse. Women who have had restrictive sexual training often develop a conflict between inhibiting sexual response and releasing full orgasm.

Emotionally the orgasm is perceived as a loss of consciousness, a yielding, a "bursting of a dam," an explosion, a "coming apart," a "going crazy," or even dying. The French refer to orgasm as "the little death" *(la petite morte).* Some women describe a sensation of "melting" or "drawing downward" just prior to orgasm. Others liken the sensation to having their bodies "flooded with light" or "washed over with a warm wave"; still others speak of dizziness, "spinning," or "flying."

For the woman who feels insecure, a total release of control in strong orgasm seems dangerous. She feels vulnerable, exposed, to allow herself to give in to such overpowering sensations. If she can lose control in this experience, she might do so anytime. This is the fear behind much orgasmic inhibition. Some 10 percent of women are estimated to have never experienced orgasm.[27] Inhibition leads to dreams of orgasm as annihilation—crashing, falling, being run over and crushed. Being blown up by an explosion often represents the orgasm for the anxious woman.

At the opposite end of the spectrum, the woman who totally accepts her sexuality and gives herself freely in orgasm may find herself with an unsuitable partner. One woman described her difficulty in restraining herself from orgasm, in holding herself back until the man was ready for release. When she allows herself orgasm at the outset, she feels bored and irritated by the man's continuing activity. Her needs are not easy to match.

When these women—extremely inhibited or extremely responsive—find a satisfying relationship with a mate, their dreams mirror this change. The delights of their waking hours resound in their visions.

Alfred C. Kinsey, it will be recalled, reported that only 37 percent of women experience orgasm in their dreams by the age of forty-five (compared with 83 percent of males of the same age). Yet humanist psychologist Abraham Maslow, founder of the theory of self-actualization, maintains that women who have the highest self-esteem dream openly of sexual intercourse.[28] And a study comparing creative girls in a writing class with noncreative girls found that the creative ones had far more explicit sexual dreams.[29] Perhaps their thinking was freer at all levels.

The number of women who have dream orgasms may be increasing. Not only is this generation more sexually active, but also women are discovering they can permit themselves pleasures in dreams. Women who learn to become conscious while they are dreaming describe incredible raptures, as Kerry did, in one of her lucid dreams:

I allow myself to become totally lost in the passion. I feel
myself existing between the tip of the penis and the mouth of
the womb. I let myself melt into the thrusting movements. The
bliss builds. . . .

Because she is aware of her dreaming state during the dream, the woman
who is lucid feels the aroused condition of her body. The sensations connect
with the imagery in her dream. She can choose what to do, and she often
chooses orgasm.

Sexual Images as Metaphors for Other Emotions

Dreams that portray sexual activity directly may carry symbolic meaning.
Of course women's sexual dreams sometimes express a craving to have
intercourse, especially during periods of deprivation or of high stimulation.
Sometimes they replay delightful revels already experienced. However,
women frequently overlook the layer of meaning beyond the obvious in
sexual dreams. In general the symbolic meaning of intercourse in a dream
is a connection, a union, with the element the dream lover represents. This
element can be a negative or a positive one.

Feeling Overwhelmed

A woman who has critical thoughts about her boyfriend may cast her
feelings into sexual imagery. Amelia, in her thirties, described a dream in
which:

I am making passionate love with my girlfriend's boyfriend. It
feels wonderful, complete with orgasm. Later on, I examine his
body and notice that his penis is huge and hairy, about the size
of a loaf of bread. It's kind of overwhelming.

Amelia went on to explain that the night before her dream she had a lengthy
discussion about this man with the girlfriend. Since he is not a person who
appeals to her in reality, his presence must be symbolic.

This dream occurred during the time that Amelia was involved with a
man other than the one in her dream. The imagery of the "huge and hairy
penis" that was overwhelming suggests she felt "overwhelmed" by something in her current relationship, even though parts of it were "wonderful."

A few months later the couple broke up. Amelia was not dreaming of a literal penis that was too big and rather repellent; she was dreaming of a man who was difficult to handle and had some qualities she disliked. Dreams always exaggerate.

Women will sometimes dream of a "substitute" man for the one who is their lover. Hesitant to comment on or be critical of a man they want to love, they dream their feelings about a stand-in. One woman in the study, when she felt angry at her sweetheart, would dream about his brother, whom she disliked. It was the brother who misbehaved in her dreams, not her man.

If you have a directly sexual dream, look for the symbolic possibilities as well as considering the obvious content.

Feeling "Ripped Off"

A woman who feels emotionally abused may express this in dream pictures of sexual abuse. For example, Brenda, in her thirties, reported this nightmare:

> I am in a parking lot in a city where I often go for my job. I leave the office and go to the fourth floor of a multileveled parking lot. It hasn't occurred to me it will be dangerous.

> At the elevator is a serviceman. The door opens and there is a black policeman. I'm relieved. "Will you take me out?" I ask. "Sure," he says. When I get into the elevator, he's joking. Suddenly I think he is going to rape me. I grab his gun. Then I think I'm mistaken, feel foolish, and give it back to him. When he gets the gun back, he does rape me. Now he is white. The elevator door opens, and we get out.

> I see a mother and child and I scream, "Help!" They are going to run get help. But now I think the policeman might kill me. The mother has to stop for the child and they duck into a room. I feel as though I set them up.

> The policeman tells me to take a right. We turn the corner and I see with horror that there are twelve men wrapped in towels, waiting for me, to rape me. They are all officers, too. "Bye!" says the man.

Brenda was badly shaken by this nightmare. Recently separated from her husband, she had had a disappointing intimate encounter with another man.

After lying to her several times and keeping some of her jewelry, his true character became apparent. Brenda finally realized what a mistake she had made trusting him.

An important fact in understanding this dream is that it was fictional in its imagery. Brenda had never been raped or treated brutally in this fashion. We know that sexual intercourse may be represented as an attack by a foreign or exotic strange man. Depending on what males represent this quality to the dreamer, she may select a fiery Italian, a Spanish toreador, an Oriental, a white man, or—as Brenda did—a black man. The choice depends upon the woman's view of what is dark, mysterious, or forbidden. After the dream rape, the man's "true colors" show. Having intercourse with this dream lover depicted Brenda's feeling that she had "connected" with something dangerous and untrustworthy.

The image of the gun—a metaphor for the penis—underscores the sexual meaning. The movement of the elevator may simulate for Brenda, as it does for some dreamers, the sensation of sexual arousal. The opening doors may refer to her initial receptivity—sexually and emotionally—to the man. The mother and child symbolize, Brenda explained, her feelings of vulnerability.

Beyond the explicit sexuality and the symbolic sexuality in this dream, there lies the overall feeling of being "ripped off," "raped," "used" by the current man. When Brenda realized how she had been misused, she felt frightened, hurt, and angry. The twelve men waiting to get her symbolized her fear for the future and her ability to cope with being on her own. Perhaps they also, like the twelve members of a jury, were ready to judge and to punish her. Brenda decided to get some therapy. Today she is jubilant with a new relationship.

If you are a woman who finds herself having this sort of sexual nightmare, you might consider professional assistance to develop new ways of solving life's problems.

Feeling Spiritually Connected

Sexual dreams may sometimes be symbolic in a highly positive mode. In this case the "union" is with a beneficent element.

The Angelic Lover. Ashley, in her thirties, dreamed

> I am making love with a man who is composed of golden light. The sensations of our movements are incredible. The orgasm is cosmic.

This dreamer's orgasm was literally "divine." Dreams with this quality sometimes represent a communion with a "higher" or spiritual value, as well as portraying love on a human level.

Sheila, too, reported dreaming of making love with a man whose penis was made of shining light; when he ejaculated, it was a shower of sparkles. Such imagery suggests positive associations to making love and to the man involved. It also implies connection with something "illuminating."

If you find yourself making love directly in a dream, be sure to observe your partner carefully as well as the activities that precede your union. They will help you make sense of the symbolic aspects of your dream. Fantasizing your pleasurable dream encounters during actual sexual intercourse enhances sensations for some women.

Women portray their feelings of falling in love and of having sexual problems or sexual pleasures in the symbolic images of their dreams. They also dream of love and sex directly—sometimes as metaphors for feelings they have about aspects of their lives beyond love and sex.

When loving feelings and sexual compatibility—or the hopes of it—combine, a woman usually feels ready for a committed relationship. For the woman who thinks she has encountered the man of her dreams, and if he agrees, the next step may be wedding bells. Today's style of living together also takes on some of the character of a marriage. We turn next to dreams of declaring a committed relationship and of marriage ceremonies.

Wedding Dreams

I am sitting in a garden with my fiancé. Suddenly a snake comes out. It crawls slowly at first, then it goes into hyperspeed. It stands up in front of my fiancé, flaring like a cobra. I can't move fast enough. The snake strikes my boyfriend, and he drops dead. I scream and find myself sitting up in bed.

One week before her wedding was scheduled to take place, Helena was terrified by this dream. What could it mean? Surely she did not wish her fiancé dead? Was it only her nerves? Was she afraid that she would lose him? Or was she dramatizing her anxiety that some disaster was sure to befall? Helena's nightmare escalated her already tightrope emotions to an almost unbearable tension. We'll come back to the implications of its imagery later on.

Wedding Nightmares

Brides are proverbially nervous. If you are engaged to be married, you know that despite your being happy, new issues confront you. Wedding nightmares like Helena's are frequent and frightening. It's no wonder. The betrothed woman is making a commitment of major import—hopefully lifelong. This step of pledging oneself to another (the original meaning of the Old English word *wed*) brings cold sweat to the calmest brow.

Most girls have been dreaming of getting married since they were in grade school; they have played with bride dolls and fantasized the future mate and marriage ceremony. Even among today's career-minded women, the socially approved marriage usually remains a deferred goal. Once engaged, although devotedly in love, many women find that conflicts bob to the surface like bubbles in champagne.

Part of the bride's anxiety is due to her desire for perfection at the ceremony. After all, this is the day when everyone's eyes will be superglued to her dress and demeanor.[1] The details of a large wedding can be mind-boggling, and even a small ceremony requires intricate coordination. Thus one of her pressures is societal, a concern about feeling judged by friends and relatives. Delicate handling of any conflicting relatives or soon-to-be in-laws is required, adding another pressure. The more mature bride may also have a need to demonstrate that her sweetheart is superior and was well worth the wait.

For many brides, however, the concerns run even deeper. We will survey some of the common conflicts as seen through the dreams of actual brides-to-be. Understanding the imagery in typical wedding nightmares will help you clarify your own feelings, your difficulties, and your unconscious attitudes toward your betrothed. Don't be alarmed by the preponderance of negative dreams. It's natural that concerns about a forthcoming marriage appear; each dream can yield useful information for the bride-to-be.

The single woman who is not engaged, and the woman who has been long married, can also benefit from familiarity with the scenarios of dreams about weddings, because the marriage ceremony is a powerful symbol in all women's dreams.

The Reluctant Bride

Despite the strong cultural demands to marry, the biological instinct to mate and have children, and love for a particular man, most women also harbor a fear of the married state. For some this fear is a tiny whisper; for others it comes full-blast through mental loudspeakers. The most fearful brides are often those who have witnessed unhappy marriages among their parents, relatives, and friends. Such a bride has seen the havoc in other lives; she may know that in America one million women or more divorce each year; or that the average duration of a marriage in the United States is currently 9.4 years.[2] She is bound to be aware that the divorce rate is high, hovering around 50 percent of all marriages. (Some experts claim the divorce rate is closer to 10 percent—still higher than any bride would like.[3]) These are hard facts; they hack away at her hope that she and her groom may build the exceptional life together.

True, some couples do dwell happily together; they find life as partners richer, more fulfilling. Still it is no surprise that the almost-wife is full of turmoil about whether *her* marriage will work well. Helena's wedding nightmare falls into this category of conflict. After the ceremony took place, in her cream satin and lace gown, with the seed pearl coronet gleaming above her dark curls, she described her dream to me in the midst of the crowded reception. Her brown eyes grew larger as she recalled the inner drama.

The Snake in the Garden. For Helena the garden of her dreams reminded her of "middle America," with picket fence and flowers. The snake she described as "your average slime bomb." She added that she is terrified of reptiles in general. Thus she sees herself in a comfortable, homelike setting when danger—in the form of a snake—literally strikes.

Like many a modern bride, Helena, who is in her mid-thirties, lived with her boyfriend before her marriage. In fact he was sound asleep beside her when she had her nightmare. Her then-groom joined our conversation: "It scared the hell out of me. I woke up to a bloodcurdling scream. I thought maybe there were burglars or the house was on fire." Her fiancé was able to soothe Helena, but he found himself shaken, too.

The well-known Freudian snake—symbolizing the male organ—had reared his head again. Since Helena was already living with her betrothed, this dream was not primarily a fear of sex, although I later learned there were some complications in this department. Her major fear, portrayed vividly in her dream, suggests a different focus. For her the danger lies hidden in the middle-American "garden of Eden." If one were to translate Helena's imagery into words, it might read, "I am afraid that by joining the ranks of middle America—by getting married—I will endanger the precious relationship with my man. Will settling down into a regular middle-class life destroy our love?" Dreams dramatize and exaggerate. Helena was not afraid her fiancé would die; she was questioning whether the relationship could survive marriage.

A few of the women I spoke with were so fearful of the married state, and/or of having children, they refused even to consider being wed. For such women, including those happily living with a man, to dream of being a bride was itself a nightmare. Most women, however, like the idea of marriage.

Had Helena understood the message of her nightmare, she might have concentrated her attention on ways of preserving the quality of her relationship within a married state. Helena, however, does not often remember or value her dreams; she dismissed this one as a simple case of nerves. All of us can profit by hearing the messages our dreaming minds provide; this is especially true for the bride who is undergoing—however joyfully—a life crisis.

The Ambivalent Bride

Another area of conflict that arises in the dreams of brides-to-be is a feeling of being unable to cope with a big wedding or to accept the obligations of marriage.

No Church. Ashley was only twenty when she became engaged, complete with diamond ring and party. About three months after the engagement, still nine months prior to the large church wedding that was planned, she seemed to drag her feet toward the aisle in some of her dreams:

> I am shopping in a department store for things. Matt and I are going to get married on Thursday and going to the mountains for our honeymoon, I think. I am happy, but distressed that we don't have everything ready.

> Then I am talking to Matt and saying, "We don't even have a church!" He agrees, and we decide we had better wait until next week, even though we don't want to. There are so many things to do.

In her associations to the dream Ashley explained that every other Thursday is her payday; therefore, it is a good day. Shopping in dreams almost always implies making choices. So Ashley was saying to herself, in her dream, that she still had decisions to make.

Just before this dream, Ashley had heard from a girlfriend about a relative's sudden marriage. Yearning for her own wedding day, she did not see how it was possible to get married so quickly. She, herself, felt overwhelmed with the preparations remaining to be done while carrying on a full work schedule.

Repulsive Suitors.   A couple of weeks later Ashley dreamed:

> Three awful men keep coming and trying to marry me. Matt
> has to keep fighting them off. One looks rather like another
> Matt I know. I am very frightened. They climb up a hill after
> getting out of a car to get me. Mother and Matt are with me.
> Then the men come after me in a restaurant.

Ashley explained that she had been helping Matt by typing a college report late that night after watching a spooky version of *The Hunchback of Notre Dame* on television.

Several aspects of Ashley's dreams are revealing. Mountains and hills appear in both of them. Such high places often represent to dreamers a struggle involved in attaining goals—as if climbing a mountain. Her first dream is more characteristic of the bride who feels overwhelmed with wedding preparations prior to reaching her goal of being married.

Ashley's second dream has more serious implications. Awake, she felt committed to her fiancé and eager to wed. Yet the fact that one of the threatening marriage-minded men in her dream had the same name as her boyfriend suggests that she was disturbed by some aspects in her fiancé. She described the television show as "a story about a deformed man who kidnaps the heroine"; it directly preceded her nightmare, perhaps triggering it. In fact, the hunchback of Victor Hugo's story was saving the heroine from an evil suitor.

Ashley was a virgin when she met and was courted by Matt. After they became engaged, she was drawn into sexual intercourse, feeling guilty about it and simultaneously being persuaded that it was a necessary proof of her affection. To back out of the wedding was unthinkable. She explained her nightmares to herself as due to the pressure of preparations and the distressing movie, rather than seeing some unresolved issues. Her marriage was dissolved a few years later.

Stuck at a Crossing.   Another bride-to-be, described by the psychoanalyst Emil Gutheil, canceled her engagement following some nightmares.[4] In one of them she caught her foot in a railroad-track grade switching. She was frantically trying to dislodge (dis-engage?) her foot when a train began bearing down. Her fiancé and another man were trying to help free her when she awoke. This woman was clearly feeling "stuck" in a desperate situation.

The Cold Sore.   Jill, in her middle thirties, had been married previously. Sometime between her divorce and falling in love again, she became involved in a demanding training program for a profession. A week or two before her remarriage was scheduled to take place, Jill dreamed:

> I'm supposed to be getting married soon. But I'm going to a lecture at the university. The speaker is Dr. X [an "attractive, witty, sweet, smart, sexy professor"]. I have arrived late, so I have to sit on the side of the stage. As usual, he is very funny. I'm enjoying the show.
>
> Then I begin to worry. I can feel that I'm getting a cold sore. It's going to appear soon, and I'll look ugly at the wedding. I walk out with the rest of the class, chatting, but I'm preoccupied with the cold sore.

Jill's dream reveals her conflict. I suspected the "cold sore" of her dream symbolized the characteristic "cold feet" about making a commitment. However, when I asked her to describe a cold sore, Jill explained it as "an ugly, painful, contagious blister. I never get them." She went on to say that *sore* made her think of being angry, of giving someone the "cold shoulder." Then she added, "I feel as though I stepped onto a treadmill and I have to do this [go through with the wedding]". Jill's associations were more to anger than to fear.

By making herself late to the lecture in the dream and placing herself to the side of the stage, Jill was reflecting the fact that she had undertaken her career later than many of her fellow students. She found the training very appealing, depicted in her dream by the attractive professor.

Meanwhile Jill felt distracted and concerned by a growing resentment (symbolized by the cold sore) that she had to turn her attention to the complexities of the wedding ceremony and associated activities. She feared her anger about it might reveal an "ugliness" she would rather not have show.

Although deeply in love, Jill was conflicted about remarrying. This was especially so since she found her career training so satisfying. She was afraid her budding career might "bump" up against her new marital commitment, hence her dream concern.

The Sensuous Colleague.   Wedding nightmares do not always deal with the ceremony directly. The week before her marriage Cindy, for instance, had a delightfully sensuous romp in a dream. Her discomfort came afterward, upon awakening, in realizing that her partner had not been her groom:

> I am at the beach, in a bathing suit, showering off my hair. I
> feel really sexy, with this guy looking at me (not fat, like I feel
> with my boyfriend). At first the man is a colleague at work.
> Then he turns into a guy from junior high school whom I
> haven't seen in fifteen years.
>
> This man and I seem to be just going toward each other in the
> water to kiss, when the phone rings and I wake up.

Cindy said that she was angry the telephone interrupted her dream until she realized she was having a sexual dream about a man other than her fiancé. "I felt so guilty!"

When I asked Cindy to describe the man in her dream, she told me that the colleague at work is "the only one who treats me as a partner, who treats me with respect." The man from high school was never interesting to her as a boyfriend, but he, too, was "one of the first men who was really nice to women." Obviously the combination of these two men would be especially pleasant.

Cindy's dream language was picturing a union with an aspect that is highly positive, a sense of respect and of being valued as a person. Although her dream gave her guilt pangs and made her feel somewhat ambivalent, it actually augured well for her relationship with her new husband.

The Insecure Bride

The bride-to-be may feel very certain about her attachment to her fiancé, but still find insecurities surfacing regarding her own attractiveness.

The Monstrous Fiancé.   Laurel, an attractive blonde in her mid-twenties, told me a spine-chilling nightmare she had three days prior to her wedding:

> I meet my husband-to-be in a bar (one that we sometimes went
> to). He says, "Laurel, I have something to tell you. I'm not
> going to marry you because I think you're ugly!"

At this point my fiancé visually changes into a sort of horrible monster. I am terrified. The feeling is sheer panic. My mother and I have spent the last five days preparing for the wedding. I'll have to tell everyone not to come. I don't want to do that! I wake up in terror.

Laurel went on to explain that her initial fright was followed by a wave of relief "because I knew it wasn't true." The nightmare was particularly bad for Laurel, however, because her boyfriend was in a different town and she was unable to see him before the wedding.

Laurel and her sweetheart talked on the phone and she described to him her horrifying nightmare. He just laughed, assuring her, "You don't have anything to worry about." Indeed Laurel has been happily married for the past three years.

This dream of Laurel's depicts two common bridal anxieties: the fear that her groom will discover some fatal flaw and the fear that she will be publicly abandoned. "I'm afraid you'll discover something wrong with me and leave me," was the message of her nightmare. When Laurel's dream lover accused her of ugliness, he himself became monstrous, as this behavior would have made him seem.

The Naked Guest. Anxieties about attractiveness are not limited to the young bride. Jill, who was concerned about concentrating on her career, also harbored some insecurities about making a commitment. The night before her recent remarriage, she confided that she had been plagued by nightmares for the previous ten days, sometimes awaking in sobs. In one of these upsetting dreams:

The ceremony has just taken place. Hank [the groom] and I are seated at a table having dinner, with him on my right.

A naked woman named Madeline comes in and sits directly across from Hank. She is bare from the waist up. I think, "How rude!" and at the same time I'm jealous.

Hank gets talking to her and then he suddenly gets up and goes away with Madeline, leaving me alone.

Jill told me this nightmare on two occasions. The first version, above, I recorded as she told it, the night before her wedding. About two weeks later, after the nuptial rites, she described the dream again. This time the beginning was the same, but the ending had changed:

> . . . Hank says he's going off with the naked woman. I motion
> her to come to the bedroom. I'm still annoyed. She comes and I
> start to counsel her. There is something pitiful or desperate
> about her. She's alone.
>
> I'm torn between wanting to yell at her and feeling sorry for
> her now. "Don't you know there are better ways?" I ask. We
> go back to the table and sit down. Maybe she gets dressed.

Jill had no recollection of the name she had given the naked woman when the dream was "fresh," nor of the different ending. Having recorded it at the time, I was sure of the content. The first version implies the notion of anger, with "mad" as a pun on the name Madeline, just as she was "sore" in the previous nightmare. In the dream language of both versions Jill seems to be saying, "Once I do make this commitment in marriage, I am vulnerable. My husband may hurt and desert me."

This thought was apparently too painful to sustain. Jill's memory substituted a more positive ending to her nightmare, where it was she who was sorry for the "pitiful, desperate" woman, rather than feeling sorry for herself. The dream woman became less of a threat. In a way Jill had begun to "counsel" herself. Happily, her husband is devoted. Jill looked beautiful at the wedding. Not a cold sore in sight, and Madeline did not attend the ceremony.

For many women the possibility of being jilted at the altar, as in Laurel's dream, or being deserted thereafter, as in Jill's dream, is perceived as the worst possible humiliation. Unfortunately this dismal fear is sometimes realized, as in the case that follows.

Five Basic Steps to Understanding
Wedding Nightmares

The Wrong-Way Wedding Clothes.   Ann-Marie, engaged in her mid-thirties, had prewedding nightmares that illuminated conflicting feelings about herself, her fiancé, and her mother. This complex dream occurred about three months before her wedding was scheduled to take place.

I am standing in a room in a house—I don't know whose. I am putting on my wedding dress. I look down at the front of it and see it doesn't look like I remembered. The torso is like a huge padded bra. I look at it in a mirror—It is not flattering, not pretty like I remember. It flashes through my mind that I look pregnant!

I look down and see I'm barefoot. I don't remember what house I left my shoes in. Guests are starting to arrive. I panic and tell them, "You're an hour early."

Like in a movie, there is a cut to the next scene. I am in a bathroom. Someone is with me or comes in—I don't know who. I'm bleeding. The blood is very bright red. I do something to stop it, but it won't stop. I'm aware all the people out there are waiting for the wedding to start. But it can't start until the bleeding stops.

The next thing I know, I am outside the bathroom in another room. I walk up to a little step where the marriage is going to take place.

I see my fiancé and I feel an instant distaste. "Oh, my God! This is horrible. It's all wrong." He is wearing a gray cloaklike outfit with a kind of pantaloons with a lot of fabric—it's a cross between an ethnic costume and a clown's. This is all wrong.

My mother jumps on the podium. Before I know what's happening, she breaks the glass [part of the ceremony]. I think, "No, she shouldn't do it. She's not supposed to be up here with me. Where's my girlfriend?"

When Ann-Marie awoke from this complicated dream, her heart was pounding wildly. Staring at the ceiling in the dark room, she pondered her future with agitation. A few weeks later she discussed the dream with me.

Here are the five basic steps to understanding a wedding nightmare that I shared with her:

1. Describe your dream in the present tense.
2. Reflect on your feelings during the dream.
3. Express waking emotions and events related to the dream.
4. Associate to key images in your dream.

5. Meditate on the meaning of your dream by substituting your personal associations for the action in the dream.

Notice that the initial letters of each step, put together, spell *dream*. This acronym makes it easy to remember and use the method. We will see how the five basic steps to understanding a dream apply in Ann-Marie's case.

....

1. Describe your dream in the present tense.
By writing or telling the dream as though it were happening at the moment, you are able to recall the dream emotions better and begin to discharge some of the anxiety associated with the imagery.

> **Example:** Ann-Marie's dream is described above in the present tense.

2. Reflect your feelings during the dream.
What was your overall feeling about the events in the dream? Notice if your emotions changed in the course of it. When were they the strongest? What was the worst part? What was best?

> **Example:** Ann-Marie said that she was upset, but not crying when she awoke. She told the nightmare to several people, hoping to relieve her distress. To her, the entire dream was frightening, but the worst part was when she beheld her groom.

3. Express waking emotions and events related to the dream.
What has happened the previous day or two in your life? What have your responses to these happenings or thoughts been? Can you see a connection between dream feelings and waking feelings? Remember that dreams exaggerate and dramatize. The waking emotions that dream pictures represent are likely to be similar, not exact.

> **Example:** In Ann-Marie's case, prior to her nightmare, she had just had a serious quarrel with her mother about the wedding arrangements. Ann-Marie's mother felt pushed aside in favor of

Ann-Marie's best friend, who was given several special functions in the ceremony. On Ann-Marie's part, she was struggling to include her mother—with whom she often clashed—as much as possible and still be comfortable. This conflict is reflected in the final scene of the dream, where Ann-Marie's mother takes over not only the assigned duties of the matron-of-honor but also one of the groom's (breaking the glass).

Aside from the recent argument with her mother, Ann-Marie was aware of another powerful waking emotion. She had just rejoined her fiancé after a long separation before this dream. She felt "as if I were in a reality warp. Who am I? Who is he?" She had fallen asleep after making love with the thought, "Am I going to spend the rest of my life with him?" Ann-Marie says she has "always been afraid of making a wrong decision." As the wedding date drew near, she, like so many of her sisters, began questioning her commitment.

4. Associate to key images in your dream.

First, consider the main action. If the wedding ceremony proceeded smoothly in the dream, you probably have a positive attitude and expectations about the upcoming ceremony. If the nuptials were disrupted by obstacles, your attitude is more likely to be negative and fearful. You may simply be experiencing the usual anxiety, or you may have some issues that still need to be resolved with your fiancé or within yourself.

If you have time, associate to all the images in your dream—the characters, settings, objects, colors, and so forth. Ask yourself who they are, what they make you think of, or what they mean. More than with any other dream theme, the characters and places in wedding dreams are likely to relate directly to actual people and places. Be sure to associate to key images. These are the ones that seem the oddest or the ones that give you the strongest emotion.

The Groom. At the least, query yourself about the bridal couple. Who was the groom? How was he dressed? If he looked good and was dressed appropriately, you probably feel acceptance of what he represents. If he was ugly or weird, or inappropriately dressed, your dream mind is probably suspicious—rightly or wrongly—of some negative qualities in him. Dreams are not necessarily accurate; they tell how we *feel* at a moment in time. If the groom is someone known to you, but not one you would pick as a marital partner, think over his characteristics. If these qualities are negative, they may be something presently in your life that you do not want to have there. If positive, these qualities may be something currently missing in your life.

> **Example:** Ann-Marie's ambivalent feelings toward her groom while awake are graphically displayed in the dream by his wedding garb: he is dressed in a combination ethnic costume and clown's outfit. She is appalled and repelled by its wrongness. Rather like Katharina in Shakespeare's *The Taming of the Shrew* confronting Petruchio's tattered costume, she sees her bridegroom's strange garb as foretelling his even stranger behavior.[5]

The Bride. Were you the bride in your dream? How were you dressed? Was your costume flattering, unattractive, or inappropriate? If the bride was not yourself, you may be feeling less desirable than you would wish or may be distancing yourself from the event. Whether you were the bride or not, her appearance and clothing will reveal your insecurities or confidences.

> **Example:** When Ann-Marie and I explored the unattractive padded-bra wedding dress of her dream, she explained that bras are what you wear when one is at the "mysterious transitional point" of growing up. Padded ones are "used to make you look like you have more than you do"; she had never worn one. She saw menstruation and pregnancy as maturational steps.
>
> In reality when Ann-Marie had tried on her wedding dress, her mother had criticized it for not showing enough of her breasts. Mother suggested she get a special bra to correct this, and Ann-Marie responded with mild irritation, although she did not express it at the time. Thus the bridal gown in the dream incorporated her mother's resented advice and seemed less attractive to her.

Wedding Party. Other characters present at the dream wedding and their behavior are important, too. They express not only themselves and how you feel about these people, but also those parts of yourself that resemble qualities in these people.

Example: When Ann-Marie associated to the gray color of her groom's attire, she thought of a gray skirt her mother once bought her that she never wore "because it looked absurd." This reminded her that her mother was also wearing gray in the dream. It is a color Ann-Marie dislikes and considers unflattering. Thus her mother and her groom were linked in a negative way. We can only touch the highlights of Ann-Marie's associations here.

5. Meditate on the meaning of your dream by substituting your personal associations for the action in the dream.

By associating to the key images of the dream and then substituting these associations for the images and actions in the dream, you will find that a clear message begins to emerge, almost as if you were making a translation from a foreign language.

Example: Here is a brief review of the meaning of the sample dream:

DREAM TEXT

I am standing in a room in a house— I don't know whose. I am putting on my wedding dress. I look down at the front of it and see it doesn't look like I remembered. The torso is like a huge padded bra. I look at it in a mirror—it is not flattering, not pretty like I remember. It flashes through my mind that I look pregnant!

I look down and see I'm barefoot. I don't remember what house I left my shoes in. Guests are starting to arrive. I panic and tell them, "You're an hour early."

Like in a movie, there is a cut to the next scene. I am in a bathroom. Someone is with me or comes in—I

INTERPRETATION

In the opening scene Ann-Marie observes herself in a mirror. (Looking glasses and mirrors in dreams are almost universally a symbol for "self-reflection.") She is assessing her situation and sees that she is at a transition point (the padded bra suggests she is not as far along as she would like to be); it is unattractive. Furthermore she is not ready for it. (Ann-Marie associates being barefoot—a situation that delays the ceremony—with freedom.)

In the bathroom scene Ann-Marie is trying to stop other evidence of maturation (the bleeding). Although don't know who. I'm bleeding. The blood is very bright red.

I do something to stop it, but it won't stop. I'm aware all the people out there are waiting for the wedding to start. But it can't start until the bleeding stops.

The next thing I know, I am outside the bathroom in another room. I walk up to a little step where the marriage is going to take place.

I see my fiancé and I feel an instant distaste. "Oh, my God! This is horrible. It's all wrong." He is wearing a gray cloaklike outfit with a kind of pantaloons with a lot of fabric—it's a cross between an ethnic costume and a clown's. This is all wrong.

My mother jumps on the podium. Before I know what's happening, she breaks the glass [part of the ceremony]. I think, "No, she shouldn't do it. She's not supposed to be up here with me. Where's my girlfriend?"

Ann-Marie did not make this association, the heavy bleeding she described could have been a miscarriage, since she reported previously looking pregnant. In either case there is a further delay in the service.

Finally when she confronts the ceremony, it is all wrong. Her groom reveals a foolish side (the clown suit) that reminds her woefully of her mother (the gray color).

Condensed, Ann-Marie's dream message translates to read, "I am not ready to be grown up in terms of marriage. There are serious limitations to this man and this situation which have something in common with my relationship with Mother." We have derived a "translation" from the language of dream pictures to the waking language of words—a message that can guide us.

Repercussions of Ann-Marie's Dream

A Living Nightmare. At the time Ann-Marie had this dream, I discussed only the aspect of feeling unready that it expressed. I hoped she would resolve some of her doubts regarding her fiancé.

Ann-Marie's dreams fluctuated, containing both positive and negative elements, up to a few weeks before the wedding. Once, she had a horrific nightmare in which her boyfriend betrayed her by making love with her mother. Generally, however, things seemed relatively normal until the last week, when her husband-to-be became increasingly restless and fearful.

Arrangements were complete, and parties were held to celebrate the event. During the final week her groom reported an ominous dream:

I am trapped in jail and want to get out.

Then, two days before the ceremony was scheduled, the groom startled everyone by withdrawing. A "sudden illness" on the part of one of his absent parents arose. Although the couple could have wed if he were willing, they did not do so, and he departed, leaving the unwed bride in despair to explain to friends and relatives. Ann-Marie felt that the "social" part of calling off the wedding was almost worse than losing the relationship. "I felt so much shame." The betrayal had become a reality.

Happily there is more to Ann-Marie's story. Through an inner strength Ann-Marie discovered in herself, with the help of supportive and loving friends and family, as well as a good therapeutic relationship, she was able over time to move to a new level of comfort, confidence, and productivity—and eventually a more satisfying relationship.

Banishing the Ghost Lover.   For months after the wedding cancellation, Ann-Marie was tormented by nightmares of her ex-fiancé. Usually he was doing something totally inappropriate—such as seducing a child. In one she was trapped into an arranged marriage to a man who combined negative aspects of her ex-fiancé. Sometimes he tempted her to love him again, "like a siren." These dreams became especially intense the minute she started to seriously date a new man. Finally she was able to say with conviction in one of these dreams, "I want you to get out and never come back! I'm with a different man now!" This decisive action seems to have dispelled the dreams that plagued her.

Awake, Ann-Marie realized that she was truly better off without that particular man and started building a solid and happy life. In retrospect she said, "He has characteristics like my mother that I wasn't willing to confront." She felt that her dreams during this time "were the only thing that gave me access to the unseeable. They showed me where I was." Ann-Marie's dream journey during this life crisis provides a valuable record for all women. She had achieved considerable psychological growth within a year of her potentially tragic disappointment. Moreover, she later established a truly loving relationship with a committed mate.

The Poison Oak.   Almost a year after the aborted wedding ceremony, Ann-Marie was seriously considering marriage once again. Her situation stimulated another powerful dream:

I have poison oak. It is not on me, but beside me. There are
giant blisters on a patch of skin, with water pouring out, almost
like a tap running. I see there is a little poison mixed in with
the water.

At first I say, "Look. It's a mess." Then I realize that the water
is my tears. It is my old wound opening up. "Oh, it's draining
out!" I understand that the wound is getting cleansed.

Ann-Marie's dream is a dramatic depiction of healing. The image of poison
oak is associated with an actual episode in which she contracted a bad
infection of poison oak just prior to a romantic rendezvous with her former
lover. Her dream came at an anniversary. The memory of her almost-
wedding, her dream says, was like "an old wound" with some poison still
festering. It was no longer a part of her (on her body), but is still with her.
By letting it drain out, along with her tears, Ann-Marie was cleansing herself
of the infected past. Once the wound had released its old poison, she would
heal. Ann-Marie was ready for her new commitment. I took special joy in
watching her radiance at her recent wedding. We all need to let go of the
past in order to forge the future.

Final Farewells.   How much luckier Ann-Marie is than the woman in her
fifties who told me of recently dreaming that she received a telegram
announcing that her ex-fiancé was dead. Some thirty years after the event,
married to another man, she at last accepted the finality of being jilted in
that long-ago relationship.
   Sheila, in her thirties, had just been happily remarried when she dreamed:

I am at a bus station saying good-bye to a former lover. He
looks short and not too well. I am glad to say good-bye. He
presses my hand several times, and that's that.

She, like Ann-Marie, was able to let go of a love of long ago after much
inner development and after finding herself happily situated with a better
person.

Time Pressures

Most brides find themselves feeling squeezed by all the details that require
their attention the last few days before the wedding. These normal pressures,

too, appear in their dreams. Amelia, for instance, dreamed of sorting through old files, pulling out things that belonged to a former boyfriend—an activity that could make her late to the wedding. "I was getting rid of all this old stuff." Like so many brides, Amelia felt, "If I just had a little more time, I'd be completely ready." Amelia was making sure she was prepared emotionally in the midst of the bridal flurry.

Betsy, the night before her wedding, dreamed:

> I see a huge movielike image, as if I am sitting in the front row of a theater. It is an enormous "to-do" list. As each item gets checked off with a gigantic marker, another will magically appear. It seems endless. I wake up thinking I might as well be doing my list, instead of dreaming about it.

Betsy, like most brides-to-be, felt overwhelmed by the numerous chores. Dreams of this type are quite typical. They are a normal reaction to the many waking-life preparations that are necessary for the bride and, as such, should give no cause for alarm.

The Value of Wedding Nightmares

Uncomfortable as a nightmare may be for the soon-to-be bride, her dreams can help her understand herself. We have seen that wedding nightmares frequently express the bride's sense of being overwhelmed. They also sometimes reveal the bride's fear about the success of her marriage, her own insecurity, or her uncertain commitment to her mate. Occasionally, wedding nightmares alert the bride to a danger in the relationship—even prompting her to break the engagement. We saw also that by discussing a nightmare with her groom, the bride can sometimes dispel her worries and draw closer to her loved one. When she contemplates the imagery of her dreams, the bride-to-be can find warnings and guidance.

Happy Wedding Dreams
The Blissful Bride

We must not forget the bride who embraces her fiancé wholeheartedly. Although she, too, will have small concerns and perhaps misgivings, at some point she goes to her man without serious reservation. Her dreams have a different flavor. Nonetheless, they still convey messages about her feelings.

New Clothes. Sue, for example, when she was twenty, was approaching her wedding with eager anticipation, despite parental objections. She had her photograph made and an announcement put into the newspapers, which forced her mother into a position of acknowledging the situation. Somewhat reluctantly the mother held a bridal shower for her daughter.

Sue remembers dreaming at that time a lot about clothes and hats that were all in black and white—she saw black dresses with big white spots and complicated hats with bows and veils. In her waking life Sue had been buying her trousseau. Since she never wore black, however, she was puzzled by these dreams.

In retrospect, Sue—a sophisticated dreamer—believes that trying on these new hats with veils and dresses symbolized her trying on the new role as wife and wished-for motherhood. Hair, headpieces, and hairstyles, I find, often represent the thoughts of the dreamer. From this point of view Sue's thoughts are positive.

Sue thinks of the black as a symbol of death that represented a "good-bye to my childhood"; the white she associates with purity, innocence, snow. "I was saying good-bye to all these, too." The strong contrast of black and white she sees as an expression of her "either-or" situation—either stay in her small hometown as "Daddy's little girl" or move to a big city with her fiancé. "It was all strange and exciting." Sue's choice was made.

Rainbow Shorts. A few days before her wedding, Naomi told me that she had been having a prolific "dreaming spell," and the dreams were becoming more detailed. "The closer it gets to the wedding, the more Brad [her groom] and the ceremony come into it." She described the dream of the previous night:

> Brad and I are at an amusement park. A small, amateurish opera company is putting on a performance. We are in the audience. Brad becames bored with the production and takes off his trousers. He is naked from the waist down. I am really embarrassed. Should I be marrying someone I don't know this side of? He gets dressed.

So far, Naomi's dream is nightmarish. She sees her lover overexposed in a strange way. Her intricate dream continues through various escapades when, toward the end,

> We look into a glass window where we see a pair of boxer shorts with padded rainbows. Brad asks, "Would you mind if I paraded in these?" I imply that it would be better than nothing, but I prefer proper clothes.

> Then we are in a resort area in my hometown. We have a meal of steak and are not charged for it. Throughout the whole dream I am concerned Brad and I will be late for the wedding. We meet one of my relatives, who is very concerned that her son is not yet there. We are going to get married anyhow. I think how she is making a big deal about nothing, and wake up.

Although several elements in Naomi's dream reveal ambivalence, there are strong positive elements present, too.

By plugging Naomi's associations to the dream images into the action of the dream, we will see that she is making several comments about the wedding ceremony and reception, as well as her groom. I will describe the "translation" of Naomi's dream, with her original dream images in parentheses.

In the opening scene Naomi and her fiancé are in a place that should be fun (the amusement park). They are watching a kind of make-believe (the opera company). Many brides, I have observed, dream about the marriage rites as a kind of play or theatrical performance. Here the groom becomes "bored with the production"; this leads him to reveal a personal side (the removal of his trousers) that seems strange to the dreamer; he is exposed (naked from the waist down). She wonders about her decision to marry him. If Naomi's dream had ended here, it would be a typical nightmare. However, she goes on to resolve some of her own concerns within the dream itself.

Naomi examines something valuable (displayed in the little glass window, like those used for jewelry). Here she sees that an intimate part of her fiancé (the underwear) contains a magical (the padding) sign of happiness, an omen of good fortune (the rainbow). Naomi is accepting of this aspect of her groom. She went on to tell me that Brad "has a delightful, whimsical side to him." Although she is rather shy of having this aspect of him appear in public, she likes it.

The dream continues in a place Naomi used to go to for solace (the resort), where she incorporates (eating the meal) something earthy (the steak). Furthermore, in the dream, Naomi and Brad go ahead with the wedding in spite of any latecomers. One part of Naomi is "making a big deal about nothing" (the relative is a person who has "nervous tirades even when everything is okay"). Naomi is commenting about her own anxieties. She has used the relative who has "nervous tirades" to symbolize her own worries; in the dream she dismisses them as unjustified. Thus Naomi made positive strides in reassuring herself within the dream. She gained confidence to proceed without further misgivings.

Bright Outlook. Janna found herself having happy dreams the month before her wedding. She would see herself with her fiancé sitting on a hilltop surveying a beautiful scene, or sketching together, or going sailing. When brides go forth with a happy excitement in their dreams, like Sue, Naomi, and Janna, the future looks bright.

The Jittery Groom

While the bride-to-be is pledging her troth in her dreams—more or less happily depending on her circumstances—the bridegroom is having his own premarital jitters. My collection of groom's dreams is smaller, but those I have suggest that getting married is less appealing for the man. We have already mentioned one groom's dream of being in jail. Here are two other examples.

The Shooting Gallery. Jim, entering his second marriage in his late thirties, shared his wedding-eve dream. Standing on the sweeping green lawn where the ceremony had taken place, he was still in his pale gray silk tuxedo with pink cummerbund when he told me, "It was the weirdest dream. I was in some sort of shooting gallery. It was like a huge panorama. Everywhere bombs and gunshots were exploding."

Jim is a man who had great difficulty controlling his temper. Getting married again, it would seem, triggered for him fear of replicating a situation in which his explosive anger might have free range.

The Red Shoes. A couple of nights before his wedding, one groom dreamed of standing in his white tuxedo at the altar waiting for his bride when he suddenly realized his cummerbund and shoes were red, as though he were performing in a nightclub act.[6]

This man had courted his young sweetheart for seven years before finally winning permission from her father to marry her; he wanted everything to be perfect for her. Not only was his anxiety running high, but his dream suggested that he felt a little out of place at the wedding "act."

Obviously bridegrooms share many of the bride's anxieties. They commonly consent to participate in elaborate ceremonies to please their fiancée, without taking the same pleasure the woman derives.

Happily Ever After? Postwedding Dreams

Fairy tales traditionally end with the bride and groom living happily ever after. Life is rarely that simple. The wedding dreams are not over once the ceremony is completed.

Breaking Through Her Shell.   One still-nervous bride reported a nightmare that she had just three days after her marriage. Mimi is fortyish. This was her third marriage, and it was causing her some trepidation; her new husband was a few years younger than she. She believed this nightmare to be a landmark—after it, she felt fully commited to him:

> I am a spirit flying up in the air. I see myself below sitting in a green meadow. I am twenty (instead of my age). "Oh, that's me," I say. I swoop down and say to the young-me, "Who do you love?" The young-me says, "No one." "What, not even Sean [her new husband]?" I ask. The young-me says, "I love no one!"

> Then a middle-aged lady, plain and a little plump, with short brown hair—more my true age—says, "All right, if that's the way you want it, look at this!"

> I seem to see an alternate future, what will happen if I don't love Sean. I see him surrounded by friends who are congratulating him on being newly married—but not to me. They are laughing and having a good time. (No bride is in sight.) I say, "Oh, no. He's supposed to be *my* husband!"

> I run up to him and begin pounding on his chest. He doesn't feel it or see me or anything because I am invisible. I'm

> surrounded by a kind of crystal shell. I'm saying, "No, Sean! I
> love you! I love you! I do love you!" But he can't see me.
>
> I start to cry. The crystal shell that makes me invisible cracks
> around me. We hold each other and say we love each other.

Hurt and bewildered following her second divorce, Mimi said, "I didn't know if I could ever trust a man again." Her dream revealed to her the danger of protectively withholding herself from her new husband.

Mimi dreaded being hurt again, as do we all when once scalded. Yet her dream dramatically displays the consequences of holding feelings back in the new relationship—she might lose her husband to someone else. Mimi described the crystal as a "hard shell" she put around herself for protection. By breaking through it in the dream, with her emotions, Mimi was able to make contact with the man she wanted and loved. So, too, in life. Mimi realized that, like everyone, she must risk being hurt in order to love and be loved.

The Joyful Rerun. Miriam, in her thirties, was entering her second marriage—also to a younger man. She shared Mimi's concerns about being the older partner. But, in addition, she faced an unusually difficult situation following her wedding: her groom broke his foot.

After a "magical weekend," just when they were to leave on their honeymoon, her husband was confined to hobbling around in a cast for six weeks. They felt forced to postpone the rigorous honeymoon trip they had planned to a foreign country. Miriam found it hard to accept the injury, explaining that "all the good feelings [of being married] drained away."

A few weeks into her husband's convalescence, Miriam dreamed:

> I am getting married again. It is like an instant rerun, a replay
> of the whole ceremony. Very similar to the original. I feel
> waves of love that are still with me when I awake.

Miriam added, "It was so wonderful to have the good feelings flow back again." This dream helped restore Miriam's equanimity, just as Mimi's had helped stabilize the new relationship. If we allow them, our dreams can sometimes heal our frustrations and bring us back to balance with new energy.

The Extra Guest. Naomi, too, found herself dreaming "reruns" of her wedding ceremony. In one of these:

> I am looking at pictures of the wedding. I see a guest in my
> dream that I don't remember inviting. He resembles my
> husband, but about ten years older. I enjoy that presence. He is
> the spirit of what I imagine Elijah or the spirit of God would
> have been. His expression is very approving. I wake up happy.

Naomi explained that a person ten years older than her husband would be in the middle of life, between old and young, wise and knowledgeable, with time ahead. She was feeling extremely happy in her newly married state, perhaps even more than she expected. Not only did she feel closer to her mate but to her religion as well. The "spiritual presence" in her dream was not specifically invited, her dream says, but it is approving and it brings her joy.

Brides are not the only women to dream of being wed. We see in what follows how marriage dreams have significance to women of all ages.

The Symbolism of Wedding Dreams
for Nonbrides

Women of every marital status dream about getting married. Even those women who have been long wed or those who have no intention of doing so may find themselves playing the bride or watching a wedding ceremony in their dreams. If wedding dreams reveal a bride-to-be's attitudes toward her fiancé and the married state, what meaning do they have for the woman who is not engaged?

Watching a Wedding From the Sidelines

Another Woman Takes Over. At times a woman who is already married dreams of watching someone else's wedding. Nina, a contented wife, found herself quite angry after this dream:

> I am in my home and I look outside, where I see that my
> ex-boyfriend's wedding is taking place. I also seem to be
> attending the service at the same time, when I notice I am
> wearing my pajamas.

Then I am back inside the house. The bride is moving my furnishings around. She is setting up housekeeping right under my stairs. This *young* girl is taking my grandmother's sewing machine!

I am furious. I am running around to get some help to get someone to stop her. I want to hit her! I am getting help when I wake up.

Nina had recently learned that a man with whom she "has carried on a flirtation for seventeen years" was getting married. She had met him when she was in her teens and had romantic ideas about him. The date for the wedding was approaching. Nina, although she had been invited, decided not to make the trip to attend. She thinks that he invited her with the intention of stirring up her jealousy.

If so, he succeeded. In Nina's dream language she feels left out and angry. First of all, the wedding is taking place on her doorstep. Secondly, she is inappropriately dressed in her pajamas, indicating how left out and exposed she feels. Worse yet, the bride—with emphasis on her youth—is moving around the dreamer's "belongings." Nina is angriest when the bride touches her grandmother's sewing machine. This instrument is the only memento Nina has from her beloved grandmother; she treasures it. Nina seems to be saying to herself, "How dare this woman touch my precious belonging—this man? Hands off!"

When Nina took a good look at the meaning behind the dramatic pictures of her wedding dream, she had to laugh. She had, after all, decided to marry another person herself. Realizing this, she no longer felt distressed about the situation. The wedding had stirred up her insecurity, but she was basically happy with her own decision, her own mate, and accepted the marriage of her former boyfriend with good grace.

If you have a dream of watching someone else's wedding, examine the imagery carefully to find out what's going on in your feelings.

Wishing to Get Married—Or Be Unmarried

Wedding Rings Lost and Found.   Of course dreams of getting married are sometimes, especially for a young girl, simple wish-fulfillment dreams. For instance the unmarried woman who dreams of being given a wedding ring or of finding one is usually expressing a wish for the relationship it represents.

Because the wedding ring symbolizes union, the unbroken wholeness and continuity of a loving relationship, its appearance in a dream is always significant. The gold, from which the majority of wedding rings are made, adds to the symbolism of the circle the further meaning of this precious metal—durability and unchangeability.

People in different cultures have traditional ideas about the meanings of certain dream images. Tiah, a young woman from Thailand, tells me that in her country the dream of finding a diamond—whether loose or in a ring—is a sign that something nice will happen soon. After she broke up with a boyfriend, she dreamed:

> I'm swimming underwater and I find a beautiful antique ring. I
> am very pleased and enjoy it. Later it is gone.

Tiah found this dream comforting and expected good luck to follow. I suspect the dream related to her lost (antique?) relationship, as well as to the probable wish for a replacement.

Married women who dream of losing their wedding rings or finding that they are somehow deformed or broken often refer to a current marred condition in their relationship with their mates. To dream of finding a lost ring may represent the rediscovery of something valuable in a relationship.

Dream Marriages: A Mirror of Inner Union?

Just as dreaming of getting married when you are planning to do so refers to the significant life event about to take place, to dream of getting married when you are *not* planning to do so refers to a significant *inner* event taking place. When such a woman awakens from a dream of getting married, she may find herself less depressed or less anxious or more at ease, or she may feel outright joyful—all for good reason.

Carl Jung regarded dreams of marriage, especially involving the marriage of a royal couple, or a brother and sister, as a pivotal image in the process of "individuation," of becoming a unique individual. Wedding dreams, he said, can be a "transforming symbol."[7]

According to the Jungian view, the bride and groom in a wedding dream symbolize different parts of the dreamer. Their wedding ceremony depicts the union of these opposite elements.

Verta, for example, had a powerful dream of this sort:

My spiritual teacher married my design teacher. The wedding
took place in a beautiful teahouse that had a
Japanese-Filipino-African flavor. It was so lovely.

Following this dream, Verta began to design jewelry that had an exotic
quality, like the Japanese-Filipino-African structure in her dream. No one
element could be clearly identified, as the designs were a blend uniquely hers.
Heretofore, her energies had been divided between artistic and spiritual
endeavors. This dream helped her to see the potential in "wedding" the two;
this union yielded a unique product line that has brought Verta much
commercial success. The personal integration her dream represented is perhaps even more important.

Other symbolic wedding dreams may include a woman discovering a
new relationship to her body when she has formerly lived a mainly intellectual life. Her dream marriage would portray the freshly found unity of her
physical and mental selves. Likewise a dream wedding can represent the
union of working skills and romantic life, or between the emotional and
spiritual selves, or between the feminine and masculine qualities or other
opposing tendencies that were previously in conflict. The five steps outlined
on pages 143–44 will help a woman comprehend the nature of her internal
union.

Some additional questions for nonbrides who have a wedding dream are:
Have you formed an emotional relationship with a new person in your life?
Do you seem to be encouraging or discouraging yourself in this relationship
in the dream? The content of the dream—the action and the images you
use—will tell you which. If you are already married, consider whether you
want to begin again with a new mate.

Also, ask yourself whether there are any aspects of your life that are fitting
together better than they used to do. For the mature woman, dreams of
getting married are sometimes a mark of inner development. They may
show her commitment to full growth, her movement toward psychological
wholeness.

Outer Change or Inner Change.   Thus, when you dream of getting
married, the probability is that you are either anticipating an important
change in your outer life or are experiencing an important change in your
inner life. Whether we are actually to be wed or not, dreams of getting
married offer us a chance to peek inside our hearts.

We turn now to the results of committing oneself to a mate—producing
babies or other creative projects.

Pregnancy and Childbirth Dreams

I give birth to a baby boy. It's so easy—he just pops out, fully dressed. He's a big baby, about four months old, who crawls around.

The young woman who had this dream had just learned during the day that she was pregnant. Mindy, in her late twenties, had never been pregnant before. She was luminous with pleasure. Several months later, in fact, Mindy gave birth to a healthy baby boy. We shall see how dreams of giving birth to a mature baby or a full-grown child are characteristic of pregnant women.

Women who are not mothers—or never plan to be—can nevertheless benefit from familiarity with the dream symbols of childbearing. Almost all women, mothers or not, dream at some point in their lives of giving birth to a child. Newborn babies have special significance in women's dreams. Those dreamers who are more interested in the symbolism of childbirth dreams may prefer to turn directly to this section at the end of this chapter. Dreams about the conflict between work and mothering appear in chapter 7, "Career Dreams."

Today's woman is less likely than her elder sisters to follow the traditional pattern of marrying, housekeeping, and childbearing in rapid succession. The modern female often chooses to work intensely at a career for several years before pausing to have a baby. She may choose to give birth as a single mother or even elect not to produce a baby altogether. Whatever her individual time schedule, when a woman becomes pregnant, it occupies her dreams as well as her daily thoughts. She shares a pattern with women of all time.

Being pregnant is one of life's greatest adventures. For the woman to produce another life from within her own body seems magical. To grow and nurture a child out of herself—with a start from her mate—is almost incomprehensible. Many women, despite worldly success, regard giving birth as their most significant accomplishment, the event that makes their whole existence worthwhile. For these women the wonder of bearing a child is overwhelming.

The dreams of a mother-to-be trace her momentous journey—from the first meeting of egg and sperm to the emergence of the offspring. With hope and fear she follows the developments inside her womb. Her dreams relate her internal story. Here's how it begins.

Changes in Sleep and Dreams: The High Dream Tide

During the nine months of pregnancy enormous changes permeate the mother-to-be's body. Some researchers think that women who are pregnant dream more than at any other time in their adult lives.[1] Probably because the female sex hormones are at flood level during her pregnancy, the woman is served a banquet of dreams. This bountiful feast of rapid eye movement sleep (REM) often results in more remembered dreams than usual.

"I Can Hardly Hold My Eyes Open"

Pregnant Women Need More Sleep.   Excessive drowsiness is one of the earliest signs of pregnancy. There is good cause for feeling overwhelmed with weariness. Progesterone, the hormone that stimulates development of mammary glands in the breasts and helps form the placenta, also acts as a sedative; it is secreted in large amounts during pregnancy.[2] This same hormone rises in the latter half of the menstrual cycle, after ovulation, when dream time also increases. It may account for the fatigue women often feel before their menstrual periods are due.

In the first few months of her pregnancy a woman spends more time in the deepest stages of sleep than when she is not pregnant. Mothers-to-be who are able to do so add one or two hours to their sleep time each night. Whenever people focus inwardly, as women do during pregnancy, they require more sleep.[3] As the woman's pregnancy advances, she gets less deep sleep—perhaps because it is difficult for her to be comfortable while lying down. Movements of the baby, or pressure on her bladder as the baby gets larger, cause the woman to wake frequently. This may explain why one team of investigators noted an increase of REM during the second trimester, followed by a decrease in the third trimester, when sleep was poorer.[4]

Do Pregnant Women Dream More?   While the pregnant woman is sleeping longer and more deeply, she is also probably dreaming more. Studies with humans show that the more we sleep, the more we dream. Also, researchers find that when people undergo an accelerated learning program, they dream more than usual;[5] perhaps pregnancy is such a learning period. Furthermore, researchers studying pregnant cats found that as the animals approached delivery, they showed a rapid increase in REM sleep.[6] The cats were dreaming more than usual and they continued to do so into the postpartum period. Although the evidence from humans is not totally in agreement, women's dream time is likely to follow a similar pattern of expansion.

Dreams Change as Bodies Change.   Throughout her pregnancy a woman's dream topics change. They echo the changing conditions of her body and express her anticipations about her forthcoming child. Some themes and images are typical of the first three months; others are more characteristic of the middle months; still others are more likely to occur during the last few months. Specific dream themes often begin at a characteristic time and continue for the remainder of the pregnancy.

By examining the table *Women's Dream Symbols of Pregnancy* you can get an overview of dreams themes during the entire pregnancy. Dreams, however, are as complex as the minds that produce them; themes may occur at any time and the categories blend in ways difficult to convey on the printed page. Let's see how.

Women's Dream Symbols for
PREGNANCY*

1st Trimester Typical Dream Images	Probable Stimulus
easy labor and childbirth	awareness of conception
mature baby or full-grown child	hopes for easy childbirth
large vehicles, buildings, constructions	awareness of growing body
gardens, fruits, flowers, seeds	fertility, internal growth
driving big vehicle	feeling awkward
carrying heavy bag, trouble walking	awareness of weight gain
dangers or intruders	fear of motherhood
open doors, falling, drowning, loss, blood	fear of miscarriage
factories, construction	awareness of growth of fetus
small, structures, miniatures	awareness of small fetus
water, swimming	the womb's internal fluids
small aquatic animals —tadpole, fish, lizard	awareness of small fetus

2nd Trimester Typical Dream Images	Probable Stimulus
love affairs with former lovers, others	desire to feel attractive; sexual deprivation
husband being helpful	need for support
husband being difficult	feeling insecure, unstable
husband having love affair	insecurity about attractiveness
cuddly animals— puppies, kittens, chicks	awareness of enlarging fetus
mother being helpful or harmful	reassessment of old conflicts with mother; new hopes for own motherhood

* These are general trends, not isolated categories; themes and images overlap between trimesters and vary with individual dreamer. List is not conclusive.

3rd Trimester Typical Dream Images	Probable Stimulus
baby's sex and appearance	hopes and fears for baby
baby's name	thinking about names
special communication with baby	wish to know baby
large animals—lion, ape, monkey	awareness of large fetus
great waters	anticipation of amniotic sac breaking
details of labor and delivery	hopes and fears about labor; Braxton-Hicks contractions
journeys, being lost	fear of the unknown
rituals, ceremonies, holidays, birthdays, rites	anticipation of joy of birth

The First Trimester: Changing and Growing
Conception Announcements

A woman's dreaming mind sends out announcements of having conceived—sometimes before the waking mind is aware of the fact. Several women described dreams that convinced them they were pregnant prior to their suspecting it or to having it confirmed by laboratory tests. One, for example, reported a dream that her physician poked his head around a door, in the midst of unrelated action to announce, "Oh, by the way, you're pregnant!" In other cases women who did not yet know they were pregnant told me of dreams that they were pregnant or had given birth to a baby; these dreams were later proved to have appeared immediately or within days of conception.

Birthing Mature Babies.   Many first-time mothers, when they discover they have conceived, dream of giving birth to a fully mature baby or grown child. Early in their pregnancy these women rarely know much about the childbirth experience; they often feel apprehensive. The combination of hopes for an easy delivery and incomplete understanding of the actual process leads to dreams of the baby "popping out" or simply appearing. Donna, for instance, when she was first pregnant, dreamed:

I give birth to a full-grown child. He is like a miniature adult, dressed like an adult, and walking and talking like a grown-up.

Perhaps an older baby or child seems less threatening than a fragile newborn to the inexperienced mother. Donna thought the adult baby in her dream reflected her anxiety that she would have to go back to work and would therefore miss her child's growing up. Whatever the reason, first-time moms typically dream about older babies or easy childbirth.

Back to the Conference.   Experienced mothers, too, may exhibit this dream theme. Just before Bonnie and her husband decided to try for a second child, she dreamed:

> My husband is at a conference. There is a hospital right next
> door. I don't look pregnant at all. I walk through double doors
> to the hospital, have some kind of labor—not much—get up,
> take the baby girl, and hurry back to the conference. She looks
> like a newborn, but I'm not that attached.

Although she is familiar with labor, in the dream Bonnie undergoes a simple childbearing process; she gets right back to her husband. Significantly Bonnie's husband, who is, in fact, exceedingly busy, does not come with her to the hospital in the dream. Hence her haste to be at his side again, to not miss a thing. During the dream, Bonnie is not "attached" to the newborn, but afterward she liked the idea so much, she seriously set about having a second child—a boy, to her surprise. Notice the double doors in Bonnie's dream. Doors often represent the opening to the womb in dreams, as we'll see later.

In addition to dreaming about grown-up babies or easy birthing, women also speculate, like Mindy in the opening dream and like Bonnie, on the sex and appearance of their child-to-be. (We discuss these dreams in a later section.) By the time she has been pregnant a few months, the mother-to-be is more likely to have realistic dreams—if not outright frightening ones—about her forthcoming labor and infant. She may also have dreams of incredible beauty in which she shares secrets in a mysterious communication with her unborn child. These modern mothers follow in an ancient tradition.

Holy Mother Dreams.   Long before there were laboratories to measure dreams or therapists to interpret them, people in olden times believed that the dreams of pregnant women were predictive.

Almost every great religious or legendary figure is reputed to have been forecast by one of his mother's dreams. Familiar examples are the biblical account of an angel appearing to Mary to announce her being impregnated by the Holy Spirit, as well as Joseph's dream of being reassured by an angel that his future wife was carrying the Son of God.

Less well known in the West is the story of Queen Maya, the pregnant mother of Buddha, who is said to have dreamed that a rare white elephant with seven tusks, resplendent with radiant light, entered her side while she slept; her seers interpreted the dream as indicative of a forthcoming savior of mankind.[7]

Likewise in Irish and Scotch legend the pregnant mother of the future Saint Columba, named Eithne, reputedly dreamed that she was given a beautiful cloak; it lifted into the sky and spread above the land and sea.[8] In retrospect this dream seemed prophetic of the influence her son "spread," bringing Christianity to the highlands and islands of Scotland. Whether such dreams actually occurred to the mother-to-be or whether they were attributed by later legends is impossible to say.

We do know that all pregnant women conjure up dreams anticipating the characteristics of their unborn child. The contemporary mother-to-be shares the same hopes for her future child, and the same fears, as those mothers of long ago. The holy mother—who is informed in a dream of the spiritual quality of her forthcoming child—is an archetypal pattern that is alive in the modern woman, as we shall see. It has a powerful impact upon the pregnant woman who dreams it.

After all, a woman with a child in her womb faces a major life experience—a milestone in womanhood. Body and emotions undergo upheaval. This life crisis brings unprecedented opportunity for personal growth as the woman sets out on her great adventure.

Big Buildings and Bulky Vehicles: The Pregnant Woman's Changing Body

"I feel like a stuffed olive!" pregnant Leah announced to me one day. In her olive sweatsuit with red collar and cuffs covering her rounded belly, she conjured up quite a picture in my mind. The woman who has conceived clearly notices the changes taking place in her body and the different way it is beginning to function. These changes are paralleled by alterations in her body image and how she feels about herself.

Feelings of self-esteem are closely related to how a woman perceives her body. Unfortunately most women—pregnant or not—have a distorted image of their actual shape. One team of investigators found that two out of five women overestimated the size of one or more body part by 50 percent or more.[9] In general women saw themselves as 25 percent larger than they actually were; men saw themselves as 13 percent larger. Women consistently overestimated their measurements compared with men.

Another study found that women are more critical of their bodies than men are of theirs.[10] Investigators concluded that women judge themselves more harshly in appearance, in physical fitness, in health, and in sexuality. The researchers commented, "Little boys are taught to be proud of themselves because they are strong and athletic. Little girls learn to value beauty." A woman's feelings about her body may either improve or deteriorate during pregnancy.

The emotional response of a mother-to-be to her changing figure is determined in large part by her experience of gestation and her attitude toward being pregnant. Contrast these two comments I collected from women:

> I hated being pregnant! I hated the way I felt and the things
> that were happening to my body. I felt it was an intrusion, an
> invasion—like a cancer.
> [This woman terminated her pregnancy at two and a half
> months.]

> I loved being pregnant! I never felt better in my life. My
> complexion cleared, my hair got glossy. People told me I
> looked radiant. I loved the sensation of the child growing
> within me—it was magical.
> [This woman carried to term and delivered a healthy child.]

Most pregnant women are somewhere between these extremes. They feel both happy and anxious; they are ambivalent about the impact of a child upon their love life or their career or their figure.

Nanette, in her early eighties, recalled that despite being thrilled to be pregnant with her first child, she felt "ashamed people would see my big belly." She had a dressmaker make a large navy blue cape that concealed most of her figure, adding, "I never went on the street without it."

Today's woman may think of her fertile figure as a badge of pride. However she, too, is highly conscious of how her growing shape affects her comfort and mobility. These attitudes are vividly portrayed in her dreams.

The Spare Tire.   When pregnant with my daughter, I dreamed:

> I am driving a car. At the same time I carry a spare tire around
> my waist.

Awake, it was obvious that the "spare tire" was my expanding midsection. Driving a vehicle is often a metaphor for the way the dreamer is moving through life at the moment; with the spare tire, my movement was rather clumsy.

Pregnant women frequently picture themselves driving trucks, buses, or other vehicles that are more difficult to maneuver than cars in their dreams—reflecting their perception of awkward movement. Such dreams usually start early on and may continue throughout the pregnancy.

The Handicapped Dreamer.   Another image women employ to express their sense of ungraceful movement is that of difficulty walking. Joan, in her thirties, dreamed the following near the beginning of her sixth month of pregnancy:

> I line up for a scan search (in an airport) for weapons. It seems
> like a school situation. I have great trouble walking, like a
> woman I know who has multiple sclerosis. Since I am at the
> front of the line, everyone is held up because of me.

Joan's feeling of growing awkwardness in getting around led her to picture herself as handicapped. The comparison of the airport to a school situation suggests that she saw herself in a situation where she was learning, as well as undertaking a journey. Perhaps she also thought of her pregnancy as a kind of "hidden weapon."

Many women describe dreams of having too much to carry—toting unwieldy packages or heavy suitcases. These, too, portray a woman's awareness of extra weight as her baby grows bigger.

Confronting the Intruders.   When Leah was about three months pregnant, she was worried about her weight gain. At the same time she was reading material about influencing the mind. One technique involved focusing on a word that epitomized a desired change; Leah chose the word *confidence.* She asked herself, "If I were more confident, how would I act? What difference would being more confident make in my life?" She pondered this before bed, went to sleep, and dreamed:

I seem to wake up in my bed with the impression that someone is in the house. I get up and go out the bedroom door. Instead of there being a porch, as there actually is, there was another room. A kind of violent, evil man is there, like the character from the film *Blue Velvet*. I chase him out.

A few days later I dream the same thing:

There is an intruder in the house. This time I chase the person through room after room. I finally confront a kind of pudgy woman with drab blond hair. Instead of being afraid, I go right up to her and ask, "Are you the terminator?"

Many pregnant women, like Leah, find themselves dreaming of an intruder in the house. Since a house or room in women's dreams often represents the dreamer's body, the "intruder" is a typical initial reaction to the presence of the fetus. The British even use the phrase *a little stranger is coming* to refer to the condition of pregnancy. Leah, instead of being terrified by the stranger, copes with his presence.

In Leah's dreams there are extra rooms that do not exist in her actual home. These are probably a reference to her expanding body. In fact, when I asked Leah to tell me about the pudgy female character, she explained that the woman looked tough and uncomfortable; she added that it was difficult for her to gain weight even though she loved being pregnant. So one of the things Leah was confronting in her dreams was the change in her body, her "internal room." The phrase *the terminator* may be a pun on carrying a baby to "term." Leah would certainly be pudgy by then. It could also be a reference to the fact that Leah plans to "terminate" her job and become a full-time mother.

Leah felt good about these dreams. "The part that struck me is that I was aggressive, how I'd be if I were more confident. Usually I'd be so afraid, I wouldn't do anything." Without realizing it, Leah had come upon an effective way to help herself be more comfortable in frightening dreams. Later we will see how a similar method of increasing dream assertiveness is thought actually to be associated with easier childbirth.

Construction Under Way.   Researchers who have studied the dreams of pregnant women observe frequent references to buildings in them, from simple rooms to soaring skyscrapers. The dream buildings are often places where things are made, such as a factory or a shipyard, probably parelleling the "making" of a baby that is taking place inside the woman's body.

In a landmark investigation of the dreams of sixty-seven women, psychologist Patricia Maybruck found that 18 percent of the 1,046 dreams she collected contained references to buildings or other architecture.[11] Her study is important because she personally interviewed twenty-five of her subjects, in addition to collecting dreams from the overall group, whereas many dream studies rely solely on questionnaires, on dreams collected without personal discussion with the dreamer, or on dreams submitted by mail.

Perhaps pregnant women dream about buildings because they are hypersensitive to their "enlarging inner space."[12] Indeed the type of building pictured in the woman's dreams may increase in size as her pregnancy progresses. Maybruck found that dream buildings became larger and more complex the closer the woman was to term; skyscrapers were especially common.[13]

Among my subjects Joan recorded her dreams throughout her pregnancy. She belongs to a dream group and keeps a regular dream journal. One of her earliest pregnancy dreams included miniature buildings, but her latest pregnancy dreams had buildings no larger than a restaurant and a small house. Her thirty-three pregnancy dreams did not show a marked tendency for buildings to increase in size or complexity, so this trend must vary from dreamer to dreamer.

Joan contributed a special dream from her sixth month that refers to a part of a building; she called it "Home Sweet Cubicle":

> There has been another shift of desks and people at work. This time my cubicle is in a very quiet, isolated part of the floor. I welcome the peace and solitude. My furnishings include a bed and a stove. I lie in bed, feeling very relaxed. A good friend from work, who is also a member of my dream group, tucks me in. There may be lots of activity all around my area, but within my own sphere reigns peaceful calm.

Here we see the shift of Joan's attention from the outer world of her work to her inner space. Her unborn child had quickened and moved within her. She stocked her dream with all that she needed nearby—the bed to rest in and the stove to prepare nourishment—and she felt the peace of a contented mother-to-be. Pregnancy is the time for withdrawal from the outer world of activity to focus upon the marvels taking place within.

Plants and Doors: The Growth and Stability of Pregnancy

Abundant Growth.   Plants, flowers, and fruit have long symbolized the fertility of the earth and of woman. Mother Earth gives forth food to feed the animals and the people who walk upon her surface. Ceres, the Roman goddess of growing vegetation, from whom we get the word *cereal*, is typically pictured with sheaves of grain; her name comes from the same root as the word *create*, indicating her role as giver of life.[14]

This fruitfulness of woman is depicted in Botticelli's famous painting *La Primavera* (Spring). When I saw the original of this picture on display at the Uffizi Gallery in Florence, I was impressed with the figure of Spring. The artist shows her belly great with child, her head wreathed in flowers, her neck in garlands, her body covered with a flowery print dress, and her arms full of blossoms. The trees above her are heavy with fruit; the grass below her is lush with bloom.

This same fruitfulness characterizes the dreams of pregnant women. Walking through grasslands, pastures, or fields; filling flower boxes, tending gardens, or growing vegetables or fruit—such dreams are typical of pregnancy. A "nursery"—a word that means a place where children are cared for as well as a place where plants are raised—is sometimes used as a pun in the pregnant woman's dreams. If you are a woman who thinks she might be pregnant or who already is, look for images of growing things in your dreams.

Delicate Seedlings.   Even suspecting that she is pregnant can lead a woman to a fertility dream, as it did for Sheila the month before she conceived:

> I see brown earth being watered. Tiny shoots of tender grass
> appear. I say to myself, "The seed springeth up." I know we
> must be careful not to overwater the delicate seedlings and wash
> them out. Then other things get watered. I stick a knife into
> soft mud. . . . Later I see green algae forming in a glass above a
> sink.

Sheila had had intercourse with her husband without using a contraceptive the morning preceding this dream. She was not sure exactly when her period was due, but she felt that if she did become pregnant, it would be all right. Notice the typical symbols of sexual intercourse and fertility in Sheila's dream. Her body was the "brown earth" that provided rich soil for planting. The water represented the semen that was deposited; the knife in the soft mud was a metaphor for the penis in the soft female body; the delicate seedlings and the green algae were the potential embryo that might have formed; the glass was the container that, like her womb, could enclose growing things. Sheila expressed concern in this dream that the seedlings could be washed out. The following month she actually conceived and carried to term a healthy infant.

Ripe Grapes.   Maybruck describes similar imagery in one of her thirty-seven-year-old subjects who had been trying unsuccessfully to conceive for three years. When the woman dreamed, "I look down, and huge, ripe bunches of grapes are growing from my belly!" she knew for certain conception had finally occurred.[15] Later on in pregnancy, Maybruck observed fertility dreams that included lush jungles.

Miniature Gardens.   Joan, during her first few weeks of gestation, dreamed:

> I am bicycling through the shipyards containing miniature
> gardens and streets. [This reminds her of shipyards in Pearl
> Harbor she has seen and of a miniature village in Holland.]
>
> The shipyard backdrop dissolves. I am now swimming indoors
> in a curved pool, which is bordered by tiny model villages. This
> time I would imagine I am in a movie set.

Here we see Joan moving through life under her own power (the bicycle) into an area where construction takes place (the shipyard), paralleling the building of the baby within her. The miniature gardens symbolize the little, growing being inside her body; the image of water (the pool where she swims) represents the uterine waters gathering in her body at the time. We shall observe how water is a popular image throughout pregnancy.

The Open Doors.   As a pregnancy progresses, women often express their concern about its stability in their dreams. Shortly after my daughter, Cheryl, conceived, she dreamed:

> A girlfriend and I are driving a school bus. Her two-year-old
> son is playing up front. The bus doors open and he starts to fall

backward, out of the bus. "Look out!" I shout. We grab the child.

Cheryl had experienced some common early pregnancy spotting around the time of this dream; the images probably represented her anxiety over a possible miscarriage. Luckily this did not occur, just as she managed to save the child in the dream.

Notice the school bus that usually contains children—this dreamer's version of the bulky vehicle typical in dreams of pregnant women. The open doors represent the "doors" to the womb that could open too early to release the precious child, as well as signifying the risky situation in general.

Other themes that express this same concern have to do with dreams of lost children or children falling or drowning.

Unhappily for some mothers-to-be, a miscarriage does occasionally take place. Robert Van de Castle, in a speech to the Association for the Study of Dreams in 1986, documented dreams from his vast collection that were associated with miscarriages.[16] They included: recurrent dreams that the dreamer was starting her period; dreams of being in a bathtub when the water turned red with blood; and a dream of a strange lady telling the dreamer three times, "You can't take care of it!"

Van de Castle also described a dream in which the pregnant woman saw her infant baby on the examining table with her obstetrician; he discontinued the exam because the baby was too cold. This woman's fetus died in the womb. In another case the dreamer saw her mother baby-sitting her child; the mother put the baby into a refrigerator, where the dreamer found it icy cold. This woman's child was born dead. It seems these women sensed the coldness of the fetus in their wombs. In yet another case the pregnant woman dreamed that her grandmother poisoned her to kill the baby; later it was discovered that she was carrying twins, one of whom had died.

Let me emphasize that these instances are unusual. It may be small comfort for the mother who suffers such a loss, but physicians assure us that most spontaneous abortions or death of a fetus are nature's way of eliminating imperfect babies. Most pregnant women have alarming nightmares that prove totally unfounded. Frightening dreams may even be actively beneficial, as we will see.

Lost Baby Found.　Dreams are part of the healing process. When she was pregnant in her early thirties, Cassie underwent a therapeutic abortion at four months. She did not want to do so, but her doctors insisted. Later she dreamed of her baby many times:

Sometimes it's a boy, sometimes a girl. I will be holding the baby, not sure if it's mine. It seems to be partly my baby and partly someone else's. I don't feel sad during the dream, but afterwards it is very painful.

Such dreams, grievous as they are on awakening, pave the way for the dreamer's acceptance of a sad reality. They facilitate the healing process in the same manner that a soldier's traumatic experience may be relived in nightmares; eventually the event is incorporated, and life can go forward constructively. For Cassie, now in her middle thirties and pregnant again, the future may be better. So far her physician thinks she can carry to term without endangering her life.

Rising Waters: Awareness of Amniotic Fluid

From goldfish bowls, to family wash, to swelling oceans, the pregnant woman's dreams refer to water throughout her pregnancy. The mother-to-be will often find herself swimming, as Joan did in the curved pool, in her first-trimester dreams. Where animals appear in a pregnant woman's first trimester dreams, they are often aquatic creatures, such as tadpoles and fish. This water in her dreams possibly depicts the pregnant woman's awareness of the water gathering within her womb.

In her second trimester Cassie had an impressive dream with water:

I am going to a girlfriend's house. I think, "After I deliver the baby, I will live here. I go inside. It is really big (much more than it actually is). On a big bed are many, many babies, all naked and playing. They are crowded.

I go into another room, where I will be staying. This is smaller. I see a four-year-old boy floating in a golden fish tank. His body is in the water with his face sticking out, with a plastic bag containing air over it. I think, "Oh, no, he will drown!" But he looks very comfortable, smiling. He is happy there.

Part of this imagery is characteristic: the house that was bigger than reality probably related to Cassie's own growing body; the many babies implied the growth within her womb (perhaps her potential for more children); the water symbolized her amniotic fluid. I was puzzled, however, by the boy who seemed to be drowning. From amniocentesis Cassie knew that the baby she was carrying was a girl. Past experience has shown me that dates and figures are almost always symbolic in dreams, so I asked Cassie, "What happened four years ago?" Without hesitation she replied, "That's when I had the [undesired] abortion. It was a boy." The four-year-old in her dream represented the child she had lost. His smiling attitude suggested that Cassie has accepted the past. Pregnant with a new baby, she looks forward with happier feelings. In a later dream Cassie was having fun bathing a little boy.

Water in dreams may take on a dramatic form as pregnancy progresses. Toward her due date, the pregnant woman is more likely to dream of water as a symbol of the "breaking waters" that announce imminent childbirth. At the end of her second trimester Cassie dreamed of carrying a heavy schoolbag when big ocean waves rose and endangered her. In one of her third-trimester dreams Joan was in a region where the projected rainfall was 700 inches—a heavy gushing of waters indeed. Maybruck observed among her subjects, instead of the calm lakes or pools of early pregnancy, dreams of bursting water tanks or turbulent rivers.[17]

We begin our lives as water creatures, suspended in a sea of liquid within our mother's womb. Even embryos fertilized in a culture dish outside the womb require return to the inner ocean for nourishment. The pregnant woman is drinking fluids for two, herself and baby. Small wonder that her dreams overflow with images of water.

To summarize, then, during the first three months of a woman's pregnancy, her typical dream pictures and their possible causes include the following:

Dream Image	Probable Stimulus
Easy childbirth and mature babies	Conception; hopes for easy labor
Large vehicles, buildings, luggage	Awareness of changing figure
Gardens, fruit, and flowers	Fertility and inner growth
Dangers or intruders	Fear of motherhood
Open doors, blood	Fear of miscarriage
Small animals, often aquatic	Awareness of small fetus
Water	The womb's gathering fluids

These images ebb and flow during the following months. After the changes in her body and the growth of her fetus are well established, the pregnant woman's dreams focus more on the main people in her life: her unborn child, her previous children, mate, mother, and other significant folk.

The Expectant Father's Dreams During the First Trimester

In their own dreams fathers-to-be are busy reacting to their woman's pregnancy. During the first few months men with pregnant mates are likely to have many more sexual dreams than usual, according to an intriguing study conducted by psychologist Alan Siegel in Berkeley.[18] The fathers-to-be in his study dreamed of having sex with their wives, with other women, with prostitutes, or sometimes with homosexuals early in their wives' pregnancy. In contrast, mothers-to-be tended to have sexual dreams toward the end of their term.

Siegel speculates that the protective feelings a man develops toward his wife and unborn child may be threatening to his masculinity. His sexual dreams and other macho visions (such as triumphs on the football field) may be expressing a need to be more "masculine." They offer reassurance.

At the same time he is having an unusual number of sexual dreams, the expectant father often dreams of protecting and caring for his wife. The sexual dream theme usually drops out as the pregnant wife moves into her second trimester, whereas the protective themes continue. The pregnant woman can help her mate avoid feeling left out—a typical reaction—by sharing dreams and recognizing that these common sexual themes are not a threat to her in themselves. Sharing dreams can help the couple understand each other's feelings throughout pregnancy. The husband's and wife's relationship becomes an important focus in the couple's dreams during the second trimester.

The Second Trimester of Pregnancy: Dreams About Important People

Baby Animals: Dreams About the Fetus

Kittens, puppies, chicks, tadpoles, fish, lizards—these are some of the animals that typically wander through the dreams of pregnant women. These creatures probably represent the fetus within the woman's womb.

Hungry Babies.   During the time I was pregnant and preparing to nurse, for instance, I dreamed several times:

> I see dozens of tiny starving kittens. I wonder desperately how I can feed them.

My fondness for kittens probably accounted for their appearance in these pregnancy dreams: kittens also feed on milk, as human babies do. Lack of confidence in my ability to nurse successfully is the likely explanation for the overwhelming number of tiny, hungry creatures in my dreams. I felt somewhat overwhelmed with becoming a mother. The fear proved unfounded, as I later happily nursed my daughter for her first year.

More Animal Dreams in Pregnancy.   Dreams about baby animals are especially characteristic of the mother-to-be. Both little girls and boys frequently dream of animals. Some studies report that more than 60 percent of children's dreams have animals in them, whereas adults typically report about 7 percent of their dreams to contain animals.[19]

However, when a woman becomes pregnant, her dreams of animals increase. She dreams more about animals than the nonpregnant woman. Among the expectant mothers in her study, Maybruck found that animals, including fish and amphibians, appeared in 17 percent of their dreams.[20] Participants in my study showed a similar larger number of animal dreams. Joan, for instance, had animals in six of her thirty-three pregnancy dreams, a rate of 18 percent.

Each age group dreams of animals for different reasons. Children, theorists speculate, identify with the instinctual elements of animal behavior. Girls and boys probably use animals in their dreams to represent the self, free of social regulations and able to express anger toward adults; at other times the dream animals probably symbolize people the child perceives as threatening.

For most adults dangerous animals in dreams symbolize a "wild" emotion arising within themselves or else a sense of threat in their environment. But for pregnant women animals seem to symbolize the fetus.

Different Animals at Different Stages of Pregnancy.   The type of animal the woman dreams about usually shifts with her stage of pregnancy. During the first trimester, women commonly picture fish or reptilelike creatures in their dreams. It is as if they could telepathically see into the womb where the tiny embryo, floating in fluid, undergoes transformations that recapitulate the evolution of sea creatures to land mammals. At the same time the pregnant woman is often reading illustrated books and learning about the stages of development of the fetus, reinforcing her awareness of the changes that are happening to her unborn child.

Whether the dream animal is aquatic or not, it is typically small in the dreams of the first trimester. When Cassie was two months pregnant, for instance, she dreamed:

> I go out the back door of my house and I see in the neighbor's yard their pet dog with many small black animals. They are a triangular shape, a kind I never saw before. They are playing with some rats on a little hill of dust.
>
> When I open my door to go back in, they try to follow me. They climb up over the fence after me. Many, many of them surround me. I am afraid they will come inside. I close the door again. I don't know how to deal with them. They don't look harmful. What happened?

Although Cassie has very much wished to become pregnant, her dream imagery of the strange, small black animals suggests she feels puzzled about how to cope with the situation. She may have felt a mild threat as these animals invaded her space—a common reaction to the child in the womb.

During the second trimester, the pregnant woman's dreams contain animals that are more babylike, such as pups, chicks, and kittens. Depending upon her attitude toward the pregnancy, her mate, and her situation, the animal may be either threatening or lovable. In one of Joan's dreams during her fourth month of pregnancy:

> While visiting Mother, I sit by myself in her living room. Near me on a chair is a pet of hers, a gibbonlike creature. I keep my distance from him, afraid he might bite. He climbs around on the furniture, and nibbles on some squash in a hanging basket.

This dream suggests Joan felt some ambivalence about the effect of the strange new creature coming into her life. Would its presence be destructive?

The quickening of the child within the womb is often described in animal terms by pregnant women. Kerry, for instance, said the first small movements of her fetus felt "like butterfly wings." Eva said they felt "like I swallowed a bird and his wings are still going, fluttering." Perhaps these small internal sensations make it easy to dream of the fetus as a small animal.

The final three months of pregnancy may be marked by dreams of larger animals, such as a lion, along with dreams of the actual fetus itself. There is no hard and fast rule, however, only overall tendencies. Animals of every size may appear in dreams throughout gestation.

Friendly Animals During Pregnancy. The presence of friendly animals—rare and charming creatures in dreams—is generally thought to represent a good relationship between the dreamer and his or her instincts.[21] In the dreams of many pregnant women, animals are frequently cuddly and cute. Maybruck found that although dream animals were sometimes threatening to the pregnant women in her study, during the second trimester they were most often of the appealing, adorable variety.[22]

Cheryl, for instance, during her fourth month of pregnancy dreamed:

> I am somewhere with my husband and friends. It is a weird place in Mexico, almost a hovel with poor people. We are smuggling dogs back home—one for everyone. They are young puppies, not little ones. I bring them. They are so cute! At the end we're in an apartment of mine in Canada.

The strange place where Cheryl found herself was undoubtedly the land of pregnancy, where she had never been before; it seems foreign yet near home to her. She was the one carrying the puppies for everyone, just as she carried her unborn child. The fact that they were being smuggled suggests the hidden quality of her pregnancy at this stage. Finding the animals cute reflected her positive attitude toward the child-to-be.

Friendly dream animals foretold easy childbirth among the Ojibwa Indians. They believed that to dream of an animal that had easy labor and delivery—such as a bitch, a mare, or a cow—could bless the woman with childbirth powers. A woman who aspired to be a midwife was required by her culture to have one of these favorable dreams to qualify for her post.

One popular midwife, for example, described to investigators a dream of a "she-wolf" who resembled a person with a wolf's voice. The dream creature informed her that she would bear five children—which she subsequently did. Licking her hand, the wolf added that she would assist her in childbirth. A dream of this sort would surely encourage any pregnant woman in her waking-life task.

Even today, in some parts of Japan, the pregnant woman may use as underwear a special *obi* (a bellyband) inscribed with the character for *dog*. Since it is believed that dogs have an easy labor, people hope the writing will help the woman to have a comfortable delivery.[23]

Joan, in a dream two days after her baby girl was born, saw herself as the helper: she called it "The Cat in the Fat":

> I enter the house and in the kitchen see a jar of fat drippings with the top of a small cat head protruding from it. I think at first that one of our cats has climbed into a jar and become stuck, and I laugh.
>
> I realize I must get the cat out, so I grab it by the head and gently pry it loose. It looks like a newborn baby, covered with cheesy, fatty substance. The creature was so helpless—I saved it.

Joan drew a charming sketch of the stuck cat. Her rescue of the dream creature and her compassion for it paralleled the childbirth and her sense of bonding to her helpless newborn. She gently pried it out of her body. This dream vividly dramatizes the fact that dream animals symbolize the fetus.

If you are pregnant, you may find that the animals in your dreams develop from sea creature to land mammal, repeating the journey of primeval ancestors; at other times you may find you dream of your unborn child directly. Your feeling about the animal or baby reveals something about your attitude at the time of the dream. From birth onward the baby often appears as himself or herself, a human being with body and spirit.

Former Lovers, Spouses, and "Other Women" in Dreams: Relationships With Mates

The Lover From Long Ago. Veronica spoke to me in a low, confidential tone so that her husband, who was talking in the next room, might not overhear her words. Nearly six months pregnant, Veronica was troubled by her dreams:

> For weeks I've been dreaming about my old boyfriend. Wild, sensuous dreams. I'm with him again, kissing and making love—it's as passionate as ever. When I'm awake, I have fantasies about wanting him to see me with a child. What's going on?

Dreams about former lovers, delicious as they may be while in process, often torment the dreamer when she awakens. The pregnant woman has difficulty understanding why she should choose this time of supreme intimacy with her mate to hark back to loves of long ago, or else to fantasize about new dream lovers, celebrities, or seductive strangers.

The Masterful Magician.   Erotic dreams are more likely the larger the mother-to-be gets; they tend to occur most often during the final three months. Like most dream themes, however, they may surface at any time during the pregnancy. This one is from Joan's first trimester:

> I am in bed with an old magician; he does a masterful job of
> bringing me to a climax. I never expected he would have such a
> great touch!

The reasons for erotic dreams in the pregnant woman are as varied as the women themselves. Nevertheless most mothers-to-be share a concern about their changing figure and its effect on their sex life. Intercourse is necessarily more awkward during the final months of pregnancy. Many couples are fearful of hurting the child within the womb and so curtail their usual activity. Deprived of her accustomed regularity or intensity of sex, the expectant mother sometimes compensates for it in her dreams.

Beyond whatever physical deprivation they may feel, pregnant women often feel insecure about their continued attractiveness to men. Gripping furniture for support in raising or seating herself, her ankles swollen, the mother-to-be finds her body increasingly difficult to maneuver. She sometimes feels less comely as a woman. Her dreaming mind offers reassurance in the ecstatic lovemaking of sexual dreams. Sensuous dreams are fairly common during pregnancy.

In addition to the pregnant woman's concern about her attractiveness and to feelings of sexual deprivation, she may have erotic dreams that are stimulated by the increased blood flow to the vaginal area, the swelling and sensations that become stronger in the genitals as her pregnancy progresses.

Joan may have dreamed about the masterful magician for one of these reasons. She might also have been portraying sexual climax as a metaphor for the climax of bearing a baby. In her middle thirties, Joan had postponed childbearing to near the comfortable limit. Her husband, formerly married with several offspring, was not eager to add more. Joan might well not have expected this great touch to her life.

A few pregnant women dream of former lovers because something is missing in the romantic relationship with their husbands. Such dreams may even indicate unfinished business with a youthful love. Few married women maintain a liaison with a lover while pregnant; the sensual dreams of those who do may express a wish to be with him more often. Unmated mothers-to-be understandably yearn for a supportive, affectionate relationship; their dreams may provide compensation. Sexual dreams in the pregnant woman may also be a response to the increased fullness in her genitals.

Mostly, however, erotic dreams during pregnancy simply offer the comforting reassurance, "Don't worry. You see, you are sexy, alluring, and lovable."

The "Other Woman" Beckons.   Sometimes the expectant mother finds herself tortured by nightmares that her husband is having a love affair. Or she may picture strange women propositioning her man.

Such dreams also express a sense of insecurity about holding the husband's love and attention through a time of great change. The pregnant woman has a realistic sense of vulnerability. She is more dependent than ever upon the goodwill and support of those around her, especially her husband's. She may fear his loss.

Unfortunately, for a few women these fears prove true, as they did for the heroine of Nora Ephron's autobiographical novel *Heartburn*. [24] The husband, who frequently feels neglected while the wife is preoccupied with their forthcoming child, sometimes chooses to philander during his wife's pregnancy. Needing attention, he seeks it elsewhere. Under such circumstances the pregnant woman faces a complicated situation that usually requires professional help.

For most women, happily, the insecurity is unfounded and passes. In fact many women find that going through the experience of preparing for and giving birth to a child bonds her and her husband in a deep way. Those pregnant women who understand the husband's tendency to feel neglected will find ways to include him in preparations for parenting.

The Husband as Helper or Handicap

Every couple has mixed feelings about each other. A woman and man living in daily intimacy are bound to have occasional conflicts that have repercussions in their dreams. When they are feeling intimate and loving, this, too, finds dream expression.

Most of the time the pregnant woman's mate is simply present in her dreams. The participants in Maybruck's study depicted their husbands in 24 percent of their dreams; usually they were merely on the scene, neither actively helping nor harassing.[25] Joan's husband, for example, appeared in 27 percent of her thirty-three pregnancy dreams.

Excess Baggage.   In most of these dreams Joan's husband simply accompanied her, as he did in a dream of visiting a bookstore, entitled "Here and Now." In an early pregnancy dream he assisted her:

> I am lugging around heavy baggage, several items, and so is
> John [her husband]. I put one bag inside the other and offer this
> to John. He takes the doubled-up bag, thus lightening my load
> considerably.

Joan thought that taking over the extra bag might symbolize John's plan to take over the whole wage-earning "burden" for several months after the baby was born. Here the baggage, which often refers to weight gain in pregnant women's dreams, appears to refer more to financial burden. Joan's husband was to carry a "double load," and she felt grateful.

Clutching Her Purse.   In a few dreams Joan's husband evoked ambivalent responses or outright anger and misery. At the end of one of these,

> . . . Later I am wandering around dark streets, clutching my
> purse. I meet John again in a bar under the theater. He tries to
> explain what is happening in his head, but I cannot listen. I am
> crying too much. I wake in deep sadness and frustration.

Joan must have been experiencing some tension in the relationship with her husband when she had this dream. Although her prevailing feeling is tearful distress—revealed in the fact that the environment was so dark and in her fear of losing her valuable purse—her husband did find her and tried to communicate. Actions of this sort reveal positive elements at work even in nightmares.

Husband Sick and Dying.   Leah, when she was about five months pregnant, had some nightmares about her husband. In one,

> My husband is dying of a dread disease. He has a really good
> attitude, very positive. I am sad for him, that he is going to die.

Then I realize it's contagious, and that means I will die, too, and so will the baby. I wake up with a terrible headache.

During the day Leah had been worried about her husband's safety while he was out sailing. On one level her dream probably reflected that waking concern. However, her husband was quite well, while Leah herself was experiencing some uncomfortable symptoms with her pregnancy.

At this time Leah was bothered by headaches at the end of each day's work. Her dreaming mind probably made an association between the discomfort that she was experiencing and the idea of fatal illness. In their caricature mode, dreams sometimes liken pregnancy to a disease. Soon Leah depicted herself as the one who was ill.

Sick and Unloved.   A week or so later Leah commented, "The last two nights I've had dreams that were so bad, I didn't want to write them down." All she could remember of one was:

My husband doesn't want me anymore. I am sick and he doesn't care. It doesn't matter to him.

Leah went on to explain, "I woke up feeling miserable. I don't recall the details now because I didn't record them, but the feeling was awful, like I used to feel when I broke up with a boyfriend."

Husband Goes Berserk.   In yet another dream of the same time period Leah dreamed:

My husband is a crazy person. He talks about killing people. I don't believe him, at first, then I do. We live in the house my parents lived in. Here I am with this maniac, but he has a dependency on me. I know he won't hurt me, but I can't react like I want and tell him to get away. I have to sneak out, and he comes after me.

These dreams sound on the surface as though Leah's husband is behaving badly toward her. In fact he was loving and patient. It was she who was extremely sensitive, in need of abundant attention, and finding herself yelling at him to reduce her tension. She felt pressed and resisted going to work; there were demands she had to respond to and didn't want to deal with. The house in her dream is one associated with a difficult aspect of adolescence, thus a fitting setting for a disturbed dream.

When a person attributes to other people behavior and feelings that originate in the self, psychologists term this attribution projection. People often project in their dreams as well as when awake. Leah is dreaming of her husband as sick or in trouble, when it is she herself who is distressed.

In Big Trouble. This explanation became clear in Leah's case because a couple of nights later she dreamed:

> I am Oliver North's assistant. I am in a room full of high
> school people, in a cafeteria. I am eating and looking through
> North's papers. On a stage there is a skit taking place, but
> nobody is paying attention. The players say, "Look, you have to
> pay attention." But nobody does, so they stop. North shows me
> all this s__t I have to sort out, things to unravel. The
> entertainment is mad. They want to be appreciated, but I have
> to unravel the problems of life.

Here Leah is expressing her need for attention and her difficulty in handling things more directly. Oliver North and the Iran-Contra hearings were much in the news at the time of this dream. Leah's main association to North was, "He's in big trouble." She went on to elaborate. "He screwed up. I feel a little compassion for him because he's taking the brunt. He has to keep a lot of things organized and sorted." Each dreamer, of course, would have his or her own associations.

For Leah, North in her dream symbolizes a person in trouble who has to "unravel life problems." Casting herself in the role of his assistant in this dream, she must work to organize and sort everything out. High school was not a happy place for her. In her dream language, then, Leah is saying, "I can't even focus on the entertaining part of being pregnant (the skit). I have to deal with too many complexities (the paperwork). I'm in big trouble (like North is). I want people to give me their attention and recognize my situation."

These two themes—being ill and being in trouble—are only one side to Leah's pregnancy dreams, as we will see. When she feels pressed, overtired, and fed up with work, themes of being in trouble arise; when she has headaches or other unpleasantness from her pregnancy, dreams of illness are likely to occur; when she feels sensitive and neglected, ambivalent dreams about her husband unfold. Yet there are other times when her dreams are full of happy expectation. Dreams show our momentary moods.

Other pregnant women in my study portrayed conflicts with their husbands by storms, natural disasters, or other catastrophes. The expectant mother needs to keep in mind that dreams overdramatize; a small fuss with a mate can cause a dream earthquake. The images in dreams depict how the dreamer feels at a moment in time—the following night can be full of joyful imagery.

In positive dreams about husbands, pregnant women saw themselves being rescued from danger by him, helped over obstacles, or being treated with great tenderness and affection.

If you are pregnant, you can expect your dreams to echo all the nuances of your constantly changing relationship to your spouse. Being pregnant brings out special needs. Your dreams will show you where your feelings about your husband are at the moment, reveal areas that need working on together, and sometimes soothe and nurture you when you most need loving care. Sharing dreams with your husband can be a good way to stay in close communication about your emotions as you go through the experience of pregnancy side by side.

Whose Life Is This, Anyhow? Relationships With Mothers

The Dreamer Gains Control From Mother.   When a woman becomes pregnant, old emotions about her mother resurface—anger, affection, guilt, jealousy, dependance, and the need to be a separate individual. At the same time, especially during her first pregnancy, a woman begins to experience directly what her own mother has gone through to produce her. She gains a new appreciation of what is involved in bearing and raising a child.

In some ways, therefore, the expectant mother feels more understanding and tolerant of her mother; in other ways former resentments reawaken. Her mother becomes the model to react against or to copy. The mother-to-be may still feel like a child herself; fears of being overwhelmed, inadequate, or too immature to have a child are common.

Pregnant women dream about their mothers according to their various feelings about them. Good mothers, bad mothers, and indifferent mothers abound in dreams. Fathers occasionally make dream appearances at this time, too, but their role is less striking, probably because they are less of a role model. Van de Castle estimates that in the dreams of pregnant women a ratio of five mothers appear to every one father.[26]

Maybruck found that her pregnant subjects dreamed about their mothers in 14 percent of their dreams,[27] a somewhat lower percentage than most studies report. The roles that the mother played varied from being confidante and helper to being an outright villain. She observed that her subjects who had mothers living nearby were more likely to dream about their mothers as allies; those whose mothers lived farther away tended to have more anxiety-provoking dreams about their mothers.

In Control of the Steering Wheel.   Some pregnant women dream of their mothers in different roles on different nights, as Joan did. In one dream she was a young child; her mother let her down, leaving her deeply disappointed and bitter. In another dream her mother helped her prepare food and take out the trash. In yet another dream Joan displayed a discernible shift in her ability to cope regardless of what her mother did:

> I am in a small plane with Mother flying over the Hawaiian
> Islands/Columbia River. She is at the controls. I tell her to fly
> more slowly, but she speeds up instead. Finally I gain control of
> the plane and I turn it around.

The person at the steering wheel of dream vehicles always indicates the aspect the dreamer feels is "in control" of life at the moment. Joan might have been dreaming about her actual mother or of the "mother quality" within herself. In either case she has made rapid strides in sensing her capability. From the "disappointed child" of an earlier dream, she has become "pilot" in control of a plane. She has actively succeeded in achieving her needs and determining her own direction, instead of passively accepting her mother's control and feeling frustrated. Dream behavior of this kind suggests a corresponding growth in maturity.

On the whole, when pregnant women dream about their mothers, they are trying to find an answer to the question "How much do I want to be like my mother?" The mother serves as a role model to rage against, to emulate, or to modify.

The Flying Pogo Stick.   The whole issue of being in control of one's life becomes important to the pregnant woman—whether or not her mother appears directly in her dreams. Leah, for example, pregnant for the first time in her early thirties, was about five months along when she dreamed:

> I am at a beach where there are lots of people. I see something
> and very intentionally walk toward it, making my way through
> the people and kids. It is a mechanism, a kind of pogo stick,

with a place to put my hands and a place to stand on. I step onto it and begin to move it around to get the feel of how to operate the mechanism.

Then I am flying up in the air. People, kids, are below me playing. I see houses right by the water, people working, a lot of activity. At first it's kind of adventurous feeling. I'm interested in looking at all that's going on below. I see a client I had a lot of trouble with milling around on the beach. Birds are flying on the same mechanism.

Then I observe I'm getting way too high and I feel scared. I don't quite know how to operate it. I call out, screaming. My husband shakes me awake.

Leah went on to draw me a picture of this flying pogo stick and explain the very delicate, vulnerable mechanism that operated it. At first she was having fun in her dream, perhaps corresponding to the adventure of pregnancy. She was rising above her problems, represented by the troublesome client left behind on the beach. However, she soon felt she was moving too high, into an area where she didn't "know how to operate," and she panicked. Pregnancy can give many a first-time mother the feeling that things are out of their control. Luckily many gain confidence in the process, as Joan did, taking over the controls from her mother. For many women pregnancy becomes a final step in the process of growing up.

During the second trimester, therefore, many of the pregnant woman's dreams center around the following:

Dream Image	*Probable Stimulus*
Animals	Awareness, concerns about unborn child
Her husband	Mirror of ever-changing relationship
Her mother	Old conflicts; new hopes for own motherhood
At a steering wheel	Wishing to be in control of her life

The Expectant Father's Dreams During the Second Trimester

The Family Ghost.   At the same time that the mother-to-be is dreaming about the topics listed above, the expectant father's dreams are becoming less dominated by sexuality and more protective and nurturing. Nat, the husband of one of the participants in my study, was very involved with his wife's pregnancy; during her second trimester, he dreamed:

> I am sitting talking to my [deceased] grandmother, who is
> reclining on a couch. I tell her all about the baby. I notice how
> very thin my grandmother is, a skeleton with just light skin
> over her bones. It's okay. I know she is dead. It feels good to
> tell her about the baby.

In the same way that being pregnant stirs up a woman's feelings about her parents, the expectant father may find himself thinking and dreaming about his family of origin. In this case Nat wishes his beloved grandmother were able to share in the new development in his life—the continuity of her family.

Giant Lobsters and Alligators.   Larry may have been feeling more threatened by the impending birth of his wife's baby. When Eva was about twenty weeks pregnant, Larry dreamed

> I'm in a market. The store manager is in a wheelchair. In a big
> tank, twelve-foot lobsters are being kept. Suddenly a
> twelve-foot 'gator jumps out of the tank and leaps eight feet in
> the air.

The alligator, Larry told me, is a "slithery, unpredictable reptile with big teeth." Animals with big teeth, we have said previously, usually represent a threat of danger. The store manager, confined to a wheelchair, was described as a person who "should be in control, but is not." The tank containing the aquatic creatures probably represented the womb containing the fetus. Larry's imagery suggests he was coping with some angry feelings at the time of the dream. It was undoubtedly he, symbolized by the store manager, who felt out of control of the situation. Perhaps his dream was expressing momentary unvoiced resentment about the forthcoming baby because the same night Eva had a very happy dream.

The Pregnant Father. In a dream when his wife was six months along, Nat saw himself being pregnant and giving birth:

> I am nine months pregnant. I feel a drip of water on my ankle and say, "Oh, it's time to go to the hospital."
>
> Next I am in the hospital, on a bed with my legs up in the air, relaxed, with no pain. But the baby is right at the exit, and I can't get it out. I give it back to Sonny [his wife]. She has to take over.

Obviously Nat identified with his wife. He recognized her unique role as childbearer, yet wanted to share the experience.

Expectant fathers often feel left out at this stage of their wife's pregnancy. More than half of Siegel's subjects dreamed of being excluded and alone.[28] Dreams like Nat's can help bridge the gap. Confiding troublesome dreams with one's mate can overcome feelings of loneliness and keep partners in touch, while trading happy dreams can increase confidence and intimacy.

The Third Trimester of Pregnancy: Dreams of Babies and Journeys

Dream Babies: The Unborn Child's Gender, Looks, and Personality

"What will my child be like? A boy? A girl? Will my baby resemble me or someone else in my family? What name will be right?" These and similar questions fill the minds of parents-to-be.

Modern methods such as amniocentesis may unveil some of the mystery of the unborn child for a few pregnant women, but expectant mothers still have much material to dream about regarding the infant in their wombs. Researcher Robert Gillman analyzed the dreams of forty-four pregnant women, comparing them to the dreams of a group of nonpregnant college women. He found that 40 percent of the pregnant women dreamed about babies, whereas only 1 percent of the nonpregnant group did so.[29] Such dreams about the child may begin as early as conception; they tend to accelerate during the last trimester.

Pink, Blue, or Yellow Booties?

The pregnant woman is making many decisions during the final three months of her term. She is usually preparing clothing, choosing a layette, and setting up an area for her baby with crib and changing table. Choices between pink for girls and blue for boys or "unisex" yellow or white or pale green must be made.

Some mothers feel quite certain of the sex of their forthcoming child based upon their dreams. Meg, at forty-one, was sure that her child would be a girl because her dreams were filled with dancing, quite different from her earlier pregnancy with a boy; she later birthed a girl. Mindy, at twenty-nine, dreamed from the outset that her first baby was a boy. So did her husband. During the first trimester he dreamed:

> I am at work when an announcement comes over the
> loudspeaker saying that Mindy has just given birth to a boy, so
> I'm a father. I feel really happy.

This couple was obviously in tune with their wishes; sure enough, their dreams of a son came true.

Lucy, however, was equally certain that she would birth a boy. Already the mother of two girls, she wished to complete her family with a male. Throughout her pregnancy she dreamed of having a boy; she also carried the weight of her unborn child more to the front, unlike her former pregnancies, giving her the impression—from folklore—that her child would be a son. Two weeks after having given birth, she smilingly told me, "Well, I was wrong. It's another girl!"

Sometimes the pregnant mother's dreams about the sex of her child are vague. Maggie, in her thirties, described this dream she had when eight months pregnant with her first child:

> I am running in a meadow and feeling ecstatic. It is an idyllic
> scene—my dream of motherhood. I wear a flowing gown. I can
> see the back of my child skipping before me happily. I can't tell
> from the back whether it is a boy or a girl. I always want to
> know, but it is usually masked in my dreams.

In an effort to verify how frequently pregnant women correctly sensed the sex of their unborn child, Maybruck asked her subjects about predictive dreams.[30] She found that 50 percent of the expectant mothers whose dreams she investigated had accurately dreamed of the baby's sex. Since the chances of having a child of either sex are also fifty-fifty, these subjects—as a group—predicted no better than chance.

A few pregnant women, however, had highly prophetic dreams involving details of their labor or delivery, such as going into labor early, the exact date of a premature labor, being put into a community labor room, the specific circumstances under which the waters broke, having an unplanned cesarean section, developing toxemia, and so forth. It would seem that at least some women have a keen ability to anticipate their future.

The Face of the Unborn

Pregnant women, Maybruck found, see their babies in about 15 percent of their dreams.[31] Other researchers have reported an even greater number of baby dreams during the third trimester. Sometimes the expectant mother depicts the appearance of her forthcoming child with surprising accuracy. Ginny, for instance, commented,

> I give birth to a baby daughter with black curly hair like her father and blue eyes like mine.

Ginny went on to explain that she did give birth to a daughter looking exactly like the baby in her dream. Later, when the girl was older, her hair changed to straight brown hair like her mother's and her eyes darkened to brown like her father's.

Some mothers-to-be worry in their dreams that the child might inherit an undesirable characteristic. Donna's concern was that the child in her womb might have his father's eyes, one of which wanders. She dreamed:

> The baby is born and he has bizarre eyes. It is very frightening.

Not long afterward Donna gave birth to a son with perfect eyesight. She had been expressing a waking fear in her dreams. In his study of the dreams of mothers-to-be, Gillman found that 12 percent of his pregnant group dreamed of crippled and deformed infants; most of these women had feelings of apprehension in their dreams.[32] Among Maybruck's pregnant subjects, 40 percent of their dreams were nightmares.[33] Pregnant women can take comfort in the fact that nightmares are typical during this time and rarely contain prophetic material.

Cassie, when she did not yet know she was pregnant, dreamed:

> I give birth to a baby girl. Her eyes are round like mine, but
> the shape goes downward, like my husband's. She looks peculiar.

In fact Cassie had just conceived when she had this dream. She actually wanted to have a girl, but worried that it would resemble her husband, since, she believed, girls often favor the father, boys, the mother. Her husband's looks, she told me, would be better for a boy. This dreamer, too, was undoubtedly picturing her concern.

Leah anticipated the appearance of her child with more delight:

> I'm having a sonogram [something she had already done].
> Instead of being all cloudy like it is, it's absolutely clear, like
> Kodak film, in color. I can see our baby girl, and she looks just
> like us. She has my eyes, all dark and sparkly, and my husband's
> cute little bow mouth. She is a mixture of us in miniature. It's
> so thrilling!

Like most mothers-to-be, Leah had been wondering what the baby will be and what it would look like. In another dream of the same night she saw herself playing with her baby, who this time was a boy she was dressing in cute clothes. Dreams offer a chance to check out one's child in imagination.

Some pregnant women seem to have extrasensory communication with the child in their womb. Such dreams are less frequent than the common dream themes of pregnancy, yet when they arise, they are emotionally powerful.

Jill, for example, pregnant for the first time, dreamed that the child crawled out of her womb. The tiny creature capered around her mother's body playfully, then, like a baby kangaroo returning to its pouch, went back into the womb. Jill felt she had experienced a direct contact with her child.

Leah tried saying to herself, "I want to communicate with my child," as she was falling asleep. She imagined a big building, a medieval church or school. She saw a little girl standing outside in a costume, a kind of brown robe. The child was about four years old, with straight bangs, brown hair, in a short pixie cut with a slight wave.

Leah continued speaking to her drowsy self, "I want to see that," and brought the picture in closer:

"Yes, I'm your daughter," the girl said. I feel happy about it. "My brother's coming soon," said the child. "Not too soon, I hope," I replied. I was afraid to ask her about twins.

Leah told me that when she began this imaginary process of communication with her baby, she was conscious but by the end that she was asleep and dreaming. The decision to interact was deliberate; the imagery seemed to run on its own. Leah had earlier dreamed about having twins, and her physician suggested this possibility, hence her concern in the dream. She eventually gave birth to an adorable daughter.

Pregnant women who are curious about their child might enjoy setting up a dream as Leah did to see what happens. Another woman who was already the mother of twins told me that throughout the pregnancy she kept dreaming of things in pairs or doubles. She was aware of the fact that twins were forthcoming. It would be intriguing to investigate whether there is imagery characteristic of women about to give multiple birth.

Among the women in Maybruck's study, a few reported dreams in which their stomach became transparent so that the mother-to-be could look inside.[34] Like Leah observing her baby in a clear sonogram, the dreamer could observe the face of her unborn child. Such dreams left the woman with a feeling of deep joy and serenity.

Name, Name, Who's Got the Name?

Pregnant women spend many waking hours contemplating possible names for their forthcoming babies. Harmonious fits to the last name are weighed as carefully as the child's future education. Family names and fashionable ones are tried on for sound; parents consider how a given name may be susceptible to teasing or to a sense of uniqueness in the years ahead. Meanwhile, in sleep, dreams suggest, and sometimes demand, other choices.

Convinced that her unborn child was a boy, Bettine selected her favorite name: Benjamin. Her dreams thought otherwise. The night she had made her final decision, she dreamed she held her baby in her arms. Suddenly he spoke to her, saying, "Mommy, please don't name me Benjamin. Please!" Needless to say, Bettine awoke somewhat shaken. When she eventually gave birth to a baby boy, she decided to call him Christopher instead. Although she still preferred the name Benjamin, she hesitated to go against such strongly expressed wishes, from wherever they derived.

Kit, who was pregnant with her first child when we spoke, dreamed of having a baby girl who announced to her, "My name is Shannon." Awake, she confided, "It's a pretty name, though I never would have thought of it. Maybe I should name her Shannon if it's a girl." Kit did in fact birth a little girl. She named her child Jenna, which was not too dissimilar from her dream name.

When Sue was pregnant with her first baby, she had struggled under the double handicap of severe financial problems combined with the discovery of her husband's unfaithfulness. This strain brought her near the breaking point. One night in her distress, Sue knelt at the bedside to pray for help. When she retired, she dreamed:

> I give birth to a baby boy. He tells me that his name is Jesus Christ.

Sue felt comforted by this dream. By the time her child was born, she had forgotten this dream and christened the little boy Jeremy Clark, using family names that she liked. Months later, in reading over her journals, she encountered her dream. Startled, she realized that she had used the same initials, J.C., for her child's name. Her dream baby may have symbolized the birth of her hope.

Although Sue's marriage eventually collapsed and she endured many difficulties before remarrying happily, her son remained a source of solace. A grown man today, she describes him as "very spiritual," in the mode of his dream introduction.

In olden times American Indians regarded names given in a dream as having "power." Today's parents, too, often find that names arising in a dream hold special resonance for them.

Archetypal Dreams

Some pregnant women nearing their due date find their dreams taking on a mystical character. The word *archetype* derives from the Greek word *arch*, meaning "chief." It was originally used by Plato to describe ideal forms thought to exist in the mind of God. Centuries later Jung used the word in his psychology to indicate "inherited tendencies of the human mind to form representations of mythological motifs."[35] Dreams with archetypes impart a feeling of awe to the dreamer.

Baby From an Ancient Couple. Jayne Gackenbach-Snyder, current president of the Association for the Study of Dreams, for example, told me that when she was almost eight months pregnant, she dreamed:

> There is a young couple who are virgins, and they wend down
> to the river, where he kisses her. As I watch all this, I see the
> images of an older couple (they are from an ancient culture,
> perhaps Egyptian). They have a baby and they put their baby
> into the young woman. I don't know if the young man and
> woman make love or not.
>
> Then it is twenty years later, and I am taking part in the dream.
> I am on some sort of world council—we need to decide
> whether or not to change Easter from the day it is to a new
> day that the populace wants. The new day is the birthday of the
> infant. . . .
>
> A spaceship is collecting information on the configuration of the
> planets and stars to deliver to the council in pictures. I am to
> get it and deliver it to the council.
>
> The rest of the dream is taken up with this attempt. People
> keep trying to steal the film from me. It is in film cannisters in
> a clear liquid that when you put something in it, you can't see
> there is something in it.

In Jayne's multifaceted dream, she supported the decision to change the date of Easter. (The word *Easter*, by the way, derives from the name of the Anglo-Saxon goddess of spring, *Eostre*. [36]) Jayne's dreaming mind felt that she was participating in an event of universal import—a kind of resurrection. As a creator of a new life, she may even have felt goddess-like herself.

Familiar symbols of pregnancy overflow: the spaceship, as well as the cannister of film, probably represent the expectant mother's body; the clear liquid is likely to symbolize the amniotic fluid in which the fetus floats—as yet undeveloped, like the precious film. Jayne, in addition to her demanding post as a university professor, editor of several books on lucid dreaming and role as president of the Association for the Study of Dreams, does photographic work, so the film in her dream is a symbol from everyday life.

The archetypal flavor of this dream comes from the young virgins, the couple from the ancient culture who give the child as a gift to the young woman, the configuration of the planets and stars, and the idea of changing the date of the "rebirth" of Christ to the birthday of the infant. This dream left Jayne with a special feeling of being part of a sacred rite.

Gift of the Precious Cradle.   Leah had a similar experience during her third trimester, when she dreamed of a "metaphysical delivery person" from outer space who brought her an expandable cradle worth $2,500:

> . . . First I tell him I don't want it. I didn't order it. He explains it is really special. It converts into a dining room table and a china cabinet. He begins to sway me. I need more space for dishes. Also I feel sorry for him, for all the trouble he's gone to. I write him a check for $210, adding extra for the delivery. It really was coincidental. He just didn't have my name right.

Leah really enjoyed this dream. She had had several earlier dreams about basinettes decorated with skirts; these were usually small, inadequate ones—one the size to hold a cat, one that was a soap dish, one a shoe. In waking life she had already purchased an expensive designer crib, so her dream was speaking symbolically. As we discussed these images, it emerged that they represented for Leah the small "space" in her life that had been allotted for her baby. So far, work had taken up most of her time. She wanted to have greater room to concentrate on her pregnancy. The "metaphysical delivery person" in her dream brought her exactly what she needed—more space for the baby.

The expandable cradle opened up into a dining room table that Leah defined as a place for families, a place to receive nourishment, to gather around to communicate. A china cabinet was, in addition to being something she needed, "a place where fine things are kept." Dishes, an item Leah loves, are "used for providing the food we need. I have many beautiful dishes that were wedding gifts." The cradle in the dream was very costly, beyond what she could have afforded to order; the price she was charged was an amount she could manage without strain.

Putting these symbols together with the action in Leah's dream, we see that she was "coincidently" receiving, along with her baby, the nourishment she so badly wanted: she was creating a family that would increase communication and provide for her needs. Her dream seemed to be giving her permission to expand the role of her forthcoming child, as if it were a valuable gift from another time and space.

Just as the dreams of holy mothers, which were described earlier, inspired the dreamer to feel that her child would make a special contribution to his or her world, so, too, modern women reenacting the childbirth ritual of time immemorial may feel significance in their pregnancy dreams. They are participating in an event of monumental import in their lives.

The Final Weeks of Pregnancy
Destination Unknown

During the last weeks before her term ends, the pregnant woman turns inward. Her obsession with the forthcoming child becomes all-consuming. Withdrawing her attention from those around her is essential preparation for the task ahead: birthing a child. It requires all her concentration to gather inner strength. For she is truly alone.

The woman about to give birth to her first child is face to face with the unknown. There is no way out now. No one can do it for her; she cannot call in sick; she cannot make an excuse; she cannot plead prior commitment. She must labor and bring forth to become complete—woman with child. Small wonder the prospect shakes an otherwise mature and skilled adult.

In olden days the risk was far worse. But even with modern methods and loving support, childbirth often seems overwhelming. So, for a multitude of expectant mothers, dreams of journeys arise.

Foreign Travel Required. Five days before Cheryl gave birth to her son, she dreamed:

> There are two mixtures of dreams, and they come out as one. In one of the dreams Bill [her husband] is getting onto a bus. He comes and tells me, "Some woman keeps trying to sit next to me." I reply, "Well, tell her to go away!"

> In the other dream that is happening at the same time, I am boarding a plane, going off to a foreign country somewhere. I am pregnant but not so much as I am. I have a bad feeling, like I don't really want to go. I am not an exile. People are escorting me. I have to go, but it is not for long.

> On the plane are all these movie people, not superstars but people you recognize from adventure stories. It is confusing, like *Raiders of the Lost Ark*. They are talking about scripts. There are

these things that look half like people and half like apes. Both dreams go on at once.

Cheryl's double dream expresses an emotion women typically experience toward the end of gestation: reluctance to confront the unknown. For a first-time mother, giving birth is rather like a journey to a foreign country. Face to face with her own adventure, she has an important starring role, even though it is with reluctance, since she must go alone. The fact that Cheryl knows she is "not an exile" in the dream and that the trip is "not for long" suggests that her attitude is basically positive and that she expects to return safely.

The half-person/half-ape creatures aboard the airplane undoubtedly represent the unborn fetus. The airplane itself can be seen symbolically as the enclosing womb, the "mother ship" where this dreamer's adventure and confusion take place.

Simultaneously Cheryl's husband is on a trip, too. But the dream likens his journey to a bus ride rather than an airplane flight, underscoring the difference in their roles, or "scripts," at this stage. Cheryl's associations to the annoying woman who kept trying to sit next to her husband led her to comment on the reduction of sex during the last few weeks to avoid injury to the baby. At almost nine months pregnant, she was sensitively attuned to wanting her husband's complete attention. Although their journeys are of a different nature, they are parallel.

No Substitute. Joan depicted the common journey theme of the last trimester in a different way. When she was six and a half months pregnant, Joan recorded the last entry in her dream journal prior to the birth of her daughter:

> I am offered a chance to go to Hawaii for one or two weeks
> with two friends and my sister. I queue up in the Seattle line,
> while they stand in the Portland line. Just at the last minute I
> remember that I am committed twice a week to teaching a
> geometry class. Thinking it would be impossible to find a
> substitute, and not right to just cancel class, I decline the chance
> to go. It would be nice, but the timing is not right.

For Joan, who travels frequently to Hawaii in her waking life, the trip is seen as a pleasurable distraction from work. Here she makes the decision to keep her commitment to do a job. It is too late to cancel.

The pregnant woman who accepts that no one can act as a substitute for her in childbearing, that there is no longer a way out, that she must do it herself—that woman has reached a milestone in becoming a mature woman.

Giving birth, in addition to being depicted as a journey or an important commitment, may be represented as traveling through tunnels and corridors or the bursting of great waters.

The Waiting Game.   Sonny, in a dream reported only three days before her son was born, anticipated the pleasures of being able to have and hold her child:

> In the dream we have had the baby two days ago. I have gone somewhere while Nat [her husband] is taking care of the baby. He's taken it to a sporting event, with a bunch of his buddies.
>
> I go to the stadium. It is a beautiful, sunny day. There is a combination football and baseball game going on. One team wears bright red uniforms and the other yellow.
>
> I walk up the bleachers, and Nat tells me where the baby is. I look behind where there is a cabanalike arrangement with three babies. It is easy to pick out mine. It is time to feed the child, and so I nurse it. I think that I must ask Nat how the labor went. He comes in. The whole dream has a feeling of great happiness.

Sonny said that this dream left her with a marvelous aftertaste of joy. "We had had the baby and adjusted. Nat and the baby were able to function without me, and yet I was important and needed to feed it."

There is much symbolism in this involved dream of Sonny's, but the main points here are the sensation of joy at having finished childbirth, and the complex game. Sonny explained that she likes football and knows a lot about it. Baseball she sees as boring; it takes a long time before anything happens. Thus the combination is something with interesting elements but that requires a lot of waiting before there is any action—just as pregnancy does. The ball in the game probably represents the fetus, whose motion will determine the end of the "waiting game." Being nine months pregnant, Sonny expresses here a wish for her baby's arrival and the pleasure she anticipates. The game is not over, and the outcome remains unknown.

Trial Runs

Sometimes the pregnant woman depicts labor and delivery directly, instead of in symbols. Such dreams often give vent to fears or hopes for the forthcoming experience.

Giving birth to a child today is far safer than it was during the last century, when many women died from infections. Nonetheless, the first-time mother goes into the unfamiliar experience with a degree of trepidation. Some women develop extreme fear of the possibility of pain during labor, not realizing that they can learn to reduce (or even, some say, eliminate) discomfort by training.

The experienced mother may find labor dreams realistic, yet unalarming. Bonnie, for instance, was seven months pregnant with her second child when she had a lucid dream:

> I begin going into labor in my own bed. There are no doctors
> or hospital. Feels so real. "Oh, my God," I think. "I'm in labor.
> I don't want to go into labor now. It's almost three months too
> early." Then I realize I'm dreaming, and it changes from a real
> sensation to a more dreamlike one. It isn't painful, just routine.
> The dream continues, and the baby is born. My husband isn't
> there until the end.

Bonnie thinks that she was experiencing "false labor" pains, which triggered her extremely realistic dream. Indeed it may be that labor dreams are stimulated in part by the periodic tightening of the uterus during sleep. These contractions are the so-called Braxton-Hicks contractions, which are believed to strengthen uterine muscles in preparation for labor.[37]

A research team headed by Ismet Karacan recently demonstrated that healthy young women who are not pregnant have rhythmic contractions of the uterus during REM sleep.[38] They found that the uterus contracted from one to three times each minute. Contractions during REM were more often than during any other sleep stage, especially deep sleep, and they were also more numerous than during the waking state. This constant activity of the uterus may be a kind of exercise to prepare it to meet the demands of menstruation, reproduction, and labor. Researchers also think that these contractions keep the uterus healthy, preventing atrophy, because their frequency decreases after menopause.

Compared with the nonpregnant woman, the pregnant woman has even stronger regular contractions of her uterus, which intensify toward the end of her term; it is these contractions that probably stimulate the woman's dreams of childbirth. Most of the pregnant women in my study related dreams of labor during the last trimester.

Dress Rehearsal. The pregnant woman's dreams of labor may help prepare her by a kind of rehearsal. Such dreams are a sort of "practice run" for the physical separation of mother and child at birth. Pregnant women can accelerate the positive effect of their dreams, as we will see.

Early in her pregnancy, delivery is often visualized in the expectant mother's dreams as a baby who just "pops out" the way Mindy's and Donna's did. Later on, her dream scenarios about delivery are more realistic, sometimes outright terrifying. The pregnant woman who understands what can be done about these can actually benefit from dreams of childbirth. Researchers find that women who are assertive or even aggressive when they are threatened in nightmares have a different, and usually more positive, childbirth experience than those who remain passive victims.

When a pregnant woman is having a nightmare, she can react in one of two main ways: she can accept the threat, allowing herself to be victimized by the villain or danger confronting her; or she can assertively stand her ground. This self-assertive behavior may range from simply refusing to be victimized, to yelling, to aggressively counterattacking, to outsmarting, to befriending the dream villain. The key element is action.

Taking Action. By becoming an active participant in the dream, the expectant mother mobilizes her resources. Maybruck, a childbirth educator who currently runs a consulting service in San Francisco for pregnant women, advises her clients to behave assertively in their nightmares.[39] She also tells groups that she leads on the topic of preparing for childbirth to suggest to themselves before sleep, "Even if I have a nightmare, I will not be victimized." Actually writing down, before going to bed, "I will not be victimized in my dreams tonight," helps imprint this intention. Guidelines for dreaming such as these can profoundly effect the dream plot, especially when reinforced by discussion with peers.

These concepts are based on Maybruck's findings in her study of pregnant women. After the participants in this study had given birth, Maybruck observed the length of each woman's labor and placed her in one of two groups: those who had labor of ten hours or less and those who had labor of eleven hours or more. (Current estimates of average length of labor for a first-time mother are about twelve hours.) She noted that thirty-six of the women labored ten hours or less, while thirty labored eleven hours or more.

One of her sixty-seven subjects, who had induced labor, was eliminated from these measures.

Nearly half (40 percent) of the over one thousand dreams reported by the pregnant subjects were nightmares—defined as a dream containing fear, terror, or physical or emotional pain.[40] In some of these nightmares the dreamer was victimized; in others she behaved assertively when threatened. Maybruck scored the nightmares as containing assertiveness or not, depending on whether the dreamer defended herself.

When short- and long-labor groups were compared to nightmares of being assertive or not, Maybruck found that there was a strong connection between the dream content and the length of labor. Among the women who had short labor, 94 percent had been assertive in at least one of their nightmares. Among the women who had long labor, only 30 percent had been assertive, whereas the remaining 70 percent allowed themselves to be victimized. Self-assertion was connected with shorter labor.

Breath of Life.   Of the women who participated in my study, Leah had a threatening labor dream just two days before her delivery:

> I go into labor. I'm walking around the living room and I feel the baby's head come out. I reach down and pull it out—it's a little girl. The head is flesh and skin, but the body is just bones.
>
> I'm worried. "This is not right." I blow on the baby or breathe on her, and she fills out to normal-looking. I'm still kind of concerned she will stay okay when I wake.

Although "blowing" or "breathing" on a newborn may be a simple behavior, the important fact is that Leah took action in her dream. In so doing, she transformed the dream baby. Subsequently she gave birth to her first child—a girl—in a short, six-hour delivery.

Taking charge, having confidence in herself, and being in command may help a woman to cope with the job of giving birth to a child. If you are a pregnant woman who finds herself being threatened in a nightmare, you may find that, instead of letting yourself be victimized, assertively reacting to the situation will make a profound difference. Not only will you feel better about your nightmare, you may actually help make your labor shorter and easier.

In an earlier study, researchers Carolyn Winger and Frederic Kapp reported that women with anxious nightmares about childbirth seemed to have shorter labor.[41] In retrospect, perhaps it was primarily those women who were active in their nightmares who had shorter labor. We cannot be sure, because exact dream content was not recorded in this study, only the presence or absence of nightmares.

The whole issue of taking action in nightmares is extremely important, especially to the pregnant woman, for whom a more active stance may be connected with shorter and easier labor. Hopefully future investigators will explore this issue with care and map it clearly.

Meanwhile the expectant mother has nothing to lose and potentially much to gain by becoming an active participant in her bad dreams. By telling herself before she falls asleep, "If I do have a nightmare, I will not be victimized. I will remember to cope with the threat," she may change her waking experience as well as her dreams. She can choose for herself the means to deal with danger in her dream. Some mothers prefer questioning the villain, instead of assertive counterattack, asking, "What do you want?" One theorist suggests surrounding the threatening image with golden light.[42] Whatever her mode of response, if the dreamer takes action to cope with the threatening dream figure, she may accomplish more than banishing her nightmare; she may help herself to function better in her task of labor.

During the last trimester, a pregnant woman prepares for the adventure of childbirth in dreams, including the following:

Dream Image	Probable Stimulus
Large animals or buildings	The enlarged fetus
Newborn baby's appearance	Expectations or fears about baby
Communication with the fetus	Wish to know forthcoming child
Great waters	Anticipation of breaking of the amniotic sac
Details of labor and delivery	Hopes or concerns about experience; Actual early contractions
Journeys	Fear of the unknown
Rituals, ceremonies, holidays, birthdays, rites	Celebration of the joy of birth

The Expectant Father's Dreams During the Third Trimester

The father-to-be anticipates the birth of the child in his dreams, just as his pregnant wife does. The fathers-to-be in Siegel's study often dreamed of finding babies or of being given them, sometimes during elaborate ceremonies or rites. While the woman may be dreaming of the work involved in her forthcoming labor, her mate may be concentrating on dream celebrations of the baby's birth. Dreams of this kind indicate acceptance and valuing of the child whose arrival is imminent.

Once again, sharing dreams during the last months of pregnancy gives a couple a unique way of staying in close contact with one another. Partners can better understand the feelings of their mates by hearing their dreams. Dream sharing can intensify their intimacy, making the adventure mutual.

Does the Fetus Dream?

While expectant mothers and fathers are dreaming throughout the pregnancy, expressing their hopes and fears for their developing baby, the fetus may be dreaming, too.

From the thirty-second week of pregnancy onward, tiny rapid eye movements (REM) can be monitored from the brain of the fetus. The brain of the unborn child is active during the third trimester, with slivers of memory being laid down. Scientists think the minute mind is exercising; it wakes and sleeps and has REM.[43]

Of course we cannot say whether the fetus actually dreams during REM, but perhaps there are sensations of stretching legs and arms, or of sucking, or of hearing sounds reverberating through the watery environment.

Could the fetus already be in synchrony with the mother's dreams? We know from studies comparing nursing mothers with bottle-feeding ones that infants who breast-feed synchronize their sleeping and dreaming (or REM) cycles with their mothers'. Many a mother has noticed her nursling awaken just as she does.

Couples who are in close harmony tend to synchronize their sleep and dream cycles, too. In some families, mother, father, and baby may be dreaming together. Perhaps they are communicating in ways yet to be discovered.

The "Golden Child": Symbolism in Dreams of Pregnancy

Women who are pregnant frequently dream of giving birth to a child, but so do those who are not pregnant. Whence do such dreams emerge? What do they mean to the nonpregnant dreamer?

Sometimes the answer is that the nonpregnant woman is stimulated by ovulation. Donna, for instance, tells me that she always dreams about having a baby when she is ovulating, her wish to have another child being greatly enhanced by her current physical receptivity. A week later she feels much more practical, thinking of all the reasons it would be inadvisable to bear a second child at present. Many women, like Donna, dream of having babies when their bodies are ripe to do so.

Dream Pregnancy as an Escape. Beyond the physiological basis of ovulation, dreams of being pregnant or of giving birth have a powerful symbolism.

The woman who has never delivered a child may dream persistently of this event as her "biological clock" runs out of time. A woman's capacity for childbearing is limited to roughly thirty years, from about age fifteen to forty-five, plus or minus five years at either end. It is well known in our culture that the risks escalate for the older mother carrying a first child. In their mid to latter thirties most women must make the decision to proceed if they are to experience motherhood. The question becomes "now or never."

Nina, who found herself facing this dilemma, had put off childbearing until she was at her outer biological limit. Having had a teenage abortion, she focused all her energy on a business career. In her late thirties she was a successful businesswoman. Recently a crisis had arisen at work that shook her to her dream roots. She had a violent argument with an employee, culminating in the need to fire the girl. That night Nina dreamed:

> I am pregnant, about to have a baby. I don't have my bag
> packed, but I am not upset. I go to the store to buy a
> nightgown and other things for the hospital. I feel happy.

The pleasant emotional tone of the dream was partly a compensation for the distress experienced in the daytime. Beyond this, the imagery suggests a need to prepare for an important new development. As we spoke, Nina said, "Maybe getting pregnant is a way to get out of this nightmare of business. It's a good excuse—the only one." It emerged that she had been in conflict about whether to quit business and have a baby or not. Thus the pregnancy in Nina's dream was partially an escape route.

One month later Nina's business problems had been resolved. The following month, she announced with twinkling eyes, "I'm pregnant!" Her dream had been more than a way out; it was also a reality. She had in fact been pregnant during the time of her dream without intending it, knowing it, or expecting it. Her dream was both symbolic (an escape from work) and realistic (she was pregnant).

Other women have described to me dreams of becoming pregnant when they had difficulty at work; these dreamers did not turn out to have conceived. Having a baby seems to remain in the back of women's minds as an alternative to a career situation when it becomes frustrating.

Dream Pregnancy as Idea Development. At times dreams of giving birth to a child do not represent a wish to do so nor a respectable means of escape from a difficult situation. Pregnancy and childbearing dreams can symbolize the "birth" of a new idea or project.

German sculptor and graphic artist Käthe Kollwitz recorded in her diary:[44]

> I repeatedly dream that I again have a little baby and I feel all
> the old tenderness again—or rather more than that, for all the
> feelings in a dream are intensified.

It was a "very fine" period of her life when she was deeply engrossed in her work—her dream babies were probably art projects.

Val, a contemporary professional writer, who has never birthed a child, was hard at work on a major magazine piece when she dreamed of being pregnant; it was her "baby." Writers of both sexes have often likened their large-scale projects to the "gestation" of a child. A book grows from an inner fantasy to manifest form, one that requires laboring over, nurturing, and delivering. Creative artists in all fields compare their products in paint, stone, or song to their "children." The woman who undertakes an important project—mother or not—may well dream of her creative "child."

The Divine Child. For Jung, dreams of a child are archetypal.[45] The birth of a new potential within the dreamer, the potential of wholeness, the Self, the unity of opposites, a transformation of the personality—these are some of the terms Jungians have used to interpret the child in a dream. In ancient alchemy the product of the elements mercury and sulfur formed, it was said, the philosophical gold or "golden child." Jung likened this to the divine child that appears in dreams.

From a biological point of view a child is truly the "union" of opposites of his or her parents. The mother and father, female and male, are brought together in a new way in their baby. Psychologically a child may symbolize reconciliation between two conflicting attitudes: spiritual versus material ideas, work versus play, love versus hate—such opposites may find a resolution that is symbolized by the dreamer as a newborn child.[46]

In the dreams of a woman who is not pregnant a special child may symbolize her inner development. Thus a woman may dream of giving birth to a child when she is undergoing change, as Miriam did just before her birthday:

> I have a baby on my own, and she is so smart. She has her full intellect in four days. I am so proud of her.

Miriam, who was not yet a mother, felt her life was changing in significant ways at the time of this dream; her bright baby was her own inner growth. Cheryl, several months after her son was born, dreamed of looking into a bedroom in her girlfriend's house:

> The baby girl is lying on the bed playing with her toes. She is counting them. "One-two-three-four-five. They don't know I can talk!"

Cheryl, too, was discovering new capacities within herself in her role as mother and growing rapidly. The mystic child who speaks to us in dreams, who solves riddles, or who grants wisdom is the internal sign of healthy new potential.

Whenever a woman dreams of a child, new life stirs within her. Pregnant or not, mother or not, to dream of a miraculous child speaks of new life born within the dreamer.

Career Dreams

I am flying on a mattress high above newsmen and crews
who are scurrying around frantically. I feel wonderful!

Bibi, a television news producer in her middle thirties, was feeling frustrated
with her job when she had this dream. After she had invested a great deal
of effort in an innovative show, it had just been canceled. In her aggravation
she was seriously considering leaving the news department. The mattress,
Bibi told me, was "like a magic carpet, a magical way to transport yourself
above and away." In her dream Bibi had made the escape she longed for;
it felt wonderful. She left the frantic folk far below as she soared off to better
horizons.

Our dreams monitor our work, as well as every other important area of
our lives. They comment when we feel we are working too little or too
much; they alert us to excess stress; they point out imbalances between our
jobs, our love lives, and our parenting; they clarify our conflicts. They tell
us when, like Bibi, we want to change something or to escape. Have we
been neglecting our responsibilities? Have we been procrastinating on an
important job? Our dreams will jangle our minds to alertness more insist-
ently than an alarm clock. Of course we must know how to listen. If we
turn them off, they will keep replaying the same message in different pictures

210

until it penetrates. Dreams may jolt us into focusing or even inspire us to clever innovations.

For many a modern woman, her career is primary. But even happily married homemakers find that skills enabling them to contribute to the family resources give them valuable feelings of self-esteem. Some women remain in difficult marriages because of their economic dependence. In these cases work skills may play a crucial role in a woman's emotional health— they may offer the only route of escape. Here, too, our dreams can elucidate issues. Ability to work well helps us feel good about ourselves.

Neglected Work in Dreams

The Unattended Garden.   Sheila was curled under her comforter on her king-sized bed after her husband's early-morning departure when she began to dream:

> The garden is full of weeds. I have so many to pull to set it
> right. I wake with a startle, realizing I must get to work
> immediately.

In dreaming of her neglected garden, Sheila realized she needed to get to her task of meeting a deadline. Since she worked at home, it was easy to let time slip by—but not without a dream reminder.

The Forgotten Baby.   In the midst of working on this book I was forced to stop writing for several days because of jury duty. The night of the first day I was able to return to work, I dreamed:

> I am in a busy downtown area. I go into an open-front store,
> rather like an arcade, and stroll around. Then I enter an elevator
> and go to different floors. As people get off, I notice, to my
> surprise, there is a baby carriage sitting there beside me
> unguarded. I wonder who could have left it.
>
> Something prompts me to lean down and touch the covers.
> There is a wriggling, and suddenly a baby begins to cry. "Good
> God! The baby's still inside!" My mind races with what to do.
> I know we were at the fourth floor. Perhaps that's where babies'
> clothes are.

I wonder whether to pick up the crying infant; I press the
control button to return to the fourth floor in hopes the mother
will return there. At that moment the doors open again, and a
woman [resembling a colleague who is a working mother] gets
in and says with tremendous relief, "He's still here!" I'm
relieved, too.

When I woke up from this dream, I asked myself, "What important thing
have I forgotten?" Knowing that the image of a baby represents a precious
new life for me, as it does for most dreamers, I knew I must have forgotten
something. The answer was easy: I felt guilty for not having put enough
hard work into the writing project on my first full day of being free of the
court. I had forgotten my "baby," that is to say, my book, leaving it
"unguarded." The working-mother colleague in my dream is an especially
diligent worker; even she could momentarily forget her child.

"But why the fourth floor?" I asked myself. Numbers in dreams always
have some relevance. Suddenly I burst out laughing: "It's my *fourth* book!"
The metaphor of the forgotten baby inspired me to get back to work
promptly the next morning. Dream reminders like this one can give us the
nudge we need.

Overwork in Dreams

The Steamroller. We usually know when we are overworked; we
hardly require a reminder. Nevertheless our dreams sound a warning when
the pressure becomes excessive.

A few months ago, after several days of writing a special speech on
children's dreams for a national conference of pediatricians, preparing new
slides, and getting little sleep followed by a long, tiring day of travel to
another city, I had a vivid warning dream:

Everywhere I go, construction is under way. Sidewalks are
being repaired. Many things are dug up. As I walk, I reach a
point where I can't comfortably continue and will have to go a
different way.

I see Ian [a hard-working and efficient man who has done recent
reconstruction outside our house] leading a team of workers.

They have filled a large section of the path and are just coming to the end. They are moving a huge steamroller that requires keeping up the pressure until the last minute to get the space filled properly.

Ian is encouraging the team, "Push! Push! Push!" They make it to the very end. He, exhausted by the effort, collapses to the street. I bend over and embrace him, pressing my cheek to his, saying, "Ian, would you like to come inside for a minute and rest and have a cool drink?"

This dream, just like a sign in big red letters, spelled danger. "Slow down. Ease off or you'll be in trouble," it shouted in dramatic pictures. I must "go a different way," "rest and have a cool drink," or I would soon collapse like the dedicated work leader in my dream. I was glad to see the "teamwork" in my dream that enabled the laborers to "construct" the new program and "keep up the pressure, to push" to the end, but I had to stop now. Accordingly I treated myself gently, resting, eating well, taking pleasant walks, and reading light books for the day that preceded my presentation. Refreshed, I found that a quick review was ample to do a good job and I returned home well.

Stress Levels.   Some jobs, like my own, are only stressful periodically; others exert a consistently high level of stress. Recently a group of British investigators from the Manchester University's Institute of Science and Technology rated 150 different occupations on a stress scale of 0 to 10. According to their findings, miners were at the top of the scale with a stress score of 8.3, whereas librarians scored the lowest level of stress, at 2.0.[1] How would you rate the stress level of your job?

Whatever tension your work entails, your dreams will offer clues when limits are exceeded. Each dreamer has individual symbols for overwork or excessive stress. One man who was overexerting himself dreamed of a huge prehistoric beast hauling a heavy burden. He felt himself to be a "beast of burden" whose work "load" was too heavy. Tidal waves are among the work-stress dreams most frequently relayed to me. Dreamers who feel "overwhelmed" by work—or some other personal situation— often picture this condition by images of inundation with water. We have seen how some women dream of becoming pregnant when they want to escape dissatisfaction with work.

Learning to recognize and heed one's own symbols for overwork can save dreamers much future aggravation and may even help evade illness.

Work Conflicts in Dreams

Dreams about work often contain both elements of the dreamer's conflict, just as in my dream about the sidewalks there was active "construction" taking place that contrasted with the exhaustion of the leader. Looking for both positive and negative aspects in the dream pictures will help you to comprehend the nature of any conflicts.

The Enormous Meadow.   Author Diane Wolkstein describes a dream she had while involved with a major project.[2] She was working with Samuel Kramer, an expert on the ancient culture of Sumer and translator of several cuneiform texts dating back to 2000 B.C. As a folklorist and storyteller, Wolkstein was seeking an ideal story of her namesake, the Moon Goddess, Diana.

In collaboration with Kramer, Wolkstein spent two years condensing sections of his translations, adding, editing, and seeking to perfect the text. She says,

> During the first year I dreamed of being in an enormous green
> meadow and having the task of cleaning the meadow blade by
> blade.

In Wolkstein's dream each translated word was likened to a single blade of grass. Her task of polishing single words was depicted as cleaning individual grass blades.[3] Although the green color undoubtedly represented growth, the imagery suggests that she felt overwhelmed, at the moment, by the details of her job. The positive growth depicted in the green meadow was in conflict with the enormity of her chore. Perseverance prevailed.

The book that resulted, co-authored by Wolkstein and Kramer, is *Inanna, Queen of Heaven and Earth: Her Stories and Hymns From Sumer.*[4] The story itself contains a five-part "great dream," the dream of the shepherd-king Dumuzi. Surely this author's own dreams were helping her carry forward and complete the task that at first seemed overwhelming.

Colliding Fighter Planes.   Hilda elected to picture a stressful situation in her work as armed combat. She was preparing a large conference where several "star" performers were to appear when she dreamed:

> I am flying a small plane, enjoying myself. After some time I
> encounter some fighter planes doing wild acrobatics. Then more
> fighter planes come along. I know they will crash.

Sure enough the fighter planes collide, and the whole
atmosphere shakes with the repercussion. I feel the shock waves
and wake up in distress.

Awake, Hilda realized that she was anticipating the "clashing of egos"
of the stars on her program. Her conflict became literal in the dream. When
working by herself, she was able to "fly" along happily. When she encountered the wild "fighter" airplanes—the people who wanted to be most
important—the trouble began. The ensuing crash and "shock" was rough,
but it was important, I pointed out, that she survived in the dream. As we
discussed this symbolism, she pondered, "So what should I do? Keep a
straight course?" In fact Hilda was able to follow her own good advice.

The Gestapo Intrudes.   Fiona began having nightmares while she was
undergoing heavy stress in her profession, being harassed and literally threatened with legal action by a man who wanted her position. In one of these
her husband ran off with another woman. In actuality her second husband
is devoted and supportive, but Fiona was shaken in every area of life by the
trouble at work. In another dream just prior to the return of the troublesome
man after an absence,

> I am with my daughter, who is very young again, in a familiar
> house when someone arrives—it's the Nazis. One has a grizzled
> beard [like the threatening man at work]. We only have a little
> time to gather our things. They're going to relocate us.
>
> My daughter is oblivious, blissfully picking out treasures to take
> along, while I am aware of the danger.

We see here Fiona being "persecuted." The "relocation" in her dream refers
to her waking fear of losing her job; the "Nazis" represent the threat she
feels. In her dream language Fiona is saying that her more childlike aspect
(symbolized by her daughter) is unaware of the full extent of the danger
(blissfully loitering). Dreamers often use their youngsters to represent the
more vulnerable part of themselves.

House Under Attack.   A few nights later Fiona dreamed:

> I am at my mother's home with two members of my staff who
> are my friends. Chuck [the difficult man] drives up.

He tries to get in the front door of the house. He's pounding
and shaking the door on one side while I hold it on the other.
Somehow I can see him, but he's not aware I'm holding the
door. I am in between him and these vulnerable people. I must
protect them. I feel responsible. I wake up in a sweat.

Fiona described this dream as "real disgusting." She saw her mother's home,
where the dream was set, as "a haven." The threatening man from work was
depicted as trying to break into this sanctuary. The vulnerability of her staff
members in this dream paralleled the blissful unawareness of her daughter
in the earlier dream. Although Fiona felt responsible for these people in
waking life, they also probably represented the vulnerable part of herself
that was in danger, as well as themselves.

The positive sign in this dream was Fiona's active struggle to keep the
door shut—an improvement over accepting the persecution of the Nazis—
that suggested she would fight for what she believed. Progress of this kind
over a series of dreams indicates that the dreamer is rallying her resources
to cope more effectively while awake.

The work situation eventually resulted in the man's position being dissolved and Fiona's being restructured. The aftershocks are still reverberating
in Fiona's life, but she is grateful for a period of stress reduction. Her anxiety
about the situation, along with her nightmares, were becoming too much.
Many women share her feeling of emotional vulnerability at work, despite
actual superior capability. Dreamers who are attacked may find that counterattacking the dream villain, as Fiona did, helps reduce their waking
anxiety.

Falling Behind at Work

Losing Precious Time.   Dreams have layers of meaning. Bess, in her
middle forties, had a frightening dream the night before our interview:

I get into a taxicab. The driver seems way up ahead of me and
I'm far in the back. Two kind, handsome men get in where I'm
sitting. There is some amorphous sexual stuff with one of them,
the younger one, I think. There is no fear and no morals about
it.

Then they turn into two mafia-type men. The older one starts
to rip me off, taking my watch and other valuables. The

cabdriver tries to help, but he's too far away, and I don't put up a strong enough protest. They get out. I feel turned on and ripped off.

Although she was a very attractive woman, Bess had never married. Her work had priority over the men in her life. Recently she had been dating two men. One was an old boyfriend, with whom she had broken up the previous summer; the other was farther away, and she only saw him occasionally. As Bess was explaining this, she said of the old boyfriend, "My priority is work, and he wanted more. Like my mother, he made me guilty I didn't give more. There is something evil and sinister about this quality in him."

These facts of Bess's life made much of her dream apparent. She was traveling along in life (as she was in the cab). Since someone else was at the steering wheel, she probably felt that she was not wholly in control. The two men that joined her were her current lovers, the older one probably symbolizing her "older" boyfriend, that is, the one she had dated for a long time. At first they seemed delightful, but after the sexual encounter they turned dangerous, like the "evil and sinister" quality in the former boyfriend.

"As I was on my way to meet you," Bess said, "it suddenly came to me what the dream meant. They were stealing my precious time!" Bess had made the association between the stolen watch in her dream and her fear of losing valuable time by investing it in a relationship. In fact her watchband had recently broken; this became a dream symbol for lost time. She felt simultaneously "turned on and ripped off" by her relationships.

As we continued to talk, it emerged that Bess had come down with a life-endangering disease a few years ago that required a hysterectomy. Her physicians told her that she was now clear and she looked well, although her energy was still limited. The image of "losing time" took on an extra dimension. This dreamer was not only struggling with the conflict between the time needed to succeed in her career versus the time invested in her emotional relationships, she was also concerned about her long-term health—"How much time do I have in the future?"

Missing the Bus. Kay, a charming woman in her thirties, had originally trained and worked as an anthropologist. Later she took a job working for a brand-new magazine. When the first issue was due out in a week, Kay fell ill with the flu. Lying in bed at home, she dreamed,

> A bus is pulling away from the curb. Inside I can see all the
> older people at the magazine. I grab ahold of the pole. The bus
> is going swiftly while I'm trying to keep up and get inside. I
> don't know if I make it, but I'm hanging on.

Dreams about missing a bus, train, airplane, or ship usually refer to the dreamer's sense of missing out on an opportunity. In this case Kay saw the older people at her work as having an advantage; they were more experienced at the job than she; they had a head start. If, through being sick, she was unable to complete the work she had to do before her deadline, she might fall behind and lose her chance. When we spoke, Kay still had a bad cough, but she was back on the job and doing her best. The fact that this woman "hung on tightly" in her dream augured well for her future good performance.

Singing the Wrong Role.   Ada, in her fifties, is the wife of a famous performer. Her "job" is to accompany him on his worldwide tours, arranging all the details in order to spare him, and to appear at his side at social functions, being endlessly gracious. An opera lover, she confided one of her worst nightmares:

> I have to sing a role in *La Traviata*, or else in *Don Carlos*. I
> don't know the words. My husband assures me he will help me,
> but I feel very upset.

Ada thought this dream came simply from tension. Questioning her, I found that she disliked the music of Verdi, the composer of these operas, finding it "too marchlike." In her dream language, then, she was being forced to play ("sing") a role that was unpleasant to her. Her husband was supportive and encouraging, but she still found it distressing.

Dreams of performing poorly, I notice, often occur when people feel they are "being tested" and fear they might fail. For many dreamers this emotion takes the form of being back in school taking an examination. Hunting for the right room, not knowing the answers to the test, not having read the books the test is based upon—these are typical dreams when dreamers are facing a life situation that makes them feel as they used to when they were in school.

People who actually perform in waking life—singers, actors, speakers, musicians—will often dream of themselves doing poorly in their work setting when they sense they are being "tested" in waking life. Musicians tell me dreams of arriving late for the concert, not knowing the piece, forgetting the score, or sounding a wrong note. Singers describe singing the wrong role, not knowing the music or lyrics, being in the wrong costume, and so forth. Actors dream of forgetting lines or of speaking the wrong part.

Whenever we face a difficult situation—a lawyer presenting a summary of a complex case, a publicist giving a presentation to a tough client, going out on a blind date, having the boss to dinner at home—we are likely to dream of being tested or performing. We feel our behavior is going to be judged. When we do poorly in our dreams, our waking expectations are likewise low. When we sail along in our dreams, feeling great and doing well, our waking hopes are also high.

Sexual Discrimination at Work

Pigs at Work. Women still have an uphill struggle to succeed in the world of work. Victoria, like Fiona, found herself in a power conflict with a male colleague. Although she was nominally in charge and he held a lesser rank, the man frequently managed to take over meetings. As her frustration grew more intense, Victoria dreamed:

> I literally pick up Hugo [the man she is in conflict with] by the
> lapels and scream at him, "You sexist pig!" I continue to berate
> him in a loud and obnoxious way.

When she awoke, Victoria felt a little uncomfortable by her uncharacteristic behavior in the dream; at the same time she felt as though "I got something out of my system." A dream of this type can help the dreamer discharge some of the accumulating tension. At the very least it vents anger in the dream. It may even give the dreamer confidence enough to act forcefully— in appropriate ways—so as to improve the frustrating situation in waking life.

The Isolated House. Ruth, in her forties, is a lawyer. Her career and her relationship to her husband are central in her life; she has no children. Recently Ruth dreamed,

> The house that I used to live in, in the South, is relocated in
> Dallas, Texas. Instead of all the other houses like ours around it,
> with shutters and roses, dogwood and azalea, it is surrounded by

all these high rises. It is isolated. There is an ugly schoolyard
covered with concrete nearby. I wake up crying.

As Ruth and I discussed this dream, it emerged that it dealt with her sense
of sexual discrimination at work. First I had her describe the house in her
dream. It was "just the way houses should be, traditional, with sloping
roof, a screened porch, an upstairs and downstairs, a yard, a garden." Next
I asked her to tell me about Dallas. Of course, her answer is idiosyncratic.
Each dreamer needs to make her own associations to the elements in her
dream to get at its meaning. For Ruth, Dallas, a city she had only been
to once for a conference, had "nothing old, there's no history. It's the
grossest place I can think of." Ruth was very interested in architectural
preservation, so the location of her favorite house was in a repellent setting in her dream.

Then I asked Ruth to tell me about high rises. These, she explained, were
"big, refrigerator, cratelike objects made of concrete." Concrete, she felt,
was "hard, cold, impersonal, and unapproachable. No grass can grow on it."

Putting Ruth's associations to her images back into the dream, we see that
she was saying, "I find myself (symbolized by her past home) with the things
that make life worthwhile and beautiful (the traditional features, the flowers), in a place that is hard, cold, and impersonal (among high rises and
concrete). Nothing can grow. I feel overshadowed and isolated." No wonder this dreamer woke up feeling sorrowful.

Ruth's large law firm consisted mainly of men; all the partners were male.
These were probably symbolized by the "high rises" in her dream. Although
she was a long-term member, her rank was lower than it should be, as the
little house was in comparison to the high rises of her dream. She felt treated
"like an employee." The few other women in the firm were younger and
less committed. The gap Ruth felt between herself and her associates was
reflected in the isolation of the house in her dream. The issue was an
emotional one that Ruth would have to act upon to improve the current
situation somehow or reestablish herself elsewhere.

Notice how the concept of rank in the business is represented by relative
size in this dream: the *high* rise versus the *small* house. This is a characteristic
device of the dreaming mind to symbolize importance by means of literal
size.

Several months after this dream, Ruth told me with pleasure that she had
been made a partner in her firm. She had gotten a "raise." Hopefully her
new position will provide opportunities for productive new growth.

Losing the Game. Dreams can point out potential threats we miss while awake. Theresa had just finished collecting the material for her dissertation for a doctoral degree. After she met the core faculty who would be working with her, advising her how to proceed and judging her final product, she dreamed:

> There is a volleyball game. The players include the core faculty, my sister, and myself. The men have a volleyball, while the girls seem to be batting tins, like hubcaps, back and forth. They are not doing so well.
>
> I think I can do better than the others but find that one of the men from across the net is standing on my foot. How can I move?
>
> I decide to sit down. Someone says, "Oh, Terri, get up!" I do and then I'm able to move around.

Theresa was much puzzled by this dream. Part of it she understood. She was "playing ball" with her faculty. The men who were "playing the game" of academia (symbolized by the volleyball game) had better equipment than the women. This imagery obviously mirrored the sexual discrimination she felt existed at her university.

But the faculty member who was hindering her from movement in the dream seemed to be extremely helpful in waking life. In the course of the next two years, however, he continually changed the rules by which Terri and other students were to work. She found herself enormously frustrated but was finally able to extract in writing his conditions for satisfactory completion. Then she swiftly fulfilled the written rules and was awarded her degree.

"In the dream I had sensed the trouble he would give me," Theresa explained. In retrospect, the dream image of the man stepping on her foot to prevent her movement had become a reality. Her dream also anticipated that by responding to the urgent plea to get up, she would be able to move, to "play the game" and "win." Taking action in appropriate ways solves more than dream problems.

Office Flowers. In Japan, a large number of young women are hired by businesses to serve tea, make photocopies and answer the telephone. Called "office flowers" these women work only a few years and are expected to retire upon marriage or the birth of their first child.[5] Until 1966, retirement at marriage was compulsory. American working mothers have more choice—and also more conflicts.

Working Mothers' Conflicts in Dreams

Climbing the Ladder.   Our wishes for success take many forms in our dreams, according to the strength and direction of our goals. Desire to excel often involves the imagery of height, as we saw with Ruth's "high rises."

Joan, when her baby daughter was about one month old, had serious intentions of returning to her profession. Simultaneously she had become emotionally invested in her affectionate care for her infant. Her concerns were portrayed in this dream:

> I am waiting in line to climb a public ladder and look at the
> view of the city. I climb up with my baby and find, to my
> dismay, that her movements cause the ladder to sway
> precariously. I cry out for help, but discover that I can
> counteract baby's movements and stay relatively balanced.

Here Joan appears to wonder whether it is possible to "climb the ladder" of success while remaining close to her baby, indicating a work-child conflict; waiting in line probably refers to the delay in resuming her career. Ladders, high shelves, pinnacles of mountains—such imagery often reflects the "high goals" of the dreamer. Joan finds it difficult to manage, but discovers the way to "stay relatively balanced." This dream augurs well for Joan's ability to cope with family and work life.

The Tiny Basinette.   Leah, who was six months pregnant and still working full-time, was already struggling in her dreams with the same issue of work versus mothering. In one, for instance,

> I am in a kind of house-store on an upper floor shopping for a
> basinette for the baby. What we are looking at are basinettes
> about the size of a soap dish or the size to hold a cat. My Mom
> and Dad are there. I am perplexed. I don't know what to get.
>
> I hear my husband's voice talking on the telephone one level
> down. I go below to ask his help. I pass my two nieces, who
> are on the next floor, taking a nap. No beds, they're resting on
> the floor. They ask, "Can we get up?" "No, not yet," I tell
> them.
>
> When I find my husband, I am very upset to discover that he is
> on the telephone making appointments for me. "Oh, no!" I
> wake up in distress.

When I asked Leah what she thought was going on in her dream, she replied, "It's so apparent. There's a real tug-of-war going on inside me. Consciously I want to stop work. But I get a lot of satisfaction from it. I love doing it and get lots of positive comments. But I don't want to listen to other people when my child is at home."

The dream depicts Leah shopping—an activity in dreams that usually suggests making choices. She is looking for something she actually needs—the basinette—but in the dream her options are too small for a real baby. This indicates that Leah feels her baby is not being given enough room in her life. Her nieces, who are special favorites of hers, do not have beds either. When she turns to her husband for help, she finds he is committing her to work activity rather than assisting her in creating space for her baby. Leah must feel that her husband is more supportive of her working than of her mothering. The conflict, however, is mainly within herself.

Leah spent the next few days after this dream "doing a lot of nesting"—she cleaned out her closet, her drawers, and entire bedroom with great vigor. Then she went out and bought a large, expensive basinette. Perhaps this behavior was her way of making sure she has the space in her life that she wants for her child. A few weeks later she dreamed of having delivered a cradle that could expand into a whole dining room table and china cabinet. Awake and asleep, Leah was clearing room for motherhood.

In a recent study of families with dual careers, psychologist Betty Allen-Trembly found that the majority of women she interviewed have a profound feeling that they should "do it all."[6] Their ideal was to provide a nurturing home, doing as much as or more than their mothers had done, plus succeed in a career. These women often felt inadequate when they were unable to handle both home and work life comfortably. Such conflicts are bound to be revealed in women's dreams. It is important for the dreamer to realize when she is placing an overwhelming demand on herself.

Work is a more conflictual area for women than it is for men. Deciding whether to work or not; whether to pursue a career or simply take a money-earning job; whether to strive for creative work or accept a "practical" occupation; whether to try to juggle full-time work with full-time mothering; whether or not part-time work is more appropriate—all these are complex issues for the modern woman. They cry out for resolution. According to the United States Department of Labor, Bureau of Labor Statistics, as of March 1986, almost 55 percent of all women worked; about 45 percent of these had children under eighteen years old.[7] Current estimates indicate that 68 percent of all American women will be in the work force by the early 1990s. Women who work need answers.

The Closed Office.   My husband, who is a psychotherapist, tells me that his women clients are in much more conflict than men between taking practical, money-making jobs and doing creative work. This ambivalence was given dramatic form in a series of dreams by a woman therapist who participated in my study. Theresa was trying to decide whether or not to give up private practice for writing.

In her forties, Theresa had been practicing therapy for years. Her move to the Bay Area of San Francisco was part of her plan to switch her career to writing. She commuted for a period of time to her town of origin, where she continued seeing clients. During this time she began having recurrent dreams about her office:

> I will arrive and find that my office is closed. Or else I discover
> I have to share my office with other people. Sometimes I have
> no chair. At other times the office is inconveniently located
> down the hall. Once, when I get to my office, I find a
> stenographer's pool is set up in the midst of my things.

> Finally I am set up in a space outside of the building where my
> office actually is. I am with my husband and a group of artists.
> This feels like home. I woke up encouraged.

Theresa explained that the setting with the artists represented the more creative work she hopes to do. She was yearning to bring out the "artist" in herself. The fact that her husband was present in this same space suggested that she felt she will have more time for him as well as for the work that appealed to her more. She was "home."

Several of the women in my study who were having difficulty in their work described dreams of a similar nature to Theresa's. Some crucial change had been made to their work space—it was empty, had been cleaned out of essential equipment, things had been destroyed, or they had been moved elsewhere. Working women who find themselves having such dreams need to confront the situation seriously and reassess what they want from their careers.

Dream Clothing and Self-Identity

Business Suits Versus Housedresses.   Dream clothing—or lack of it—always makes a statement about some important aspect of the dreamer's emotion. Women, because they dream about clothing more than men do, are especially prone to express feelings by the style of their dream garb.

Sexual dreams are often populated with female characters in provocative garments; romantic dreams with ladies in beautiful gowns; household dreams with characters in aprons—or whatever the dreamer habitually wears doing household chores; spiritual dreams with women in flowing robes. Likewise women's emotions about work are frequently depicted by business suits. Men, by contrast, are more likely to "change hats" in their dreams, or to wear uniforms, as did the man who was feeling depleted by low energy and boredom when he dressed his dream men in army "fatigues."

The Straight Skirt. With her baby a few days old, Joan dreamed:

> I'm trying to put on a straight skirt (as in a business suit), but
> find it hard and uncomfortable to do so.

Her figure not yet back to her usual trim shape, Joan was saying more than something she already knew while awake. In dream language she was saying that the business role did not "suit" her at the moment; it would be hard to fit into it.

In another dream a few nights later, Joan wore "a bright red knee-length muumuu and a murky green knit or crocheted poncho" while carrying a portfolio to a school. In the dream she observed how these colors did not flatter her complexion. For Joan, the portfolio did not go with her casual, unbecoming outfit, suggesting she was grappling with the issue of business (represented by the portfolio) versus baby (symbolized by the at-home type clothing). Outfits that are mismatched, ill-fitting, or inharmonious suggest the dreamer is struggling with some aspect of self-identity.

The Pink Suit. Likewise Brenda dreamed of wearing a pink business-type suit. "It wasn't a bad suit, it just wasn't my style, didn't fit me, didn't bring out my good features." Pink was, she felt, the wrong color for a business suit; therefore she was wearing inappropriate and unbecoming garments.

Brenda and her then-husband shared a business they had created. "The marriage was the job; the job the marriage," she explained. For her, it emerged, the marriage as well as the job was "unsuitable." In fact Brenda separated from her husband—and the job—a couple of years after this dream. She was no longer willing to "wear" an inappropriate role in her marriage or her work.

The concept of "dress for success"—in which women are urged to outfit themselves like male power figures, in dark, severe suits—imposes a code standard that may not seem natural. Many working women feel they must sacrifice their femininity on the altar of their ambition.

In general, clothing in women's dreams symbolizes two facets: it reveals the dreamer's current feelings about her body; or it indicates what sphere she is identifying with at the moment. Women's self-concept is in the process of changing.

Changing Roles, Changing Dreams. A series of recent studies demonstrates this shift. As described more fully in chapter 2, researchers in Canada headed by Monique Lortie-Lussier, compared the dream content of women who were homemaker-mothers with that of working mothers.[8] The difference was striking:

....

Homemaker-Mothers' Dreams	*Working Mothers' Dreams*
More residential settings	More vocational settings
More familiar characters	More unfamiliar characters
More female characters	More male characters
More friendliness	More unpleasant emotions—sadness, anxiety, anger
More misfortunes	

....

The investigators concluded that dreams change with a change in the woman's role.

In a further study Canadian investigators compared the dreams of working mothers with the dreams of women students.[9] Equally demonstrable differences were observed. Of special interest were the findings that:

- Working mothers' dreams showed much more autonomy
- Working mothers' dreams had more male characters
- Working mothers dreamed more about their work, as well as their husbands and children
- Students tended to idealize the male, acting more friendly to him
- Students dreamed more about peers of both sexes and had more sexually seductive and marriage scenes

It may not seem surprising that working mothers dream differently from women students or from mothers who remain at home. The findings of these studies are important, however, because previous studies of dream content—often conducted with students—have reported women's dreams as uniformly similar to each other, in contrast with men's dreams. These former studies implied that dream differences were a result of inborn sexual characteristics. The Canadian studies show this conclusion may be wrong.

For example, most studies of dream content in the past found that women report an equal number of male and female dream characters, whereas men usually report twice as many male characters as female characters (about two to one).[10] This result is claimed to exist across all cultures and is often interpreted as a result of sexual difference, with women being more social and men being more competitive.[11]

In contrast the Canadian studies' observation that working women have more male dream characters, while homemaker-mothers and women students have more female dream characters, demonstrates that dream content may be, instead, a function of social role. The woman's daytime experience may be the determinant of the greater number of dream men, since women who work often have contact with more men than those at school or at home.

Furthermore the results of the Canadian studies show a higher level of hostility or aggression in the women's dreams—students, homemakers, and working mothers alike—as well as more themes of achievement and success than have been previously found.

Our dreams, it would seem, are a continuation of our waking lives. Our social roles impact our dreams. As women's social roles continues to change, so will their dreams.

Dream Inspirations for Work
Shapes and Colors

Whatever material fills our minds during the day finds its way onto our nightly dream screens. We may not recognize it until we learn to read our personal dream language, but it is there with fresh ideas, guiding or warning us about days past and days to come. Since I have written extensively about inspiration from dreams in my first book *Creative Dreaming*, I will only mention a few instances in which women have discovered concepts in their dreams that have enriched their working lives.

Ideal Marriage.   Dreams may inspire a line of work, as one did for Verta, a jewelry designer who models her own line of exquisite necklaces. Tall, slim, dark-haired, she is an admirable backdrop for the intricate garlands of colorful beads she devises. Verta tells me that her jewelry business began when she dreamed:

> My design teacher marries my spiritual teacher.

(This dream is described more fully in chapter 5, "Wedding Dreams.") The symbolic meaning of marriage in dreams—almost always positive—inspired Verta to unite two strands of her life in a deeply satisfying way. Instead of her interests in art design pulling her away from spiritual expression, Verta found a plan to integrate the two interests in a single activity. Weddings in dreams, for women who are not currently brides, usually represent the union of two formerly contradictory elements; they are a resolution of conflict.

Unique Pattern.   Dreams may offer a delightful new product, as one did for Monique. A dress designer who moved from France to the United States, she told me that one of her best-selling patterns came from a dream several years ago in which she saw the design—one she claims would never have occurred to her while awake—on display. Making it up soon after the dream, Monique found that the mode of cutting the fabric created a particularly flattering drapery, and she has made variations on the model ever since.

Setting the Scene.   Dreams may give the creative person the seed idea for a new project. Author Judith Guest described, in a published interview, seeing the young boy who became the protagonist for her popular novel *Ordinary People* sitting on steps in her imagination. Some of the conversations with his therapist, she says, she first heard in her dreams; like Robert Louis Stevenson, who devised "The Strange Case of Dr. Jekyll and Mr. Hyde" based on a couple of nightmare scenes,[12] Guest follows in a tradition of creative artists of all time. George Eliot obtained the title of her first story, "The Sad Fortunes of the Rev. Amos Barton," from a dream,[13] and Mary Wollstonecraft Shelley gleaned the concept for *Frankenstein* from a nightmare.[13] All dreamers can pluck from their dreams useful ideas for their working lives.

Blessing the Earth.   Dreams may help conceptualize the solution to a problem, as one did for me. I had just sold the idea for this book on the basis of a brief proposal; details of the contract were being discussed. Knowing that the book was going to be produced, I had to do some hard thinking about how to organize it, how to flesh out the proposal. I had started work on the first chapter without being sure of how to proceed when, toward the end of an unusual dream,

> I am a good spirit flying through the air. I am in a churchyard hovering in the air under stone arches that open to the sky above me and on all sides; below me is a burial ground. There are no markers on the graves, only a general sign for each section. The portion I am suspended above is marked TIL. I somehow know this means "girl" in some language [does it?]. It is as if a mass of people were buried here—perhaps a grave from a concentration camp.
>
> I am blessing the dead. I fly upright in a white ankle-length gown, barefoot, tilting slightly forward, my arms extended down with the palms parallel to the earth. From my palms stream energy. As I fly, I recite, "Til, Til, Til," as though blessing each individual buried child. Nearby lie buried women.
>
> When I have completed blessing the ground, I withdraw my hands inward to my own body. It feels very good to have made energy flow through them. I wake exhilarated.

Hands are particularly important to me. As a college student my long, tapered fingers got me well-paying jobs as a hand model; they are said to be beautiful. These days I create books or paintings with them.

The book I was writing at the time of this dream was not yet "brought to life"; it was "buried," concentrated, within primal soil. To "till" the earth is, for me, to prepare it for planting, to make it receptive to bringing forth life. To "bless" the earth, to pour energy into it with my hands, was conferring a kind of resurrection. The different sections of ground in the dream, one marked by the strange word indicating girl, another portion labeled "woman," and others, drew my attention, when awake, to the possibility of organizing the material around age, developmentally, rather than by issue. The dream provided an inspiration to tackle the work of creating a book, as well as a framework for the material.

Although my dreams are likely to offer me literary or artistic solutions to my problems, all dreamers have their own "graveyards" where ideas from their work can be brought to life. Dreamers who discover inspiration in their dreams dance with the shadow of great figures of the past.

Every woman, by using her dreams on a regular basis, can bring vitality to her daily tasks. Our nightly images show us when we are neglecting aspects of our work; they warn us when we are pressing ourselves beyond our capacity. In dramatic "movies" our dreams reveal our conflicts between work and parenting, between work and relationships, between competition and cooperation, between drudgery and creativity. They may point out a clever notion to apply to work or even signpost the path to a new career. When we work with our dreams, our life's work prospers.

Divorce Dreams

I am lying on my back in an endless sea, paralyzed with
fear that I'll drown. There's no land in sight, no airplane
or ship to be seen. I wake in great fear.

—Woman undergoing a divorce

Divorces do not happen overnight. Long before the tidal wave crashes into
married life, the wind blows, the waves whip, and the rain batters the dreams
of each partner. Women in my study described the ominous nightmares that
foreshadowed the death of their marriage, in some cases years before the final
break.

Gretchen, whose dream is described above, was tormented by her husband's request for a divorce. Although they continued to live together for
several years, Gretchen felt "lost." She found herself unable to carry on her
profession—one that involved writing at home. During this time she had
the above dream.

Gretchen recognized the connection between her feeling of helplessness
in the dream and her daytime feeling of hopelessness about the future. She
contemplated the symbolism, telling herself, "If I had started to swim, I
might have seen land, an airplane, or a ship." This idea, she says, made her

sense of paralysis in the waking state disappear. She understood she must start to "swim" to get rid of her fear of "drowning" within her marriage.

The very day following the dream of being in an endless sea, Gretchen began to write again. Looking back, she believes this dream not only helped her "keep afloat," it marked the start of positive growth. Despite the fact that the divorce eventually took place, she experienced herself as becoming stronger, a fact that also strengthened her work.

No Home.   This affirmative development growing out of the divorce required time and effort. After Gretchen's marriage dissolved, she continued to live in the house that she had shared with her spouse. One night she dreamed:

> Because of the divorce, I have to look for another home. I find a new development with attractive white houses where I would very much like to live. All the available houses, however, have an option on them already—by my husband or one of his friends. There is no house available for me.
>
> I have to look in what seems like a threatening area to find a place to live. I feel very frightened and cornered.

This dream impelled Gretchen to go into therapy. She realized the necessity of distancing herself from her past marriage along with the influence of her former husband. She needed access to the new "development" instead of continuing to live in fear (symbolized by the threatening area). With time, Gretchen resolved her problems and developed the inner capacity to cope successfully with her profession and to establish a new loving relationship.

Women who undergo the exceedingly painful experience of divorce— about 50 percent of all wives—hope it will eventually make life better. If we do not learn from the trauma of parting, we remain stuck, unable to embrace life with vitality. Our dreams can, as they did for Gretchen, help light our way forward.

Dreams of the Husband as Victim
"Why Don't You Just Drop Dead?"

Every wife has ambivalent feelings toward her husband from time to time—as he does toward her. Women in long-term relationships share much of the same patterns as married partners, so the concepts discussed here apply equally to them. I will use the terms *husband* and *divorce* throughout, but the statements apply as well to "long-term lover" and "separation." Separation from a live-in lover can be almost as piercing a crisis as divorce.

Within the most loving relationship, legal or not, an occasional bolt of lightning will flash. One husband, on his fiftieth anniversary, was asked by a reporter whether he had not contemplated divorce at least once. Purportedly the old gentleman, eyes atwinkle, replied, "Murder, yes; divorce, never."

During the moments of anger, bitter resentment, frustration, fear, or jealousy toward the spouse, our thoughts and dreams sometimes depict the unspoken words "I hate you. I wish you were dead." Like the impulsive child who stamps and rails against a parent, the partner yearns to be free from what is temporarily perceived of as a trap. Should the loved one actually die by accident, a profound guilt response arises, as though the wish had magically slain the person. Such dreams or thoughts almost always produce guilt in the adult as well as the child, although they are normal reactions to being thwarted.

Making a Fatal Error.   Zoe endured several years of this type of misery. She had had a wild love affair with her future husband prior to marriage. Once they were legally bound, however, he became impotent. Zoe discovered that her mate was unable to have intercourse with a female he respected, a phenomenon that clinicians refer to as the "virgin-whore" (or "madonna-whore") complex.

For a few years the couple had sporadic sexual contacts, even managing to produce a child. After the baby's birth, Zoe declined further stress-laden attempts at intercourse, and her husband, relieved, complied. They continued to live together many more years in a *mariage blanc*—as the French call a nonsexual or "white" marriage—regarded by their unknowing friends as an ideal couple.

When I asked Zoe why she finally decided to get a divorce, she explained, "I began having constant daydreams that he would drop dead." When this wish became obsessive, Zoe knew she had to get out. "If I stayed in that marriage, sooner or later, *I* would have ended up dead." Every night during this period Zoe had what she calls "screaming nightmares":

> I always do some small thing wrong, like I forget to push a
> button, or I forget to fasten my seat belt, or I step over a line.
> As a result, I'm going to die. With my last gasp of breath, I
> scream. I wake up screaming.

These recurrent nightmares caused Zoe horrendous suffering. Unlike most women who feel locked into an unhappy marriage because of economic necessity, Zoe was financially free to leave. Yet her emotional commitment held her captive. At the same time she began grinding her teeth all night long. Her dentist commented, "You must be fighting the war in your sleep." The war was indeed in Zoe's mind.

Whether Zoe's guilt over her obsessive wish for her first husband's death stimulated her screaming nightmares or whether it was her fear that the marriage was killing her in "little things" is unclear.

Eventually Zoe's nightmares drove her to divorce. The nightmares even lingered several years into a new marriage, although she thinks this was because of her concern about difficulties she was then having with her child. Gradually the nightmares decreased in frequency, and for the last decade they only troubled her a few times a year—a significant improvement over every night.

Being Buried Alive. The kind of thinking and dreaming Zoe underwent are sure signs that the dreamer's mental health is imperiled; it demands change. The same emotional danger existed for the unhappily married man who had recurrent nightmares of being buried alive. He would awaken to his own muffled sounds of terror. In his dream language, being trapped in his marriage was a living death. His nightmares ceased, as they frequently do, upon divorce and the subsequent establishment of a loving relationship. Dreamers who suffer recurrent frightening dreams of this type require professional attention.

Dream Reminders

It is important to understand that an occasional dream or thought about the death of a loved spouse is normal. It usually symbolizes either a sense of threat to the mate (such as danger to his physical health) or else a momentary wish that he would "go away." It is not usually a wish for his literal death but, rather, a wish to escape from the situation. Dreams of the death of a husband may even serve as a reminder of how deep the affection runs and so help the dreamer construct a reconciliation.

Dead on the Freeway. Dee, for instance, was feeling resentful that her husband's work required long hours away from home; in addition he sometimes chose to extend these by evening business engagements, leaving her with extra child care as well as her own strenuous job. The night he was attending a charity club meeting and not expected home until almost midnight, Dee fell asleep waiting for him and dreamed:

> My husband is killed coming home on the freeway. I wake up
> in a sweat.

Terrorized by her dream, Dee rethought her situation. When her mate finally did appear, she was delirious with loving feeling. Her warm welcome overcame the tension they had been building. "It put things into perspective—I knew what was important."

Hands Cut Off. This same dream theme may occur when a woman is having ambivalent feelings about her boyfriend. Maggie's worst nightmare arose when she and her boyfriend were in the midst of difficulties. "I felt a lot of the time that I hated him. I was about to leave him." In her dream,

> I am in a car ahead of Sid [her boyfriend], driving fast. I look
> out at a tree-lined boulevard, like in Europe. In the rearview
> mirror I see there has been an accident. He is thrown to the side
> of the road.
>
> He is leaning on his elbows, looking up at me like a puppy. His
> arms are bloody stumps—the hands are cut off. He is a sculptor.
> His whole life is gone, and it's my fault.

In this nightmare Maggie anticipates going off on her own (symbolized by driving in a separate car). Looking back, she views the emotional damage (represented by the accident) that she is leaving behind. She sees the pain she would cause, the "cutting off" of something essential for her lover's work (his hands in the dream); she responds with guilt.

Maggie explained how this dream made her "think twice about leaving him." For the first time she felt compassion for her boyfriend, seeing him as a victim rather than a villain out to make her miserable. Soon Maggie and Sid were back together, eventually marrying. Dreams of this kind can have a powerful impact.

Shot and Killed. Nora, who was visiting the Bay Area where she had accompanied her boyfriend from Ireland, had been away from home for over a month. It was Christmastime, and Nora was homesick for her family across the ocean, whom she would not see until Easter. Her eyes filled with tears as she told me this dream:

> My boyfriend and a lot of other people are shot and killed. I
> have to figure out how to send his body home to Ireland on
> my insurance. I wake up crying.

Nora, who loves her boyfriend, acknowledged, "I would *have* to go home if my boyfriend were killed." Her dreaming mind provided the longed-for wish fulfillment—not a wish for his death, but for a way home.

A woman has dreams of her mate's death or victimization when she feels that a threat—physical or emotional—is endangering him. Or she dreams of his death when she is upset with him, or thwarted by him, and she wishes he would "disappear." In dramatic dream language she tells him to "get lost." In relationships that totter and fall, dreams of the partner's death may accelerate.

Dreams of the Husband as Villain
"I Killed Her Because I Love Her"

At times the spouse may play the role of murderer rather than victim of accidental death or injury. A wife's dreams of her husband murdering her are responses to fear of literal injury; fear of emotional injury; or feelings of anger toward him, followed by guilt, with subsequent fear of retaliation.

The Wife With a Brutal Husband. A woman who fears her husband will literally injure her is frequently tormented by nightmares of being murdered by her mate. Battered women—unfortunately a large group—are victims in their dreaming as well as waking lives. They are, indeed, endangered.

Sexually abused women, likewise, suffer nightmares of being tortured or murdered by their molester. Those who were abused as children and then "forgot" the incidents often relive them in dreams as adults, allowing themselves to remember specifics as they became more capable of coping.

Slaughtered Loved Ones. Ginny, who was subjected to her husband's verbal threats of murder when she sought a divorce, still has occasional nightmares about him, her worst, many years after having happily remarried:

Usually he destroys all the people around me, with a gun or knife—a lot of violence. He slaughters my current husband and child and others to get at me, and whisks me away.

Ginny's first husband had a drug problem, along with an obsession for guns, so that her fears have a realistic basis when combined with the man's fixation on her. Her response is typical of women whose husbands have threatened to kill them, either directly with weapons or verbally. These nightmares often occurred when Ginny's child was behaving badly, as described in the next chapter, "Parenting Dreams."

One of the tragedies of our society is that murderous threats are sometimes carried out. Most murders are in fact committed among those who are related to one another.[1] The murderous husband, one study found, usually kills his victim in the bedroom; the murderous wife—when she does act out—usually chooses the kitchen. Each, it would seem, selects the arena of their greatest familiarity. Since threats are potential acts, women who believe their mates to be capable of harming them should take immediate steps, following a death threat, to get professional assistance in protecting themselves.

The Wife With a Difficult Husband.   A spouse who has never raised a hand toward his wife may be cast as a brutal murderer in her dreams if she is anguished by his behavior. The husband who has liaisons with other women, ignores or ridicules his wife, or is harsh, cold, or alcoholic may make the wife feel emotionally "murdered." She may suspect he is capable of acting out against her.

Locked in Prison.   Fay, who had been married for some twenty years, had clear-cut plans to leave her husband eventually. Feeling trapped in a "depressing" marriage by children who required financial support, she was already emotionally divorced from her mate and had recurrent nightmares about him. In one of the worst,

I am locked up in prison, and a man comes by wearing a rat hood. I'm his prisoner and I'm trying to figure out a way to get out. I somehow know *he* will be in prison. I feel sorry for him and stay put.

Obviously Fay's marriage had become a prison for her, even if it was she who elected to remain in the barred cell. She thought of her husband, who had serious problems of addiction, as a "wounded man," hence her pity and her reluctance to leave him. Rats are common dream images for women who are having difficulty with a man who is "acting like a rat."

Squeezed Into a Gas Oven.   In a later nightmare of Fay's the rat hood is removed; it is the husband who is clearly the villain:

> A woman, possibly me, is making herself very small in order to fit into an oven. She has to squinch up very small to fit in. She's totally cooperative.
>
> Her husband is there and he's telling her to get smaller. Then he turns on the gas. She knows she has to keep her breathing even. If she does, she'll survive.

Here Fay is depicting an emotional life in peril. By compressing herself to fit into the oven—probably symbolizing the limited nourishment in her home life—she is putting herself into a position worse than in jail. She feels that she has to "squinch up" her personness to "fit in" to her husband's notion of what she should be. Making herself smaller in the dream suggests that her waking "growth" is stunted by her relationship. The husband, by turning on the gas, is murdering her. The only positive element—and it is an important one—is that Fay can survive by continuing to breathe evenly. If she can hold on until the divorce, her dream says, she will make it.

Trapped in a Corner.   Kiko, who is in her forties, was born in this country but raised in a traditional Japanese household, where she was taught to be subservient to men. She was beaten when her behavior was not submissive enough. Her more Americanized husband found her quiet ways difficult. Eventually the marriage collapsed. Undergoing the divorce she herself wanted, Kiko went to bed nightly curled into a fetal position. Her recurrent dream:

> I am being chased by a man who gets me into a corner where I am trapped. I wake up in terror, exhausted. My shoulders ache with pain from the tension of trying to escape.

Although the pursuer in Kiko's dream is not her husband and does not succeed in killing her, this theme expresses her inner turmoil. Her whole life was in chaos—her house sold, her bills unpaid, and she was uncertain that she could earn her own living. Small wonder she felt trapped in a corner.

Cut Into Pieces. Robin was divorcing her husband of ten years when she began having a recurrent nightmare:

> I am being chased by a man with a knife who cuts pieces out
> of my arm—little pieces. I can feel the knife going up my arm.

Robin explained that the first year when she and her husband were separated, "it wasn't too bad. But when the lawyers got involved, I felt as though I were being cut into little pieces!" With or without mask, the husband may play the villain in the dreams of the divorcée.

Other Women Flaunted. Another form of the husband as villain is in his dream flirtations with other women. When Maggie was eighteen, she married a man almost ten years her senior. Barely out of high school, she had little confidence in herself. The husband, she says, "made me feel stupid and untalented."

Maggie began having horrendous nightmares that her husband was flaunting women in her face, coming up to her openly and proudly with a girlfriend. She woke up sobbing from these tormenting dreams and, during her waking hours, felt unbearable jealousy over her husband's flirtatious behavior with other women.

After six years of marriage Maggie discovered, from an anonymous phone call, that her husband was in fact "cheating" on her. It emerged that he belongs to the type of male who claims to love his wife dearly but simultaneously wants all the freedom of a bachelor.

When Maggie finally found the courage to get out of the marriage, her husband resisted violently—physically threatening her and later overdosing himself with sleeping pills in an attempt to get her back. Finally he found a girlfriend he liked enough to release his wife. "Thank God, I'm free!" was Maggie's response.

Slowly Maggie was able to rebuild her life. She took some college courses and became convinced she was not stupid after all. Eventually she remarried with a trustworthy man and is now the proud mother of a long-wished-for baby. The torturous nightmares seem to be far in the past.

Yvette, who also had good cause to feel betrayed by her husband, told me a horrifying vision. She had discovered her mate's infidelity, yet dreaded to confront him. Lying in bed late one night at his side, she suddenly felt herself "projected" from her body, hovered over his sleeping form, and swooped down to strangle him.

This violent action startled Yvette out of her reverie. Distraught by the intensity of her murderous impulse, she decided it was better for her to get out of the relationship quickly. Playing the role of villain herself was something she did not want to happen in waking life.

Nightmares or daytime fears about the husband having love affairs, it must be remembered, also occur without foundation, when the woman is feeling particularly insecure or vulnerable.

Dream Images of Strained Marriages

Aside from dreams of the husband being victimized or being villainous, other images are characteristic of strain in marriages. Some of these represent a passing emotion; others become a permanent attitude.

The Wife Who Feels Guilty and Afraid

When a woman has done something she knows will anger her husband—having damaged the car, having overspent, having had a love affair, having made him suffer—she feels guilty. The same sense of guilt may come from having wished he would die so that she could escape an unhappy marriage without the trauma or social stigma of divorce.

Feelings of guilt, as mentioned, often become transmuted into feelings of fear of retaliation. Punishment may appear in the wife's dream in the form of a murderous husband who does not yet know how "bad" she has been.

Running Away. Amberly, several months before separating from her husband, dreamed:

> My husband overhears a conversation I have with my lover. He acts as though he will agree to leave me. I can see him standing on top of a truck that is going away from the apartment where I am. I watch him out of the window. He is naked. When it gets a distance away, he jumps off and doubles back and is going to kill me. I am dialing the operator for help to get the police.

Then I am running away with my child. My husband is close
behind, jumping into cars, pursued by the police. It is dark and
snowing. We duck into a store and change into other clothes so
that people won't recognize us. We are going to try to eat
dinner at the Red Cross. I wake up frightened.

Here Amberly expresses her sense of guilt, her fear of retaliation or punishment, and her need for help. The darkness, the snow, the disguise—these
depict the danger in her environment. The nakedness of her husband suggests
she thinks he may be capable of acting out against her in anger, that is, his
motive is "exposed." By dialing the operator for the police, by running
away, by changing clothes, by trying to get nourishment at the "Red Cross,"
Amberly seeks help—all good signs. Her lover, however, seems to disappear
when the threat becomes obvious. Amberly may wonder how supportive
he will be if the facts are known.

Dreams of the husband as murderer sometimes arise from trivial events.
Sheila, in a much loved and loving relationship, had decided to "play
hookey" from some commitments and go to a movie with a girlfriend
without mentioning it to her husband. The night before her planned escapade she dreamed that her husband wanted to murder her. In her dream
language, she was saying, "If he only knew, he'd 'kill' me." Her own guilty
feelings had created the pictures. The dreamer herself knows best the degree
of severity involved in such dreams.

The Pink Refrigerator. Fiona, also in a loving relationship, felt guilty.
She and her husband were going through a financially difficult period.
When he was out of town for a few days, she indulged herself in some
personal shopping and knitting lessons that he would have thought frivo-
lous. The night of her splurge, she dreamed:

I run out and buy a big refrigerator and a big stove. When it is
delivered, I realize the refrigerator is shocking pink. It was on
sale and can't be returned. My husband is not going to be
happy!

Instead of the small purchases she actually made that would probably pass
her husband's notice, Fiona buys something in her dream that is unavoidable
because of its obvious color. She actually does need a refrigerator. Pink,
however, is a color Fiona would never choose in appliances or apparel; she
thinks it is unflattering to her complexion. Fiona's guilty feeling is "vividly"

apparent; her dreaming mind judges her behavior as "shocking" (symbolized by the shocking-pink color) and unattractive to her. Dreamers who feel momentarily guilty in the daytime express it in exaggerated form during the night.

Dreams of the Marriage Collapsing

Instead of depicting the mate directly as victim or villain, women sometimes personify their marriage as a dream object that collapses.

Falling Apart.   Robin lives in a house built into a hillside; its precarious position requires sturdy structures to support and protect it. Rainstorms sometimes undermine this support, and it needs to be rebuilt. Following her divorce Robin became involved with another man, who, one evening, deeply disappointed her. That night she dreamed:

> My retaining wall falls down again.

To Robin the "collapse" of the new relationship felt like a repetition of the collapse of the marriage.

Lost in a Hole.   This imagery of things coming apart or falling down is typical for men as well as women who are undergoing strains in their relationship or divorcing. Matt dreamed of seeing himself, his wife, and a strange woman walking on a rickety, rotten fence that was about to collapse. "It was like skating on thin ice," he said. The fence came down, and the couple's child was plunged into a deep hole, lost. The unhappy man awoke terrified, with his fears of losing his child, as well as his wife, seemingly confirmed.

Bulldozer on the Lawn.   Brenda, in the midst of a particularly bitter divorce that eventually was tried before a judge, dreamed:

> I seem to wake up in my house and go downstairs to get the
> newspaper. There is graffiti all over the stairwell and hallway.
> It's supposed to be intellectual because it's about art, in red,
> black, and white. I know that the man who rents the basement
> apartment did it. "That's it. You're out of here!" I say. I bite
> his arm and try to hold on like a rodent.

I take his wet laundry onto the lawn and dump it. That's when I see that a pack of mad lesbians driving a bulldozer are on the front lawn. They want to use my telephone. The garage door is missing and covered with cardboard. My car has been stolen. The whole place looks like a war zone!

Brenda woke in considerable distress from this nightmare. As we talked about the images in the dream and her current situation, the scenario began to make sense. During the same time that her divorce proceedings were under way, Brenda had gotten an abortion. Her job and other loving relationships were in transition. Her life, like her house in the dream, seemed to be under siege.

Brenda explained that the man who rented her basement apartment was not someone she liked; he was "imposed in my life." More importantly, this man was living in the space that her husband occupied before they separated. The graffiti in her dream she defined as "a way unsophisticated people communicate—it's supposed to be art and therefore acceptable, but it's not; the colors were unpleasing, standard street colors." Her husband was in the art field. Thus Brenda has gone to get the news (picking up the newspaper in her dream) to be confronted with an unacceptable type of communication from her husband (the graffiti). In actuality he was trying to get legal possession of the home she had purchased.

In the next scene Brenda expressed her angry response to her husband by attacking the tenant who lived in the same space. Dumping clean, wet laundry, Brenda said, was "particularly offensive, cruel, makes the person do the chore over again." This probably symbolized her rejection of the offered terms, as well as her wish to retaliate.

The remaining images in the dream may refer to Brenda's recent abortion. Broken, damaged doors, shifted earth—such images sometimes refer to bodily destruction. The garage door perhaps symbolized for this dreamer the opening to the womb. Her car, Brenda tells me, is "my freedom, my mobility." Perhaps, also, the stolen car represented the fetus torn from its container. The angry lesbians driving the bulldozer suggest that the abortion gave Brenda a feeling of diminished femininity.

The bulldozer on the front lawn was being put to destructive use. It is a machine "used to change things radically, to pull a home apart or put it together." The cardboard covering left Brenda feeling "totally vulnerable." So far, only the lower story of her home had been destroyed in the dream; her fear was that now she was open to total attack. The acrimonious divorce, the decision to abort, the current instability of her job and her loving relationships, left Brenda feeling—awake and asleep—as though she were living in a war zone. Luckily she heard the clanging alert signal in her nightmare and sought help. Months later her life had begun to stabilize.

Lost at Sea.   Loss of precious possessions—children, homes, cars—are often an element in dreams of collapse. Moira, feeling trapped in an unhappy marriage because of her large family, dreamed:

> Some kind of furniture—some belongings—that are beside my bed are sliding down to the sea. It is almost as if I were in a boat or ship. It is going under. I am startled and jump out of bed. "Oh, gosh, it's lost!" I wake up to find that I am really out of bed, over at the wall, trying to hold the things from going under. My husband wakes up, too, and tells me to get back in bed.

For Moira her valuables were in danger of "being lost at sea." Precious belongings lost, houses tumbling down, bridges crumbling, walls and fences tottering—such imagery depicts the "breakup" (or "breakdown") of the relationship for many dreamers.

Dreams of Emotional Distance

"Alone, Alone, All, All Alone, Alone on a Wide Wide Sea!"   Like the Ancient Mariner of Coleridge's poem, who must endure the "Nightmare Life-in-Death" in loneliness, marital partners drifting apart feel isolated. In the way that Gretchen in the opening dream saw herself paralyzed "at sea," the spurned spouse may liken her state to a living death.

Wilma, being divorced from her husband of six years, dreamed:

> I am on the beach with my husband and yet not able to touch him. We are physically and emotionally remote.

The beach is a setting that Wilma used to enjoy with her husband. In her dream the partners are "out of touch," even in a favorite place.

During or just preceding a divorce the couple almost always suspend sexual relations or contact one another only sporadically. Dissatisfaction and frustration with sex are typical. Wilma's dream probably expresses her sense of deprivation as well as emotional distance.

At this same time Wilma was also troubled with recurrent dreams of other significant men in her life—her brother and her father—drowning. They probably were "stand-ins" for the emotional "death" she was feeling with her husband. After her divorce Wilma restructured her life in positive ways. She eventually remarried and freed herself from the drowning nightmares.

Dead Body Floating. Hester, during the time she felt a growing emotional estrangement from her husband, also used water imagery in her dream:

> My husband and I are standing on a bridge, watching the water flow below. In it is my body, floating away.
>
> My husband becomes very agitated, saying, "We've got to stop it." I remain calm, "No, let it go."

Although this dream occurred about three years prior to a divorce from an eighteen-year-long marriage, it accurately anticipated the partners' attitudes. Hester was "drifting apart" from her husband. When she eventually decided on divorce, she felt calm. Her husband strongly resisted leaving the marriage, but was subsequently persuaded to "let her go," to let the marriage die.

Bridges in dreams frequently mark transition points for the dreamer. Hester's associations to her floating body led her to think of British author Virginia Woolf's suicide by drowning, an act that ended her marriage to Leonard, as well as her life. Drowning dreams underscore the resemblance in dreamers' minds between divorce and death.

Waking Desertion. For some women, the sense of abandonment may come upon awakening from a happy dream of the lost lover. The French writer George Sand, in despair over the break-up of her relationship with the poet Alfred de Musset, wrote in her diary:[2]

> Last night I dreamed that he was beside me, that he embraced me. I awoke swooning with joy. What a dream, my God.

The pain that returned on waking from this dream must have increased the unhappy woman's sense of loss.

Alone, deserted, lost, drowning, unable to connect except for a moment in a vision—such imagery conveys the dreamer's sense of isolation.

The Monk and the Spider.   Divorcing men, too, often experience a sense of isolation. Their dreams of being alone may have a different quality from those of women. A few months after his divorce, for example, Bert—a professional in his late forties—had this dream:

> I'm walking on a twisting, narrow mountain road, like some scene from a James Bond movie. It's dangerous, with a cliff on one side, a stone wall and a drop on the other.
>
> I come to a turn and find an old man dressed like a monk cross-legged in the road. He's got a bald head and a beard and wears red. I sit down beside him. Then I lean back on my arms and look at the sky.
>
> It's beautiful—all over red. A large spider comes into my vision. It's very big because it's near. It fascinates me to watch it.

Bert was intrigued and pleased with this dream; he made a painting of it. As we discussed the images, he told me that a monk is "a man who may or may not be wise, who goes off to live alone." A spider, Bert explained, is "a lone hunter, is useful, eats insects, can be compared to the cat in the animal kingdom." Whenever dreamers employ images with similar associations, as Bert does here with the monk who lives alone and the spider who hunts alone, it is a sure clue to the meaning of the symbols.

When I asked Bert to tell me about the color red and what makes it different from other colors, he said that it is "a warm color, more natural than other colors, as in a sunset." I noticed, as we spoke, that Bert was wearing a red tie with his professional white jacket.

In his dream language Bert is saying that he finds himself traveling a difficult, somewhat dangerous path (symbolized by the narrow mountain road). When he comes to a decision (the turn), he encounters the man who lives alone (represented by the monk who may or may not be wise). There is something natural about this state (symbolized by the warm red worn by the monk and then seen in the sky). He finds being a lone hunter (the spider) important (its closeness and largeness) and fascinating.

Although Bert now finds himself alone, he pictures this condition less as a desertion, isolation, or destruction and more as an interesting possibility. Perhaps being alone in one's late forties has less of a negative charge for the male dreamer. After a year or so of "lone hunting," Bert settled on a new woman and remarried.

Most of the women in the study, especially those whose husbands chose to leave them, dreamed of being alarmingly alone, lost, unable to connect, or drowning—images that conveyed the dreamer's sense of isolation.

"I Can't Stomach Him!"

What is the secret of a long-term marriage? Nanette, at almost eighty, evolved her own view. One of my favorite sayings in this collection comes from a whimsical story she related.

Nanette was standing in line at the supermarket behind her husband, who was checking out, and in front of a young couple who were arguing. After a few minutes she was unable to bear the quarrel any longer and looked directly at the pair, hoping to stop their fuss.

"How long have *you* been married?" the husband asked Nanette.

"Fifty-five years," replied Nanette.

"Fifty-five years!" said the astonished young woman. "How could you do it?!"

Nanette fixed the woman with her bright blue eyes. "You swallow a lot, darling, you swallow a lot." Turning to the man, she added, "You, too." The young couple's grim mood dissolved into good-natured laughter with the elderly woman.

Recent research suggests that the most frequent reason for an enduring and happy marriage is a positive attitude toward one's mate, viewing him (or her) as one's best friend, and liking the partner as a person.[3] Along with Nanette, I agree that a happy marriage also involves compromise. However, some women are forced to swallow too much.

Choking on Coins.   Some partners have great difficulty "swallowing a lot." Moira, who dreamed of her belongings sliding into the sea, had recurrent nightmares—every few months—that she was choking. At times dreams of having difficulty breathing or choking have a physical cause.[4] Moira's description of her marital relationship, however, made me think that her periodic choking dreams were a metaphor:

> I dream that I have something in my mouth, a coin—like a penny or a dime. I swallow it and suddenly realize it's gone down.

Recently, Moira continued, her husband blamed her for a minor accident suffered by one of their children, even though he was also present and was physically closer to the child. That night Moira dreamed of swallowing and choking on the coin.

Moira defined coins as "money used to buy things. You give it in exchange for something." She saw choking as indicating that "something inside you is wrong. You may have to have it out by operation. Steps have to be taken to save you." In describing her marriage as "atrocious," she commented that her husband often accuses her of things she did not do. "He *rams it down my throat!*" This information, together with the fact that she remained in the marriage for economic reasons, makes the meaning of her nightmare apparent.

In Moira's dream language she is saying, "Staying with my husband in exchange for money is causing trouble within me. Swallowing his unfair accusations is harmful." Moira feels forced to "swallow" things she detests along with accepting her husband's financial support.

As we worked with the dream images, Moira herself had an insight into its meaning. "Could it be that I need an operation to get separated from my husband?" she asked with a wry smile. She had left him once before and been persuaded back. Her recurring dream says that the issue is still unresolved. Obviously it is possible to swallow too much.

Economic dependency is a major factor, along with religious concerns and fears of the unknown, that cause women to allow themselves to remain trapped in miserable marriages.

The Voices of Divorcées

The alternative—terminating a marriage or relationship—is painful. Suffering is almost always acute, whether the woman chooses the divorce or has it thrust upon her. (Divorces are not usually mutual.) It is a sort of death whether—to use a friend's terms—one is the "dumper" or the "dumpee." In fact one researcher ranks divorce as second only to the death of a spouse in the degree of trauma.[5] "Dumping" a husband who is no longer loved is hard on the woman, who often feels regret or guilt at causing pain; being "dumped" by a man—especially in favor of another woman—initially angers the wife but ultimately leaves her feeling rejected and worthless.

For some women obtaining a desired divorce, anger was a chief element:

I wanted it, yet when it came, it was extremely painful. A lot more withdrawal and dependence than I thought was there. It really made me mad.

I didn't love him. I wanted something more. It was very difficult—I was very angry and hostile over the process. It was hard to be alone, even though I didn't want him.

Women who had a great deal of anger were likely to dream of being injured by their mate or of terrible things happening to him.

Other women seeking divorce experienced collapse:

It was my choice, but only by resignation—he was having a love affair.

I wanted it very much, but it was still totally draining. I couldn't drive to the courthouse. How much your life can change with a stroke of a pen! It was like the death of hope.

It was a nightmare. I was totally stifled, physically paralyzed. I had wanted it for years before I had the courage to demand it. It was the first independent thing I'd done in my life. Then I felt like I was going to die. I couldn't get out of bed. I would get so dizzy, I passed out. However, I went through with it.

These women were more apt to dream of buildings and other structures collapsing or of great upheaval and destruction.

Only one mentioned surprise that her husband did not resist the legal proceedings:

The third divorce was the most painful. I got it before I had any ground under my feet. I was trying to scare him because he was running around with other women.

Dreams of being alienated or lost were typical here.

Depression is a common reaction when the woman feels abandoned by the partner's departure:

I was so downcast when my boyfriend of five years left me for another woman; it was worse than my divorce. I had given up trying to get my degree when I married. I was shy and afraid in public, and miserable to be alone. I remember walking my dog

in the rain in November, feeling dismal. Then I saw a tiny bit
of sun with two birds singing. Suddenly a great joy came into
my heart.

Women who react to divorce with profound depression were those who
were likely to dream of being lost or drowned. Luckily this woman saw
a ray of sunlight.

Still other women in the study who wanted to divorce were relatively
detached:

I left my first two husbands. I was hurt but not devastated—I
wasn't that involved, and it was not that difficult to get
uninvolved.

I was already in love with another man. It was only later that
my reaction set in.

Women who felt this way were more prone to dream of other lovers or
concerns. Eventually, however, they had to go through an inner separation.
One woman commented,

We just drifted apart. I fell in love with someone else and he
did, too. The divorce was very friendly.

Others, especially those who had suffered heavily in the marriage, celebrated
the divorce or separation joyously:

Free!

It was hard to get, but wonderful to obtain.

It was a relief . . . liberating.

Women who had these feelings were more likely to dream of new plant
growth or buildings being constructed as their lives without their husbands
expanded.

These emotions—anger, fear, hopelessness, exhilaration—form the raw
material of divorcing women's dreams. The many images that express these
emotions may appear in the same woman's dreams at different stages of her
divorce.

The Sleep and Dream Patterns of Divorced Women

Getting divorced seems to affect sleeping patterns as well as dream themes. In general, women sleep longer than men do. A Gallup poll on sleeping habits found that a greater number of women than men say they sleep eight hours or more each night.[6] The reason for this finding may be simply that nonworking women have more time available for sleep; working women's sleep patterns more nearly resemble those of men.

Even when they are happily married, women report more sleep difficulties than men, despite the fact that more men have actual sleep problems—such as apnea (stoppage of breathing) and snoring.[7]

Under conditions of divorce or separation, people's sleep becomes disturbed. They tend to go to bed later than when they are married. Their habits of sleep become more irregular; they retire at different times from night to night. Furthermore, divorced and separated people report a greater number of sleep problems than when married. Women, more than men, are likely to discuss these difficulties with their physicians.[8]

Distorted Dream Mechanisms During Divorce.   These complaints are based upon actual changes in the dreaming mechanism. Rosalind Cartwright, a psychologist and sleep specialist in Chicago, has done extensive work with the dreams of women undergoing divorce, and the following findings from her research can help us understand what is happening.[8]

In one of her studies, twenty-nine women in the process of divorce were selected from volunteers to spend six nights in a sleep laboratory. According to their own descriptions, the majority (nineteen) of the group were depressed— although none were taking antidepressants (a requirement of participation). Most of the women measured as "traditional" on a scale of sex roles, while fewer of them scored as "liberated." For comparison, nine happily married women were also interviewed, tested, and recorded in the sleep laboratory.

Cartwright first observed that the divorcing women who were depressed displayed a malfunctioning in their dream mechanism. They had rapid eye movement (REM) periods earlier in the night than normal; and their eye movements were more intense early in the night, rather than building gradually. Both of these changes in the function of sleep are characteristic of people who are depressed for any reason. In addition, the depressed, divorcing women tended to be traditional instead of liberated; the women

who scored traditional in their feminine role showed greater sleep disturbance.

A psychotherapist friend of mine points out that for a female who thinks
of herself in the traditional role, getting a divorce is equivalent to being
fired—without a reference. Her "boss" is saying, "Your performance is
unsatisfactory." Depression and poor sleep are much more likely for her than
for the woman who chooses to divorce and has alternate roles in her
self-concept. The woman who has liberated views may "quit" her job as
wife, or feel free to take a different one if she wishes, acknowledging it was
not the right job for her.

Distorted Dream Content in Divorce.   Cartwright, in her study, examined the reports of the divorcing women's dream content with care. All the
women had been allowed to dream for the same amount of time before
being awakened to describe their dreams. Yet, significant differences were
observed between groups in the length of their dream reports, the time
setting of their dreams, the emotions, the motives, the characters, and the
progression from dream to dream throughout the night.

The divorcing women who were depressed gave shorter dream reports;
they saw themselves in their dreams as helpless, damaged, in need of care;
they were not motivated to relate to others, but instead abased themselves
in order to be nurtured. They had *less* emotion in their dreams—a finding
that is characteristic of depression. Anxiety in dreams is a sign that the
dreamer is actively struggling to cope. As depression lifts, dreams become
more emotional.

The depressed women were preoccupied with the past and with former
relationships in dreams (whereas happily marrieds set their dreams in the
present); they had one or few dream characters; they blamed themselves
excessively, and did not show progress in resolving their problems from
dream to dream.

In contrast the nondepressed divorcing women gave dream reports that
were twice as long; they set their dreams in the present and future as well
as in the past; they had many more positive, hopeful emotions; they had
needs for esteem and control, not only for safety; they rarely saw themselves
as inadequate; they had many dream characters. Most importantly, perhaps,
the nondepressed divorcing woman worked through her problems in her
dreams, reaching resolutions. Her dreams energized her for change.

The Cartwright study demonstrates that dreams have a meaningful relationship to waking-life stress; they reflect the way positive or negative
emotions about divorce are handled by the dreamer. When a woman

undergoing divorce is depressed, her dream mechanism malfunctions and the structure and content of her dreams change. These stunted, sparsely populated dreams clearly signal need in the depressed dreamer.

Antidepressant medication is usually of a type that suppresses rapid eye movements (REM); when taking such antidepressants, dreaming is lessened. This medication may temporarily help relieve dreamers of the repetitive, self-damaging dreaming and thinking patterns observed in Cartwright's depressed dreamers. However, best results are achieved when depressed divorcing women also obtain therapeutic guidance, as Gretchen did, to become more active in dream behavior as well as waking life.

Danger of Illness Following Divorce.   Divorce is a major life crisis. A recent study at Ohio State University indicates that divorce is so stressful, it can lower a woman's resistance to disease. Researchers Janice Kiecolt-Glaser and Ronald Glaser compared blood samples from a group of married women with samples from a group of divorced women.[10] They found that the women separated from their husbands had poorer immune responses; they were more susceptible to illness than the married women.

Moreover, among those married women who said their marriage was poor, a weaker immune response was found than among the married women who gave a high rating to their marriage. Being happily married, it would seem, is good for the health; getting divorced may depress it—depending on the woman's attitude about getting divorced.

Women undergoing divorce will want to seek out whatever emotional support is available—from friends, relatives, community groups, or the helping professions. Divorce, like other crises, offers the person an opportunity for growth when it is dealt with in a positive way.

The Dream Alert

What can we watch for in dreams that might alert us to trouble in a relationship? What signs can a divorced woman look for as she heals?

We have seen how our dreams are profoundly altered by friction in a relationship that may lead to divorce. When women feel afraid they will be physically hurt, or when they are emotionally hurt, or when they—either with or without justification—feel jealous, they cast their mates into the role of dream villain. When, rightly or wrongly, women feel guilty and deserving of punishment, they may "accidentally" destroy themselves in dreams.

When their anger is strong enough, they slip over into playing the villain themselves.

We saw, too, that a woman's ambivalent feelings toward a partner may appear in dreams of her husband's or boyfriend's death. When she is angry or frustrated with him, she kills him off in her dream pictures. Such dreams may also occur when she fears that something—ill health, for example—is threatening her mate.

Finally, women may portray their discomfort in a marriage by images that depict the emotion they feel: being lost at sea, being in jail, squeezing into a small space, or choking on something difficult to swallow. Such dreams are strong warning signs to the woman who has them.

As the divorced dreamer begins to heal and to adjust to her altered situation, she can expect to observe corresponding images in her dreams. New construction going on, extra rooms discovered, new developments, plants sprouting and flourishing, moving with ease, gliding, flying—these are a few of the dream pictures that accompany a more positive development.

Many divorced women continue to dream about a former spouse, even when they are happily remarried. Like the first wife in the Thurber cartoon who is parked on the bookcase as if she were a trophy, memories of marriages past hang around in the dreamer's mind. Such "ghosts," especially after several years in a new marriage, usually symbolize some current stress. It is as if the dreamer were saying to herself, "Hey, my current husband is acting like so-and-so used to about this issue." A dream of this type may serve as a reminder to avoid or to do certain things that have caused past trouble—a timely warning.

Large numbers of women and men divorce each year. Although authorities differ on the exact amount, the figure is too large for anyone's comfort.[11] Partners in the process of divorce go through typical reactions. If you are contemplating a divorce, have recently been divorced, or are undergoing a divorce, it is urgent that you familiarize yourself with these phases so that you can better cope with each stage: accepting the "death" of the marriage, mourning its loss, seeking the potential for new behaviors, and so forth. (See, for example, Mel Krantzler's *Creative Divorce*[12] and *Learning to Love Again* or Marilyn Jensen's *Formerly Married: Learning to Live With Yourself*[11]) Divorces, as these authors point out, can become valuable opportunities for personal growth.

Listen, as well, to your dreams. They are a barometer of your inner emotions. They will tell you where your heart is at the moment. Only you will know if it is a passing feeling or an ongoing state that requires action.

If you are troubled with nightmares about your mate that become worse or more frequent, seek professional counseling. You will be more able to judge whether your issues can be resolved or whether you and your spouse are better off apart.

The Symbolic Meaning of Dreams of Divorce

A married woman may dream of getting a divorce either when there is a momentary wish to do so or when she is "divorcing herself" from a particular situation or person. When a single woman—or one who is engaged—dreams of divorce, she may be warning herself against a certain relationship.

To dream of someone else getting divorced suggests there is something for the dreamer to gain from this action. As always, the dreamer must ponder what the characters represent. One should also consider whether one of the marital partners who is getting divorced is of romantic interest to the dreamer. If so, the dreamer may be hoping the couple will break up so that she will have a chance.

Whether married or single, a woman's dreams of divorce sometimes have little to do with love or marriage. Instead divorce dreams may refer to a wish to separate from a job, from an outmoded value, or from some problematic aspect of life that is no longer productive. The dreamer needs to contemplate the symbols of the dream carefully in order to decipher the meaning that applies.

Parenting Dreams

> I give birth to a boy. I see the hospital from the front
> and notice it is raining. Then I see the nurse and my son.
> In the dream I name him, calling him Michael Sean.

From even before they conceive, mothers begin to dream about their children. Chloe, for instance, had the above dream about her son five months before she actually became pregnant with him. She had been trying to conceive for some time. After the dream, "I decided I didn't have to worry about getting pregnant—it would happen. In a conscious state, I would have picked a more unusual name for a boy, but the dream name seemed perfect."

Whether Chloe's dream was actually predictive or whether it relaxed her enough to conceive is impossible to know. An interesting aspect of the actual birth, however, is that Chloe went into labor on a clear, sunny day, two days before her child was delivered. She went to the hospital and was sent home three times; on the fourth trip her son was born and—as in her dream—it was raining.

Once mothers begin to dream about their children, before or soon after their birth, they never stop. Daughters and sons become major characters in women's dreams throughout their lives.

Children Star in Mothers' Dreams

Dennis the Menace, in a recent cartoon, confided to his friend Joey, "Moms are funny. They're either hollering at you, bragging about you, or worrying about you." Hollering, bragging, worrying—these attitudes find their way into mothers' dreams as well: frustration and anger at the child's behavior, pride over accomplishments, fear for the child's safety, and hopes for the child's future. Mothers, in their common role as the primary caretakers and frequently also the disciplinarians, are much occupied with these topics.

Most dream researchers agree with Calvin Hall's finding that the members of a dreamer's family make up a high percentage of the characters in one's dreams. Unmarried young dreamers, in their teens and early twenties, tend to dream about their mother and father most often, whereas middle-aged and married dreamers more often dream about their mate and their children.[1] In general, women dream more about their families than men do.

We dream about the people with whom we are emotionally involved. This is especially true when we have mixed or changing feelings toward them. Younger dreamers, who are trying to establish independence, resist the authority of their parents or feel guilty about leaving them. Older dreamers have already resolved many of the conflicts with their parents and concentrate more on relationships with their spouse and children.

As the intensity of a relationship escalates, we dream about the person more. When we fall in love, the object of our affection appears more and more frequently in our dreams. So, too, does the person with whom we are in friction. When we clash with our mate or our child, that person's presence becomes even more frequent in our dreams. As we dream, we express our emotions about the person and try to resolve any tension. We dream about our children when we are most concerned or most involved with them.

The mother of a young child is invested with his or her development; she has a multitude of concerns about the child's safety and well-being. Mothers raising teenagers find adolescence can be as strenuous for an adult as it is for a youngster; the inevitable clashes become a regular element in her dreams as well as her days.

Stepchildren are often even more of a mixed blessing than natural offspring. Many of the remarried women in my study reported aggravating or tormenting dreams about their stepchildren. They would agree with the contemporary wit who claims, "Happily ever after was invented by someone who did not have a stepchild."[2]

Our dreams about our children and stepchildren not only alert us to current feelings, but also reveal possible solutions to problems. We can improve relations with our offspring or extended family by hearkening to the messages in our dreams.

At times our dreams about our children do not refer to the daughters or sons themselves; our children become symbols for our more youthful self or for some aspect of our personality. The symbolic meaning of dreams about children and youth is discussed toward the end of this chapter. Even those dreamers who are not parents can benefit by becoming familiar with the symbolism of children in dreams. All of us, parents or not, populate our dreams with boys and girls—characters who always have significance for the dreamer.

Dreams About Children
Concerns About a Child's Welfare

Crystal Ball Forecasts.   During the first few years of a child's life the mother's dreams about him or her are often happy as well as frightening. Mindy, for instance, reporting a dream about her six-month-old son, said,

> He is one year old, walking around. In the dream I think, "Oh, that's what he'll look like. He's really cute!"

Dreams of this type are fun. They pleasurably anticipate the hope or expectations of a mother for her child's future.

The Lost Baby.   Probably the first type of dream a new mother has— when she can get some sleep—involves fear for her newborn's welfare. Especially among first-time mothers, dreams of concern over the where-abouts and well-being of her infant are paramount. Several dreams in my collection from new mothers express fear that the baby is lost, as in this typical example of Cheryl's:

> I seem to wake up. I look over to the crib and see that the side is gone. The mattress lies on a slant from the crib to the floor. I think, "Oh, my God! Where's the baby?!"
>
> Then I see a single bed in the corner of the room where Baby is with his daddy lying beside him, talking. What a relief!

Responsibility lies heavy on the new mother. Cheryl had just nursed her two-week-old son and tried, unsuccessfully, to get him to sleep. Her husband had taken over, put the boy into the crib, kissed her good-bye while she was in a semiconscious state, and gone to work. The weary mother's subsequent dream had picked up the unfinished feeling—of not having returned the baby to his bed—and then registered the probable explanation that the father was in charge and all was well.

Although Cheryl recalled having this common dream only once, Maggie had recurrent anxiety dreams that her newborn baby was lost in the bedcovers while she searched in vain. As a long-awaited child, the infant daughter was a precious possession that Maggie feared might disappear. Happily, like most babies, the infant kept on growing into a healthy child. Mothers who dream about their baby being lost are usually expressing their concern for the child's safety.

The Blue Butterfly. Joan's version of the lost-baby dream took an animal form:

I have a very small moth in my care, downtown. I fuss over it, but wonder why I am involved with such a small creature.

The moth disappears and as I look frantically for it, I see a large blue monarch butterfly—that's my moth, I think. It was a monarch butterfly all the time.

Instead of her baby daughter, Joan searches for an animal that probably represents the infant. Many mothers describe the early fetal movements as feeling "like butterfly wings fluttering." Joan's dream adds the concept of transformation—from moth to monarch—from ordinary to regal. Perhaps this dreamer is thinking of the transformation from womb to outer world. Blue is an unusual color for a monarch; the dreamer prefers it to the characteristic orange. Joan's dream, coming about five months after the birth of her daughter, suggests a transformation of feeling—from the weary, sleep-deprived first few months of parenting to greater joy in the developing life of her child.

Dreams of hunt-the-baby, or animal, are so common I suspect they may have something to do with sensations about the "loss" of the fetus from the womb and the "finding" of the newborn. They are surely connected with the new mother's sense of responsibility.

Schoolroom Woes and Wows. Mothers of school-age children may find themselves troubled—or delighted—by dreams about their child's performance.

All parents identify with their child. The mother whose dancing career was frustrated may push her daughter into an overly rigorous ballet program at an early age, less for the child's interest or aptitude and more for the parent's vicarious satisfaction. The mother hopes her daughter will achieve in her stead and that she can shine in the same spotlight of fame. For such a mother, dreams of her daughter's outstanding dancing, for instance, may be wishes to be applauded or appreciated herself. Symbolically the same dream might suggest that the woman's "inner child" is performing well. Only the dreamer's associations to the images can clarify the dream's meaning.

The mother who is dissatisfied with her husband or with her father may concentrate enormous energy on directing her son into a career that is inappropriate for his skills but that she regards as prestigious. Dreams of the son being a great leader or spiritual figure may spring from the mother's needs. The child may become the parent's stand-in, a compensation for past failures and hopes for future stardom.

To a certain extent, it is desirable to have ambition for our children and to live through their accomplishments, but we must learn to recognize when something is truly in the child's best interests and when it only serves our own pride. Mothers need to find ways of fulfilling themselves directly.

Concerns about a child's academic performance in school or about the child's popularity stimulate negative dreams. These, too, may originate in realistic anxieties about the child's welfare or from the mother's own sense of inadequacy. The child's difficulties may reawaken painful experiences in the mother's past.

Dreams of the child failing an examination may warn the parent that the child needs help in a subject. From a symbolic point of view, the same dream may refer to the mother's sense of being "tested" in some situation for which she feels unprepared and fears she will "fail."

Child Hurt or Killed. As babies grow into young children, parents continue to have occasional alarming dreams that arise from concerns for the child's safety. Mothers typically dream about injury or danger to their child. Now, however, these scenarios involve more complex settings than the bedroom. Department stores, city streets, fairgrounds, seashore resorts, and other places serve as the setting for a child in peril. Such dreams can be warnings to the parent about risky people or situations they perceived but did not attend to during the day. Other frightening dreams about children replay minor or major disasters that have already taken place.

Danger Zone. Mothers report that they sometimes feel more anguished over dreaming about their child's injury or death than from any other kind of nightmare. Among the "worst nightmares" I recorded from women in this study, two were of the dreamer's children being hurt. For example, Moira dreamed:

> I'm standing in a place. Nearby are a line of men from a state prison. I'm with the children. My oldest son runs over near the prisoners. I call him to come back. He ignores me. One of the men rapes him. It is excruciating. He's just a little boy. I wake very upset.

The pain of such dreams is considerable. Moira's dream was probably triggered, in part, by the fact that there had been an incident in her hometown in which a man had climbed into a bedroom and molested a small boy; it was much in the news. Beyond this, Moira may have been feeling particularly vulnerable herself. When we are feeling emotionally "hurt," we sometimes dream of a child in danger.

Rescue From the Cliff. Whenever possible, the dreamer should take action to help an endangered dream child. For example, Chloe, who dreamed about her son before he was conceived, cited her worst nightmare:

> Something happens to Michael. He is playing with friends on a cliff. Somehow he falls off. I see it happening and am able to catch him.

By acting to save her child in the dream, Chloe is beginning to resolve the situation the dream symbolizes. She is mobilizing her resources to cope in the waking state, whether the dream is expressing fear about her "inner child" or fear about her actual one.

Explanations for Dreams of a Child in Danger. Dreamers may take comfort from the fact that most mothers have dreams about their children being in trouble. Literally hundreds of the dreams in my collection are those of a mother's bad dreams about her child. It is essential for a mother to realize that such dreams rarely predict future events. We dream of our child's affliction or destruction when:

- We fear for the child's actual safety
- We fear for the child's emotional well-being
- We fear we have neglected the child
- We are expressing emotional damage to some part of ourself

Wrong Number.   When I remarried in my middle thirties, my daughter Cheryl was only twelve. I had a series of dreams about her that definitely had to do with my daughter herself. I was worried about the effect of the divorce on her, the relationship with her father, and how to establish a good relationship between my loved child and my beloved husband. During this time period my husband and I were on a short holiday when I dreamed:

> I am talking to Cheryl from a pay phone. We get disconnected.
> I'm trying to tell the operator the number of her telephone. I
> have it written down, but the numbers are mixed with other
> numbers and it is hard to decipher. I wake in frustration, trying
> to recall the number.

Dreams of this type almost always have to do with emotional communication. Here I am "in touch" by means of a pay telephone rather than one at home, suggesting that the contact with my preadolescent child is "costly." The connection between us—the emotional communication—exists at first, but then is "broken." I am desperately trying to figure out how to get in contact with her once more, but the means to do so is "hard to decipher."

On the surface, I was away from home and did want to stay in contact with my daughter during my absence. But the frustration of this dream indicates that more was involved—I felt that the communication between us might break down. I had good reason to worry.

Despite efforts on all our parts, a great deal of suppressed hostility was developing. Furthermore, my daughter reached menarche just a few weeks before turning thirteen; the hormonal storm accompanying this, combined with the other major changes in her life, proved to be too much. Right before an escalation of the problems and a confrontation I dreamed:

> A house is coming apart; chairs and tables and things are coming
> off the walls where they were attached. Everything seems weird
> and distorted. At one point I am holding onto a chair on which
> Cheryl is seated.

I am very angry that she is blithely ignoring her position and
chatting away. I say, "Do you realize that you're here entirely
because I'm holding you? Do something to support your own
weight!" If I let go, she would drop and she felt heavy.

In this dream I seem to be anticipating the coming eruption. My dream says
that I feel as though "things are coming apart." I am doing my best to "hold
her in place" and keep the child from getting hurt. But I resent that I have
to be continually defending my daughter and "supporting her position"
without any help from her. She is making it difficult for me, yet I do not
want to "drop" her.

Like many a remarried woman I felt torn between the needs of my child
and those of my new husband. Happily, for us the issues were eventually
resolved. After many years, much pain, and some sound help we all came
to love and respect one another. My daughter grew into a fine young
woman with a family of her own, one of my favorite people. The dreams
that paralleled this journey would fill a book. Variations on the same themes
are replayed in the minds of dreaming mothers throughout the world.

In other instances when I dream of my daughter in danger, it is not
actually about her as a person, but rather a part of myself that feels vulnerable. This type of dream is discussed in the section on symbolism.

Intruders Break Into Home.   Lorene, in her late forties and a mother
of four children, tells me that she has recurrent dreams:

Intruders are breaking into my house, threatening my family. I
rout them. I'm always organizing the four children to escape.
Sometimes my husband is there, sometimes not.

Recurrent dreams always suggest there is some situation that remains unresolved. For Lorene, who married when she was only eighteen, her family
is paramount. She has been constantly concerned with their welfare. Although in the past few years, as her children go off to college, she has
developed a successful career as an art dealer, her children continue to be
foremost. On one level, her dream could express her ongoing concern about
their welfare. Understanding Lorene's recurrent dream is complicated by the
fact that a few years ago she was diagnosed as having breast cancer.

Since Lorene's children are grown up and seem to be doing well, her
recurrent dreams are less likely to be about them per se. Whether her dream
refers to her general sense of insecurity or to the threat of danger to her

physical body is unclear. Houses frequently represent the woman's body in dreams, and her body has certainly been "broken into" and "threatened." The positive aspect of her dream is that she is taking action to protect her valuable property (represented by the children) and routs the illness or whatever danger the intruders symbolize. Dreamers who can cope with perilous situations in their dreams have a better chance of succeeding in dealing with the waking-life situation they represent.

Dreamers who learn to assess when the picture language of their dreams refers to their own child, as distinct from when it refers to the childlike part of themselves, or when the two blend, will be able to extract the best guidance from their dreams.

Concerns About a Child's Behavior

Dreams about teenagers are frequently negative. Because the parent–teen relationship is so fraught with conflict in our culture, it becomes a major topic in a mother's dreams. As a child enters the teenage years, his or her behavior becomes increasingly challenging to parental authority. Yet gaining independence from the parent is one of the major tasks of the teenage child. It is the only way the youth can become a responsible adult. The mother's and father's ideas of correct behavior often clash with the teenager's, so the parent must find a way of permitting and encouraging a healthy independence while simultaneously guiding the youngster toward wholesome development.

The Gutter Kid.   Ginny, in struggling to cope with the rebellious behavior of her thirteen-year-old daughter, found herself agonized in this nightmare:

> My daughter is living with my sister in the house where I've grown up. I've sent her there because she's been in trouble.
>
> When I go back to take her out, I find that she has changed for the worse. She is promiscuous and mouthy. She blows smoke in my face. She's wearing cheap perfume. A real gutter kid!
>
> She says, "Too bad if you don't like it!" I think, "What have I done?" I don't like her. She's the total opposite of everything I want rolled into one.

In fact Ginny's daughter was not behaving as badly as depicted in her mother's dream. The nightmare, like most dreams, exaggerated certain tendencies, illustrating her worst fears come true. Dreams of this sort can motivate the dreamer to take necessary action to prevent the fear from being realized by such things as initiating confidential talks with the child, consulting the child's teacher and school counselor, or seeking professional therapy.

During this same period of time Ginny also had repetitive nightmares about being chased and hurt by a murderous ex-husband. When I asked whether anything stressful was currently going on, she told me about the difficulties with her teenage daughter. "It's *his* daughter, and the traits that bother me about her are traits of his." In her dream language she was likening the distress over her daughter's behavior to being "attacked" again and again by her former husband. Understanding the connection between the threatening nightmares and the current stress made Ginny feel considerably better; it relieved her mind of the fear that the dreams about the former husband were predictive.

The Growing Baby.   A mother's dream concerns about her child's character and welfare are frequently lifelong, whether she is asleep or awake. Fleur, a woman in her forties who is the mother of four adult children, has recurrent dreams of having a baby:

> The infant is just born, very small and weak. In the first dreams I had about this baby, it was always frail. I nursed it and cared for it. Lately the baby has grown. It has gotten stronger and older. These days the baby seems pretty healthy when I dream of it.

As Fleur and I talked about the possible meanings of her repetitive dream, she had an insight that made the symbolism obvious. At first her thoughts centered around her desire for more children. In addition to the four she had delivered, she had had three miscarriages, two following the birth of her last child. Maternity and nurturance were especially important to Fleur, although she carried on a career as well.

I explained that dreams of nurturing a child may symbolize the development of a creative project. But when I mentioned that recurrent dreams usually suggest an issue that is unresolved, Fleur flushed and became teary-eyed. She told me then that one of her daughters recently underwent an abortion. Fleur, wanting more children herself, experienced a considerable trauma over her daughter's abortion. Her recurrent dream, it now seemed to her, stood for a wish to nurture the child that her daughter had sacrificed. The fact that the child of her dream grew healthier and stronger was a good sign. It suggested that Fleur was developing some inner strength herself.

Locked Out.   One of the older women in my study, Ada, reported a dream about her adult daughter:

> I go to visit my daughter, but she has locked all the doors. She refuses to answer when I knock and won't let me in.

Ada was having difficulty communicating with her daughter at the time of this dream. She was trying in every way she could to "reach" her daughter, but the younger woman "refused to answer" or respond to the efforts. The dreamer felt "locked out." Ada told this dream to her daughter, no doubt with the hope that it would compel her to relate in a more satisfactory way.

The Angry Alligator.   Men, too, struggle with relationships to their children in their dreams. Franklin, the father of an adult daughter in her late twenties, told me his dream after having a quarrel with her:

> An alligator is chasing after my daughter and gaining on her.

In retrospect, Franklin thinks he may have been too harsh in expressing his disapproval of his daughter's behavior. He was likening himself in his dream to the alligator in vicious pursuit of the young woman. Animals that devour others with sharp teeth—alligators, crocodiles, sharks, wolves—often become the characters that represent anger for dreamers. The big teeth are a metaphor in the dreaming mind for "biting words," "cutting words," or, in slang terms, "being chewed out." At times we are the victims in our dreams of the beast of prey. As parents we are more apt to play an aggressive role toward our children in dreams when we judge ourselves to have been unreasonably angry. Fathers in particular are more apt to dream of physical aggression directed toward their children; mothers dream more of verbal attacks.[3]

If a parent's conflicts over her children are severe, those regarding stepchildren are extreme.

Dreams About Stepchildren

The Wicked Stepmother and the Fairy Godmother

Wicked Stepchildren.   The bad repute acquired by stepmothers is familiar from fairy tales and folklore. For many stepparents, the feeling is reciprocal—they dislike the stepchild as much as they are disliked. Modern marriages proliferate stepchildren at a fantastic rate. Often, especially after the first few crises, stepmothers feel as enthusiastic about their stepchild's behavior as the Queen did about Snow White's beauty.

The new wife confronting the husband's children by a former marriage acquires a surprise parcel. She unwraps it with anticipation, hoping for the best, but is sometimes shocked by the contents. Likewise the new husband, facing his wife's child or children by a former marriage, may find the bonus less than a bargain.

Prospective stepchildren who appear delightful during the courting stage may actually like and encourage the candidate for their parent's mate. Once the couple has wed, however, and the stepparent is forced to exercise authority, the stepchild can turn resentful and use every ploy available to sabotage the new marriage. Stepparents and stepchildren commonly resent the mate's time and attention being given to the "rival." In fact, friction over stepchildren is a major area of conflict in remarriage.

Running away, ignoring the "intruder," acting delinquent, stealing jewelry from the stepmother, inventing lies about her, defying the new father's regulations with curses—these are some of the tactics the stepchild may adopt. The parent is in the middle between the child of the first marriage and the new mate. As in the ancient Roman form of execution in which the four limbs of the victim were each tied to one of four horses that were then driven in opposite directions, the conflicted parent sometimes feels torn asunder.

This strife over stepchildren tends to be even fiercer than disputes over a couple's natural child. With a child born to the original parents, both mother and father share a common history with the child. They carry the softening influence of experiences nurturing a helpless infant, they remember the nights of fever, the joyful first steps, the sweet embraces of childhood. Shared memories like this serve as a shield against the harshness adolescents may fling. The "new" parent, unarmed by loving remembrances, faces the teenager's assaults full-force. Many a stepparent falls wounded.

Sinking in Raw Sewage.   Fiona found herself in this kind of turmoil once into a second marriage with a loving mate. She exerted herself strenuously to please the three acquired stepsons. They, on their part, regarded her with suspicion. She seemed strangely unlike their mother.

Although she was eventually able to overcome the resistance of two of the boys, Fiona was anxious at every appearance of the third. He chose to act with hostile indifference on his visits, making a good relationship virtually impossible. "He surreptitiously knifes me," she confided, speaking for many a stepparent.

On one occasion when the youth's arrival was imminent, Fiona dreamed:

> I am driving a car with my dog along the canals near the airport. In the dream there are many more canals than actually exist.
>
> Suddenly the car goes off the road into a canal with green, bubbling, raw sewage. I struggle to get myself and the dog out of the car and try to make my way to the shore.
>
> Then I see my husband standing on the shore. He tells me to stay still; he'll come. He saves us.

Here Fiona is in danger of drowning in the raw sewage that, it emerged as we discussed the dream, represented the "shitty" feelings she had about her troublesome stepson. The setting is on the way to the airport, where the couple will be meeting the expected stepson. The car, as dream cars frequently do, stood for her way of moving through life at the moment; she lost control and swerved into a mess.

Her dog, Fiona explained, is a valuable creature to her, one she takes care to protect. On a deeper level, pets often represent the dreamer's instincts—here her dog might symbolize the instinct of self-protection. The most positive element in this dream is the husband's active role to extricate his wife from the mess. This imagery indicates that Fiona feels her husband is supportive.

Septic Tank Explosion.   Dreamers develop their own preferred symbols for particular emotional events. Excrement is a common one to refer to a situation one finds repulsive. The same symbol recurs in a later dream of Fiona's following an uncomfortable encounter with the stepson:

My husband and I are in a very large house, in an upstairs room. The furnishing is not great; it looks like a sparsely furnished shell that makes me uncomfortable. There are septic tank pipes coming up through the floor, like exposed plumbing.

A workman is there to plunge the pipes. It seems there is a clog in all the cesspool material from the past one hundred years. He is trying to relieve this pent-up material that is clogging the pipes.

I know it is going to come out in a volcanic eruption. My husband knows, too, but is matter-of-fact about it. I feel much more apprehensive.

Suddenly there is a blinding flash—like an oil well erupting—it bursts everywhere. All the stuff from the explosion is flying in my face. It feels like my eyelids are searing. I wake up.

"I don't usually think in scatological metaphors," Fiona hastened to explain, "but he [the difficult stepson] treats me that way. He dumps shit on me." Fiona's associations to the one hundred years of the dream led her to mention the Hundred Years War. "My husband and I have had this conflict forever. It has always been and will always be," she added.

Fiona's septic tank dream gives graphic expression to her anxiety that her suppression of negative emotions about the stepson is "building up to an explosion." Sometimes, indeed, such explosions are essential to clear the air. This may provide the basis for a better understanding between the couple. In other cases, marital partners may have to accept that discussion of the stepchildren is potentially dynamite and treat the topic cautiously, regard it as untouchable, or get professionals to handle it with them. A general rule might be, "Never criticize the stepchild to your mate."

Humor helps. In her delightful book *Funny Sauce: Us, the Ex, the Ex's New Mate, the New Mate's Ex, and the Kids,* Delia Ephron serves up a potful of stepparenting adventures. Her definition of the extended family is classic: "It consists entirely of people who are not related by blood, many of whom can't stand each other."[4]

Among the true stories of her family life, Ephron cites a diary entry of her daughter's dream about her future stepfather:

Last night I had a dream that I found Joel [the fiancé] kissing someone else, and poor Mom was so upset. I had to kick him out.[5]

Many a stepchild wishes "poor Mom" would relinquish her suitor, and would be delighted to "kick him out" for her. Sometimes, however, the tables turn.

Magic Wands

From time to time a dream provides the inspiration that solves a serious stepchild-stepparent problem.

Multiplication Rhymes.   Jeff had recently acquired a ten-year-old stepson, Lewis.[6] The boy, just enrolled in a fourth-grade class that was much more advanced than his previous school, was having trouble; mathematics, in particular, was causing him grief. Vainly the child struggled to learn the multiplication table while adjusting to his new home life. This generated tension that caused quarreling among the family members.

One night, after an especially frustrating session trying to help his stepson learn his times tables, Jeff had a dream that included some characters singing a jingle:

> You can't remember the words of this song,
> 'Cause we make them up as we go along.

The amusing jingle stuck in his mind all the next day. That evening, as he again tried to help Lewis with his homework, Jeff had a sudden inspiration. He began composing rhymes for the multiplication table. Soon Lewis was making up his own verses:

> Nine times eight is seventy-two,
> If you don't believe me,
> I'll kiss your shoe!

Inventing several nonsensical but memorable verses imprinted the times table into Lewis's mind at last. Literally overnight he went from the bottom of his class to the top. As if a magic wand had been waved, the problem was solved. Jeff's dream-inspired jingle making marked the beginning of a long-term friendship between stepson and stepfather. Our dreams are intimately connected with our daytime difficulties.

The goal for stepparents is to develop a friendship with the stepchild.

Stepparents can never be a replacement of the natural mother or father; they can—if they work on it and dream on it and are lucky—become good friends with their stepchildren.

The Symbolic Meaning of Dreams of Children

Children are always significant in women's dreams. The little girls and boys who populate the dreams of women may symbolize a variety of emotions. For women who are not parents, the symbolic meaning of children in dreams is simpler to comprehend than it is for mothers.

A woman who is not a mother may dream of a child:

- When her body is physiologically receptive to pregnancy, at ovulation during the reproductive years
- When she yearns for a child
- When she fantasizes a child that was lost in miscarriage or aborted, or one she is unable to conceive
- When there is an actual child in her life, a niece or nephew, for instance, with whom she has an emotional relationship

We shall see how additional meanings may also arise.

A mother, we have said, often has nightmares about her child:

- When she feels concern for the child's physical safety
- When she feels concern for the child's emotional well-being
- When she feels she has been neglectful of the child
- When she feels angry toward or guilty about the child

Mothers may have good dreams about their children when they are feeling happy about them or are sharing a joyful event with them.

In these cases the woman's dreams—parents and nonparents alike—refer to an actual child. At other times a woman may dream of a child as representing:

- A younger aspect of herself, her "inner child," perhaps vulnerable or immature. The dreamer may be referring to emotions that were active when she was the age depicted in the dream. This is especially true of a woman's dreams about her daughter.

- A characteristic of herself that resembles a strong characteristic of the child. For instance, dreaming of a child who is "a spoiled brat" usually indicates that the dreamer feels she acted in a spoiled way about some situation.
- A developing idea or concept. Dreamers often cast their projects into dreams as "my baby" or "my child."

Eventually a mother's dreams about her child come to represent, at least sometimes, herself. Dreams about one's child being lost, injured, kidnapped, or killed may symbolize danger to the dreamer's "inner child" as well as to the actual child. The youngster frequently stands for a precious and vulnerable or innocent part of herself that is at risk.

In pleasurable dreams the child may symbolize a valuable growing or developing aspect of the dreamer. Whether the dream is happy or frightening, the age of the child is meaningful. A woman with a grown son or daughter who dreams about her child at age ten, for instance, may be dealing with her own issues that were important when the child was that age; something in the present has revived similar emotions. We saw that when Cassie was pregnant with her second child, she dreamed of a four-year-old boy in an aquarium tank who was the age her previously aborted child would have been had he lived. Her current pregnancy stirred up memories and feelings associated with her previous pregnancy.

The age of the child in a dream sometimes represents the length of an important relationship or project. It is helpful to ask oneself, "What happened in my life ten years ago?" or "What has gone on in my life for the past ten years?" Although we may not recognize it at the time, no detail is meaningless in our dreams.

More important than the relevance of the age of a child to the dreamer is the child's behavior in the dream and the responses the dreamer made. Was the child sad, hurt, troublesome, or totally unaware of what was happening? Was the dreamer loving and nurturing or rejecting and neglectful?

When Cookie dreamed of a baby dying in her arms, she was expressing her sadness over her physician's diagnosis that she was incapable of bearing a child. The dying baby was the death of her hopes to become a mother. When Miriam dreamed of giving birth to a baby who had her full intellect in four days, she was expressing happiness about a new lover and other good changes in her life. The gifted child was the birth of her hopes for a second marriage with a desirable mate. When I dreamed of finding a baby that had been forgotten (see chapter 7), I was reminding myself to get back to work on my current project, to attend to my "baby." Noticing the condition of the dream child and your behavior toward it will help you understand the children in your dreams.

Jung's Views About Children in Dreams

From the Jungian perspective, children in dreams are the formative forces of the unconscious. He sees them as beneficent and protective figures.[7] We dream of a child, he says, when some great spiritual change is about to take place.

The archetype of the divine or mystic child who solves riddles and teaches wisdom or who, in heroic aspect, liberates the world from monsters, sometimes appears in the dreams of modern women.

The promise associated with childhood, the youthful reawakening force, may stir in dreams when a woman feels hopeful. In art symbolism, children are symbols of the future, in contrast to old men, who symbolize the past. The child is the beginning of new life, in fact and in dream.

The child unites the opposites of mother and father, growing beyond conflict to form a new life. The child has the potential of wholeness. So, too, when women dream of a youth, they identify with the eternally youthful power. A woman may see the young women in her dreams acting as erotic figures, fatal sirens, or as spontaneous, warm, loving beings. The young men of her dreams may be drifters and bums, or mighty heroes.

Each figure contains seeds of potential growth that the dreamer may choose to disperse or gather. Children and youngsters in our dreams tell of the young parts of ourselves and how they either wither or flourish.

CHAPTER TEN

Menopausal Dreams

I am startled to see that there are several sinks filled with
dirty water. They need to be drained.

—Author's dream diary, age forty-six and a half,
immediately prior to menopause

The woman whose season of childbearing is complete changes hue like the
autumn leaves. Her hair touched with silver, her skin marked with the lines
of living, she is nonetheless full of beauty. Much joy may abide in this phase
of life. Sad, indeed, that few women are prepared for the process of menopause; few understand what to expect, how to cope with it, or how to make
the most of the glory of their autumns—fall can be spectacular.

Menopause is a critical turning point in a woman's life cycle, equal in
significance to the menarche, the first intercourse, and the birthing of a
baby. For many females it becomes a crisis of major proportion; for some
it marks the beginning of self-discovery. We shall see how this process of
menopause—its physical manifestations and its psychological responses—is
charted in our dreams. As explained in a later section, the menopausal
dream described above reveals much to the woman who can "read" its
imagery.

The Hidden "Passage."   In our society menopause remains a nearly taboo subject. Young women generally regard the topic with a kind of horror, often equating the cessation of their reproductive years with asexuality, useless old age, and death. Adult women seldom know more about menopause than the whispered family stories of how Aunt Lizzie "went bonkers at the change of life." Menopausal women themselves seldom challenge these assumptions. Those who confront the issues glean information unobtrusively from older women of their acquaintance—who were themselves usually uninformed—or from peers, books, and their gynecologists. Few would carry literature about menopause in public or discuss the topic in mixed company. Men are frequently mystified by the process.

The stereotypes about menopause harm all women. Those who must inevitably face it in the future feel condemned to fear without cause; those who are going through it suffer needlessly in silence; those of us who have finished menopause are prevented from freely sharing our experiences and from finding the fulfillment that is our birthright.

We do not cease being women because the blood or the milk no longer flows from our bodies. If anything, we are more complete women. We have tread almost full cycle. We know what was unknown to us before. We have experienced another crossing in the great life spiral. Another "mystery" of womanhood stands revealed. We survive with wisdom.

Rites of Passage Needed.   In some societies this life passage is celebrated with ritual. When a woman turns sixty in China, I am told, it is considered a momentous event. Family and friends gather, not simply to mark a significant birthday as we do, but rather to honor the status and wisdom of the elder.[1] So, too, many of the Native American tribes give special privileges to their older women. Having passed menopause, the woman is allotted greater freedom; she is honored for her knowledge. When people in India have fulfilled their duties as "householder," having married, had a family, and contributed to society, they are expected to seek inner wisdom. The older woman or man who renounces all to search for spiritual understanding is highly admired.

When a society or tradition reveres the elderly, special positions of status exist for the older woman, whose worth and power are appreciated.[2] Our "tribes" have no ritual passage for our women's transition to "wise woman." We have few models to embrace. Part of the reason for this deficiency is the fact that as recently as a few decades ago, women did not need to trouble their minds about life after menopause. In 1900 few women survived to experience it. The average life expectancy being fifty, a female was considered truly old by this age.[3] Two hundred years ago women rarely lived through their childbearing years, let alone beyond them.

Today a woman is likely to pass through menopause sometime between 45 and 55 years of age; she will probably survive an additional 20 years or more beyond this. The current average life expectancy for an American white newborn female is 78.7 years (1984 census)[4]; for all other American women, it is about 75 years. If a white American woman reaches the age of 65, she is likely to live until almost 84.[5] Depending on her heritage and physical health, she may live much longer. After menopause, then, one-third to one-half of her life may lie ahead of her. Whether these years are filled with decay or active living depends on many factors, the most important of which may be her determination.

The population in the United States has a rapidly expanding segment of middle-aged and elderly persons, especially—since they are more long-lived—women. We desperately need new values that give these "elders" their rightful voice.

Role Models Needed. Throughout life women have had few models of power to inspire and guide them. In a study of children's dreams that I conducted in 1984,[6] the dreams of boys were filled with heroes from the media: Superman, Captain Kirk of the *Enterprise,* characters from the Star Wars saga, and countless others. Boys from India had dreams of gods and goddesses rather than media stars. Most boys had some sort of individual dream hero.

The girls, in contrast, had few heroines in their dreams. When heroines appeared, they were most often of a general type, such as princesses or brides. Their importance came only from their relationship to the bridegroom, king, or prince. A handful were movie stars or actresses or ballet dancers. Only one girl cast herself in the role of Wonder Woman; another saw herself as a good witch. If the girl approaching maidenhood has few strong female figures to follow, the menopausal woman and her older sister have even less.

Now is the time to define the new old woman. Not as witch, or hag, or crone—a word derived from words meaning "withered old woman," "useless old ewe," "carcass," and "carrion." Let us seek instead the best in our elder sisters—the wise woman, the sibyl, the one who comprehends the mysteries.

By learning from those who have gone ahead of us in life's dance, by respecting their findings and their essence, we prepare for ourselves a place of value and accumulate a legacy of hope for the daughters who follow. No longer mainly a maiden or a mother, our role now—if we but embrace it—is that of the wise woman.

Physical Changes at Menopause

The Two Main Symptoms of Menopause
Result From Low Estrogen

The Seven-Year Shift. Simply put, menopause means the cessation of menses. Like her younger self approaching menarche, a woman's body undergoes changes. This "change of life" takes place over several years, just as pubertal changes do. The ending of menstruation is the culmination of gradual shifts that began when the woman was only twenty-five; around that time her estrogen level began to decrease in minuscule amounts.[7]

Sometime between the ages of forty-five and fifty-five (for a few women it is earlier or later), the woman's estrogen level falls low enough that her ovaries stop ripening eggs and cease production. They no longer respond to the hormones put out by the pituitary gland beneath the brain. The woman's adrenal glands continue to manufacture a small amount of estrogen, but after menopause, her ovaries have reduced their estrogen output by about 75 percent.[8] Now smaller, the older ovaries still manufacture androgens, which are converted by the fat cells into a weaker estrogen called estrone.

These natural biological changes take place in a woman's body over a span of approximately seven years.[9] Thus a woman may experience premenopausal changes as early as her late thirties. Since the average age of menopause is fifty, about half of all women are beginning to go through premenopausal changes by forty-three or earlier—although few of them recognize this fact.

Of course a woman may experience aspects of menopause at any age if her ovaries are completely removed. Many women who undergo surgery for removal of the uterus or portions of the ovaries mistakenly believe this brings on menopause. Their menses may indeed cease, but unless the ovaries are entirely absent, they continue to produce estrogen; this hormone will decrease and eventually result in other symptoms of menopause at the age they would have naturally undergone it.

Women should also be aware of the fact that smoking brings on an earlier menopause than they would ordinarily have from genetic causes.[10] Several studies demonstrate that women who smoke reach menopause earlier; other studies reveal that even those women exposed to passive smoking—their spouses smoked, for example—reached menopause a couple of years earlier than those married to nonsmokers. Smoking and excess exposure to the sun are also the two most common causes of wrinkling and aging skin. Smokers beware—cigarette smoking adversely affects a woman's hormones.

Reduction in the amount of estrogen in a woman's bloodstream imbalances the body's "thermostat." As a result the woman undergoing menopause, and sometimes for a few years afterward, experiences "hot flashes" (or hot flushes, as they are called in England) and perhaps also night sweats.

The hot flashes are experienced as a sudden flooding with warmth, often accompanied by sweating and dizziness (described in greater detail below). They may occur several times a day and at night drag the woman repeatedly from her sleep, leaving her restless, damp, and weary. Theorists speculate that these flashes are triggered by biochemical events in the brain.[11] Other symptoms are frequently reported, but hot flashes, night sweats, and vaginal dryness have been discovered to be based upon the reduced level of estrogen; other symptoms may be caused by lack of sleep consequent to frequent awakenings from night sweats.[12]

Hot Flashes in the Laboratory. Researchers in 1975 recorded measurements of a menopausal woman during her hot flashes.[13] She lay nude on top of a nylon net bed; connections to various instruments allowed monitoring of her physiological changes. The investigators found that each hot flash lasted about 3.5 minutes. When the flash began, there was a sudden increase of the woman's skin temperature all over her body by 1 to 4 degrees Fahrenheit; her heart rate simultaneously accelerated.

This sudden change triggered the body's reflex response to fever of any kind: internal heat radiated to the skin; the heated skin began to perspire; and finally the evaporation of the perspiration cooled the skin. Sweating was most profuse on the woman's forehead and nose, less on her chest and nearby areas. She lost about one teaspoonful of water with each hot flash. Further studies have confirmed the same general pattern. We can understand from this process why many women dream of dryness and fire during the time they experience hot flashes.

Other investigators observed that hot flashes are aggravated by certain conditions. Hot weather, for example, tends to bring on hot flashes; a study of several menopausal women during June and July verified that more hot flashes were experienced on hotter days than on cooler ones.[14] Some women find that hot drinks and hot or spicy food have a similar effect. Emotional stress can also trigger hot flashes, so that women whose circumstances are tension producing—such as trouble with teenagers, divorce, or a death in the family often have a more difficult time. Such women simultaneously must cope with physiological changes and psychological difficulties.

Women report hot flashes more than any other symptom.[15] It is estimated that 85 percent or more of women have them, with greater or lesser frequency. Hot flashes reach their peak near the cessation of menses, although they usually begin before and may last for five to ten years beyond. Some women have only a few a month, others are troubled with several an hour. About 30 percent of women seek medical advice or treatment for their hot flashes.

Extreme caution is needed in selecting physicians or psychotherapists for help with menopausal problems. Many health professionals still mistakenly believe that a woman's menopausal symptoms are neurotic complaints. Freud, for instance, said that menopausal women were "quarrelsome and obstinate, petty and stingy . . . sadistic and anal-erotic."[16] An analyst who follows in this tradition would only damage a patient who seeks help. Some analysts refuse to treat women of menopausal age and older.[17] Menopausal women who feel they can benefit from psychotherapy should seek counsel with a person who understands that many symptoms are hormonal and who also believes in the potential for change at any age.

Night Sweats in the Laboratory. Scientists are certain that hot flashes and night sweats are physiological, not imaginary, because laboratory studies show that they occur during sleep. These symptoms are not neurotic complaints but real events. Physician Howard Judd and his colleagues at the University of California School of Medicine in Los Angeles monitored the all-night sleep of nine women with severe hot flashes.[18] Their measurements proved that numerous episodes of changes in skin temperature (the hot flash) occurred during sleep. In forty-five out of forty-seven episodes, the woman awoke within five minutes following or sometimes just prior to the hot flash. When the women suffering hot flashes were given estrogen, they had significantly fewer flashes and fewer awakenings during the night.

In a study by Joan Thomson, along with physician and dream researcher Ian Oswald, at Royal Edinburgh Hospital in Scotland, one group of women ingested a placebo for six weeks followed by eight weeks of estrogen.[19] A control group took the placebo (an inactive substance) for the entire time.

Once again, the researchers documented that the women taking estrogen awoke from sleep less frequently and returned to sleep more quickly. These findings are crucial because many physicians and lay persons still attribute menopausal symptoms to a distraught mind. The evidence for the physiological origin of hot flashes and night sweats is incontrovertible.

Estrogen Stimulates Dreaming. Researchers Joan Thomson and Ian Oswald also demonstrated (in 1977) that taking estrogen shifts the proportion of sleep time that is spent in rapid eye movement (the characteristic sign of dreaming).[20] When women took estrogen, they dreamed more; when they were estrogen deficient, they dreamed less. Here is the strongest evidence we have for estrogen's connection with dreaming.

When we are deprived of dreaming at night, we suffer during the day. Our whole sense of well-being depends upon sleeping well, especially on our having dreams. Numerous studies have validated the role dreaming plays in making our sleep refreshing. Considering the enormous impact lack of sleep or insomnia has upon people—making them irritable, anxious, under par, and inefficient—the benefits from estrogen therapy for the menopausal woman may outweigh the small risks. Every woman, however, should assess her case with her gynocologist.

Fire and Water: Dreams Depicting Physical Changes

Dreams Associated With Missed Periods

Dirty Water. Each woman's pattern of menopause varies. Some women find that their periods simply stop; others notice their menses growing lighter and lighter until the flow ceases; still others are troubled with excessively heavy periods that require curettage; yet others alternate heavy bleeding with extremely light flows. Most women begin to skip occasional periods a few years prior to menopause itself.

My own pattern, for instance, was mixed. Since this material is generally unfamiliar, especially as related to dream life, I describe it here. My periods ceased completely in 1981 when I was forty-six and a half, but as early as 1975, six years prior to menopause, my extremely regular menses were no longer reliable. Whereas the usual flow was every twenty-six to twenty-eight days, that year it once came at a fifty-day interval, followed by a normal interval, then twice in one month, followed by another normal interval, and then twice in the next month. This erratic bleeding continued for the next year. In 1977 the usually heavy flow concluded with exceptionally light days. Then toward the end of the year there were a couple of months with exceptionally heavy bleeding. In 1978 there was one month with two periods and four months with skipped periods; 1979 was similarly erratic. The last six months of 1980 were marked only by light spotting or no period; this spotting continued for the first two months of 1981, and there the menses stopped completely.

This variation of heavy and light bleeding, as well as missed periods gave me a chance to observe the physiological process in my dreams. For example, on the occasion when I had nothing but one day of spotting for six months, I had the dream described at the opening of this chapter, about sinks filled to the brim with dirty water. For me, as well as for many women, sinks are frequently a symbol of the womb—corresponding to the womb's capability of being filled and emptied. This dream suggested that there was still a need to release some material. Sure enough, two light but relatively normal periods followed a few weeks later—then, complete cessation.

Later on in the same dream of the dirty water there was another obvious womb symbol:

> I learn that the emblem of a secret order is a vase, an urn, of a
> deep, almost-maroon red that is set into ceramic tile above the
> altar. Somehow this understanding entitles me to be initiated
> into the group. I wear a red velvet gown with a short cape, and
> a small golden circlet on my head.

Aside from the mystical imagery, the red urn—the container—is of the color of dark menstrual blood. The gown I wear is blood red as well. Vases and urns as well as sinks often serve as symbols for the womb in women's dreams. They, like the womb, function as receptacles for contents. The fact that the water in the sink is dirty suggests accumulated blood; the fullness of the sink indicates the likelihood of another flow. At other times when I have been bleeding heavily, I dreamed of sinks overflowing. The mystical imagery implies a positive attitude toward the natural process of menopause.

Dreams Associated With Heavy Bleeding

Red Doors. At another stage of approaching menopause, when I was bleeding profusely for longer than normal, I dreamed:

I am climbing up a ramp in a narrow tunnel, on my stomach. At the top I open several layers of red doors to a restaurant.

Then there is a mystery story about some missing jewels. Much searching. One place resembles a home where I once lived that has an all-red meditation room. Later someone asks me if the pearls are pinkish. Yes, they are unusual. A man sets out to hunt.

Narrow tunnels and hallways often represent the vagina, as in this dream; the layers of red doors may have stood for the days of heavy bleeding; the restaurant is the nourishing womb. The missing jewels probably symbolized the lost eggs (the female sexual cells)—there were few ripening in my body at the time of this dream. The pink pearls—ovum-shaped—confirmed this hypothesis. The all-red room of my past waking-life experience relates, no doubt, to the all-red womb.

Sinks, vases, tunnels, hallways, doors, jewels—the woman approaching menopause may well be able to assess the condition of her womb from the condition of these images in her dreams. Because each person has their own individual dream language—in addition to the symbols that are commonly shared because of similar shape and function to the womb—it is important to learn one's personal images. Women can do this most easily by monitoring their dreams carefully, especially during ovulation and premenstrual and menstrual times. She will soon notice what her dreams are saying about her body.

Dreams Associated With Hot Flashes and Night Sweats

Fire Alarm. The chief symptom I experienced was a night-time restlessness—awakening damp, warm, and fidgety—that reduced my usual ample dream recall and left me tired during the daytime.

Daytime hot flashes were, for the most part, exceedingly mild. Since the estrogen level dropped gradually in my case, I rarely mentioned the presence of this symptom in my journal or tied it to specific dream imagery. An exception, however, appears in an entry a couple of years after the menses ceased. It was four days after I noted a hot flash accompanied by heavy perspiration brought on by exceptionally hot weather:

I am in a house with problems. My husband has just gotten out of his car when a whole pane [pain?] glass window in the house falls forward and hangs at right angles, as though on a hinge. I call to my husband to come help me and he does.

Later I hear firemen at the door of the house. Now it seems to be a kind of cottage in which an alarm has gone off. Because the firemen get no quick answer, they circle the glass—I hear it ringing—and cut a hole through which they open the door to enter. Inside they spray a preventative liquid. I think there is smoke. A fire person—perhaps a woman—tells me to be careful where I step, that the liquid can burn if it touches the skin. In a later scene we are saying good-bye to a fictional teenage son as he goes off to camp. Much affection among us.

The dream house, which usually represents the dreamer's body, has problems. In fact, later on the same day of the intense hot flash, I had sprained my right ankle (the "right angle" of the dream) on a holiday outing. Like the large window pane, it is a "big pain" that required repair. I am warned in the dream to "watch my step."

Furthermore the dream says that my house is smaller, shrunk to cottage size. This, along with the fire alarm that has sounded, indicates that the change in the body, more specifically the womb—is one that has to do with heat. The positive aspects of the dream include my husband's helpfulness, the appearance of firefighters to control the problem and the preventative liquid that can burn the skin (as the hot flashes do). The farewell to a youth may be saying good-bye to the part of myself that began during the teenage years. From another point of view, the teenage boy could be the son we might have had—we have been married for 19 years—but now will not.

A few months after this dream I accepted my physician's urging to take a minimal dosage of estrogen, which resulted in not only elimination of hot flashes and increased sense of well-being but also in greater dream recall. All symptoms vanished.

Fire in women's dreams often represents an emotional heat, as well as a sexual state of feeling "hot." In menopausal women the stimulus for dreaming about fire may be the hot flashes occurring during sleep. Depending upon the woman's experience of menopause and her attitude toward it, the conditions of the fire will vary.

Dreams Associated With Feeling Burned-Out

Destructive Fire. For some women, fire in dreams brings devastation. One of the few accounts of menopausal dreams in the literature is described by Jungian analyst Ann Mankowitz in a small book, *Change of Life: A Psychological Study of Dreams and the Menopause*.[21] Worthwhile as Mankowitz's contribution is, it relates only three dreams from one fifty-one-year-old woman who had just completed her final menstruation. This patient, who was considerably depressed, reported a dream containing the destructive results of fire. Following a scene in which she viewed a blackened and burned-out farmhouse, with a woman who died in the fire, the dreamer reported:

> The next tableau is in a high barn next to the bedroom. It is not like a painting, but has the tactile quality of real things. The barn is scorched dry, and full of dust and ashes. From the roof hang four twisted dusty ropes, and clinging to them, one on each, are four wisps of what look like fragments of mummified bodies and hair. I know they are children, caught trying to escape the fire. I'm horrified by the gruesomeness and can hardly bear to look.[22]

This segment is referred to as "The Dead Babies." The dream continues with scenes of lost souls; a womblike coffin; neglected grass and wild bushes with a wooden sculpture composed of live trees, of brilliant orange and red colors, like autumn leaves, that have been caught and petrified by the flames; in the final scene the dreamer is led to inspect the new foundations of a building submerged in water with a source of light underneath.

For this dreamer the four corpses in the scene of the dead babies represented her four pregnancies—three children born and one miscarriage. She saw the "fruit of the womb" now "shriveled, juiceless, lifeless." She also remarked that her children called her "Mummy," an association to the mummified children. The dreamer's sense of barrenness is symbolized in the images of scorched, burned-out buildings, dust, and dead children. The ashes were not only the remnant of her reproductive capacity but also her view of her life being burned out. Mankowitz makes no mention of whether her patient was experiencing hot flashes during the time of this dream, but it seems to me quite probable.

The few positive elements in this dream set, which the therapist was able to point out to the dreamer, included the neglected grass and bushes that must have emerged from fertile soil, the new foundations upon which a new structure of self could be built, and the light of understanding. After a period of therapy this woman was able to tackle life with a new spirit.

Dreams Associated With
Changing Life Conditions

Women of menopausal age frequently have to cope with dramatic shifts of scenery in every act of their lives. At the same time that their bodies are undergoing physiological changes, their children are growing up and leaving home; they may find themselves or their mates dissatisfied with their relationships and choose this time to divorce or wander; their parents are usually aging, ill, or dying. Although these changes may eventually be liberating, they can temporarily add to the stress and confusion of the menopausal stage.

Alone in a Rocky Land. For women who find themselves on their own, this phase of life can be especially difficult. Hilda, who in her mid-fifties had been once widowed and twice divorced, struggled against despair. Her menopause started at age forty-nine, and over the next four years she was troubled with hot flashes and depression that abated somewhat with hormone replacement, although she had not been consistent with her medication. Hilda suffered a recurrent nightmare of ending up "alone, abandoned, left out, and lost." In one version,

> I'm supposed to take an airplane, but I can't because I'm looking for my father. (He has always been critical of me in waking life and is so in the dream.)
>
> I know he is hiding behind a rock. Then he disappears completely. The plane is gone. I make a futile search. I am trying to reach out, but I am left all alone.

Hilda's father was still living, but they have never been able to communicate in a way that is satisfactory to her. His quality of being "impenetrable," emotionally inaccessible, was depicted in Hilda's choice of a rock as her father's hiding place. He was unreachable, and then disappeared—probably revealing the daughter's fear of his inevitable death. Landscapes in dreams often communicate the dreamer's sense of emotional environment. Jungian analyst Marie-Louise von Franz says that landscapes in dreams as well as art frequently symbolize an inexpressible mood.[23] Here the rocky landscape represented Hilda's "rocky" interaction with her father.

Dreams of missing a connection—buses, trains, ships, and airplanes—

usually indicate, as in Hilda's dream, the sense of "missing out" on some opportunity in life. They dramatize the common saying, "I missed the boat."

Stepping Into the Void.   In a nightmare Hilda had about a year after her last divorce, an event that was close in time to her mother's death, she took a risk:

> I am walking on a narrow ridge near the ocean. I come to an
> edge with the ocean far below. Where can I go? I jump off.
> Surprisingly I find that I float down to the sandy beach below. I
> feel a resilience as I land softly. It's miraculous—I could have
> died but I took a chance and survived. I continue walking on
> an entirely different level.

This dream gave Hilda a greater sense of confidence. She saw her act of jumping into space like the chance she took in getting divorced, since she had no job, no money, no future, and no hope. "I was stepping into the void," she explained. Her dreaming mind made a concrete picture of the pun. Although her balance was precarious, her dream said, she could manage to find her way to another level without damage. Fortunately, there are some supportive forces in Hilda's life. An attractive woman, her warmth draws new friends. She has a loving daughter. Yet, like so many women of her age and situation, Hilda needs to build a strong inner center on which she can rely.

Spit in a Bucket.   Barbara, in her late forties, is experiencing the physical changes preceding menopause. Her periods have become heavier, then lighter for the past two years; her hair is thinning and nails beginning to break; she has found her sleep disturbed by waking "feeling totally wet." She commented, "I don't seem to dream as much as I used to," another indication that her estrogen is lowering. Unlike Hilda, Barbara has remained in an unhappy marriage her entire adult life. She shares with Hilda, however, some discouraged feelings about her future, reflected in a recent dream:

> My dad is standing with a pole over a bucket. In the bucket are
> some camisoles of mine with shoulder pads—they're the
> natural-colored ones (I also have black). The figure fluctuates
> between my dad and my husband. He pokes in the bucket with
> the pole and then spits into it.

On one level Barbara's dream is sexual. Containers, like the bucket in her dream, often represent the female genitals in dreams. A pole that is "poked into the bucket" is a characteristic dream symbol for the phallus. Spit in dreams is considered to be an equivalence for semen. The action in the dream, from this point of view, describes a father-husband figure performing intercourse in a mechanical way.

Barbara was not aware of this possible explanation. Her associations to the images in her dream revealed another dimension. When I asked Barbara to describe a bucket to me as if I were a child who did not know, she said, "a bucket holds something that you don't want to lose, spill, or destroy. It allows you to carry things from one place to another." A pole, she said, was "used for lots of different things. It could be something to support you as you walk along. You could hang something on it." Spit, in her perspective, is "something the body won't take, something you don't need, something you want to get rid of at the moment, to spit is to show disdain." A camisole with shoulder pads, the dreamer explained, is a garment "I hate to wear. Yet I'd put it on when I needed support." Her father, Barbara told me, never treated her mother right; he was always jealous when her mother spent time making her clothes. She says that her husband resembles her father in ways.

Understanding Barbara's associations to the key images in her dream adds richness to its sexual meaning. Her repetition of the concept "support" in reference to the pole and the shoulder pads was a critical clue. Whenever associations repeat a theme, it is central to the overall meaning of the dream.

In her dream language Barbara is saying, "My relationship to my husband resembles my father's relationship to my mother (the alternating father/husband figure). Our sexual interaction is mechanical (like poking a pole in a bucket). Yet I depend on his support (the pole that can help one walk and the pads of the camisole). I feel as though he treats me with disdain (the spit)." As we worked on getting at the meaning of her dream images, Barbara herself added, "He was maligning something precious that I own."

Barbara felt stuck in a marriage with no escape. Economically she could not afford to live comfortably on her own; it seemed better to stay where she was than to face the unknown. Barbara regretted not having gotten the advanced education she now wanted and not having developed a career. However, she was motivated enough to complete an undergraduate degree over the past few years and, since her grown children had left home, had launched an attempt at a serious career. Perhaps these new efforts led to another recent dream:

There is a flat scene with no action. I see a brick wall. On the left it is well built. Above this section I see a very positive head floating; it has lots of hair and a happy glow—bright, shiny, a female above the wall. I'm down below, in front of the wall looking up. During the dream I think, "I'm looking up to happiness."

On the right the bricks are broken off and there's this male head. It's down in front of the wall but not so much as my head. The wall's coming apart on this side.

As we talked, it emerged that this scene pictured Barbara's situation. She told me that a wall "is put up to stop things, separate things, divide." Bricks "can be strong when cemented with other bricks, stacked together they support each other and become strong. Apart, they break." A brick wall differs from other walls in that "it can fall apart on its own."

Barbara has a well-built, strong wall that separates her from the happiness that hovers above her. She sees the falling-apart section of the wall as representative of "the relationship coming apart." Although the dreamer cannot reach the happiness she seeks, it is within sight. "I'm not desperate, because there is hope," she adds.

When I asked Barbara to describe her marriage in a word or phrase, she volunteered, "Turmoil. However, it has fulfilled some section of both partners." Her dream gives a similar picture. The crumbling section of the wall is near her husband. Yet she gains some strength from the complete section of bricks that "support each other to become strong." Barbara had not yet found the way to make her marriage fulfilling, nor the courage to leave it. But she did recognize the need to find a strength within herself, to develop herself. She saw the hope of becoming the positive, happy woman she had glimpsed in a dream.

Brick walls, rocky places—the menopausal years can be hard with their physical and environmental changes. One of the major events of this time of life is often the illness or death of a parent.

The Loving Touch: Dreams of Deceased Parents

Parents may die at any age, of course, but middle-aged people are the most likely to find themselves confronting the death of their mother or father. Unresolved problems with parents often make this circumstance extremely difficult. Dreams can sometimes provide the missed chance to connect for the first time in a meaningful way. For those adults whose relationship with a parent was good, a dream encounter may be the reestablishment of a profound connection. Such dreams of the dead can give deep content.

Mother Is Young and Sweet.   In chapter 2, I described the dream of Lynette about her deceased mother. I repeat that dream here to add some information. Lynette, shortly after the surgical removal of her uterus, had to cope with her mother's illness from lung cancer and subsequent death at eighty-two. This delightful European woman who spent several years in America was helped through her mother's death by a powerful dream. Nonetheless the process was strenuous, involving oxygen tents and constant nursing care. At times the dying woman became nasty.

Lynette had felt alienated from her mother for years. She saw her as "possessed by her ego, living only for her husband and physical comforts." She regarded herself as more like her father, mentally and physically active. About two years after her mother's death, Lynette dreamed:

> Mother comes to me, dressed as she was when I was a child, in the 1930s, young—in a long dress with a low waist and a Basque beret. She has a loose sweater on top, with a pale blue, rather gray, scarf tossed over her shoulder, and white sport shoes with dots—she always was an elegant woman. Her hair is grayish.
>
> Most of all Mother has a sweet, sweet expression—she lost that in her long illness. I can vividly see her image and at the same time feel her atmosphere, what she represents. I sense a real contact is established—one that I had lost since her death.
>
> This dream leaves me with the feeling of a close contact. It makes me understand what she meant to me, what she represents in my life . . . my roots. She was very intuitive and I'm trying to develop that. I'm more like my father, physically and mentally active, more concrete. I need mother's sensitivity and subtleness. This seems like a real, true, deep contact with that—the mother in me—what I can learn from her. The link between us had been broken and now it is mended again.

Lynette went on to explain that she had no pictures of her mother from the time depicted in her dream—that almost all of them had been confiscated by Nazi troops. This vivid dream felt real to Lynette, like a living connection that "made me understand—feel—appreciate my roots." She remembered how her mother was very intuitive; she recalled her subtleness, her sensitivity—qualities that Lynette was currently trying to develop. This "true, deep contact" in the dream helped Lynette feel for the first time that she had learned something of value from her mother, something she currently needed.

No Face.   Sophia, a beautiful woman in her early sixties, also lost her mother in the Holocaust. Although she and her mother and brothers at first hid from the Gestapo together, they had split up on the last night before they were taken. Sophia, only about seventeen, survived; the others were killed. Like many survivors, Sophia is burdened with unwarranted feelings of guilt for not having perished, too. Like Lynette, she has no photographic mementos of her mother.

Sophia confided a painful thought, "The one thing I cannot dream about—I can't see the face of my mother. I want to see her in my dreams and I can't. Awake I can't visualize her face. She was such a loving, giving person." For this woman who has endured so much horror, the tender memory of her mother is still too painful to bear even in a dream. Perhaps the day will come.

Meanwhile Sophia had rebuilt a full life, fallen in love, married, and given birth to a son. Recently widowed, she was amazingly resilient. When I asked her how she had managed, she replied, "If I had given up then, the Nazis would have won after all." She is still learning and growing and giving, a radiant example of the indomitable human spirit.

Mother With Long Hair.   Michi, who is now in her middle forties, was having a rather difficult time with menopause. A slender and youthful-looking businesswoman who spends half of the year in the Orient, Michi felt dissatisfied with her job and her husband; her physiological symptoms of nighttime restlessness and nervousness seemed to increase her agitation. She yearned for more stimulating work and passionate romance. Her dreams of her mother had been disturbing.

When she was in her early teens, Michi had a predictive dream about her mother's death:

> Mother is lying in bed. She has very long hair in the dream.
> She is combing this long, long hair while she says to me,
> "Daughter, I'm going to die soon."

In actuality, Michi explained, her grandmother had very long hair, according to the old tradition, while her mother wore her hair short and modern. So in the dream the mother was being likened to an old person ready to die. This nightmare distressed Michi on awakening, but her mother came to comfort her with reassurance of her presence and that all was well. Unfortunately the mother did fall ill and died two years later.

Mother Goes "Home." Many years later Michi dreamed again of her mother:

> I see Mother on a beautiful Chinese pulling cart—it is high and tall on two wheels with someone running. The graveyard is behind me and the cart in front, with Mother coming toward me.
>
> She wears beautiful silk in lush colors—a lot of yellow and red with touches of green— and she has colorful ornaments in her hair. She looks radiantly happy. She looks rather like the paper dolls we burn when people die.
>
> I am with a man who was a neighbor of ours, someone my mother liked and wanted me to marry. I hold a camera. I ask, "Mother, where are you going?" She replies, "Home!" meaning the graveyard. "Please take the camera home and give it to someone." She goes on.
>
> Then the man and I walk together back to Mother's grave.

Michi was so impressed with this dream that, despite her marriage and children, she called the man in her dream to tell him about it. He suggested that they visit her mother's grave. They went together and placed some of her mother's favorite flowers upon it.

This contact, stimulated by Michi's dream, led to an intense emotional relationship with the man. Although it was never consummated, their intimacy took on all the emotions of a love affair. "I realized that even married women can have genuine love," she said. Suddenly, after deluging her with attention, the man broke off all contact. Michi was left feeling deserted and more lonely than ever. At this time the unhappy woman virtually stopped dreaming.

For several years Michi had no dream recall except for three short fragments, two of them involving forbidden, but pleasurable, physical contact with the man. Since these dreams were no longer capable of being realized, they evoked pain. "I probably decided not to have any more dreams. They made my life so complicated," she explained. Cessation of dream recall is a reaction some people have to a shock—physical or emotional. It is sometimes a part of severe depression. Whenever people tell me they used to dream frequently but then stopped completely, the suspension of dreaming can almost always be traced to a specific waking event or to a specific dream.

In Michi's dream of her mother going home, she seems to be giving herself approval to reach out for a romantic mate that her mother had already commended. The camera may have offered the dreamer another "picture" of her life, or its boxlike shape may have been a symbol for the womb. It is as though her mother said, "If you had listened to me and married this man, you would have been happy." The awe-inspiring image of her mother in ceremonial garb evoked Michi's respect for the older woman's opinion. In waking life Michi found it painful to let go of the possibility of happiness with that man, to bury it.

Michi had been strongly moved by the dream of her mother but, in this case, it provided a suggestion that did not resolve her problem. Eventually Michi undertook efforts that led to a more satisfying answer. She found a program of artistic training that could be adapted to her sporadic work schedule; she invested much energy in developing skills. Her vitality returned. She found new friends and fascinating activities.

Red Explosion. Michi's dreams recommenced with a literal explosion:

> A nuclear explosion goes off—perhaps it is my anger with my
> home-life situation. I hear people running. I look out and see
> pink, orange, and red clouds. A friend and I start to run,
> holding hands.

After several adventures in the dream, Michi and her friend survive. "At the end it is beautiful. I feel in a whole piece. We're safe." Michi thinks of warm red colors as expressing anger or excitement. Symbolically the explosion may represent sexual climaxing as well as anger. In either case things are changing in the dreamer's internal landscape as well as her outer life.

Michi had begun to express her own anger, to exercise new skills, and to relate to the opposite sex on a basis of her own choosing rather than her mother's. She joined a group to study dreams. Most recently one dream included scenes of a cement room changing to a stage with bushes: she saw green floors, workers dressed in green who turned into dancers, and green woods. The "gray, unfinished, solid, hard, plain" quality of concrete was replaced by living things. Michi's associations to the color green were of joy, of peace, of healing. In truth Michi, in a new stage of life, was growing; she was finding peace and joy as she healed herself.

Father Is Warm and Loving.   Fiona, in her mid-forties and beginning to experience menstrual irregularity, was distraught to learn of her father's death while she and her husband were away on a holiday. She returned for the funeral to find that he had been ill for some time but had forbidden his wife to confide it to their daughter, intending to tell her himself when she returned. Fiona felt, as people usually do under such circumstances, bereft of a chance to say good-bye. "I wish I had known. His death left a black hole in my life that will always be there."

Fiona and her father had always shared a deep love, but his style was distant and formal. After childhood he rarely touched or held her; she, a lovely, mild, and compassionate woman, felt reticent and shy to impose any contact. After his death Fiona had several dreams of her father:

> He is so real—I can even smell him. In some dreams I know he
> is dead, that there's something different in our status. He is
> laughing. I am able to touch and hug him, something we were
> never able to do in waking life. I wake up feeling good.

Poignant as these dreams are for Fiona, they, like Lynette's dream of her mother, give her a sense of precious communication. They fill a need as well as her arms.

The Chopped Trees.   My own dreams of my father since his death are special to me, too. His gentle sweetness and fond greetings feel like a genuine visit. I remember dreaming the night I learned of his death:

> Something about an old people's home. There are large trees on
> the lawn. Someone has cut them down to make more room, but
> they took all of them and chopped them into tiny pieces. I am
> very annoyed and upset that they didn't leave a few of them for
> shade.

Awake, I thought of the marvelous oil painting my father had made of a forest filtered by sunlight. Trees are often a male symbol in women's dreams;

to chop them down and cut them into bits is a total destruction. Surely I would miss his sheltering presence.

I had had a premonition of his death the last time we were together, only five days before his fatal heart attack. We had spoken by telephone two days after we parted. Despite the shock of his death, I had a sense of having said good-bye.

The Loving Essence. Shortly after my father's death I had a nightmare about almost being smothered by the kind of paper used in lithography. This was clearly a reference to my father, whose work was lithography, and also to the many legal papers I had to cope with after his death.

Later on, dreams about my father were of him directly. He would appear, smiling, loving, helpful, as he was in waking life; I would awaken feeling good. These days, some eighteen years since he died, I dream about him less frequently. Yet, when they come, these dream "visits" provide a valued communication. They remind me of his loving essence. Dreamers can still learn from their images of the deceased.

Discovering ways of coping with the illness or death of a parent or the rebellion or wild antics of teenage or college "children"; relating to a mate who may be undergoing midlife crisis; adapting to physical changes—the middle-aged menopausal woman has her hands and her heart full. The women in my study had definite opinions about this phase of life.

The Voices of Menopause

Some of the women who participated in my study were just beginning to have symptoms of menopause:

> My periods used to be very regular, every twenty-one days. Now they're further apart, maybe thirty-two days. It used to be a gradual stop and start; now I bleed very heavily for two days and immediately stop.

> My periods are still regular, but in the past few years I've started to get some facial hair. I'm told it was male hormones. [A few women are troubled with this symptom as their estrogen level falls.]

> My periods started to be disruptive about two years ago—first they got heavier and then lighter. I've gained weight since then,

and my hair is getting thin. My teeth and nails break more
easily. Who knows what's going on with the bones? Sometimes
I wake up feeling totally wet.

Such women have some signs of physical changes in their dreams, but they
are more apt to deal primarily with relationships to mates, family members,
friends, and colleagues at work.

Others experienced menopause as a result of surgery:

I had a difficult time following the hysterectomy. I got heart
palpitations, like a panic, along with night sweats. I couldn't
sleep well. My skin and the membranes of my vagina became
very dry. I was celibate for a year, and the first time after that I
tried to have intercourse, I nearly went through the roof. Now
I use an estrogen cream and it's fine.

My womb was removed, but the ovaries were left. Every
month I felt like I was having a period, with my breasts
swelling and me getting emotional. Then recently, several years
later, I started having hot flashes.

I had a hysterectomy in my middle forties after excessive
bleeding that wouldn't stop. I felt so much better afterward,
because my hemoglobin had been low. I've taken a low dose of
estrogen ever since.

Women whose menopause is brought on partially or suddenly by surgery
are likely to dream about their symptoms, along with a sense of bodily
invasion from the disease or the operation. Unfortunately most of them do
not realize that their bodies continue to experience cyclical changes when
the womb is removed prior to what would have been the time of their
natural menopause. Knowing this can help women be more tolerant of their
mood swings or other symptoms they may experience. Women with a
surgically induced menopause can still observe pattern changes in their
dreams throughout a month.

Some women had a difficult time with their natural menopause:

I was very miserable, went mentally bonky. My period would
come, zoom! Once I was in a theater wearing a white suit. I
had to turn the skirt around and hold the jacket over it while I
went home to change. I didn't have many symptoms except
depression, I felt lost.

I'm having a hard time, lots of hot flashes and night sweats, horrible, hopeless dryness. I put on ten pounds, especially around the tummy.

It was during the same period as I was going through struggles with my boys. I was very emotional. Night sweats were the worst symptom. I felt similar to the way I got before my period. I had a lot of water retention—my ring still doesn't fit. I gained weight.

I felt anxious for the past few years. I think it's more because my husband wants me to help in the business. I need to be alone, to have time for myself. My eyes got weaker, and I felt really tired, couldn't center myself. It's much less now.

Women in situations like this tend to dream about their physical symptoms as well as their strained relationships with mates and children.

Yet other women seemed to glide through their menopause:

It was easy. Once in a while I'd feel hot and open the window and put my head out. My mood was a little nervous and irritable but not to make a fuss over.

I had no problems—an occasional hot flash. I always had a tendency to water retention and gaining weight. I started to use a vaginal cream. My mother was ill and died during this time, but there was really no difficulty with the menopause.

I'd wake up in the middle of the night feeling sweaty and clammy. I had other problems, but not with menopause.

It was a mild nuisance. I gained weight and my hair thinned. At times I felt like screaming—an exaggerated premenstrual feeling. I had hot flashes and a lot of night sweats, but as soon as I went on a low dosage of estrogen and calcium, the symptoms disappeared.

Women in this category were likely to dream of their difficulties in other areas with a modicum of dreams about their physical symptoms, only when these were intense.

Few of the women in this study had taken estrogen or calcium for any length of time, if at all. They seemed to know remarkably little about what caused the symptoms of menopause and what relief could be obtained. Most were eager to discuss the process with me and to understand it better. Those who are interested will find pertinent information on this topic in the reference notes. There are excellent books now available as well (see the bibliography).

As the menopausal phase passes, with or without treatment, what changes can be expected in the woman's dream life? What shifts occur as a troubled woman consolidates her self-understanding? What of the woman whose life is basically good, whose attitude is sound and outlook already positive? What forms arise in her dreaming mind that indicate increasing psychologi cal maturity?

Initiations and Goddesses: Dreams Linked to Self-development

The Dream as Inner Ritual

Women who are able to turn to their dreams for nourishment, understanding, and guidance often find that the menopausal stage brings dreams of staggering impact. In addition to dreams reflecting their physical symptoms and changing conditions, such women discover an inner transformation unfolding at this stage of life.

Deprived of outer rites of passage, women can draw upon the rich inner ritual available in dreams. This nightly panorama sometimes reveals the role models and archetypal patterns that bring a sense of wholeness to life.

Jung has spoken of the value of the second half of life, how this is the time of finding the center of one's being that he called the Self, the whole that was previously hidden or scattered in several directions.[24] He emphasized in particular the affinity women possess for contacting this through dreams.

The woman who communicates with this realm gains wealth beyond compare. She may find herself truly at peace; she may be inspired to strike out courageously in new directions based on guidance from within; she may undertake creative projects; she may discover spiritual joy.

Goddesses, temples, initiations, magical objects, descents and ascents, ritual dances, chants—this sort of imagery is found in the dreams of older women who open themselves to the treasure buried in sleep.

When a woman has struggled to "find herself," when she listens to the words and contemplates the pictures of her dreams long enough, and wrestles to understand their messages well enough, the character of these images undergoes change. A new center emerges. What was buried is reborn. Von Franz tells us that:

> In the dreams of a woman this center is usually personified as a superior female figure—a priestess, sorceress, earth mother, or goddess of nature or love.[25]

This quote did not come to my attention until long after I began to observe such a transformation taking place in my own dreams. I have described my image of the goddess of love elsewhere.[26] Briefly, she was in the form of a large white stone, roughly hewn or natural on the outside with a smooth, flawless hole in the center—a simple, perfect hole. Several more realistic-type goddesses appeared in dreams that I have described in my *Pathway to Ecstasy: The Way of the Dream Mandala.*[27]

Among the women in my study who had evolved an "inner work," a philosophy of life or religion that genuinely expressed themselves, I observed a similar type of imagery. Lynette offers a good example.

The Salvaged Trunk. The charming Frenchwoman whose dream of her deceased mother is described above, Lynette, at fifty-five, was full of vitality. Her salt-and-pepper hair topped a lively, loving face, and her brown eyes sparkled with mischief. Having spent a score of years doing skilled but routine work in the financial world, she turned with some trepidation to interests in psychology and health. Several years ago she was remotely involved in a spiritual group when this dream plummeted her into direct participation:

> There is a kind of graduation ceremony, like in Sweden. I am one of the girls in white dresses holding candles. The principal of the school is there wearing a square black hat.
>
> The ceremony involves his burying a trunk, lowering it into a stream about six feet wide. The water is very sparkling—light, transparent.
>
> Afterward I go home and remove my gown. Late at night I return to the river. I dive down to see what is in the trunk. (I'm rather good at underwater swimming.) I find the trunk and open it. Inside are important documents from India. I have to get them out and back to where they belong.

It turns out that the principal of the school is evil, trying to bury the documents so that no one can know where they are. I take and hide them somewhere where I can find them later to put them somewhere safe.

I go back to the house—an English-style place with dark carved wood. It's still dark. Suddenly there is a black man with a knife chasing me upstairs. I run up calling my husband, crying out his name when I wake up.

This dream had such an overwhelming impact on Lynette that she sent a description of it to the leader of the spiritual group, who was in India. He responded by telegram asking if she would assist in working on getting some special material published (the actual documents of her dream). Prior to this dream he had judged her incapable of the task, but now changed his view. Lynette joined a team working on the project, and it became the focus of her work for the next decade.

Lynette regards this dream as a "battle in the occult world," with a spiritual message—it certainly became a life-changing message for her. From a symbolic point of view, there are several interesting aspects. The girls in white dresses holding candles seem to represent good, innocent forces within the dreamer; the evil principal (= principle) is marked by his square black hat, the color of darkness, the house, and the villain who later threatens her. Thus negative and positive parts of the dreamer confront each other at the ceremony in which the precious trunk may be forever lost.

Here it is important to be aware of the dreamer's menopausal history. Lynette had had her womb surgically removed when she was in her early forties. Her ovaries, however, were intact, so that her hormonal fluctuation continued as normal. Although she had no bleeding, she still experienced monthly swelling of her breasts and became emotional. During the last year Lynette had noticed hot flashes. She found herself having two or three days each month with headaches and sweating in what would have been her period. This subsided, but she still had sensations of heat (probably hot flashes), for which she took no medication. "All my life I've been cold, so now I feel warm. I like it!"

We know that trunks, suitcases, and purses are typical symbols for the womb. They also represent the containers for valuable objects in general. Jung tells us that the womb and its symbols frequently represent the "creative aspect of the unconscious."[28] The removal of the dreamer's uterus —her precious trunk—is a kind of "burial." The dream water may be an indication of the fluid accumulation that is typical during the menopausal years, but the clarity and sparkle of the water suggest that it refers to a more general representation of the unconscious.

In the dream Lynette is not willing to lose the valuable trunk; she will not remain ignorant. She returns secretly and, using a personal skill—her ability to swim underwater—she identifies the supreme worth of this belonging. Instead of accepting the death of this part of herself, she opens up a new possibility.

The idea is frightening, Lynette's dream language says, because she is pursued by a fearful would-be attacker and cries out for help. Awake, she contacts the person who could, in fact, help her implement her wish. Her dream struggle led to a satisfactory resolution. She was able to dedicate her energies in a direction that she desired. Her dream provided the impetus to make a change in her life.

The New Land. In a later dream Lynette appears to have found the center of her own strength:

> I am at some villa at the seaside with my mother and my father. All of a sudden I see the waters are coming in, and the level is going up. I notice that if we stay there, we are going to be stuck. You can't open the doors anymore.
>
> I tell my parents, "Don't be afraid, we can open the window." We have to leave all our belongings, just let them go. If we jump out very quietly and just float on the water surface, we'll be safe. (I'm a good swimmer and had taught my parents how to swim by first floating with their hands on my shoulder.)
>
> I jump out of the house onto the water and I am just waiting in the sun. I feel a beautiful liberty to float in the sun.
>
> Curtain. Act 2. The waters have gone; the house is gone; my parents are gone. Now I'm in a beautiful countryside. You can tell that the waters were there. The road is still wet, shining in the sun.
>
> It's beautiful! It's like spring. I see white and purple lilacs, soft and tender, and rose tulips with pale green tender leaves, apple blossoms, and cherry blossoms. There is a lot of rose and purple and tender green. It's like Ireland, so very green.

I'm walking on this barely wet road with grass on the sides. Everything is glowing, shining, like pearls and glistening like diamonds. It is like a beautiful new country.

I wake up with a sense of joy and beauty, of freshness, like a new world, a new life. I have a quiet happiness. A phrase comes into my mind, as if someone inside were speaking, "You are going to help your mother to die." I feel no sorrow; I didn't know she was sick.

In fact six months later Lynette's mother was diagnosed as having cancer. She went through a painful dying process. Lynette feels she was able to support her mother because of her dream, to smooth her mother's transition, and to better prepare for death herself.

Aside from the possible extrasensory perception of her mother's impending illness and death, this dream reveals much about Lynette's psychological state. In the first scene she is again threatened, along with her parents, who may represent older parts of herself. The villa is being flooded, in a way that is similar to the trunk being "buried" in the stream. She refuses in this case to get "stuck," even as she refused to remain ignorant about the contents of the trunk. Encouraging the fearful parts of herself, she leaves attachments behind and trusts to the process, as readily as floating on water, and she gains a great sense of freedom. By using her ability to cope with the unconscious (represented by skill in swimming in the sea), the darkness of the earlier dream is gone. The warming sun suggests not only pleasant heat (perhaps her body's heat) but also illumination of the mind.

This action seems to open an incredible world of beauty for the dreamer. Notice all the symbols of luxuriant, healthful growth—sun, fertilizing rain, flowers, fresh greenness. Lynette's dream is a strong contrast to the neglected grass, scorched patches, and petrified trees in the dream of Mankowitz's patient "Rachel" at the same phase of life. These symbols of growth are likened to glowing jewels—almost always a symbol of supreme value. Jungians speak of stones, precious or not, as a frequent and high-level symbol of the Self.[29]

Other symbols of the emerging self, according to Jungian thinking, include the wise old woman (or for a male, a wise old man); a supernaturally gifted girl (or for a male, a beautiful youth); a miraculous child; a cosmic man; a helpful animal; and a mandala (a magic circular form).

Lynette sees the heavenly country as preparing her to cope with her mother's illness and death. It also speaks of the inner peace and beauty she senses in her own life and death. It is a space all dreamers can—if they are lucky—discover for themselves. During the menopausal years women have the maturity to seek, find, and treasure this inner realm. The change of life may become a real change—the dreamer may discover her own center.

The Woman in the Sarcophagus. Sheila Moon, a Jungian analyst who describes her own dream experiences in *Dreams of a Woman: An Analyst's Inner Journey,* cites another version of this sort of dream from sometime between her forty-ninth and fifty-second year:

> I am going to see the Cassetta Stone (or a stone of Cassetta marble) as it contained a clue to some mystery I need to solve. Connected with this, I was looking down into a newly excavated, square sarcophagus containing a statue of a woman in a fetal position. The statue was cradled in a delicate powder blue material. I felt it was Greek.[30]

Moon says that her dream described what was happening in her own analysis, at the time with Gerhard Adler in England; she felt that the birth or rebirth of a new feminine dimension of consciousness was taking place, one that had still to be lifted from its coffin. She painted scenes from this dream, trying to fully comprehend its symbols. Perhaps the mystery-containing stone represented the self for this dreamer. Since Moon gives no information regarding her menopause, we can only speculate that the womblike sarcophagus also related to the "death" of her own womb and the rebirth of the new phase of creativity that soon followed—a resurrection of her Self.

Moon, who is now in her seventies, says that it was during this time she began to write. In dreams that came shortly after this one, she saw "hungry children and an infant who would always be with her." In her last hour of analysis before she set out on a trip she and Adler discussed the possibility that the hungry children were part of an urgent need to write crying out for existence—something she had once tried and now wished for more.

At a stop in Switzerland, where Moon slept in Küsnacht, the small town where the Jungs had lived, she dreamed she was with Mrs. Jung. In her dream Mrs. Jung—who, prior to her death, had been Moon's analyst—urged her to "begin writing, and do a little bit every day."

Inspired, Moon followed this dream advice. She intended the writing to be only for herself and was astonished when a knowledgeable friend who examined it said it was a children's novel. When edited and typed, Moon sent the material to a publisher and was surprised to have it accepted. Since then she has published several books. She says that "out of the most difficult and desperate inner work, something emerged that was to become an important avocation-vocation." Writing was a fresh dimension that she felt became one of the most worthwhile in her life. We might add that, using her dream language, the woman in the coffin had been reborn.

The Bread of Life.   Although the dream I am about to describe is not a typical initiation dream, it was "life sustaining" for the dreamer, and as such may help others to comprehend the power of dreams. When Sophia, now in her sixties, was in her late teens, she was confined in the concentration camp in Auschwitz. Among the incredible horrors was the constant starvation. "I would have given my life for a loaf of bread," she told me. "I created a bakery out of my imagination. When we had to stand for hours in the morning, listening to the guards talk, witnessing beatings, I would will myself to think about this bakery. At night I dreamed of it. We all dreamed about food. It was a life-sustaining dream that filled me."

Years later, after Sophia's release by the Allied troops, recovery, marriage, move to the United States, and the birth of a son who had grown to manhood, Sophia was on a holiday with her son in Switzerland. She was walking around the streets of Basel waiting to meet him at a certain time when she smelled the scent of fresh-baked bread. Following the fragrance,

> I came into a narrow street where I found the smell was coming from a bakery. I looked into the display case and saw the little crunchy breads, the black crumbly loaves, the raisin scones. "I've seen this bakery before," I thought. Then I recognized it was the bakery of my dream. The day was warm and sunny but I began to shiver. I thought, "I must be dreaming! I must be back in Auschwitz!" Suddenly I heard an inner scream. It all came back. I began to run.

A few minutes later Sophia's son grabbed her on the shoulder and she "awoke" from this replay of the dream that had sustained her through catastrophic days and nights. Sophia and her husband, who had also been a prisoner, rarely spoke about those tragic days. She had deliberately not burdened her son with details of her experiences. During the day of this "flashback" the tone was set for it by small things—she had noticed books in a store, leather-bound German editions of volumes she had once won in school for prizes. These remnants of her past probably stimulated the memory of the bakery dream.

Like many survivors of disasters, Sophia had to relive the pain in order to truly set it aside. The nourishing bread of her dreams was more than food for her aching belly—although that function was paramount. Some 500,000 persons starved to death in that concentration camp, in addition to the 2.5 million who were executed.[31] The bread also symbolized home and emotional nourishment, the lost family, and the love that was equally essential to her. By allowing this "forgotten" dream to come back to her, along with its suffering, Sophia released some of her still-pent-up energies. She could live her good life with more complete vitality. The power of the imagination to sustain us in darkness and lead us to light is immense. The force takes many forms.

The Twin Goddesses.   At the conclusion of my menopause on the day after Christmas, following six months of no periods or very light spotting, and just prior to the final spotting, I had a remarkable dream of a ritual:

> I am outdoors descending a complex arrangement of circular stairs. It is constructed as though it were around a temple, although no building is there. There are numerous doors and compartments that are waist-high.
>
> Many people descend with me. A fat woman catches up and crowds me. I feel uncomfortable as she pushes into some small compartment with me as I go through. I try to think why her fatness bothers me so much and I realize I fear that she will smother me. I decide to let her pass, and she does, which pleases me.
>
> As I reach the bottom of the strange descent, I see members of a family of artists I know, particularly noticing the man. They are welcoming some returning voyagers. We greet and embrace.
>
> We speak of a powerful predictive dream I have had that has to do with the breakage or loss of the middle front tooth in the lower jaw of their daughter. . . .
>
> Then the scene shifts and I am seated in a room on a chair, as part of a circle of people belonging to a special group. We discuss the same predictive dream of mine. It emerges that I am being accepted because of my skill in dreams, this one in particular.

The leader, a man with the bizarre code name of Cucumber, proposes a toast to two woman who embody the principles of intellect and beauty. I say, "I'll drink to that," and picking up my wineglass set beside me on the floor, I proceed to drink the red wine that fills it. All join the toast.

Then the leader says something like, "Let's do a little 'Loga-Shana.' A little Loga-Shana can't hurt anybody." Everyone rises and, still in the circle, we turn to face his direction. He, with his back to us, demonstrates certain movements and gestures that we follow. The idea is that this secret ritual is safe to communicate to others. Now the women are goddesses. The leader turns partially to the right, at a forty-five-degree angle, and utters, "Loga!" as he spreads his arms open wide at shoulder height and lifts them upward. This is the invocation of Loga. He then withdraws his outspread arms to his body in an embrace, as though to incorporate Loga's essence of intellect; simultaneously he bows his head and dips his body reverently.

Turning to the left, with the same arm-opening gesture, he utters, "Shana!" and then withdraws his arms to his body once more in the identical movement to the left. Doing this incorporates the essence of beauty of spirit. We join the procedure, repeating it over and over.

Ethereal music begins. I know it comes from real singers somewhere in the house because this group does everything with quality. I sense that now at last I can learn some of the things I have yearned to know.

As we continue the repetitive gestures, crying, "Loga! Shana!" I feel myself slipping into trance. I see green fields with people moving over them. At the same time I seem to be writing a description of the ritual, in order to retain it, waking up with the effort.

This complex dream has for me many fascinating dimensions; I will mention only a few. My first impression was awe at the way the dreaming mind can express a partially formed concept. I never heard the word Loga before, but it reminded me of the *Logos*, the word of God that was said to create the universe; perhaps it could be a feminine form of intellect. Shana made me think of the Yiddish-German word for "beauty" *(schön)* that in the dream implied more than physical loveliness. Surely wisdom and beauty of spirit are principles I wish to embody. Awake, it would never have occurred to me to think of them as goddesses who could be invoked and incorporated.

In this dream I find the descent into my depths made more difficult by the presence of the fat woman and my response to her. Not only had I gained a few pounds prior to the dream—later discovered to be a result of a thyroid imbalance that required treatment—but she had negative associations to heavy people I knew, including my mother at a stage when she was physically ill. By "letting her pass" I was able to contact the artist (symbolized by the artist family) within myself. This contact leads to the special knowledge.

From the chalicelike glass I drain the red wine, probably symbolic for the womb being emptied of blood. In the circle of the whole Self, I participate in a ritual that marks my new phase of womanhood.

In addition to all this, I was stunned a few weeks later to learn that the daughter in the artist family mentioned in my dream, just prior to leaving on a trip for Europe, awoke with her mouth and cheeks swollen with infection. She had unexpectedly developed an abcess in a front tooth that required emergency attention. My "predictive dream" was truly predictive. This signal event—Jung would call it synchronous—further marked the dream ritual as significant.

How and why such events happen we do not yet understand. I cherish the content of this telling dream and the many of like nature that succeeded it. Surely there is more in dreams than we can fully comprehend.

The Value of Menopausal Dreams

We have seen that dreams of the menopausal years often indicate the physiological changes that are taking place within the dreamer's body. They may also dramatize her sense of barrenness and emptiness, not so much of the loss of capacity to have children—the woman may have had as many as she wished—but rather a feeling of uselessness in life. If the woman who feels this way searches sincerely, either with or without the assistance of a therapist, she may find new fertile ground—a purpose—for the years ahead.

Negative attitudes toward menopause are held mainly by those who have not experienced it. Sociologist Bernice Neugarten and her colleagues, in a landmark study of attitudes toward menopause, found that younger women had much more negative concepts of menopause than women of menopausal age and older.[32] The women of menopausal age and beyond in the Neu-

garten study were all in good health, none had undergone a surgical menopause, all were married, all were mothers of one or more children, all had
a relatively high education, and most were living with their husbands.

Postmenopausal women in this group tended to see menopause as a
temporary condition with symptoms that were easily coped with or controlled. Far from being grieved over the loss of their reproductive capacity,
the majority of these women were glad to be done with menstruation and
its annoyances; they were relieved to have completed the mothering of small
children; they felt better, more confident, calmer, and freer than ever before.
They also saw themselves as sexier than what the younger women anticipated.

Loss of the reproductive capacity is not as important to middle-aged
women, Neugarten tells us, as younger women think it is. I remember a
young houseguest asking to borrow some sanitary equipment on a visit
shortly after my menopause. When I told her I did not stock it anymore,
since I had no need, she responded with, "Oh, how sad!" In actuality, it was
a relief not to be bothered any longer with the process of periods. Many
of the negative ideas about this phase of life comes from the fears of
inexperienced young women and from psychological or psychiatric literature dealing with clinical patients in distress, rather than, as in Neugarten's
study, healthy women completing a life phase and going on to the next with
relish.

The mature woman has four basic tasks:

1. She needs to value her wisdom—her experience, judgment, and emotional understanding—over physical attractiveness alone.
2. She needs to build satisfying human relationships rather than unrealisti-
   cally romantic or purely passionate encounters.
3. She needs to retain her capacity to love others when parents and friends
   begin to die.
4. She needs to exercise flexibility of mind rather than becoming rigid.[33]

With these capacities, she can flourish in the years ahead.

When I asked Sophia how she felt about growing older, she replied, "I'm
very comfortable with it—as long as I'm active. I wish I had had the wisdom
earlier. Getting older means I can please myself more; I can surround myself
with people I like and avoid those people and situations I don't. There is
so much to do yet, to learn yet, I don't feel old." In her sixties, Sophia is
going to school, writing, feeling the warmth of loving friends and family,
glowing with life.

Some women can find their internalized menopausal rite of passage in a dream. Awake, they may seek an unexplored direction, a way to revitalize their energy for abundant and luxuriant new growth. With the freedom from birth control, from the nuisance of equipment for menstrual periods, from the emotional swings of the reproductive years, and from heavy commitments to home and children, the menopausal woman finds she can pursue interests that formerly eluded her.

We shall see how undertaking new activities not only stimulates us momentarily, it literally adds growth to our brains. What we have regarded as old age is, in large part, ill health or boredom. As physical activity and good nutrition strengthen the body, intriguing mental activity strengthens the mind.

In addition to travel, to pleasurable hobbies, to time with loved ones, to creative pursuits in pottery, jewelry design, painting, language study, charitable or other projects they have always wanted to try without previously having the time to do so, women of menopausal years may find new self-development and spiritual direction. Who knows, perhaps this preparation will serve us well in the unknown beyond?

Dreams of the Elderly

My daughter tenderly places her firstborn baby—my new grandson—into my arms. The silky skin, tiny, shell-like ears, perfect little nose, tender mouth, long fingers, and downy dark hair reawaken memories. Minute rapid eye movements flutter beneath his closed lids. His search-ing, sucking mouth releases a flood of maternal feelings; I feel the old familiar tug inside my breasts.

What sheer physical pleasure it was to nurse a hungry infant, to fill the urgent need from one's own body. Yet my role is not to suckle this child, to bear it, or to raise it. I am the grandmother. The word has a strange shape in my mouth, unaccustomed to its use. A new generation is born, and I am of the old.

Although my mother still lives—a frail buffer between me and mortal-ity—there is an awareness of a new scale brought on by the small, warm being cradled in my lap. For much of humanity, making a mark on life means that their seed lives on into the future. This seed may take many forms, from children and their offspring to actions that have profound repercussions in the lives of others.

The night I first held my grandson, I dreamed of crystals and Christmas lights made of rare material, and of power in the movements of dance. Toward the end of this series of special dreams I performed a complex, repetitive ritual that involved gathering many birds and molding them into one bird that I planted in the earth; from this bird-plant grew a special new bird that somehow ensured the continuance of a group.

Later on in the same dream,

> A woman is teaching me significant secrets as we walk on the roof of a castle. I see below a group of people involved in a ritual led by a male teacher. The people raise their arms and shout in unison, "Power Be!" The leader than tells them that the symbol of their group shall be ". . . an egg and a leaf!" I see this symbol set before them, an upright egg resting atop a green leaf, whereupon I wake.

Among my many associations to the images in this involved dream were those to birth and to growth—the egg and the leaf. The power in dance movements was the dance of life. The "rare material" that was lit for the birth of the holy child—at Christmas—was related to the molding of the birds. The life force that could be gathered into one whole, or break apart to form many, was seen in the spiritlike birds that could be shaped and planted like seeds to grow new life. The newborn baby who is my grandson is, in part, a continuation of my own life, but even more, he is evidence of the life force itself flowing through all humanity. Several of the images of this remarkable dream resemble images found in the dreams of people accepting death.

At fifty-three, I hope to have years ahead, time to love my man, to write more books, paint more pictures, to celebrate with friends and family and to see this grandson grow from little boy to man. Yet the wheel of life turns.

Multitudes of older women remain vitally involved in creative lives until their time is finished. Agatha Christie wrote her famous detective novels into her early eighties. Georgia O'Keeffe painted luminous canvases into her eighties. Photographer Imogen Cunningham was clicking the lens in her nineties. Grandma Moses started her folk painting at seventy-eight. The educator Maria Montessori traveled and worked steadily until her death at eighty-one.

Sculptor Louise Nevelson was still busy hewing wooden shapes in her eighties. Katharine Hepburn is delighting her audiences from stage and screen in her late seventies. Lillian Gish starred in her 104th movie at eighty-six. Dancer Agnes de Mille is choreographing in her eighties. Probably the oldest person ever to earn the coveted black belt in Korean karate is Lucille Thompson, at eighty-nine.[1] Each of us, no matter how great or small our talent, should use our abilities as long as possible.

But regardless of how productive we may continue to be, sooner or later all of us must face the end of life. What lies beyond is part of the great adventure. Thus it is that the thoughts of elders seek naturally the next step. In like manner, so do their dreams. Before we look at the dreams of the older person in depth, let's examine what's happening in the aging woman's body during sleep and dreams.

Sleeping and Dreaming in Later Years
Less Deep Sleep for Both Sexes

"I don't sleep so well these days," confided seventy-year-old Jan, in a typical interview with an older woman. As we age, our sleep and dream patterns shift. First of all, even if we sleep the same number of hours, less of the time is spent in deep sleep. Elders are more likely to have the light sleep of stages 1 and 2 than the profoundly restful stages 3 and 4.[2]

By the time we reach forty or fifty, most people notice that they wake more often during the night, they stay awake longer during these nighttime awakenings, and they sometimes feel drowsy during the day. At sixty-five, our deep sleep is about one-half of what it was during our twenties. This lighter sleep makes us feel less rested and affects our mental functioning.

By eighty the normal, healthy adult takes about eighteen minutes to fall asleep at night, sleeps only about six hours, with a few short minutes, if any, in deep sleep; he or she spends about 20 percent of the night awake and usually takes a daytime nap. Compare this with the twenty-year-old, who falls asleep in eight minutes and spends seven and a half to eight hours asleep with at least one-half hour in deep sleep; he or she spends only 5 percent of the night awake and usually takes no nap. Of course these are averages; individuals vary considerably. One woman I spoke with in her nineties assured me that she sleeps soundly, only waking once to go to the bathroom, for seven hours or more.

Many people among the older generation, however, are chronically sleepy. In the laboratory, sleepiness is tested by how quickly a person falls asleep. A study by Mary Carskadon and her colleagues showed that some of the healthy volunteers over sixty-five who were given a chance to sleep during the day fell asleep in five minutes or less.[3] Falling asleep this rapidly represents pathological sleepiness. In comparison, healthy young adults and middle-aged participants averaged ten minutes to fall asleep, whereas pre-teenage children did not fall asleep but remained optimally alert. Scientists have confirmed what most of us know from our own experience: when we are sleepy, we perform poorly.

Older Women Get More Deep Sleep Than Older Men.   Men begin to notice changes in their sleep as early as their thirties, whereas women do not usually show sleep changes until after menopause (usually between forty-five and fifty-five); thus women are in their fifties before they begin to exhibit the sleep changes that appeared in men as much as twenty years earlier.[4] Throughout the remainder of life, women continue to "sleep younger" than men. Although women take a little longer to fall asleep, they have more deep sleep with less awakenings for shorter periods.

This sound, refreshing stage of sleep, the deep sleep of stage 4, is when growth hormones are released; young people have the largest percentage of stage 4 sleep. In a study by researcher René Spiegel in Switzerland, the elderly men had about 30 percent less slow-wave sleep (defined as stages 3 and 4 combined) compared with younger subjects: the elderly women actually *increased* their slow-wave sleep by 19 percent.[5] Although stage 4 sleep is usually found to drop gradually throughout life for both sexes, the loss is more pronounced for men than for women. Stage 4 sleep disappears entirely in most elderly men, but still persists in about half of elderly women.[6] Some women show almost no sleep changes compared with younger individuals.[7]

Less REM and Less Dreaming for Both Sexes

"I used to have a lot of dreams," said Whitney, who is in her late eighties, "but these days I rarely have any." The average eighty-year-old does dream somewhat less—approximately one hour of dream time during eight hours of sleep, compared with a twenty-year-old, who dreams from one and a half to two hours during the same amount of sleep. Those elders who sleep less, of course, also dream less. Our dream time declines gradually as we age: infants have the largest amount of REM; children the next most; young adults spend about 20 to 25 percent of their sleep time in dreaming; thirty-to-fifty-year-olds dream about 18 to 25 percent of their sleep time; while older adults of fifty to seventy years dream about 13 to 18 percent of their time asleep.[8]

Older Women Dream More Than Older Men. A team of investigators, Robert Williams, Ismet Karacan, and Carolyn Hursch, plotting the amount of time spent in REM in subjects from ages three to eighty, reported a difference between the sexes.[9] Although both groups decreased in REM between infancy and puberty, slowing gradually thereafter, the males' percentage of REM leveled off through middle age, dropping again in old age. Females did not show any drop in REM after their twenties.

Spiegel, in his study of sleep in older persons in Basel, Switzerland, found, on average that the older women in his group spent 14 percent less time in REM compared with younger sleepers; older men showed a decrease of 19 percent.[10] Although the difference in REM duration for men and women was not great in this study, Spiegel noted that the elderly women in his group increased their REM periods over the four nights they spent in the sleep laboratory,[11] suggesting that women might be dreaming even more at home. Longer REM periods accompanied feelings of having slept well.

The More We Dream, the Better We Function. We know that this dream time is crucial for our good health because of the results of several laboratory studies conducted on dreaming and mental functioning in the elderly. In an investigation by Irwin Feinberg and his colleagues, the older subjects who had more REM also had a high level of alertness, as indicated by their higher brain frequencies. Fienberg found that changes in sleeping patterns in the elderly are related to impaired memory. Spiegel did not find the same correlation between intelligence scores and the amount of dreaming, but his subjects were fifteen to twenty years younger. In general, the better we sleep and dream, the better our brains can process information.[12]

In another study, researcher Patricia Prinz found that older people who have normal percentages of REM are faster and more accurate on memory and addition tests than those whose REM declines.[13] She suggests that the percentage of time spent in REM is an indicator of our mental sharpness. With the decreased blood flow to the brain and reduction in numbers of nerve cells that are functioning—changes that tend to occur with age— the person feels dull as well as functions less efficiently. We shall see how, to a certain extent, we can counteract or slow this change.

More Sleep Problems

Not only do we have less deep sleep and shorter dream time as we age, we also tend to develop more sleep problems. Some of these common difficulties, however, are readily amenable to treatment: they are not inevitable. Many of the problems blamed on old age actually arise from sleep disorders or from undiagnosed illness.

Stoppages in Breathing.   As we grow older, we are more vulnerable to the sleep disturbance called apnea (from New Latin and Greek words meaning "not breath").[14] This disorder is a stoppage of regular breathing that occurs during sleep; people with a severe case of apnea awaken literally hundreds of times a night in order to breathe.

In the older person the soft palate—the mucous membrane that begins at the place the hard roof of the mouth ends—loses its muscle tone; as the older person relaxes, the tissue droops downward to block the breathing passage. People who sleep on their backs are especially susceptible to this condition. When the breath is cut off, bodily processes signal the brain, which triggers an effort to clear the passage, usually producing a snort. Apnea is frequently associated with loud, raucous snoring.

Throughout life, men are more vulnerable to apnea as well as to snoring, but the gap narrows in the older years. By sixty-five, three out of five men snore, while two out of five women do so.[15] Snoring is more than a nuisance for the bed partner. Habitual snorers have twice the chance of high blood pressure, putting them at risk for heart disease and stroke.

The individual who develops apnea gets little rest from sleep, feels tired and irritable during the day, and thinks less efficiently. In a study at Stanford University, healthy older volunteers with no sleep complaints slept in the laboratory. Two out of five of these subjects stopped breathing more than five times in an hour—an abnormal amount. Those with many breathing stoppages functioned poorly on tests that required thinking ability. Even worse, people with severe apnea may be misdiagnosed as senile. The problem may even become fatal. Certain researchers believe apnea to be the cause of sudden death during sleep in the elderly.[16]

If you snore and sleep on your back, you might try to retrain yourself to sleep on your side. If you suspect that you or someone you love has apnea, consult a physician and consider having tests done at a sleep laboratory.

Muscle Twitches and Restless Legs.   Another sleep problem that is more common among the elderly than among younger people is referred to as restless legs, restless leg syndrome, or muscle twitches. Nearly one-third of all people over sixty-five develop this disorder.[17] The sufferer complains of deep, creeping sensations in the legs that only cease when the legs are moved: this may happen hundreds of times an hour, causing awakening or light sleep. Bed partners complain of being kicked.

Although both sexes develop restless legs, it is more common among women. In earlier years pregnant woman are particularly susceptible to this discomfort.[18] Perhaps this is more true of the pregnant woman whose diet is inadequate, because the disorder is sometimes traced to vitamin deficiencies.

Excessive use of caffeine is associated with the experience of restless legs, as are nighttime cramps in the legs. Physicians often recommend that people who suffer from these symptoms restrict their intake of caffeine. Elderly persons are more sensitive to the effects of caffeine than when they were younger. Those who suffer from restless legs may find that cutting down on or eliminating caffeine from their diet may eradicate the problem.

If reducing caffeine is not effective, a person with restless legs would be wise to seek medical advice. Sometimes the symptom can indicate the presence of certain diseases; it has been linked to diabetes, kidney disorders, and anemia. It also sometimes arises in connection with psychological disturbances, or it may simply result from previous prolonged exposure to the cold. Health care providers are divided over whether drug treatment of restless legs is helpful, but some researchers report that certain anticonvulsant medications have proved quite useful.[19] If there is a problem with this condition, a physician knowledgeable about sleep problems should be consulted.

Depression.   Women are generally more susceptible to depression than men.[20] Feeling deeply discouraged may occur at any age, but it is more likely to go unrecognized in the older person and may be mistaken for senility. Depression is frequently linked to poor sleep.

Although women are more prone to depression, and more women attempt suicide, it is the depressed older men who are more likely to actually kill themselves. In a study conducted by physician Myrna Weissman and K. Fox of 258 attempted suicides treated at the Yale New Haven Hospital Emergency Room, women outnumbered men two to one.[21] However, another study by Weissman and her colleagues showed that the majority of suicide "completers" are men. In the over-seventy age group a greater proportion of men than women actually commit suicide.[22]

All of us experience grief associated with sad events in our lives, such as the death of a loved person or a loved pet or the loss of an important job. Temporary counseling or psychotherapy may help us overcome significant losses. Normal mourning may bring on severe depression—technically referred to as clinical depression—but most cases of deep depression arise without apparent cause. Episodes of misery may last for six months or longer, if untreated, and may sometimes lead to suicide.

Depressed women have been successfully helped with estrogen, according to a study done by Edward Klaiber and his co-workers at the Worcester Foundation for Experimental Biology in Massachusetts.[23]

Recently some brain scientists conducting research on depression suggest that this condition may be a result of chemical imbalance that is triggered by the inhibition of anger.[24] In such cases drug therapy, combined with psychotherapy to help the person learn new behaviors, is highly desirable. If this link between inhibiting anger and resulting depression proves sound, elderly people who are depressed could benefit from assertiveness training. Older women are more likely to require assertiveness skills than older men. Here is an area for dreamers to practice assertiveness by coping with the villains of their dreams.[25]

There may also be a physical basis for clinical depression. Investigators currently believe that clinical depression is linked to a defective chromosome; if this is established, there is hope it can be prevented or cured with medication.[26] Depressed elderly people show a different sleep profile than those elderly who are healthy.[27]

There are distinguishing differences between normal sadness or grief over a difficult or tragic life happening and dangerous clinical depression. Clues to serious depression include:

- Feeling worst in the morning (rather than in the middle of the night or evening)
- Having morning insomnia
- Having feelings of intense self-blame, remorse, or guilt; losing self-esteem
- Having recurrent suicidal thoughts or behavior[28]

Professional attention is needed if you or an elderly person you love experiences these symptoms.

Dangers of Sleeping Pills.   Elders over sixty use about 40 percent of the sleeping pills that are prescribed, even though they constitute only about 15 percent of the population.[29] Such medication is particularly risky for the older person.

Few tests of sleeping pills are carried out on the elderly, so that little is known about safe dosage. We do know that the older body is less efficient in metabolizing medication, that sleeping pills reduce ability to respond to emergencies during the night, and that drowsiness and disorientation often carry over to the next day. An older person on sleeping medication may be more susceptible to injurious falls.

Most alarming of all, sleeping pills depress breathing. Since there is already a greater risk of a breathing problem from aging alone, the sleeping pills amplify that danger. One seventy-two-year-old man volunteered to test the effect of sleeping pills on his breathing.[30] Researchers observed some lapses in his breathing of three minutes duration; when he had a five-minute breath cessation, the experimenters feared for the man's life and awakened him.

One research team observed that elderly subjects who said they often took sleeping pills had a mortality rate 1.5 times higher than matched subjects who were not taking pills.[31]

Common side effects of sleeping pills in the elderly are confusion and hallucinations. In combination with other drugs or alcohol, sleeping pills may be lethal. In view of the fact that most sleeping medication loses its ability to promote sleep within two weeks, and that it reduces our much-needed dreaming, the older patient is better off without it. Most sleep experts recommend gradual withdrawal from sleeping medication. Fast withdrawal from many kinds of drugs can produce "drug-induced insomnia," or REM rebound, with dramatically increased dreaming, so that when the person does sleep, he or she is troubled by vivid, disturbing nightmares.

Robert Butler, a contemporary physician specializing in gerontology, points out that insomnia in elderly persons may be caused by emotional reactions of grief, anxiety, anger, or depression.[32] It can also be a consequence of sexual deprivation, frequent need to urinate, or disturbance of sleep patterns by travel. Many medications can produce insomnia, such as decongestants in cold cures. Insomnia may also be a symptom of physical disorders such as early congestive heart failure, early dementia, drug intoxication, or pain. Butler cautions a careful diagnosis of the underlying causes of insomnia and the use of the simplest measures to treat it, avoiding drugs as much as possible.

Stabilizing the Schedule and Stimulating the Brain

What can the older person do to ensure the best possible sleep and the most functional waking?

Exercise the Brain.   Our brains and the nerve cells that compose them are created for action. When this "machinery" sits idle or runs on low gear, it loses the ability to operate most efficiently.

Brain researchers have come up with evidence that is essential for the elderly person to know. Scientist Marian Diamond and her colleagues at the University of California demonstrated that if a young rat is placed in an environment enriched with toys and playmates, its cortex begins to thicken in a few days.[33] They further demonstrated that the same principle works with aged rats. Rats the equivalent of seventy-five to ninety-year-old people also showed growth of the cortex when they were placed in an enriched environment.

The rats were given bigger cages and more playmates; experimenters added wheels, ladders, blocks, and other objects the animals could explore. By climbing on them, sniffing them, and crawling under them, they used their whole sensory apparatus. After the rats had been in an enriched environment for as little as four days, autopsies showed that there was a measurable increase in cortical thickness. This was caused not by an increase in number of neurons but by an increase in the area of the neurons. The researchers judged these enriched animals to be brighter than rats who had been in a deprived environment because they could run through mazes in shorter times—the usual measure of rat intelligence.

Rats have the potential to live 1,000 days compared with the human being's rough potential of 100 years. Diamond and her team kept older rats in standard cages until they were 766 days old; this was three-quarters of the way through their lives. Then the aged rats were placed into enriched cages from 766 to 904 days. Even these very old rats showed a thickening of the cerebral cortex.

In another neuroanatomy study, Diamond and her colleagues conducted autopsies on mother rats that had just given birth and found that their cortex had grown during pregnancy.[34] This was true even for females from impoverished environments, suggesting that pregnancy itself provides a stimulating condition.

Diamond, vibrant at fifty-six, concludes that similarly, human beings of any age require stimulation: they must either use their brains or lose their ability to do so. The main factor, says Diamond, is stimulation. The nerve cells, being designed for stimulation, literally shrink at the dendrites (the connecting fingerlike projections from the nerve cell body) when they go unstimulated. She sees curiosity as a key to continued stimulation. If a person retains high curiosity throughout life, this interest will stimulate neural tissue and may allow the cortex to respond.

Interviewing a number of extremely active people who were over eighty-eight years of age, Diamond found that people who use their brains do not lose them. Common denominators among the group included: interest in their profession; a healthy body—most drank milk and ate an egg each day; physical activity; a love of life and of other people; and the feeling of being loved.

Clearly older people who develop new interests and expose themselves to intriguing activities and companions will provide themselves with greater brain stimulation. Some of the changes that occur with age are also observed in young people who undergo sensory deprivation. It may be that aging isolates people. Those of us with elderly relatives who are not able to motivate themselves may find it worthwhile to involve them as much as possible with stimulating activity. As we age ourselves, we need to keep our own minds and bodies active.

Exercise the Body.   To the extent that health permits, physical stimulation as well as mental stimulation is helpful for activating the brain. Brisk walking and mild stretching can send fresh blood to invigorate the aging mind. Programs such as the one designed by SAGE (Senior Actualization and Growth Experiences) have gentle exercises that are beneficial. A regular program of exercise should be practiced.

Stabilize the Schedule.   Most experts suggest that elderly people sleep better when they follow a regular schedule of meals and activities. This need not be incompatible with stimulation. Periods of interesting and new activities can be organized around firm mealtimes and bedtimes. Older people need other people to spark their curiosity. Making definite plans with friends or arranging to meet new people is important.

Having responsibilities is also useful. Many studies of recovery from surgery suggest the value of the older patient having a pet. It seems that the need to get up to feed and care for a bird or cat or dog can trigger healing processes. Even having plants to care for has been shown to speed recovery from operations. Within the limits of what is practical, an older person in a household can benefit from having light responsibilities. When they are given small chores they are capable of performing, older people feel useful and needed, rather than sensing themselves to be a useless burden.

By keeping minds and bodies active, by relating to those around them with loving care, by being treated with dignity, the older woman and man may enjoy lively days and refreshing nights, lulled by dreams that guide their way.

Life Changes Reflected in Dream Changes

The older woman has more changes to confront than perhaps at any other time during her life. Crisis after crisis emerges to test her endurance: parents and older relatives have already died, and peers soon fall ill or die; her mate is likely to predecease her; the normal aging process renders her own body more vulnerable to disease or disability; her living quarters and conditions may worsen; her grown children struggle with their own marital strife or difficulties. The older woman may find herself coping with bereavement, ill health, and feelings of anxiety and depression all at once. Now, if ever, she needs the wisdom of her years.

Where can the older woman find the support and comfort she requires? Some take refuge in religious practices; others seek counseling or psychotherapeutic support; still others find a system of philosophy that sustains them. Social groups, such as the Gray Panthers, the Older Women's League, SAGE, or senior programs in hospitals and community centers may provide friendships and help. Universities offer intellectual stimulation in special departments for seniors that rekindle interests and motivate the elderly.[35]

Within the older woman dreams still unfold. A rich interior life can guide the dreamer during the last vital phase of her existence. Each problem area is dealt with in dreaming. Sometimes her dreams depict loss or devastation; sometimes the nightly encounters spread a fabulous feast for the senses and emotions.

Holding Hands Into the Sunset:
Love and Sex Dreams in the Elderly

Romance flourishes among healthy seniors. Even with the infirm, the need for touching and affection is potent. My elderly father-in-law, at 103, likes nothing better than to hold my hand and kiss it gallantly from time to time. His 97-year-old roommate, crippled from a stroke and suffering considerable pain, brightens to see me, offering embraces with his good arm while planting kisses on my cheek and calling me his "sweetie." At the retirement community where my almost 80-year-old mother lives, marriages between widows and widowers are surprisingly common.

Younger people tend to regard romantic behavior in older people as repellent—the dirty old man syndrome—or as sheer folly. Juniors often think of their seniors as sexually undesirable; the older woman is seen as a kind of neuter. Youngsters doubt the ability of their elders to have inter-course or fear it would hurt them if they did. To the older person, however, new liaisons are sensuous and serious. Sexual activity, recent studies suggest, may even be health-inducing. As it has been all along, sex is still a major concern in later life. It is not shameful or perverse; it is normal.

Sexual Arousal During the Dream State

Sleep researchers, as explained earlier, have documented that male infants experience penile erections during dreaming. Adult women, too, have been demonstrated to experience vaginal blood-volume changes analogous to the penile erections—these probably also begin in infancy.[36] We know now that this sexual arousal is a natural part of the central nervous system activation that occurs during dreaming throughout the life cycle.

Older people in their eighties whose condition is healthy continue to have sexual responses while in REM; men develop erections of the penis, whereas women experience periodic vaginal lubrication and engorgement. At Mount Sinai Hospital Sleep Laboratory, psychiatrist Charles Fisher found that most of his twenty-one male subjects, ranging in age from sixty to ninety-six, had penile erections with their dreams—including the ninety-six-year-old.[37] In their waking lives the majority of this group were happy with one or two ejaculations a week, but could be stimulated to greater frequency.

Researchers find that sexual capacity has been underestimated in the aging person. Alfred Kinsey, the pioneer of sexual studies, noted that women exhibit little decline in sexual ability until late in life, whereas most men at sixty are still sexually capable. Since then William Masters and Virginia Johnson have directly observed and measured the sexual performance of older couples in their laboratory. Investigators from Duke University have examined 250 people from sixty to ninety-four years of age every three years; they found that 15 percent of this group actually *increased* sexual activity as they grew older.[38]

Changes in Sexual Capacity in the Older Woman and Man

Sexual activity, we shall see, can be beneficial for people of all ages. The older woman has fewer problems in participation than the older male. Older men take longer to obtain an erection and the volume of their seminal fluid gradually diminishes—although they have greater control over their ejaculation than a young man. The elderly man's ability to function sexually may be affected by boredom, fatigue, overeating, excessive drinking, fear of failure, and medical or psychiatric disturbances.

The elderly woman's capacity for intercourse continues until extreme old age. After menopause the older woman whose estrogen level becomes insufficient may develop a thinning of the vaginal walls. With this condition sexual intercourse sometimes causes cracking, bleeding, or pain. Lack of estrogen reduces the length and diameter of the vagina and may cause the labia—the outer lips of the vagina—to shrink. These conditions can be controlled by estrogen replacement or vaginal creams, so women who suspect a problem should consult their gynecologist.

Another common change in sexual functioning of the older woman is that vaginal secretions lubricating the vagina may decrease. However, for women who receive sexual stimulation on a regular basis—once or twice a week from young adulthood—this problem seldom occurs. Women as well as men who remain sexually active are more capable of retaining their ability.

Being able to function sexually is important for several reasons: there is some evidence that sexual activity helps arthritis (probably because of the adrenal gland production of cortisone that is stimulated), sexual activity helps keep the participant in good physical condition; sex also helps release accumulated tensions and so promotes deep, restorative sleep. Furthermore good sexual contact is closely associated with feelings of self-esteem and self-image.[39] Like the elderly population in the popular movie *Cocoon,* those older people who are sexually active feel better and look better.

Experts suggest that older women with partners who have problems in sexual functioning can benefit from treatment. Masters and Johnson report a success rate of over 50 percent with older patients, some of whom have had problems that existed for twenty-five years or more. Authorities also point out that sexual activity in the morning may be preferable for older couples, who tend to become fatigued by evening.

Three factors influence a woman's ability to enjoy sexual contact during her older years: her general physical health; her hormonal levels; and her opportunity for sexual activity. Since women outlive men of the same age, the outstanding sexual difficulty for older women is the decreasing number of available partners. In 1984 the life expectancy for white women in America was roughly seventy-nine, whereas white men could anticipate death by about seventy-two.[40] With superior female longevity, there are simply fewer men to go around.

The oldest authenticated living person today, according to the *Guinness Book of World Records* editors, may be—the title passes rapidly—Maren Torp of Norway, at 111.[41] Although many men live to extreme old age—the oldest authenticated person being a Japanese man who died at 120 years—approximately two-thirds of the oldest people who ever lived were women.

When her superior longevity is combined with the fact that she usually marries a man an average of 2.5 years older than herself, it becomes apparent that the typical American woman can expect to be a widow for about ten years. There are nearly 14 million older women in the United States; of these, more than 6 million are widows and 1.2 million are divorced or single. About 7 to 10 percent of women never marry. Some 65 percent of older women are living on their own—a deplorable fact when one considers that most women of this generation were raised to be dependent on men.[42]

Most of the men who are still available prefer younger women; few remarry in their own age bracket. Although men are free to marry younger women, society is strongly negative toward older women dating or marrying younger men, so potential partners are limited. Older women without partners are advised by gerontologists to masturbate, if they can accept it. This practice preserves sexual functioning—a desirable partner may be encountered later—as well as contributing to a feeling of general well-being.

Having established that the healthy older woman has sexual arousal during the dream state, is capable of sexual response during waking, and that sex is beneficial for her health, we turn to the sexual symbolism that is present in seniors' dreams, including love and romance dreams.

Dreams of Romance and Passion in Elderly Women

Sensuous Dreams: The Husband Chase. The first time I heard an account of a sexual dream from an older woman, I was startled. Hannah, spry and sparkly-eyed in her early nineties, was talking to me in her self-maintained apartment.

When she learned of my interest in dreams, Hannah announced she had a recent dream that "I am chasing the heck out of my husband for sex. Now, what does *that* mean?" I assured her it meant that she was still very much alive. "I don't want to be alive in that way anymore!" she said, with a wave of her hand. My companion later explained that Hannah's husband, dead for more than twenty-five years, had been a lady's man. Hannah was probably expressing, in the dream language of her younger years, a current need for loving attention. Dreams relating to former life needs usually arise when there is a contemporary need of a similar kind.

That a pattern of yearning for attention and affection from her husband still existed was readily comprehensible. That it should take the form of sexual desire was surprising to me. I have since come to understand how normal it is for all natural instincts to survive in healthy old age.

The Unfolding Flower.   Oma, twice widowed, was in her middle seventies when this study began; she contributed many dreams she had recorded over the years in her diary. This was one of her recurrent sexual dreams:

> Sometimes I have an orgasmic dream of a flower bud—a lotus
> or a water lily. As I watch, it unfolds petal by petal—like a
> slow-motion movie—until it's in full bloom and that is the
> orgasm. I like this one.

We have seen that women often represent female sexual organs as flowers in their dreams. This symbolism is common in men's dreams as well as in the art of most cultures—from the ancient Chinese paintings of the open peony to represent the receptive woman's genitals to Georgia O'Keeffe's monumental blooms. What is somewhat unusual in this dream is that Oma connected the image of the flower opening with the experience of orgasm. Younger women are not so likely to make this connection.

Waves of Perfume.   Another sensuous dream that Oma associated with near orgasm was the following:

> Great waves of perfume—a light, vibrant odor. I put my arms
> above my head and feel a lovely tingling sensation flow down
> my fingertips through my arms, but not below my shoulders.

> If the sensation had gone down through my body to my legs
> and feet, I surely would have been carried away. And that was
> my desire.

Not all older women have the understanding about sexuality and dream language that Oma had. Perhaps it is those women who have been more open about sexuality during their youth or middle years who are able to sense the relationship between certain dream symbols and sexuality.

On yet another level the mandala-shaped flower is said by Jungians to signify the Self; flowers are sometimes spoken of as the symbol of the spiritual body that survives physical death. Perhaps Oma, in her opening-flower dream and that of its perfume, was visualizing a spiritual self-development as well as a sensuous one.

Older women who accept their sensuality may also dream of sex more directly. A study by Joseph Adelson comparing creative college-aged women with noncreative ones found that the most imaginative thinkers had the most frankly sexual dreams.[43] It was as though the thinking of the noncreative women tended to remain stereotyped in their dreams, whereas the thinking of the creative woman was freer in every dimension.

Passion With a Stranger. Sophia, in her sixties, said that,

> Like most people, I have erotic dreams from time to time. It is usually with an unknown person—no face, no name. Certainly not my husband. It's exciting, pleasurable. It's been pretty standard throughout my life, perhaps more so after forty or fifty.

Many dreamers, like Sophia, choose the mysterious stranger for a dream lover.

Sweetheart Dreams: The Exotic Stranger. When Oma was about seventy, she had a romantic dream that made a strong impression:

> There is a farewell banquet being given in my honor, as I am leaving for wherever my home is. The guests and I go out into the street, where we wave good-bye, although there is no vehicle or train—a few horses stand about, but they are not mine.
>
> The town is like an old-time movie set, but not in California in some far-off state. The ladies wear bonnets and long, full-skirted dresses. There are men there, too, but I don't remember what they wore, except for one man. His name is Mr. Osh Kosh.
>
> He is an American Indian but is not in traditional Indian regalia—no headdress or feathers or jewelry. He wears deerskin moccasins, leather trousers, and a fringed suede jacket. He is the

most important man at the banquet—tall, authoritative, but
gentle. We have been great friends.

The crowd of well-wishers stand around as he takes me into his
arms and kisses me. It is not a sexy kiss but long and wonderful,
as though our spirits blend.
"You must write to me every day," he says.
"Yes, I will," I promise.
"I will come for you," he says as he mingles with the
still-waving crowd.
His wave is a blessing. I turn and go on my way to wherever I
am going.

Oma was so impressed with this dream encounter that later on in the same
night, in a sleepy, half-dream state, she wrote a love letter to Mr. Osh Kosh,
just as she had promised in the dream, describing the pleasure he gave her
and her eagerness for his arrival. As in the active-imagination technique of
Jung, this sort of fantasy can be beneficial.

Oma said that a week or so later she was introduced to a tall, slender
gentleman, a couple of years older than herself, who became her special
friend. When she eventually learned that he had some American Indian
blood, her dream took on extra significance. Whether Oma's encounter was
predicted by her dream or was simply a coincidence, her romantic dream
was comforting.

From a symbolic point of view, notice the horses standing around waiting. Horses, we have seen, frequently represent the dreamer's instinctual
energy. Certainly Oma was receptive to using her available sexual energy
when the opportunity came. The farewell banquet and departure suggested
a leaving behind of some aspect of herself: the soul-blending kiss and
expected reappearance of the dream lover anticipated some new feelings and
behavior. The qualities of Oma's dream hero were those she found attractive
in waking life. This older woman's romantic dream probably made her more
receptive than she might otherwise have been to the new man in her life.

Swiss therapist and writer Marie-Louise von Franz, who was herself
analyzed by Jung, speaks of the woman's "animus," the inner male that
appears in dreams, as having four forms:

1. The physical man. In his earliest appearance, the positive male figure
   in a woman's dreams is the handsome and virile athletic type.
2. The romantic man. Later in a woman's development, von Franz says,
   the men in her dreams become romantic or heroic.

3. The man of the word. Still later, the woman may dream of men who are powerful leaders, verbally skilled.
4. The man of the spirit. Finally, von Franz suggests, a woman may dream of spiritual men who teach and inspire the dreamer.

The man in Oma's dream was of the highly romantic type. I find that the first three types of male images that von Franz speaks of continue to appear in women's dreams as they grow older. The fourth is rare at any age.

We should also mention that some dreamers picture death as a journey, a leave-taking—especially to the West. In this dream Oma's characters are garbed in Western clothing. A dreamer facing death is sometimes guided to the world beyond by an attractive person. Death may even be depicted as a marriage. Since Oma was heartily alive, her vision was partially symbolic of her yearning for connection with a loving mate, but this dream may also have helped prepare her for the final journey—she died during the writing of this book.

One-Way Ticket. Elizabeth, also a widow in her late seventies, contributed a large number of dreams from her journal over the years. Among them were a few mildly romantic encounters. In one from her early seventies Elizabeth describes a dream that rather resembled Oma's:

> I walk up the street to the bus station with my friend's husband
> to ask if they will accept a personal check for my ticket. My
> hostess and her young daughter are crying because I am leaving
> them. I assure them that I will send money back for the
> children. They have so much that I wish I had—a home and a
> family. We pass three buses parked at our left in a narrow alley.

Notice the similar theme of a leave-taking. Elizabeth has buses standing by rather than horses. As the dream continues at the bus station, Elizabeth holds a long discussion with the ticket agent about when she can get a bus, is told dates that are past or in the future, and is unable to cash her check without personal identification. Finally she provides the agent with a passportlike photograph that resembles the agent himself. He asks to keep her/his picture:

> I begin to wonder if I really want to leave. I would like to
> know this kind of man better. His attitude is one of gentle
> teasing.

The dream continues with an exchange over a tea cart. When the dream ends, she is walking with the agent while his sister and the friends of the dreamer walk behind.

In this dream Elizabeth seemed to be leaving some part of herself behind, as Oma had done. She, too, met an intriguing, romantic man. By choosing the title "One-Way Ticket," she implied a difficulty in going back. Yet she was reluctant to let the romantic element go and seemed to wish for a relationship with a male companion like that in her dream. The dream ended with an uncertain connection. Again, we have the theme of a journey, this time with an undetermined departure date. Perhaps Elizabeth, too, was preparing herself for the ultimate trip.

The lack of personal identification (except for the card case) in Elizabeth's dream is more typical of another theme that arises in the dreams of elderly women.

Lost Purses and Handkerchiefs: Dreams of Personal Loss and Change in Older Women

"Oh, did I have a dream for you," announced eighty-four-year-old Betty as I entered the room. "I thought and thought about it in order to be able to tell you. It was a doozy. And where's it gone? Out the window!" Betty was eager to be helpful to my study, but found herself frustrated by a slippery memory.

Older people are often troubled by the diminution of their mental abilities along with their physical strength. Betty was extremely active into her late seventies, walking several miles a day, going swimming, and taking tap dance lessons twice a week. Having known her for several years, I always marveled at the brightness of her expressive eyes and the briskness of her step. Recently, however, her over ninety-year-old husband required hospitalization and placing in a nursing home; she underwent a cataract operation. Betty's energy was slowing down.

Lost in the Hospital.   The sense of loss of powers—whether temporary or permanent—sometimes forms a dream theme itself for the older person. Oma, for instance, in her late seventies, dreamed of being lost in a hospital. After opening scenes in the hospital surrounded by busy people, with the dreamer resenting the lack of privacy,

I get up and decide to leave the hospital but get lost. A man and a woman accompany me, and we search for a safe elevator, as many are unsafe. . . . When the elevator we choose starts to descend, a roof smashes down on us. . . . Later, on the ground floor we are lost again and wander about in confusion, then take another elevator. It is very large and carpeted. The woman rolls up two carpets, which she intends to steal. Filled with all sorts of knickknacks, there is a long coffinlike box on the floor. I think, "If she's stealing carpets, I'm going to help myself to some of those treasures." But a thin, poorly dressed woman comes along and rummages among the contents because they belong to her and her children. She shows me a little ledger book opened to show a list of mathematical problems. "This proves that my dog is getting too fat," she says.

We all take off to try to find our way out of the building again. Many students pass us. "They must come from someplace," I say, "So let's go in the opposite direction and we'll find our way out."

Oma told me that she has usually been very happy in hospitals, relishing the attention and care given to her. In the dream, however, she is disturbed by people invading her privacy and mocking her. Without unraveling all the detailed symbolism of this complicated dream, I want to point out the sense of damage, and of being lost and confused. Notice, too, the coffinlike box full of treasures that she cannot take. Oma owns several dogs; the dream reference to the "too fat" dog may refer to her own physical condition of recent weight gain.

In fact, at the time of this dream Oma was recovering from a hip operation and was having difficulty moving around with ease. The sense of invaded privacy, the wish to escape, the damage, the being lost and confused, all probably related to her desire to be finished with the limited mobility. The coffinlike box was more ominous, perhaps reminding the dreamer of the inevitability of death. Yet she saw the possibility of a treasure contained in it, perhaps symbolizing the soul. She was told about a problem relating to weight—a dream warning for herself.

Happily Oma's dream also included the awareness of "a way out." Something that was related to study and learning—the students—would show her that way. Oma had wide interests, including writing, reading, and painting, so her dream may have been urging her to be more attentive to these activities.

In another dream during this same week Oma saw herself going home through "a very tough part of town where a lot of wicked people hang about. They are very dirty and ragged and sly." After a pleasant, brief encounter with a well-dressed gentleman who evoked ambivalent feelings in Oma, she commented, "I hug my shoulder bag close so that the surrounding thieves can't steal it. Soon I'll be safe."

The precious belongings that are carried in women's purses make handbags, and similar objects, a common symbol for "something of value" in women's dreams. Especially because identity cards are carried within, purses come to be associated with personal identity. Pocketbooks, we have seen, may also symbolize a woman's genitals in particular, as well as valuables in general. In either case, Oma felt threatened in this dream, but did not lose her valued things.

These dreams were actually atypical for Oma, since she had many beautiful, inspiring dreams. Here we see her reacting to a specific, limiting situation—convalesence from the operation—and her effort to reach beyond it, as well as possible preparation for death, which was not many months away.

The Handkerchief Thief.   At times imagery of loss reflects the beginning of waning abilities. In her early eighties, Fanny described to me a dream that,

> A small boy stole my handkerchiefs. They were neatly stacked
> in a pile in my drawer. He took them all away.

At the time of this dream Fanny was beginning to seriously falter in her mental and physical capabilities. I was not able to elicit from Fanny exactly what the handkerchiefs represented to her, but I suspect that they were an essential requirement of Victorian girlhood. The dream poignantly depicts the disorder and sense of loss of something of value to her.

The Rotting Floorboards.   Among Elizabeth's numerous rich, illuminating dreams there are also references to a sense of "feeling rickety." In one, for instance,

> A man named Frank lives in a kind of hillbilly home with his
> three children. He sits all day on the porch in his rocker, dressed
> in his shabby old tweed suit with the leather patches on the
> elbow and smoking his pipe and reading while the floorboards
> rot in the porch.

Someone tries to fix them but he just goes on reading while the old house falls apart. Two of the children go to take a nap. I notice my red cooking pot sitting on the shelf.

Shabby clothing, rotting floorboards, an old house falling apart—such images suggest a sense of deterioration. The fact that the dream character ignores the decay around him and that the children—impulsive, young energy—are napping implies that there is something the dreamer is not giving proper attention to in her life. Since a woman's body is often depicted in dreams as a house, a deteriorating building carries the connotation of physical debility.

The dream was a "frank" (a pun on the name of the dream character) statement on Elizabeth's condition. The red cooking pot—where nourishing things are prepared—stood as idle on the shelf as the man in his rocker. Such a dream might impel a sophisticated dreamer like Elizabeth to attend more to her physical needs.

The House in Disarray. Tony, at ninety-seven, told me that he had dreamed the preceding night of being back in his home in Europe:

Three bums break into my house. They go into the basement and break everything. Then they go into the kitchen and break everything. I call the policeman, but he doesn't come.

Tony had had a bad night. He was in a great deal of pain when we spoke, his jaw almost locked from the aftermath of a stroke several years ago, his one side crippled and almost paralyzed. Some days are better for him, but this was worse than usual. His eyes felt so weak, he could hardly see. "This is no life," he told me in despair, "I hope I die soon . . . but my heart is too strong."

Tony typifies for me the tragedy of the elderly person whose body is in collapse while his mind remains clear. If those who are well take the time to hold a hand and hear a dream, the old vitality briefly rekindles.

From the symbolic point of view, Tony's dream depicted his sense of being broken in body. Confined to a wheelchair, his foundation—his basement—no longer functioned. Unable to digest well, his source of physical as well as emotional nourishment—his kitchen—was disturbed. He wanted help (the police), but it was unavailable. Houses, as we have repeatedly pointed out, frequently represent the dreamer's body.

Certainly Tony's body (his house) has been intruded upon. He may also be readying himself for death, as well as wishing for its release. Jungian analyst von Franz says that death is sometimes symbolized as an intruder. In terms of imagery that reflects deterioration and preparation for death, older men's and older women's dreams are much alike.

The House Rebuilt.   Happily not all people in their nineties are in such discomfort. Augusta, although she had a bout with cancer a quarter of a century ago, was well and going to work daily. In her most recent dream,

> A house is being fixed over. It is kind of like a barn. It's in the process of reconstruction.

Augusta defined a barn as "a place where you keep horses, cows, and hay," adding, "I like barns. I like animals." In her youth Augusta had been an active horseback rider. In her early nineties, she still exercised and was fascinated with learning; she had many interests. She told me that she felt less energy in the morning but gained it during the day, that "I get energy from life." Her motto might be, "Be aware of the moment."

In her dream language Augusta seemed to be keeping her body—her house—in a good state of repair, able to shelter and nourish the things she found worthwhile.

Dream imagery of damaged homes or property often relate to the dreamer's momentary sense of physical or emotional impairment rather than to a permanent situation. Such images do not imply an immutable state even in the elderly dreamer. Professionals and lay people alike need to become aware that elders and their dreams are subject to change as feelings and experiences change.

Dreams of being lost show up in healthy girls five to twelve years old as well as in women in their prime. Women of all ages occasionally dream of being lost or of having their purses, identity cards, or other valuables stolen. We cannot assume that such dream themes in the elderly mean more than they do in younger people, that is, "At this moment I feel as though I have lost something valuable."

Lost Purses Found.   In particular we must remember that dreams can still change in old age. I was delighted with the dream experiences described by my superactive godmother, Kathryn Lee. When she was eighty-two, she explained, "I never bothered about dreams until after I'd talked to you. Now I remember them all the time. Most of them are pleasant. If it's unhappy, I know it's a dream and I start fixing it up." In a recurrent dream,

I'll be in a strange city—someplace I've never been before—and I'll lose my purse (I travel a lot). At first I don't know it's a dream. Then I say to myself, "Now, wait a minute. I never lose my purse, this must be a dream."

I will set a place where I will find it. I tell myself, "My purse will be behind that bush," or, "When I turn the next corner, I will find it," or, "Somebody will bring me my purse," and sure enough, they do.

This dream scenario fits Aunt Kathryn's practical mind perfectly; if something is wrong, you just fix it—whether awake or asleep. Currently, having retired as a counselor, she volunteers at a home for abused children, visits nursery schools around the city to inspect their operation, teaches, and manages to keep in contact with a myriad of grandchildren and godchildren—quite a schedule for a lady in her eighties. She told me, "I only dream of lost purses when I'm feeling insecure about something." Kathryn's dream is actually "lucid," that is, she is aware she is dreaming during the dream. Dreamers of all ages could benefit from her recently acquired dream skills.

Research on Dream Themes in the Elderly. In a study conducted in a New York city home for the aged, in 1961, researchers Martin Barad, Kenneth Altshuler, and Alvin Goldfarb found that almost all of the initial dreams they collected from a group of fifty-two elderly patients dealt with themes of loss of resources.[44]

These investigators gathered dreams that were reported during one year by participants whose median age was eighty. The psychiatrist who met with the dreamers quickly became a character in the older persons' dreams. The subjects began reporting more satisfying and successful dreams for a while. However, as the participants received no encouragement to discuss the possible meanings and implications of their dreams, the scenarios gradually became less constructive again. It seems to me that a program of dream discussion with older persons that included discussion and comment upon dreams, in addition to simple recording, could have been as beneficial as it was for my Aunt Kathryn.

Later, in 1963, the same researchers collected dreams for two months from twenty-five older persons who lived on their own in New York City.[45] These participants, who attended a day center, were younger; their median age was sixty-nine. Several of the group described dreams where they were wandering in a strange place, unable to choose a road, or dreams of losing something. The researchers observed that these people were more likely to be suspected of having organic mental deterioration.

Other group members who had rich, elaborately detailed and varied dreams were more likely to be self-sufficient and busily engaged in organizing their lives. Would the more troubled dreamers, I wonder, have been able to find greater satisfaction in their dream and waking lives if their dreams had been worked with constructively? We need comparative studies to be certain that dream themes of loss and damage are actually more frequent in older people than they are in younger ones. Even if this proved to be so, they would still be amenable to change in many cases.

The White Bird. The capacity for change is exemplified in this pair of dreams from Elizabeth. In the first, there is clearly some danger to the dreamer:

> I find an exhausted little white bird. I hold it gently in my two
> hands and wonder if I can keep it alive.

To Elizabeth a white bird represents the Holy Spirit. In this dream, then, she senses some sort of spiritual malaise. She is trying to nurture and revive those feelings that are important to her; at the moment they are exhausted. In a dream shortly thereafter,

> I am driving a car, being shown the right way to go by a
> low-flying bird that flies just ahead of me. There is a highway
> on my right and an abyss on my left.

Here Elizabeth is in much better control—although she has never driven in her life, she is at the steering wheel of her dream car; although her path has dangers on both sides, she feels herself guided aright by spiritual feelings.

Diverging Paths: The Life Review in Dreams

"It must be Sunday," reported eighty-four-year-old Fanny when she came downstairs one morning. "I heard the church bells ringing all through my dreams." Inquiry revealed that Fanny must have been dreaming of her old hometown, three thousand miles away, complete with scenes of a Sunday morning, for she thought she was there and it took her some time to reorient herself.

The Life Review.   Anyone who is with elderly persons for any length of time knows how well they like to reminisce about the old days. Many younger people feel impatient with this tendency, regarding it as boring, meaningless, wasteful, or a preoccupation with the self. Even some professionals label the older person's reminiscence a symptom of dotage. Gerontologist Robert Butler, however, asserts that the natural inclination to review one's life can be an effort to seek meaning for one's existence and to prepare for the acceptance of death.[46]

Butler points out that people of any age facing death—during wartime, in illness, in a prison "death row," or other conditions of imminent peril—are prone to examine the value of their existence. Indeed, developmental psychologists state that one of the major tasks of later life is to face the certainty of personal death and so act during the remaining time to resolve conflicts, to make atonements and restitutions where possible, and to contribute to the welfare of those who will remain behind—until it is their turn on life's wheel.[47]

By summarizing one's life in a structured and purposeful way, Butler says, the natural process of life review in old age can be exceedingly beneficial. He advocates the taking of an extensive autobiography from older people under one's care. Using family albums, genealogies, old movies, and even pilgrimages to places of importance to stimulate their memory, older people are thus enabled to reconstruct the picture of their lives. The National Retired Teachers Association and the American Association of Retired Persons have produced a manual for reminiscence programs for trained "Listeners" who visit the elderly. The Listeners encourage remembering; the older person usually enjoys the process and also profits therapeutically.

Reviewing one's life can lead to tragic results if the person concludes that his or her life was a total waste. Since the process seems to occur universally in the final years of life, it is important for people close to an older person to be aware of the potential dangers and benefits. Family members and professionals need to help the older person see what can still be done to resolve issues that cause discomfort.

Some of the positive results of life review that Butler mentions include a righting of old wrongs, making up with enemies, an acceptance of mortal life, finding a sense of serenity, a pride in accomplishment, a feeling of having done one's best, and deciding what to do with one's remaining time. Emotional and material legacies can be worked out—one elderly man tape-recorded his life experiences as a story for a gift to his grandson. Memoirs can become a valuable creative project for the recipient as well as for the giver, in the form of art or music or albums or family trees. The older person may find a full acceptance of the life cycle and a sense of wisdom.

If the life review is successful, life can take on new significance and meaning; an ability to truly enjoy the present, with daily pleasures in grandchildren, nature, colors, warmth, beauty, humor, and love. Butler sees the life review as a natural healing process.

The Dream Review. Several of the older women I worked with presented dreams that seemed to recall nostalgic parts of their past, as Fanny's dream of Sunday morning at home did, or ones that replayed major life events or scanned large portions of their lives.

Nanette, in her late seventies, had a nightmare pertaining to a tragic betrayal by a family member. She found herself staring into a hole in the floor in which a man was drowning and trying to clutch at her. Although the event was well over, her dreaming mind needed to review and assimilate the difficult experience. The imagery of a black hole may sometimes be a reference to fear of death; for Nanette it was a response to a recent difficulty.

Elizabeth, at the same age, also "reviewed" a portion of her life:

> There is a parade with a large white slug in it. A woman is
> beating it. She says, "She will never have to worry about
> getting pregnant." It is an ugly experience. I am glad when that
> parade passed me by.

The imagery in this dream suggests that the dreamer, who had difficulty birthing her two children, as well as having a miscarriage, was relieved to be well past that possibility.

In a later, review-type dream, Elizabeth had some spectacular imagery:

> I cry out, "There is an eagle." We can see the glittering of his
> eye, or perhaps it is the diamond bracelet around his neck; he is
> in his aerie. There seems to be an ibis or egret—or perhaps
> three of them in the sky. A woman stands on their backs as in a
> circus act or someone driving the chariot of the sun. All are
> sparkling white.
>
> I am amazed and a little annoyed. "It is a publicity stunt," I
> say. "I wish we could get back to the old days, when you could
> believe what you see. Perhaps it is a projection in the sky."

Then I am walking with my daughter in an empty field up a lonely road that comes to a dead end. There is nothing there but an empty movie house. I hurry back down the road to a place where I will be in real life with real people.

Here Elizabeth seems to be dazzled by a beautiful vision that she rejects as unreal. Perhaps this dreamer had an illusion—the girl riding on the backs of birds through the sky—that she is now willing to let go. She says to herself that it is a "projection." In the second scene she depicts associating with her younger self— her daughter in the dream—traveling a route that leads nowhere (symbolized by the "dead end" and the empty movie house).

In describing this dream, Elizabeth commented that it explained why "there is no need to worry about me anymore." She regarded her realization that the movie house contained nothing but empty pictures—more "projections"—as a vital discovery. She was unwilling to proceed to the "dead end" and quickly retraced her steps to a more active involvement—real life with real people—in the present. Elizabeth's understanding of her dream imagery bodes well for her making good use of the time she has.

Paths followed—or retreated from—are often clues to significant life choices. Dreamers should be particularly alert to dreams containing roads and byways; they are clues to where they are heading.

Dreams About Deceased Mates

Widows almost always dream about their dead spouses or lovers. Depending upon the quality of their relationship, the mate may make the most casual of dream calls with an indifferent welcome or the couple may have a soul-shaking encounter. Sometimes the memory is too raw and painful to tolerate yet, even in a dream.

Washing the Clothes. Once they begin, dreams of deceased loved ones may last a lifetime. Marianna, in her early eighties, described this recent dream of her spouse who died over forty-five years ago:

I am in the very room I am sleeping in (overlooking the flowers and the pool and other motel rooms). I am in the big double bed and my husband (whom I lost in 1942) is with me. He says how warm it is. I say, "No, it's cold." (It was ninety-two degrees when I left home and sixty-two degrees when I arrived, so it was really cold.) I had no clothes for such an early fall. (In fact, the bus people had temporarily lost my valise with all my clothes in it.)

My husband got up to shower and afterward washed all his underclothes and hung them up. I was proud of him and envied him doing what I wanted to do.

Here Marianna seems to be taking an actual situation of mild discomfort and using the image of her long-dead husband to illustrate what she should do until her suitcase is located. She may also be yearning for his protective guidance.

Some older women in my study barely mentioned their former husbands in their dreams. He was playing tennis with a bachelor friend or he was sitting at the kitchen table—in minor roles, that is, of the ongoing action. These mates were not acting in such a way as to help their wives, as Marianna's was. Among these women, some had poor relationships with the men in their lives.

Other women found their deceased husband's absence from their dreams disturbing or puzzling. Seventy-five-year-old Kora, for instance, inquired, "I wonder why I dream more about my mother than I do about my husband?" She went on to explain that she had been happily married for over thirty years. "You might think I didn't love him, but it's not true," she said, adding, "I guess most women have complexes about their mothers." The likelihood is that Kora's emotions are more occupied with the conflictual aspects of her relationship with her long-dead mother and with her own troubled daughter than with the comfortable situation with her deceased husband.

Replays and Rendezvous.   Recent widows, as might be expected, have a strong emotional charge to any dreams of their absent mate. Some of these are happy dreams of the departed; some are agonizing. Two recent widows in their late seventies illustrate this difference. Louisa, who found her husband dying with his face distorted from a stroke, has painful dreams of finding him again in a ghoulish way. Mary, however, has pleasant dreams of talking with her deceased husband, laughing and communicating joyfully.

Although both husbands died rapidly from their illnesses, Louisa's mate had the more dramatic death—the shock probably imprinted this event. Like victims of posttraumatic shock, Louisa needs to go through the distressing dreams as part of the healing process; they will gradually shift into other patterns. Uncomfortable as such dreams are, they are at times essential to the recovery process.

Holding Hands Across the Dark.   At 74, sculptor Käthe Kollwitz recorded in her diary a poignant dream rendezvous with her husband, about nine months after his death:[48]

> Recently I dreamed that I was together with the others in a room. I knew that Karl lay in the adjoining room. Both rooms opened out into an unlit hallway. I went out of my room into the hall and saw the door to Karl's room being opened, and then I heard him say in his kind, loving voice: "Aren't you going to say good night to me?" Then he came out and leaned against the wall, and I stood before him and leaned my body against his, and we held each other's hands and asked each other again and again: "How are you? Is everything all right?" And we were so happy being able to feel one another.

To be able to lovingly touch a departed mate, even in a dream, can bring deep comfort to the older dreamer.

Replanting the Garden.   Sophia, in her sixties, was widowed about a year ago. Her husband had a long, painful illness; the visions of his suffering were hard to put aside. "Six or eight months ago," she told me, "I couldn't talk about him without a crying spell. I am beginning to heal. Taking trips helped; redecorating the house helped. I am getting better." One of the dream signs of Sophia's recovery occurred the night before we met:

> I am in the walled garden, adding some flowers. My husband comes to the gate. His face is very red (meaning he's ill). He says, "I'm not going to work anymore. I'm going to spend all my time with you." We talk about driving up the coast to a favorite beach of ours. I wake feeling comforted.

On one level, of course, Sophia's wish is for her husband to be able to be with her, so that they can enjoy life together. Yet the fact that she is gardening, planting new growth, with her husband on the other side of the gate, indicates that she is getting on with her life; she is "tending her garden," a waking-life activity that gives her pleasure. This dream gave Sophia a feeling of comfort, a contact with her loved person, that could help her toward full recovery.

Jung's Dream of His Wife.   After the death of his wife, Emma, Jung had a dream that was a kind of summary of their relationship:

> I saw her in a dream which was like a vision. She stood at some distance from me, looking at me squarely. She was in her prime, perhaps about thirty, and wearing the dress which had been made for her many years before by my cousin the medium. It was perhaps the most beautiful thing she had ever worn. Her expression was neither joyful nor sad, but, rather, objectively wise and understanding, without the slightest emotional reaction, as though she were beyond the mist of affects. I knew that it was not she, but a portrait she had made or commissioned for me. It contained the beginning of our relationship, the events of fifty-three years of marriage, and the end of her life also. Face to face with such wholeness one remains speechless, for it can scarcely be comprehended.[49]

Dream reviews that are so complete as this one are rare but highly satisfying to the dreamer.

Whirling in Space.   Exactly three weeks before his unexpected heart attack, Irv, who was in his early eighties, told me a dream that I found frightening:

> I was lost in space—just whirling in dark, empty space. It was terrible.

Three weeks after this dream Irv was dead. There was no reason to think that Irv's death was imminent, but this dream of being lost in space rang an alarm bell in my head. Was Irv expressing a fear of deteriorating health? Or had his dreaming mind picked up the impending danger? Impossible to know.

   Over a year later I came across the description of an experience Jung had had when he was seriously ill in 1944 after three heart and lung embolisms:

> During those weeks I lived in a strange rhythm. By day I was usually depressed. I felt weak and wretched. . . . Toward

evening I would fall asleep, and my sleep would last until about
midnight. Then I would come to myself and lie awake for
about an hour, but in an utterly transformed state. It was as if I
were in an ecstasy. I felt as though I were floating in space, as
though I were safe in the womb of the universe—in a
tremendous void, but filled with the highest possible feeling of
happiness. "This is eternal bliss," I thought. "This cannot be
described; it is far too wonderful!"[50]

Many other visions followed in Jung's case. Both men describe being
suspended in space, but Irv, who died shortly thereafter, was whirling and
felt frightened and lost in his dream, whereas Jung, who recovered from his
near-death state, was floating and felt ecstatic in his vision. Was it the
imminent death or recovery that made this difference in feeling?

Deceased Husband Gives Orders. Irv's wife, Nanette, in addition to
mourning the loss of the husband she had spent over half a century with,
was worried about the fate of his soul. For the next year after Irv's death
she had a difficult time coping; eventually her indomitable spirit rallied and
she got reinvolved with life. She intensely desired to dream about her
husband, but did not. Finally, over a year later, she got her wish and
excitedly called to report this dream:

Irv is all dressed up, with a hat and everything, lying on his
side, very comfortable. He is giving orders to someone—to
bring something or take something away.

I laughingly ask him, "And if he doesn't do it, what will you
do?" "It doesn't matter," he says, just exactly like himself. He
looks at me and I look at him. I wake up very happy.

Nanette explained that, to her, this dream meant that her husband's soul was
quiet, he was at peace. It emerged that she was afraid to dream of him in
pain as he was in his last few days; it would have signified that his soul was
not quiet. Her dream had reassured her that he was comfortable, in charge,
untroubled, and with her in spirit.

Some women find that dreams of their departed mates bring great comfort. They relive the lost companionship, talking together as of old and
feeling touched lovingly; they bring back from their dream a sense of
strength for the day and hope for a future life.

Forecasting the Future in Elders' Dreams
Heavenly Visions

Celebrations.   "My dreams are always happy," said Marianna, in her early eighties, going on to explain,

> I always dream of going to Paris [where she lived for many years]. There is a celebration going on, some kind of ceremony. People are in costumes with ribbons, beautiful colors. There is music playing. The strange thing is, I have never seen any of these colorful ceremonies, although I know the places—the museums, palaces, courtyards (of the Louvre, for instance) perfectly well.
>
> Sometimes I dream of traveling to London, or of visiting historic houses in the South, or of streets I know well, but which in the dream have new features of interest.

Marianna remembers Paris with pleasure, where she was married and dwelt happily. Yet these dreams, I speculate, are more than a widow's recall of happiness past. In part, her dreams reveal her positive attitude, one of continuing to discover new "features" to life. Beyond this, the motif of travel to a far place, the delightful atmosphere, the beauty and color and jubilance of the novel ceremonies, suggest that Marianna, devotedly religious, is symbolically anticipating paradise.

Shimmering Light.   Afterlife anticipations seem to be characterized by the celestial quality of light. Nanette, in her late seventies, described such a dream:

> I am lying down in a prairie. The earth is glittering like gold. I think in the dream how it would be nice to make a dress of this beautiful material.

The glint of treasure, the rare substance with which she thinks of covering herself—making a dress of it—suggest the idea of the spiritual body. The word *prairie* resembles closely the word *prayer*. The very next night, in her favorite of all dreams, Nanette saw the following:

> I am in a room in a house, probably the dining room. There are
> several white doves fluttering against the window, with light
> coming through it. I am very careful not to open the door. I
> am very concerned that they shouldn't go out of the house.
> They should stay. I feel very happy. I love it.

To Nanette the white dove is a symbol of peace. She recalled an old saying that when a little bird flies into the house, it brings luck. This dream recurred two nights in a row, leaving Nanette with a pleasurable afterglow.

The dining room setting represents for Nanette, as it does for most dreamers, the place of obtaining nourishment. Since Nanette is also a fine cook, it is also a place where her talents are appreciated. In her dream language she is nourished by the appearance of feelings of peace and bliss.

The shimmering light of Nanette's dream has celestial implications. On this level the doves of her dream may represent the spirit that she wants to remain in the house—her body—for the moment. But they seem to promise an ethereal afterworld.

Journeys to Far Places

The Homeland.   The process of death is sometimes depicted as a long journey. We saw earlier the leavetakings in the dreams of Oma and Elizabeth. At this stage of life women's dreams are more likely to resemble men's dreams than at any other time. My elderly father-in-law, Pop, when he was ninety-seven, announced one day,

> I went on a long journey last night. I am at home in the
> Ukraine. I am five or six years old, digging in the soil—the
> Ukraine has the richest soil in all the world. I am digging for
> red sand to spread on the floor of the house. There are three or
> four women working there. I am waiting for Mother to come.
> It is beautiful. I feel good.

Pop explained that it was the custom in the Ukraine to gather the rich, rose-colored sand as part of a ritual for the springtime festival. The sand was made into a liquid, he says, that then was made to cover the dirt floor. In his dream the color was extraordinary. "I never saw a color like that. It was a shame to exchange it for a floor." In one sense, Pop was "digging" into his past in this dream. Although the imagery has some elements of a dream review, there is a feeling of "something more" about it.

Pop went on to explain that he felt sad when he awakened, "because I felt something beautiful would develop. I hated to wake up. In my dream I was active, I was healthy, I was strong—and when I awoke I was nothing but a shadow!"

The precious thing that was about to happen was the appearance of his beloved mother. We know that those who have survived near-death, and sometimes those who are about to die, dream of being met by beloved relatives or friends who are deceased. Other elements that have the sound of preparation for death include the purifying of the foundation of his body—the floor of his house—and the rare soil, the incredible color, the anticipation of something marvelous, the celebration of the holiday of rebirth, as well as an association he had to the father being like a king during this holiday. One could easily suspect that this dream was near-terminal, but Pop is thriving at 103—still waiting for his mother to come.

The Gate.   Another elderly man reported a poignant dream of a journey. Following the death of his wife, Flo, in her seventies, Ben was lost. Although they had been about the same age, his wife had been the dominant partner; now he floundered. Two months later he dreamed:

> My wife and I are going to the airport. We reach a gate
> through which I am not allowed but she is. When she has
> almost reached the airplane, she turns and waves good-bye to
> me.

Ben was greatly relieved when he woke. He felt his wife had simply "gone on ahead" and he would join her later. He no longer felt lost and became actively engaged in life again—even to the point of remarrying. Notice the recurrence of the gate motif, as in Sophia's dream, separating the dreamer from the deceased mate.

Dreams of Preparation for Personal Death

Elderly people are forced to contemplate their inevitable demise: all around them relatives and friends fall ill. Those people who survive into old age must witness the slow or sudden death of many of the people they know. This, along with their increasing age, stimulates contemplation of their own future death.

Her Own Funeral. Kora, for instance, at seventy-five, commented that she sometimes dreams of her own funeral:

> I'm lying in a casket watching people mourn me. I listen to what they say—"She was a good person," and so forth—and decide whether they're sincere or not.

Kora has this dream recurrently, even though she is in good health and still works a daily schedule. In a way her dream helps her to accept death whenever it may come.

His Father in a Shroud. At ninety-six, Pop reported a dream I thought at the time must surely presage death:

> I see my [long-dead] father on the street. Apparently he stepped out of his grave and came to meet me. He is wearing his shroud. He asks me to take off my jacket and give it to him so that people won't be frightened to see him. I do and . . . [clapping his hands] I wake up.

"The amazing thing about it," Pop went on to explain, "is that in the dream my father was a seven-footer. In actual life he was shorter than I am, but in the dream, he was three or four feet taller."

When I questioned Pop about the height aspect of the dream, he stated that he thought the tallness "describes the moral goodness of the man, his greatness. He was a godly man—the first one to be buried in a new cemetery. They always seek a godly man to start a new cemetery."

In symbolic language Pop was making contact with an older and "greater" part of himself. This aspect does not want to arouse fear. At the time it seemed possible that Pop was symbolically shedding his physical body—the jacket—by removing his outer covering to give shelter to the dead.

As mentioned, survivors of near-death experiences, or those who have actually died and later been revived, often describe being met by deceased relatives and friends to be guided to the other world, so I feared this dream was a terminal one. However, as I mentioned, Pop remains alive and well at 103, over seven years later. His dream was obviously not one of impending death; perhaps it was one of several dreams he had that seem to prepare people for the final encounter.

Her Daughter's Death.   Nellie, in her early seventies, dreamed that her daughter was dead. Alarmed, she telephoned her daughter the next day to determine whether she was all right. The daughter was well and continued to be so. Nellie, however, six months later, had a severe heart attack from which she almost died. With the aid of a pacemaker, she survived. As she told me her dream, she was puzzled over whether it had been predictive or not. Although there is no way to be sure, certainly Nellie was dreaming about the younger part of herself being nonfunctional.

The Child Is Found.   My mother, who has been recording her dreams for decades, says that she often dreams of me to represent herself as a young girl. Older women who have daughters will want to be alert to the possibility that dreams of their daughters may symbolize things happening to their younger or more vulnerable selves. A girl may play a similar role in an older woman's dream. One of my mother's favorite dreams is the following:

> It is night and I am leading a little girl by the hand. We are looking for her father. She is well dressed in a light blue coat and bonnet and is about four years old. She is crying, "I want my daddy."
>
> I hear a shot in the distance and hope that does not mean that her father has been executed. We are in the city in a kind of murky Persian bazaar. I open one door into a schoolroom but find only a teacher and his class there.
>
> We continue to look and meet an old lady, who exclaims excitedly, "What child is this?" The old lady calls her Maharini, but adds that her name is Pneuma or Model or some third name I forget. I hold onto the child firmly by the back of her collar so that I will not lose her.
>
> The old lady shows me a document that proves the child's identity. It is in beautiful script, embroidered on cream-colored linen. I remember seeing the big letter O. It is a long document embroidered in a convent. The old lady tells me, "I remember when her mother did this."
>
> I ask, "Then Pneuma is rich?" and she answers, "Yes, very rich." I scan the document hastily and learn that her mother spoke French.

Although Mother tends to think of this intriguing dream as a kind of past-life memory, I wonder if it does not also cast forward. There are several fascinating symbols and archetypal elements in this dream; I will mention only a few. Mother titled this dream "A Child Is Found." She is picturing a "lost child," probably a part of herself that feels lost. The more mature part of herself (the adult in the dream) is seeking the identity of this part, clasping it tightly (as she does the collar of the coat). She finds herself hunting through a dark, murky, dangerous environment (the city with the Persian bazaar—bizarre?—and the gunshot). She begins to learn (entering the schoolroom) and finally discovers the true identity (the document) of this aspect of herself from a "wise old woman": it is royal (a Maharini), valuable (rich) and has a name (Pneuma or Model).

Mother is aware that the word *pneuma* comes from a Greek word meaning "spirit" or "soul" (also "air, wind, or breath"). Amidst all the dark, murky danger of the environment the dreamer has found and identified a part of herself that is very rich; her name is Spirit. The child in her dream may be her true Self, the wholeness she wants to discover. This is, indeed, a worthwhile part of oneself to contact—especially as the dreamer ages.

Dream References to Death or Separation in the Seriously Ill.   Psychologist Robert Smith has conducted an interesting study on the correlation between severity of illness and the presence of death and separation references in dreams.[51] He measured severity of illness by rehospitalization or actual death. Collecting dreams from subjects who were sick in the hospital, he found that in women's dreams, references to separation—saying good-bye or leaving in a dream—were related to the worsening of an illness. In contrast, men's dream references to death—of characters in the dream or of the dreamer—were related to the worsening of their illness. Why this sex difference should have been observed is odd. We need to understand much more about the connection between dream images and health or illness.

An intriguing finding of Smith's study was the fact that people who had no dream material at all had the highest percentage of death rate. Once again, the presence of dreams, just as was previously mentioned with the elderly, was an indication of better health.

Playing the Game.   Final dreams can comfort the dying. From my large collection of dreams is one that Manny, who was dying of cancer in his early fifties, reported a few days before his death. His widow told me that life had become increasingly vivid for Manny in the few days after his kidney failure. He spoke of colors being extremely vivid and the outlines of things being sharp. "The words people speak are as if they are written in capital letters," he said. Manny wanted to program a dream to explain to himself what was happening, so for the next two or three nights he concentrated on an explanation to come to him in dreams. Then he dreamed,

> I'm back at the old farm in New England that I used to visit
> every summer as a teenager. I was playing my favorite game,
> Halley Over the Bungalow. The players are not opponents. It's
> a noncompetitive game in which the players stand on either side
> of a building, like a barn and toss the ball to *the other side*
> [italics mine]. You never know who catches the ball and who
> tosses it back. You just play the game.

Manny found this dream strangely comforting. Although he did not know where he (symbolized by the ball, the complete Self) was going or where he came from, it was fun to "play the game." It was not a game to win, but rather a game to enjoy. I can only guess that the game received its odd name from Halley's comet, appearing suddenly over the barn. At the time of this dream, Manny and his wife expected him to live for several months. In fact he died a few days later, passing over to "the other side." Perhaps the dream he sought helped ease the passage.

Definitive Dream Images of Death?　In her recent book, *On Dreams and Death,* Jungian analyst Marie-Louise von Franz describes a collection of dreams gathered shortly prior to death.[52] She feels that the imagery is indicative of the forthcoming death of the body; I think this judgment requires substantial information about the condition of the dreamer. Here are some of the dream images of death she mentions:

> Death of vegetation—especially trees, wheat, corn
> Death of animals, such as horses or birds
> A struggle or fight between antagonists
> Travel through a narrow, dark, birthlike passage or tunnel
> Heavy dark spots, clouds, fog, a dark pit or hole, a dark lake
> A bridge to be crossed over
> A revolving door
> A candle that goes out
> A clock that stops
> A journey to the West
> A burglar or intruder entering the dreamer's house
> Pursuit by a wolf or dog, especially black

Encounter with a handsome youth or beautiful woman

A marriage

Being burned by fire or inundated by water

Seeing a ball of light, Christ, angels

Meeting a dead relative, often the mother or marriage partner, or recently
    deceased friend

Being fetched, guided, or welcomed by dead relatives or friends

Images of the soul, including butterflies, birds, flowers, stones

Von Franz says that all people have occasional death dreams from age fifty onward. Such dreams are said to usually depict the death of the physical body and the survival of a spiritual body.

However, the problem is that each of these images may also occur when the dreamer is young and in excellent health, as well as prior to death. We have seen that dreams of being chased or attacked are exceedingly common throughout life. In my study of children's dreams I found such dreams, including those of pursuit by wolves and dogs, burglars and intruders, to be the most common childhood dream. In their happy dreams, children often see butterflies, birds, and flowers.

Young women in love and encountering sex frequently dream of flowers. Likewise they many times in dreams make love with strange, attractive men or known lovers. They experience dream weddings, especially when they are engaged, and they have been doing so occasionally since childhood. In many folk traditions to dream of a bride coming down the aisle in white is considered a sure sign of death, yet I have spoken with several happy brides who dreamed of being married and survived to see their own grandchildren wed.

Women who are pregnant characteristically dream of going on a journey during their last few months prior to delivery. Their trip West, or to some exotic locale, is an encounter with the unknown ahead—it is a meeting with birth and seldom nowadays one with death.

Women undergoing divorce and other problems are beset in their dreams by pits, black holes, bridges, and images of struggling opponents.

When women experience menopause, they commonly have dreams of dying or destroyed vegetation. They also dream of fire and water in response to physical symptoms of hot flashes and water retention. Lush new growth returns to their dreams as they find physical balance and new vitality in living.

Women of all ages who have developed inner values may dream of precious stones, beings or balls of glowing light, God and angels, totally unrelated to ill health and impending death.

How, then, if all the symbols said to portend death are also symbols that occur throughout life, can we say that a certain dream is a death dream? We cannot. We must carefully examine the life situation of the dreamer at the moment of the dream; we must offer them the possibility that the negative images in their dreams can be transformed—explaining, for example, how dream pictures of dead plants can be followed by dreams of lush new growth—yet we must keep in mind the possibility that these images may imply the approach of physical death.

Going Forward. In general, elderly people's dreams review their past, express their present feelings, and forecast what the future will be. How can we be ready to meet death when it comes, as it surely will? Developmental psychologists tell us that three tasks are important for the elderly person to accomplish:[53]

1. *Valuing oneself as a person, not as a role.*

    The older woman who can see herself as a worthwhile human being, taking satisfaction in a broad range of activities (rather than only as "a wife," "a mother," "a lawyer," "a secretary," and so forth) can continue a vital interest in living fully as a good person.

    Each must strive to be herself, not a stereotype—the individual, unique person that she is.

2. *Valuing the mind and emotions over the body.*

    Every person will experience physical decline. The older woman who can take pleasure from social and mental stimulation rather than concentrating on aches and pains will enjoy her later years more. We must grow and learn and develop as long as we are able.

3. *Valuing the people who remain and valuing the future of humanity over the self.*

    Accepting the prospect of personal death, the older woman who makes life better for those who will survive her—through family relationships and friendships, through contributions to the culture—can make the lives left behind happier and more meaningful.

    We must make each contact with others compassionate and real. We are more than ourselves; we are part of the past and part of the future of humankind.

If we are able to value ourselves over our roles, our minds over our bodies, and our survivors over ourselves, we may live our ending years in vital absorption. Maybe this thought was best summarized by the woman in her nineties who told me, "You just live—live each day fully until you die." She was still working and traveling, busily doing her part. Our activities and friendships, if we are lucky, will leave behind many seeds to mark the fact that we have passed this way.

As for what lies beyond death—into the West, over the river, on the other side of the bridge—we will know at last. We live in hope that death is truly another stage of growth, a rebirth. If the fruit, the butterfly, the bird, the precious stone of the self, the seed of the soul finds new ground, it will flower and flourish in the shimmering light of the afterworld. Perhaps . . . just perhaps . . . we have been there already in our dreams.

CHAPTER TWELVE

A Woman's Life Cycle
of Dreams

A mighty pulse beats through the lives of womankind. Each life is an endless round of joinings and partings.

The egg and sperm from which we originate begin as separate cells; then they unite. During our first nine months of existence we are literally attached to our mother's womb. When we are born, we literally separate from her. As infants, if we breast-feed, we periodically reconnect ourselves to our mother, taking our nourishment from her body. As toddlers, we wander off on our own. Part of our first psychological task as a child is to comprehend that we are a separate physical entity from our mother.

Once we have established that we are individuals, independent in locomotion and desire, we begin to reach out to others for skills and learning. Our peers and our teachers become our models, as well as our parents. We turn back to our family for support.

As teenagers, we thrash around in our attempts to become free of our family's clutches—to be our own selves, to form our own opinions, have our own friends, live our own lives. We break away from our parents' direct influence. As girls becoming women, our wombs periodically engorge with menstrual blood; then they discharge it. The uterus itself pulsates in a steady rhythm of silent contractions and relaxations, strengthening itself for its future task.

As young women, we seek a partner. Once a satisfactory mate is found, we join again. We merge our physical bodies and our 'emotions with another. Whether within marriage or outside of it, we connect with another being.

We may evolve one primary attachment all our years; or we may come together with person after person, parting again and again. For many of us, we become a unit carrying an embryo within our womb. We gather inward, are one, and full; we open outward to bear the child, are emptied, and are two. Our breasts fill with milk; they are disgorged by our babe. For some women the attachment is less physical and more emotional, to our work or careers. We may cling to our loves or to our life's work or to both.

Eventually we must let go again. Our children grow up to find mates of their own; our children may bear children, bringing new attachments into our lives. Sometimes we must release our partners to find others. Our ability to birth more children, our reproductive capacity, comes to an end. Our work may finish or change; we may find fresh interests. If we survive them, our partners will sicken and eventually die.

As older women, we must detach once more from the ways we have known. Either the world around us will change or we will. We may retire from work; we may withdraw into personal illness. As our lives draw to a close, we will separate from existence as we know it; perhaps this will mean uniting with something else we know not, to merge once more. Our lives have expanded and contracted through all our days and nights, like our in-breath and out-breath. Who knows but what we shall part from here to some greater joining, to dwell again, to live, to dream, another time eternal?

The Pulse of Life. Scientists who study the life span observe certain phases, marked by biological and psychological turning points. Every theorist has his or her own preferred system for delineating these periods. I draw here, in particular, upon the work of Charlotte Buhler,[1] Erik Erikson,[2] Bernice Neugarten,[3] and Daniel Levinson.[4] Each step in the rhythm of our waking lives is paralleled by the imagery of our nights.

I will discuss the life cycle of dreams as seven stages. Because the capacity to give birth plays such a large role in the lives of women, it seems to me essential to consider the phases of the woman's reproductive cycle as separate stages. The overall pattern of seven stages that I suggest will be somewhat different for each individual.

There is no exact age when a certain stage begins, but, as Levinson has pointed out, there is a range within which a phase is most likely to start. For instance, stage 2, marked by the onset of puberty, currently begins at an average of 12.9 years in the United States. Yet a given young woman may begin her first menstruation (menarche) as early as ten years, or even earlier in rare cases, or, at the other extreme, not until sixteen years or slightly later. Likewise a woman may become pregnant and give birth in her teens, as many do, or she may not carry a child to term until her late thirties or early forties; she may not give birth at all.

Each phase in this version of the life cycle is marked at its beginning by either biological or psychological changes. The years immediately preceding the changes, what Levinson calls transition periods, are followed by years of development of the changes that initiated the phase. Thus periods of change alternate with periods of relative stability. The stages of a woman's life I propose are the following:

....

Woman's Life Cycle of Dreams
....

Stage	Average Ages	Markers
1 Childhood	0 to 13	From birth to menarche.
		Girl's activities are narrow in scope, mainly home and school. Parents are primary influence, then teachers and peers. The girl struggles to develop hope, will, purpose, and competence; she makes efforts to define self as separate from mother.
		Dreams often involve fears of parents, teachers, and others; fun with family, friends; holidays; pretty clothes and toys; budding ambitions.

....

Stage	*Average Ages*	Markers
2 Adolescence	14 to 19	From menarche until early adult.

Interests and activities expand. Relationships with peers dominate. Sexual exploration usually begins. Young woman makes efforts to establish self-identity. Phase ends with move from family home and/or establishment of personally chosen emotional relationship.

Dreams involve pubertal changes, initial sexual contacts; romantic interests; competition with girlfriends; resistance to parental authority.

Stage	*Average Ages*	Markers
3 Early Adult	20 to 29	From early adult until middle adult.

Continued expansion in every area. Initial commitments to studies, jobs, sexual or love partner. May marry; become pregnant; give birth. Struggles to establish intimacy.

Dreams involve experiments with life in every area, disappointments, tension, work and personal conflicts, goals. Dreams focus on pleasures and pains in the relationships with mate or lover, family.

....

Stage	Average Ages	Markers
4 Middle Adult	30 to 44	From middle adult to menopause.
		Reassessment of initial choices, new decisions made and pursued. Definite choice of vocation and/or establishment of emotional bond. Struggles to make an impact on life. Creative work: childbirth, child rearing, and/or career. Sexual drive reaches its peak.
		Dreams involve sex and love relationships; orgasms occur mostly in this phase; attempts to reevaluate present life, cope with changes made; parenting; emotional reactions to work; creative ideas.
5 Menopause	45 to 54	From menopause to late adult.
		Begins with cessation of menstruation. Activities decrease or change direction. Parents may die. May become grandparent. Grown children leave home. Emotional relationship may rupture. More assertive. Peak mental work.
		Dreams involve changes in body functioning; attempts to cope with losses or ruptures; suggestions of neglected areas of life; suggested new directions; spiritual or inspirational dreams.

....

Stage	Average Ages	Markers
6 Late Adult	55 to 64	From late adult to older years.
		Activities decrease or change in character. Relatives, colleagues, and mate often die now, if not before. Health problems for self or mate possible. Woman desires to leave legacy, make a difference in the time left. May renew efforts.
		Dreams involve coping with any illness or death; responses to grandchildren and new family members; new activities; attempts to make life worthwhile.
7 Older Years	65 to 80+	From older years to death.
		May commence with retirement. May have personal illness. Decreases activities further, more interest in hobbies, retrospection, religion. May volunteer, active helpfulness. Struggles to find meaning in one's whole life, make peace with the past, evolve wisdom.
		Dreams involve reviews of life, efforts to cope with any illness, previews of death, hopes for afterlife.

Let's see how our dreams trace this evolution at each stage.

Spiral Dream Path

The life cycle of dreams is shaped more like a spiral than a closed circle. There is a difference at each stage, like the movement from one level of a spiral to another. Certain motifs are more characteristic of each phase; other motifs return again and again but with variations on the theme. These recurring motifs, if the woman develops psychologically, eventually take on a mature form. To illustrate, I have chosen two recurring dream motifs from each stage of the life cycle: "the mother" and "the mirror."

Girlhood Dreams: Birth to Age Thirteen

During the early phase of life the young girl struggles to establish her own identity as an independent being, apart from the mother who bore her. The infant who plays Peek-a-Boo, the toddler who affirms her will with a loud "No!" the child who has secrets and spaces of her own, each is in the process of defining herself.

Charlotte Buhler, at the University of Vienna, who devoted much of her life to the study of the life span, characterized this period as one in which the child lives at home and has a narrow range of interests, mainly centering around the home and family.

Erik Erikson, psychoanalyst and developmental theorist who is now in his nineties, says that in these early stages the healthy child must resolve some primary conflicts in order to proceed to the next stage. He says that by coping with feelings of trust versus mistrust, for instance, the child develops a basic outlook of hope. The child needs to evolve will, purpose, and competence. She is busy, as well, in her dreams.

Dream Themes of Childhood: Frights and Frolics

During childhood the girl's effort to become her own person, to forge an identity distinct from that of her mother, is depicted in the imagery of her dreams. At this time she dreams mostly about her own family, along with animal and fantasy figures. Mother, father, sisters, and brothers are major characters; they remain so throughout life. Daughters of working mothers are likely to dream of relatives or other caretakers as well. Family pets often appear.

As the girl goes to school or is exposed to other situations that stir up her emotions, she is likely to have bad dreams of being chased and attacked or of being injured or killed. The peak of nightmares, according to most experts, is around ages five to seven, when the child is experiencing a new and more stressful environment in school. She is struggling to relate comfortably to schoolmates and teachers and to develop competency. Admired or feared teachers and classmates join her dream family.

In happier dreams of childhood, the girl dances, visits parks and playgrounds, goes on holidays, has birthday parties, and flies. She wears pretty dresses; wins singing contests, sporting events, or a role in a movie. She makes friends with a talking animal, eats good food, becomes a princess, or even gets married. Such dream themes reflect her activities, her wishes, and her growing ambitions.

The Child's Mother.   Fears about her parents, particularly the mother, are expressed in the girl's dreams. Eight-year-old Janelle shared a nightmare about her mother poisoning her pet mouse. Lenore, at seven, dreamed of her mother turning into a vampire. Fiona remembers her terrifying childhood dream that her mother and her aunt (who lived in the same house with the child and parents) took off their masks to reveal that they were wolves underneath. These dreams are a depiction of what analysts have called "the devouring mother."

As was pointed out earlier, animals with sharp teeth in dreams frequently represent the anger of some person in the dreamer's environment. Wolves, vampires, alligators, sharks, and vicious dogs often substitute for angry parents or teachers in the girl's dreams. Whales, too, because of their size and ability to swallow a child, may represent a parent who is perceived of as overwhelming.

Monsters and other frightening villains, too, can be thin disguises for parental figures in dreams. Six-year-old Tamani, for example, who dreamed of being chased by two giants who could take very big steps, was expressing discomfort about her parents. In another dream Tamani saw her sister and herself being chased by two pans and "a thing like a corn tortilla" (a food that her mother often cooked). They fled to a house and nailed the door shut. In both cases the dreamer managed to escape. By so doing, the girl was beginning to define her independence.

Parents often appear as monsters, witches, or giants—because adults seem so big—in the dreams of their children. Since the mother is more often the girl's disciplinarian, the girl expresses her resentment of authority in her dreams. Defying the witch is satisfying; being destroyed by her is devastating. Among the adult women in my study, several remembered their worst nightmares from this childhood stage.

When the girl is feeling vulnerable or insecure, she may dream about terrible things happening to her mother, as did the ten-year-old girl who had a nightmare that a man broke into her house and killed her mother with a knife. An eight-year-old dreamed that her mother broke her neck in a car crash, and a grown woman recalled the painful dream that her mother was beheaded in a traffic accident. Sometimes such dreams express the child's fear of desertion; at other times they convey the girl's suppressed anger and wish to be rid of her mother's restrictions.

The Child's Mirror. As it is in myth and folklore, the mirror is an important theme in dreams. Here the mirror plays less of a magical role and more one of "self-reflection." It is an image I have occasionally observed in the dreams of females ages eight to eighty, as in this mirror dream reported by Lindsey, age nine:

> I looked in a mirror and saw a ghost! It was whispering my
> name. It wouldn't go away.

Without seeing the drawing Lindsey made, one might dismiss this dream as a typical nightmare. Lindsey, however, in her drawing displayed at the Association for the Study of Dreams conference in Ottawa in 1986, showed the "ghost" as her "mirror opposite." The dreamer was depicted in tailored skirt and top, with straight black hair and glasses, whereas the ghost, instead of being monstrous or frightening, resembled the reverse of the dreamer: she wore a frilly party dress, no glasses, and had blonde curls with flowers in her hair.

Since mirrors in dreams are usually objects that show how we feel about ourselves, this dreamer seemed to be depicting fear of her feminine side. Everything that was frilly and fluffy seemed frightening to her. Lindsey, like so many of her sisters, was busily trying to establish who she is. We shall see how females use dream mirrors throughout their lives to "reflect" their feelings about themselves.

Adolescent Dreams: Age Fourteen to Nineteen

By the time she has reached menarche, the young girl's activities are rapidly expanding. The society and opinions of her peers vie for importance with those of her parents. For the majority, girlfriends and schoolbooks give way to preoccupation with boys.

Dream Themes of Adolescence: Changing and Growing

Dream themes frequently found during the teenage years involve conflicts with parents, emotional reactions to girlfriends, attractions to boyfriends, and dating. Dreams of getting married intensify.

The hormonal upheaval in the young woman's body as she reaches menarche is displayed in her dreams. If she is subject to edema, images of water or swelling fruits may arise; if she suffers from cramps, she may be troubled with dreams of being bitten. Blood and being wounded often become images in her dream repertoire.

Any sexual experiences are quickly depicted in her dream language; the images will vary depending on the nature of these encounters. Early sexual episodes often produce pain and guilt, leading to dreams of houses being broken into, damaged goods, or soiled bridal dresses. If the girl has been abused or brutalized, nightmares about the molester are inevitable; she may dream of dismemberment, choking, being paralyzed or crushed. In contrast, if her first contacts with sex are loving and tender, the girl is more likely to dream of heroic males, romance, flowers, and delicious foods.

Dream researchers find that some of the main differences in the adolescent's dreams compared with the girl's involve both greater sociability and greater hostility in the teenager's dreams. There are less sweet dreams and more sour ones as the teen turns woman.

The Adolescent's Mother.   Now is the time that most young women experience the greatest hostility toward their parents, especially their mothers. The restraints placed upon the girl's emerging sexuality and her wish to establish her own relationships are fraught with conflict.

The teenager who dreamed she was about to go out to play with the boys when her mother blocked the door, turned into an octopus, and struck her in the face, was depicting her sense of being blocked from sexual activity by her mother. The woman in my study who, as a teenager in heavy conflict with her mother, dreamed that her mother fell ill and died was so affected by the nightmare that she changed her behavior for the better.

Who Am I?   Erikson says that the major conflict of adolescence is Identity versus Confusion. Resolving this tension, he says, is the cornerstone of identity. At two the girl was saying no to demonstrate her difference from her mother; at twelve her actions speak louder yet.

Buhler points out that this phase is marked by the first independently chosen personal relations and the entrance into a self-chosen activity. The late teens often includes moving from the family home, going away to college, or setting up one's own residence and getting a job. The teenage girl's activities and relationships are still preparatory, rather than permanent.

Psychoanalyst Karen Horney says that young girls reaching puberty react toward the implications menstruation has for them in one of four ways:

1. By attaching herself to eroticism and to boys, losing interest in study
2. By attaching herself to study, religion, art, or sports and avoiding sex
3. By *detaching* herself emotionally, becoming inhibited toward both work and sex
4. By attaching herself to other girls in a homoerotic way, with crushes, and so on[5]

For the adolescent girl who chooses the first and most common route—becoming "boy-crazy"—one of the dangers she faces is forming an emotional and/or sexual relationship that is as engulfing as the parent-infant symbiosis. The girl often breaks away from her parents' authority only to become absorbed by the views of the male in her life. Believing herself in love, she "loses" herself in his personality, his needs, his perceptions of the world. Thinking herself happy to have broken free from her parents, she becomes subservient to the dominant male in her life.[6] Sometimes she does not discover who and what she is until decades later.

The Adolescent's Mirror.   Among the dreams I collected for this study is one Risa had recurrently, first with her teenage boyfriend and then later with her husband, from whom she was subsequently divorced:

> My boyfriend and I are both putting up mirrors. I am putting
> up a little mirror, and he is putting up a big one. He won't
> help me with my mirror because he is too busy putting up his
> mirror. The two mirrors are just sitting next to each other.

Risa explained that, to her, the mirrors meant the ego. She commented, "I spent a lot of time admiring those men and their qualities. In the dream I just thought it was unfair they wouldn't help me." In Risa's dream language even her pitifully little ego (symbolized by the small mirror) could not be made useful (put up), because the male was too involved with his own ego (putting up his big mirror). In a sense it was she who was preoccupied with bolstering the ego of her young man.

Risa, like so many young women, was seeing herself as no more than the "reflection" of the man in her life. She was not capable of helping herself in this dream; she simply subsided into resentment. Even many years later Risa was still struggling to find her own identity, her "image." She did not yet see herself as capable aside from whatever male was in her life.

Horney has called this response "the neurotic need for love." While the healthy person values being loved, in some young women the need may become compulsive and indiscriminate. The neurotic woman, she says, will call attention to how much she "loves" the man; she may try to extract love by appealing to his pity; she may try to force love by threatening him, as in, "If you don't love me, I'll kill myself." In truth, Horney says, the woman with these attitudes is actually too self-centered to be capable of real love.

Horney contends that such an intense need for love arises from "basic anxiety" over not having been loved freely by the mother in early life. She says the woman protects herself from the resulting anxiety by adopting the attitude, "If you love me, you will not hurt me," or by becoming overly submissive, "If I give in, always do what people expect, never ask for anything, never resist—then nobody will hurt me," or, by compensating for feeling weak by gaining power, "If I am the stronger, the more successful one, then you cannot hurt me," or, lastly, she may withdraw emotionally from people in order to feel safe and independent, "If you cannot reach me, you cannot hurt me."

Risa attempted to feel safe by submissively supplying her mate with the "big mirror," supporting his ego, with the hopes the boy would help her with her woefully inadequate self-image (the small mirror). Her dream tells her these efforts are in vain. Years later, she has begun to find herself.

During the late teens, college studies and careers may be pursued, but these often take second place to the young woman's primary emotional relationship. Jobs, too, often "mark time" until she can be married. The young woman frequently takes work simply to earn money for a future marriage or to buy clothing, rather than strive for positions that help her develop skills and find her talents. Like Risa, her dreams may remind her of what is missing in her life, but, at this stage, she rarely listens.

A woman's efforts to establish a satisfying love relationship are often lifelong. Until she first discovers who she is and what she wants from life, defining herself and building a solid center, she is unlikely to find a fulfilling partner.

The Young Woman's Dreams: Age Twenty to Twenty-Nine

The period of early adulthood is characterized by expanding experimentation. The young adult tries various jobs, makes assorted sexual and social liaisons, and may undertake graduate study. Among Buhler's subjects, the males who began sexual relationships under the age of twenty-eight persisted in them for less time (about ten years) than those relationships they established after twenty-eight (which lasted about thirty years).

When I asked those study participants who were in early adulthood what they had missed in life, typical responses included the following:

> I would like to figure out what I'm going to do.
> I'd like to get a job I'd really enjoy.
> I want to get married, have kids.

This is the time for seeking, for wandering, for testing.

Some of the young women had already learned the importance of not losing themselves in a relationship. When I asked them what they would advise a woman to avoid in order to have a good life, replies included the following:

> Avoid destructive relationships.
> Avoid being pushed around.

To have a fulfilling life, respondents of this age said a woman should:

> Find out what really makes her happy.
> Try to be balanced, to be open to change, to forgive past wrongs.

Of course, each was speaking from her own experience; each was trying to profit from past mistakes. As a young adult, the woman is still what Levinson calls a "novice" in life; he calls this phase "entering the adult world." Erikson points out that the young adult who resolves the conflict between intimacy and isolation develops a capacity to love. At this stage the young woman is testing out what succeeds in a relationship and in a career; she is making decisions about her life, with the awareness that if they do not work out, there is still time to change.

Dream Themes of Early Adulthood:
Experimenting With Life

At this stage the young woman dreams about her romantic relationships, as well as her family of origin. Colleagues at work, classmates, girlfriends, and boyfriends are members of her dream cast. If she becomes engaged, the young woman's dreams will give expression to lingering insecurities about herself and fear of intimacy or permanent commitment, as well as her hopes for a future life together. If she has married, henceforth her husband will become a major figure in her dream life. If her boyfriends come and go, so will the dream characters that represent them. Depending upon the nature of the relationship at the moment, this imagery will shift. Her happy dreams often involve hopes for the relationship and the joyful feelings it evoke; likewise her nightmares often result from stress with a boyfriend or husband.

Such tension in a woman's love relationship is depicted in various forms in her dreams. We saw how Sonny, in her early twenties, dreamed that the rat with curly hair, who had seemed friendly at first, suddenly turned on her and bit her; she was depicting the fright and pain she felt after a quarrel with her curly-headed boyfriend. Brenda, in her 30's, dreamed her pet bird lost its beak and was starving to death, after a quarrel with her boyfriend. Other women having momentary friction with their lover may picture cat fights, storms, or earthquakes in their dreams.

Falling-in-love dreams are as typical as dreams of conflict during these early adult years. Romantic episodes with handsome strangers; dancing; flowers; delicious food and drink; beautiful, warm colors—such images fill the dreams of young women in love.

Dreams about sex will be more or less explicit, depending upon the quality of the young woman's experience. She may dream in classic sexual symbolism—keys and locks, swords and sheaths, sticks and holes—or she may kiss, fondle, and proceed to orgasm. She is less likely than the young man to have explicit sexual dreams or to reach orgasm in them. She is more likely than he is to dream of being naked in public, a theme usually suggesting that the dreamer feels momentarily "overexposed."

The young woman will dream about her work or schooling if it has an emotional charge for her—competitive feelings toward colleagues and sexual attractions to workmates are frequent. If she is under pressure to perform in examinations or at the office, this tension will emerge in dreams of taking tests, hunting for the right classroom, or of laborers overworking. If her job becomes too stressful, she may dream, as we saw one woman did, of escaping on a flying mattress while her colleagues were in chaos below; she may dream of becoming pregnant as another kind of escape. If she has been neglecting her tasks, her dreams will offer reminders, sometimes of neglected gardens or forgotten babies.

If work or studies do not arouse the young woman's emotions, her personal relationships will dominate her dreams. Unlike young men, whose identity is tied more strongly to success in a career and who dream more about success and failure, the young woman is often most preoccupied with her personal relationships.

The unknown men in her dreams still tend to fall into one of two categories: the threatening stranger or the handsome, strong, romantic, adventurous type. The unknown women are often poor, victimized creatures or evil, dangerous ones.

Dreams relating to the young woman's body continue. Her menstrual dreams often contain the color red, dirty water, or disintegrating buildings, symbolizing the menstrual debris. If she is subject to premenstrual tension, the swelling in her breasts may stimulate dreams of ripe fruit, as they did for the young woman who saw trees with juicy limes about to burst just before her period began. Ovulation may be marked by dreams of jewels, or eggs, or babies.

The young woman who becomes pregnant undergoes a whole series of dreams tracing the development of the fetus within her womb. Frequently her dreams of animals increase. She may dream at first of aquatic creatures; then cute, cuddly puppies or kittens; then larger, apelike animals. She will begin to dream of the baby directly, its appearance, its behavior, even its name. She may rehearse for labor in her dreams and she may vent her fears, especially as the uterus begins to contract strongly, toward the end of her term. Dreams of water and of construction going on are characteristic during pregnancy, representing the gathering fluids in the womb and the "building" of the baby that is taking place inside her body. As she approaches her delivery day, she will probably dream of taking a journey.

If she is a working woman, her dreams will reflect any conflict she feels between her job and her forthcoming child, as Joan dreamed of trying to balance herself on a ladder while holding her wiggly new baby. The pregnant young woman is almost certain to dream more often of her mother again, as she attempts to cope with what sort of mother she will become.

The Young Adult's Mother.   Sheila, in her twenties, was still trying to define herself as separate from her overprotective mother. When she dreamed that a great spider fell from the sky onto her, almost smothering her, she was depicting her feeling of nearly being crushed by her mother's continued intrusion in her life. In a later dream she confronted her mother directly, shouting, "You're the vulgar one!" Giving voice to the anger she felt, even in a dream, helped free her from it. Such conflicts with parents need to be resolved for the young woman to become fully adult.

The Young Woman's Mirror. Sexual issues become more rather than less pressing for the young woman as her drive increases with age. Ashley, newly married and having some difficulty establishing good sexual relations with her inexperienced husband, dreamed:

> Mr. Wiseman, our new upstairs neighbor [in fact], comes into our apartment after I have been searching for an important letter in the mailbox. He sits on my bed, holds me close, pressing against my breasts. I feel tempted to respond and go to put on some protection, just in case.
>
> Looking into the mirror, I see I have on a long black velvet gown. My hair is long, pulled back, and tied with a long, black scarf. I look rather messy. I'm wearing a cross. The telephone rings and I answer it, thinking it might be my husband.

Ashley obviously felt some attraction for the new neighbor with the intriguing name, "wise man." Her dream language says she was searching in the "male box" (symbolized by the mailbox) for an important communication (the letter) when she found a man who made a pass. She considered accepting and did some self-reflection (looked into the mirror). Her dream seemed to pose the question, "What would happen if . . . ?"

Her mirror image showed that she was rather elegantly dressed for getting the mail, but not for attracting a male. However, the thought that she looked rather messy probably reflected her feeling that such behavior would be "a mess." Wearing a cross suggested that her dreaming mind was evoking religion to discourage such behavior. She was distracted from becoming involved by the communication (telephone ringing) from her husband, indicating that she felt they could still relate successfully.

On yet another symbolic level, Ashley's dream may have expressed a wish to unite with a "wise man" rather than the particular male who was pictured, to whom she had no waking attraction. This dream of the mirror portrayed the internal conflict between sexual attraction and disapproval of such behavior, as well as the yearning for "something more" than she had in her life. Dream mirrors are always revealing.

The Middle-Aged Woman's Dreams: Age Thirty to Forty-four

Middle adulthood is full. The woman's years of expansion reach a culmination. Earlier decisions are reassessed, resulting in a time of transition. Marriages forged in young adulthood may shatter and break. This period often begins with the establishment of a new personal tie—a marriage, a remarriage, or a long-term commitment.

Experience in jobs or college has led the woman to discover what she likes, or at least what she dislikes. Definite vocational choices may be made (perhaps to be reversed in later years). Fruitful creative work—childbearing and child raising and/or career development—are most likely to occur during this stage. Levinson calls the beginning of this stage of life "settling down." For many women it is the time of serious attention to work, a relationship, and a family. Toward the end of this phase a women enters her premenopausal years, heralding a new transition.

In my study, participants in the middle-adult years spoke of having missed many things in life. Typical responses included the following:

> I missed having an education—I was never focused enough or mature enough. I wanted my freedom more than an education.
> I missed having cultural advantages as a child.
> Adventures, experiences—I chose the safe, conservative route.
> Fun. Being carefree.
> Lots of sexual experience.
> A lover who could bring me to orgasm.
> Getting married and having children.
> I missed having a baby.
> Having a father.
> I wonder what having a loving mother would have been like.
> Having more money.
> Fulfillment in a calling.

Each of these perceived deficits formed a key topic in the adult woman's dreams.

By now these women had had ample experience against which to judge what would make or break a good life, at least for themselves. These middle-adult women's suggestions for a fulfilling life centered around three general topics: not being submissive, not being "a pleaser," not being economically dependent. For example, they advised a woman to:

Avoid being a victim.
Avoid domineering men.
Avoid feeling you need someone else to fulfill you.
Avoid pleasing others.
Avoid allowing yourself to be beat down.
Avoid cutting off a part of yourself.
Avoid letting others make your decisions for you.
Avoid accepting other people's judgments.
Avoid early marriage.
Avoid being financially dependent.

In general, most of these middle-aged women felt they had been mistaken to center themselves around pleasing a man. Many cautions were offered about choosing the wrong man, one who is unreliable, a playboy, or, on the contrary, one who is too serious. A few women said it was important to avoid self-blame or bitterness. One advised against subtle manipulation. Each was revealing a hard-learned lesson of her own life.

In contrast, they suggested, a woman who wants a fulfilling life should do such things as:

Make conscious choices.
Be aware of what you're doing.
Be a real person, not someone's toy.
Understand who you really are.
Explore your abilities.
Travel and learn.
Keep stimulated.
Preserve time for yourself.
Get help when you need it.

Although, by now, women of middle years had experienced a multitude of life's ups and downs, they still hungered to know themselves better, to preserve their integrity as a person. They knew the pitfalls; they sought better paths.

Dream Themes of Middle Years:
Producing and Revising

The adult woman's dreams parallel her activities and relationships. Her sexual drive reaches its peak, finding expression in happy dreams of passion as well as romance. Orgasm in her dreams is at its height.

If the woman becomes engaged, marries, and/or bears a child during this stage—more common with the current generation than in earlier ones—her dreams will be occupied with preparations for the ceremony or the development of her baby; her anxieties are given form and her hopes dramatized.

Fluctuations in her bodily state continue to be depicted in her dreams, varying with her menstrual cycle, her pregnancy, or the lack of it, as described in the previous section. If she becomes ill, that, too, appears in her nighttime images.

Women who experience miscarriage or have an abortion are almost sure to paint vivid scenes of the event in their dreams. Tonia, for instance, in her late thirties, remembers a horrifying nightmare that she believes stems from an abortion she had in her mid-twenties. In her dream, a few years after the operation, she saw a baby with a knife hovering above it; the baby was screaming at her, "Don't do it!" Although this dream content arose from the original event some ten years ago, Tonia was undoubtedly experiencing some current situation that gave her the same feeling as she would imagine her lost child having. She felt as though she herself were an endangered baby. Tonia is still grappling with this past event: "I never felt good about the decision to have an abortion. . . . I felt I violated my path. . . . I'm not peaceful about it yet." Not all women are as traumatized by such experiences. However, by middle age, regrets are accumulating in many departments.

The housewife often finds herself yearning to have a career, to be fulfilled in some way outside the home. The career woman may find her body more insistent about accomplishing its biological potential. Those working women who have had children may wonder if they could have progressed further and faster without the responsibility of child raising.

Children who are born to the woman become central characters in her dreams (as well as the mother in the child's dreams). All her life the mother visualizes her child in danger, in need of her, or she expresses her anger or disappointment toward the child in her dreams. The middle-aged mother's nightmares frequently deal with danger to her child.

Daughters in particular come to symbolize for the mother a younger, more vulnerable part of herself, sometimes her own past. Depending on the nature of the relationship between the two at a moment in time, the daughter's appearance in her mother's dream is either pleasant or conflictual.

If the woman undergoes divorce during her middle years, her dreams are sure to reflect the turmoil. We saw how dreams of collapsing structures, rotting bridges, or being lost at sea were characteristic.

If, instead, the unhappily mated woman remains in a painful relationship, her nightmares center on this topic, leading to themes such as the ones described for Fay, who dreamed of being in jail and of squeezing herself into a gas oven. Moira's dream of choking on coins she swallowed was also of this type.

Whatever our creative work, it is likely to reach its culmination during the middle years; it becomes a chief issue in dreams. The woman may dream of her work at night, getting good ideas, resolving problems, as we saw with Verta, who evolved a new career as a jewelry designer based on a dream that her spiritual teacher married her design teacher. Any conflicts at work, ambitions, and fear of failure are sure to be depicted in the woman's dreams. Ann-Marie, for instance, when she first began her career, dreamed of teaching workshops that her audience ignored or walked out on; as she gained confidence and experience, her performance in her dreams improved, too. At this phase, dreams of giving birth may symbolize new hope or new projects, as well as a wish for children.

The woman of middle years is more likely than heretofore to be developing a solid sense of herself. She is often less afraid of life, more assertive, more sure of who she is and what she wants. We have spoken of Jung's comment that in the middle of life a person's dreams begin to change. Before thirty-five, he suggests, dreams mainly help the dreamer adapt to life and move outward into love relationships and career building. After thirty-five, dreams function more to help the dreamer with inner life, to find her own meaning. Dreams can help us to evolve our unique pattern and purpose.

So it is that the dreams of the mature woman may begin to depict new types of characters and action. The unknown men in her dreams may be great leaders, ministers, or orators who inspire others. She may find herself dreaming of spiritual teachers, who become inner guides. Archetypal figures of a miraculous child or a wise old man may emerge. In particular, the mature woman, as her inner core gathers strength, may dream of powerful women—goddesses, priestesses, women of wisdom.

Whereas in her younger years, the woman populated her dreams with victimized females, she may now find herself playing the savior in her dreams. As her confidence grows, as she stops rejecting the things she has been running from in her dreams, finding she can fight back, confront the demons, or disarm and befriend the villains; her energy is freed for more creative dreaming. She is on her way to becoming her unique self, following her own star, what Jung calls individuation.

The Middle Adult's Mother.   Conflicts with parents, if they haven't been resolved in earlier developmental periods, remain an issue and interfere with the woman from going forward with her own life. Tonia, for instance, continued to wrestle to resolve the conflicts between herself and her widowed mother. In a dream she had sometime after the death of her father,

> My dad is standing on the porch on the house where we lived. I am there and I know he is dead. He is just furious because he says, "You said I'm a burden." I am crying and telling him, "You're not a burden, *she* is!" [meaning her mother] His attitude is, "That's my other half. If you really want me, you have to love her."
>
> Meanwhile my mother is walking around, modeling clothes. She has outfits that look like Reno costumes—with tights, short net skirts with sequins, flashy, like a caricature of someone who is going to dance in Reno. She is insane. She doesn't see us. He doesn't seem to see her. I wake up feeling bad, guilty.

This dream depicted one of Tonia's central conflicts. "If I wanted to have him, I had to love her. I just couldn't." Tonia explained that her mother is very fashion conscious; she would never wear outfits like she wore in the dream. Dressing her mother in a Reno costume in the dream expressed Tonia's feeling that her mother was superficial and false, as well as her resentment that her father did not seem to be aware of these traits. After her father's death Tonia had to deal with her feelings about her mother directly. "She had a lot of power when he was there," she commented, "Maybe now I can see who she is." And Tonia, hopefully, will then be able to define herself in a more fulfilling way.

The Middle Adult's Mirror.   In her middle years the woman's reflection in her dreams usually begins to show her age, as does her waking mirror. The woman who was peeved with her husband during the day saw her face as distorted when she looked into a rearview mirror in her dream that night. She was judging her reaction (looking back, symbolized by the rearview mirror) to be unattractive. From momentary strains to major breakups, the woman's dream mirror reflects her emotional face.

We have said that the woman who is in her middle years is likely to be developing a solid sense of herself. In her dreams, too, she may be discovering that she need not remain a victim, that by taking action she can change the conditions around her. As a woman's consciousness grows, she may find herself becoming "lucid," aware that she is dreaming during her dream. I have observed many cases of lucidity in which the woman first realized she was dreaming while she was gazing into her dream mirror.

The length of her hair, the shade, the style, the color of her eyes may be different in such a way as to stimulate the woman's recognition that she is dreaming. In one such dream of mine, it was noticing a third eye in the middle of my forehead that made me realize I was in a dream. Once aware, it becomes possible to use the dream state for some remarkable adventures, to stay asleep and carry out one's heart's desire. In such cases, the mirror in dreams acts as a symbol of the change in consciousness. Like Alice stepping through the looking glass, the woman confronts a new scenario with marvelous possibilities.

The Woman's Dreams at Menopause: Age Forty-five to Fifty-four

When I was traveling in Bali, a slim native guide pointed out the swaying palm trees that grow in abundance on that enchanting island. "We say the coco palm is a woman," he told me. "She grows for twelve or so years before beginning to produce. Then each month she puts out one new coconut. She continues this way for about thirty years more, then stops. She lives another span of years and then she dies. She is like a woman."

We, too, give forth monthly eggs during our fertile years, rest a while, then go our way. There is an elegant rhythm to our lives. The cessation of our periods is no less marvelous than their beginning. We are completing a pattern—expanding, contracting, unbroken.

The years of menopause are marked not only by the end of our menstrual cycles and the physiological repercussions to this, but also often by the sickness or death of relatives and friends. Parents often fall ill or die at this time. These losses are no longer so easily compensated for by new acquaintances as they were in younger years; some people are irreplaceable. Grown children, if they have not done so before, almost always leave home during this stage. Depending on how she has prepared herself, the woman may find the children's departure either troublesome or liberating.

Whereas we spent our earlier years expanding, reaching out, gaining strengths, now there begin to appear diminutions, sometimes economic losses, sometimes bodily damage. There may be feelings of unrest and discontent, retrospection and daydreaming. Decisions may be formed about what to do with the remainder of one's life; these are particularly important because now there are not many more "second chances."

Activities may decrease. Oftentimes there is a change of direction in work. Buhler observes that this is the period when the actor becomes director. Actresses, such as Diane Keaton, turn to making movies themselves; opera singers, like Beverly Sills, begin to emphasize teaching and guiding rather than performance. Independent creative work may actually reach a height during this time.

In the second half of life the woman begins to find tasks she has set for herself becoming more important than those that have been thrust upon her. She may undertake volunteer work or decide to go to graduate school or to learn how to paint.

While men of the same age are becoming softer, gentler, and more reflective, women are feeling more capable of assertion and able to stand up for their rights. The woman is no longer willing to tolerate nonsense. "I say more of what I really think these days," said one study participant who was going through menopause. She speaks for many women of her age.

For the woman whose identity has been defined by beauty or sexuality or childbearing, a crisis may be precipitated. Now, if ever, she needs interests and skills to accomplish a worthwhile purpose.

Women at this stage of life who participated in the study mentioned having missed the following:

> An emotionally supportive partner.
> A man who validates me.
> Not finishing my education.
> Not knowing how to have fun.
> Not enjoying life enough.

Thus the majority of them had not yet found a way to be happy in life, either with or without a man. Most of these women were currently married.

The menopausal women suggested that, in order to have a good life, a woman should:

Avoid being dependent.
Avoid marrying the wrong person.
Avoid letting other people direct her.
Avoid not developing her potential.

One woman who said, "Avoid being a prop for a man," added, "I didn't do this. All my life I was like a prop for a pillar. Now I can't stand up by myself." She spoke for many women. Only one in this group, by far the most successful in terms of both relationship and career, said,

Avoid seeing being a female as detrimental or limiting.

These same participants suggested that a woman would be helped to have a good life by:

Knowing herself clearly.
Being her own person, developing her potential.
Enjoying all possible things, pursuing her goals.
Getting her own growth first.
Continuing to grow, continuing to learn.
Being self-directed, determining to follow her feelings, to grow.
Expanding her sphere, developing her potential.

These women understood how their lives could be enriched, although not all of them were able to follow their own good advice. Those who had acted so as to develop themselves most were the ones who also had the best and most loving relationships.

Dream Themes of Menopause: Losses and New Directions

All of these issues find their way into the dreams of the woman in her menopausal years. Depending upon her physiological and psychological experience of menopause, the woman's dreams depict her changes differently. After my period had skipped for a couple of months, for instance, in the course of a complicated dream, I was sitting under a strong heater in the lobby of a movie house and noticed a basket of moldy yellow plums and some oranges about to burst into flame. Nearby I saw a bunch of beautiful fuschias.

My dreaming mind was picking up the sensations of the hot flashes I had begun to experience. The fruit in my dream may well have represented, as it does for many females, the fruitfulness of the womb. It was old, and, in the dream, I had thought about the slowness of "turnover" in this theater, no doubt a reference to the slow turnover of my dwindling periods. The healthy fuschias probably referred to my basically positive and happy life— full and flowering.

Dreamers whose lives feel empty and dry during these years had dream images exhibiting these conditions, as we saw with Rachel's dreams of the burned-out barn containing corpses of babies who had died. Fire—whether destructive or purifying—becomes a frequent image during the menopausal years; its presence is probably due to the bodily heat that is being generated from hot flashes that occur during sleep.

At the same time as dreams of fire arise, the menopausal woman may also have more dreams of water, due to the edema or bloating that often accompanies menopause. Depending upon her symptoms, the menopausal woman's dreams about the functioning of her womb vary. Those women who are having heavy bleeding prior to the cessation of their periods may experience dreams of water or other liquids overflowing containers. Women who are skipping periods may find themselves dreaming of dirty water that needs to be drained.

Dreams of a personal illness, whether it is a serious sickness or a passing crotchet, will appear. One menopausal woman, for example, who had sprained her back, dreamed of herself in a wheelchair having difficulty moving around. Marie-Louise von Franz described an interesting dream of her own during an illness: she was in a festival for old soldiers, men who were one hundred years old, coming home from the war. A voice said to her, "Yes, they have kept these people in active service too long!" Von Franz, knowing her personal dream symbols well, said, "I immediately reduced my work load."[7]

Although women may undergo divorce during any of their adult years, some find themselves coping with traumatic changes in their home, husband, and family especially at this time, along with the changes transpiring in their body. The dreamers who feel overwhelmed by this situation may find themselves inundated with tidal waves or lost at sea. As happens with divorce at any age, many menopausal women dreamed of structures collapsing, buildings wrecked, or walls falling down, when they were expressing how they felt at the destruction of their marriage.

Those women who remained in unhappy marriages still had nightmares of being trapped, being chased, or falling without support. Painful dreams still revolve around the problems of growing children, disappointments, and frustrations with a mate and work colleagues or superiors. Some women in frustrating relationships dreamed of being raped.

Erotic dreams still continue and may do so into old age. By now the woman's passionate dreams are likely to include direct expressions of love-making, as were Millie's favorite dreams of romantic, sexual fantasies. The menopausal woman is less shy about picturing sensuous encounters in her dream world and often continues to experience orgasm in her dreams.

Several of the women of menopausal age in my study had found new jobs or intense interests that stimulated a fresh sense of purpose and feelings of self-esteem. Some were undertaking study and pursuing entirely new careers. The hopeful feelings evoked by these activities brought dreams of fresh new growth, green fields, flowers in bloom, or flying above beautiful views. Michi depicted the transformation in her attitude in a dream of a cement stage turning into green trees with workers becoming dancers dressed in green. Some women, like Rose, painted art in their dreams. Such women may dream of helpful animals; one saw herself as a white stag. They may dream of finding new rooms or beautiful pearls.

A few of these women were having powerful spiritual experiences in their dreams, as Tavae did when she heard herself singing an exquisite rendition of the Lord's Prayer, or like the woman did who dreamed of being held in the hand of God. These were the women who were also likely to have archetypal figures in their dreams, tall, strong females, priestesses, goddesses, or wise spiritual guides.

Thus, along with depictions of her bodily condition, the menopausal woman's dreams continue to deal with the frustrations and joys in her love relationships—her mate, her grown children, her parents, or her work. When things are going badly in these areas, she often feels less hopeful than in her younger years; the possibility of finding replacements for a lost mate or a friend or for fulfilling ambitions may seem dim. Dreams attempting to cope with the death of parents, if it occurs during these years, are particularly poignant.

The Menopausal Woman's Mother.   Those women of menopausal age whose mothers were still living continued to dream about them in various roles, sometimes hindering, sometimes helping. Earlier conflicts that had not been resolved continued to play themselves out in their dreams.

Meanwhile the woman's daughter was dreaming about her. Hilda, in her early fifties, reported her daughter's dream of seeing her in a tree. The daughter pleaded to her mother to come down; the mother refused. Hilda's daughter, it emerged, was deeply concerned for her mother, worrying about her security as a newly single woman.

Women in my group whose mothers had died often had powerful dreams of their appearance. Now I observed a change: those women who had had conflicts with their mothers in waking life, even rejecting them, found themselves open and able to accept something of value from them in a dream. Lynette, as may be recalled, after years of caring for her difficult mother during a lingering death, saw her as young, beautiful, and sweet again in her dream. For the first time she realized there was a quality in her mother that she wanted for herself and was striving to develop.

Those women whose relationships with their deceased mothers had reached resolution before the mother's death, women who had come to peace and accepted their once-disliked mothers as fallible people who had done the best they could, or else who regarded their mothers as being loving and supportive people, sometimes also had comforting dreams of their presence.

The Menopausal Woman's Mirror.   Dreams of a mirror often reflect, during these years, the changes in the woman's physical appearance. Just as she notices new wrinkles and new gray hairs in her waking-life mirror, she finds her dream mirror reflecting her emotions about her changing body image.

When she was fifty-four, the English novelist Virginia Woolf, in a letter written to a friend, spoke about her "time of life." She says that season, ". . . came and passed as gently and imperceptibly as a lamb, two years ago."[8]

Woolf's dream-mirror reflected a different story than concern about her aging. Mirrors had, for her, a connection with a psychological disturbance.

In an article written two years before her death, she reported an earlier experience:

> I dreamt I was looking in a glass when a horrible face—the face
> of an animal—suddenly showed over my shoulder.[9]

Woolf, who was tortured by spells of madness in between clear and extremely productive periods, committed suicide at age fifty-nine in order to spare herself and her family another psychotic episode. The dream of the mirror was one she was not sure had not actually happened. It is particularly interesting in view of the fact that as a girl she had been sexually abused by her half brother, George, while standing on a hall table looking into a mirror. "The looking glass shame has lasted all my life," she said. This powerful feeling of revulsion she carried from childhood may have merged with her fear of madness. Like the biblical King Nebuchadnezzar, whose dream of a great tree being hewn down presaged his mental disintegration, Woolf was terrified by the "animal" within herself. Nebuchadnezzar's sanity returned; Woolf did not wait to see.

Lucky is the woman of menopausal years who looks into her dream mirror and sees radiant health, attractive hair, or kindly features. As with her younger sister, she may find the mirror in her dream a gateway to a lucid, higher consciousness. Like the queen's mirror in "Snow White," the dream mirror reflects a truth.

The Woman's Dreams in Late Adulthood: Age Fifty-five to Sixty-four

At this stage of life, the woman's activities tend to decrease. She may find herself confronting not only her parents' deaths, if this has not happened earlier, but probably also illness and perhaps the death of her mate. Earlier on in life, friends who moved or died were replaced by others; now the losses become more difficult to find substitutions for or to sustain.

This period may commence with physical illness of self or mate and/or retirement from work. Social activities may decrease, but, for those who have the physical and financial resources, hobbies and quiet activities such as gardening and care of plants and pets may increase.

Reminiscing and retrospection accelerate. The woman may decide to trace her family roots or take up the study of genealogy. Philanthropic and religious interests become stronger. An introspective attitude is important as this stage in order to help the woman integrate her life experience.

A few of the women of this age in my study had a marvelous time during these years. Some had returned to or begun college and evolved entirely new careers. Researchers tell us that some creative people, especially scholars who have accumulated much data over their lifetime, may contribute their major works at this time.

Study participants of late adult years mentioned missing the following:

Not having had a happy childhood.
Not having relatives around.
Not having had one more wild fling.

Mostly, however, these women were feeling revitalized with new interests, new careers, and new grandchildren.

Women of late adult years suggested that other women should:

Avoid mind-altering drugs.
Avoid emasculating their men.
Avoid being a victim.
Avoid avoiding things—
    pain can make you creative if you learn from it.

They advised women to make life better by:

Risking being hurt, being intimate.
Following your heart, not letting yourself be talked into things.
Combining a career with being a loving wife.
Developing resources, especially after the kids leave.

All these issues, of course, made their appearance in the women's dreams. Although they were not dreaming quite as much as in their reproductive years, these women had ample dreams to help them understand themselves and guide their days.

Dream Themes in Late Adult Years: Deaths and Births

Women in their late adult years dream less about their womb and sexual functioning than in their middle years. The body is still depicted in the dreams of the woman of this age, especially if it is threatened in some way, as it was for the woman who dreamed of being raped while still in the hospital recovering from a hysterectomy. Dreams may be integral to the healing process, as with Mimi's surgical scars that became part of the design on a beautiful dream dress. The health of the woman in late adult years, or its loss, is sure to appear in dreams.

Many women have described to me dreams that seemed to precede physical illness or depict aspects of it. Lois, for instance, when she was hospitalized for cancer and was suffering from extreme water retention, dreamed of drowning in a lake that was called by her last name. The woman who reported a dream in which she was flying when a left wing broke, causing her to plummet to the ground, was diagnosed as having a cancerous growth in her left breast shortly thereafter. Each woman's dream symbols of health or illness will vary, but, in general, flourishing plants, friendly animals, and clear waters are signs of positive health.

The woman in her late adult years continues to dream about her relationships with men and peers. If she has a well-developed sexual response, she will still have erotic dreams. The usual cast of characters now gets some additions: mates of the woman's children and grandchildren.

Although Ruth rarely recalls a dream, she had one the night before our interview. In her middle sixties, she dreamed about a good friend of the same age being pregnant. Awake, she laughed when it was pointed out that her friend was a redhead, like her daughter-in-law, who was, in fact, pregnant at the time. Ruth was expressing more than the pregnancy of her son's wife, something she was well aware of; in her dream symbols she was also speaking of the warm relationship that was evolving with her new daughter-in-law. Likening her to the good friend in her dream augured well for their future relations in the waking state.

Dreams of pregnancy, when the dreamer is not pregnant, usually indicate the "gestation" of some new aspect of the dreamer. Ruth herself is full of vitality at this age. "I went off to college at the same time as my son. It was so exciting to find that the brain can still function. I could spend my life in that kind of study!" Perhaps this discovery was part of what Ruth was giving birth to in her dream.

Grandchildren, daughters-in-law, sons-in-law, and other acquired relatives become important characters in the woman's dreams of her adult years—depending on her emotional response to the people involved. Strong feelings of affection, anger, or hatred are sure to stimulate dreams; indifference rarely does. Caring about the future generation, Erikson believes, is an important goal at this stage. Dreams about a deceased father, mother, or mate may be present.

The Late Adult's Mother.   Wilma, who was in her early sixties, reported a dream that typifies the conflict between mother and daughter that sometimes endures into late adult years. Her mother, who was over ninety, was still critical of her daughter. "She thinks I've gone overboard on psychology, that it is probing into other people's lives," Wilma explained. Such a judgmental mother continues to trouble dream waters. Wilma, instead of depicting her mother directly, dreamed:

> I am swimming in my childhood home in thick pea soup. I am
> trying to scrape it off.

Her mother, Wilma explained, always wore "pea green," even decorating
the childhood house, the place the troubles with her mother began, in this
color. Wilma, a wise and loving woman, was still trying to "scrape off" the
influence of her elderly mother. The fact that she was managing to swim
in her dream—rather than drowning—indicated that she was able to cope
despite the discomfort.

The Late Adult's Mirror.   Sue described to me a recent dream about a
mirror that should be encouraging for every aging woman. In her early
sixties, Sue had undertaken a heavy course of study and emerged with a
Ph.D. Her specialty was of interest to many people, and she found herself
in the pleasant position of being sought after to speak and to write a book
as well as the articles she was already doing. In her dream,

> I am with a good friend whose mental abilities I admire. We
> are shopping with two couples, getting ready to go to a
> sophisticated, elegant dance. Both of our husbands are waiting
> out front.
>
> The corridor in the shop is covered with black mirrors that are
> fifty feet high. These begin to revolve with a hat floating in
> front of them. We can pick any one we wish and try it on. My
> friend tries on a black cloche, pulling it over her face and
> asking, "How do you like this?" Then she opens up the hat and
> it turns into a black backdrop. It is beautiful! The whole effect
> is surrealistic, with the black marble floors reflecting.
>
> A hat for me floats up. It's made of white satin, with a flap that
> goes up, has pleats, and is jeweled. "You look stunning!"

Sue liked what she saw in this mirror in her dream. At the outset she was
considering options (symbolized by the shopping) in preparation for a very
pleasant activity (dancing, which Sue loves). She linked herself with her
respected friend who had a successful career. The husbands were "willing
to wait." The huge mirrors—large size in dreams often represents importance—revolved and offered the dreamer possibilities to choose her "hat,"
probably a symbol for mental activity as well as a profession.

The black cloche that covered the face was probably a symbol for Sue of feeling unknown and unappreciated, because *her* hat was the opposite—white, pleated, and bejeweled. Jewels for most dreamers indicate, as they did for Sue, the presence of something rare and precious. This was the style of thinking, the "hat," the choice, that made her look stunning.

The black hat had unfolded to become only a backdrop for something spectacular. The black mirrors, the shining marble floors, only served to make her white satin more beautiful. Sue was saying, in her dream language, "Looking at where I am and what I am doing now (seeing herself in the mirror), I am very happy with my choice." The imagery suggests that Sue had been feeling discouraged and was now feeling transformed. So may all women of her age find a new beauty—a precious hat to wear—in their late adult years.

The Older Woman's Dreams: Age Sixty-five to Eighty Plus

This stage of life often commences by retirement from jobs—the woman's own or her mate's. Personal ill health may mark the turning point. Although her social dimensions may decrease sharply, often because of ill health or lack of mobility; the woman's hobbies may increase. A wish to be helpful may spur volunteer activities. Women in their later years become more interested in retrospection; they may choose this time to write their autobiography or reminiscences. Friends who die at this stage are rarely replaced. Religious or spiritual feelings often become stronger as the woman confronts the inevitability of her own death.

The older women who participated in the study were all in relatively good health and were living on their own, in their own homes or apartments. They proved to be an inspiration.

Some of these women still mentioned missing relationships they wished they had experienced, including the following:

I missed having been raised by my own mother.
I missed being married to someone I loved.
I missed having the physical energy to pursue her many interests.

Others, among the oldest, felt that life had deprived them of little:

I honestly don't know of a thing I've missed.
Not much. I haven't missed anything I particularly wanted.

These women, even at the advanced age of eighty and beyond, were among the most vigorous and active, physically and mentally, of the whole group.

The same group of women, from the viewpoint of their years, offered the following advice:

Avoid dominating men.
Avoid being a victim.
Avoid being self-centered.
Avoid wrapping yourself up in yourself.
Avoid taking housekeeping so seriously. Don't make it your *raison d'être*.
Avoid running away from being a woman.

The older women's advice for having a fulfilling life included the following:

Get a good education.
Give lots of love and be understanding.
Get married and have children but have many interests. Take a share of the big world and consider what you're going to do to make it better.
Get out in the world and see how other people live, their problems. Enlarge your mental ideas, do crafts, pass along products, volunteer. Make a new friend of a different age every single week—younger people want to talk to older ones if they listen and are supportive.
Live each day. *Live*—but let the other person have his life, too.

Some of these women had begun to develop a genuine wisdom. Each of them was very clearly her own person, with her own specific skills and interests, caring about others and actively working to make the world better before she left it. One was taking art lessons and producing paintings; one painted the images of her dreams; one did creative writing; one was going to school in her eighties, studying history, philosophy, and poetry; one collected dolls and did photography; one liked to drive in her car and survey the countryside; one went to swimming class every week; one of the oldest was in a weekly exercise program and also took daily walks; one made sweaters to give to children in a home. Some of these older women did volunteer work in hospitals, homes for abused children, and shelters for battered women; one continued to see clients in a small practice. Each, despite occasional bouts with ill health, was very much alive. From the struggle between integrity and despair, Erikson says, comes wisdom.

These older women showed me that it was possible to be elderly and also vital, to be loving and still capable of making worthwhile contributions. They were involved, enjoying life in its final phase. "I don't think I've had an easy life," said one, "but it's been awfully interesting."

Dream Themes in Old Age: Reviews and Previews

Women in their later years are dreaming less than at any other time of their lives. Yet, especially among those who had an interest in dreams, their imagery proved informative and sometimes a source of much pleasure.

Naturally some of the dreams of the older women dealt with dreams of loved ones who have died. These were generally comforting dreams. On occasion they dreamed of their own death, as did the woman in her seventies who saw herself attending her own funeral, looking at herself lying in the casket, watching the people mourn her, and listening to what they said to assess how genuine it was.

Dreams about increasing physical frailty or specific injuries occur in the late adult years. Sometimes these feelings find expression in dreams of lost purses or other valuables being damaged or stolen, houses falling apart, or the dreamer becoming lost. We saw how one elderly woman was able to learn to change such dreams while they were happening; becoming lucid in a dream, she would plan to find her purse around a corner and regain her lost valuables. One of the most active elderly women saw in her dreams, instead of a deteriorating building, a barn being rebuilt; such images reflected inner energy and resourcefulness.

Reminiscing about younger years, paths chosen or not followed, become subjects of dreams. Depending on how she felt about her past, the woman's dreams were either disturbed or delightful. Nanette's worst nightmare was about the betrayal of a relative; Fanny's happiest dream was of a Sunday morning in her old hometown. Life reviews sometimes took place in the older woman's dreams.

At the same time that she is glancing backward, the older woman casts forward. Her dreams frequently become spiritual or religious in character. Archetypal figures, such as a priestess, a wise old woman, or a wise old man, sometimes emerge at this stage if they have not earlier. The psychological gains the woman has made in past developmental stages may continue.

Shimmering lights, golden doors, and white birds appeared in the dreams of some of the elderly subjects. I observed, as well, dreams with a "paradise" flavor among some of the older women, as in Elizabeth's dream of traveling to Joyville, where the town streets were lined with flowering trees, and in Marianna's dreams of colorful festivals in Paris.

Older women still have occasional erotic dreams as well as romantic ones. Of course they continue to dream about children and grandchildren and other relatives and friends with whom they are emotionally involved. The older woman persists in dreaming about her own mother, often in highly positive ways, along with other deceased relatives or mates.

The Older Woman's Mother.   Unfortunately some older women have never made peace with their mothers. Kora, in her late seventies, still dreams of quarreling with her long-deceased mother. Others are able to draw sustenance from happy dreams of their mothers. Over eighty, Kathryn's favorite dreams are of being with her mother and father, having a good time hiking in the woods, hunting specimens of flowers, a happy and simple pleasure. She wakes refreshed from these dreams of relived companionship.

Those people who have had near-death experiences, or who have clinically died and been restored to life frequently report dreamlike experiences in which they pass through a long, dark tunnel to a beautiful, sunlit place, where they are met by loved ones who have died earlier—a beloved grandmother, a loving father, a dear friend seem to welcome the newcomer.[10] Perhaps, when death does come, even those women who in their eldest years continue to wrestle with feelings of anger or competition with their mothers will finally be able to feel welcomed, accepted, and truly loved in their mother's embrace.

The Older Woman's Mirror.   The older woman's dream mirror reflects not only her changing features but also how she feels about them. Oma shared this dream from her late sixties in her long dream diary:

> There is a friendly, congenial group of people enjoying a picnic on a lawn by the sea. Although uninvited, I join them. They offer me food and wine, but I tell them I can't eat or drink yet as I have to go look in the mirror, since I haven't seen myself for quite a long time.
>
> As I leave, a young, pretty woman asks, "What does she mean she hasn't seen herself for a long time?" A very catty, bitchy lady answers, "Her mirror self-destructs!"

Here Oma seemed to be given the opportunity to participate in something pleasurable (the sea is one of her favorite spots). She was offered emotional nourishment (symbolized by the food and wine). She declines, however, in order to assess herself (look into her mirror). She has not done any self-reflection for a long time. The youthful, attractive part of the dreamer (represented by the young, pretty girl) wonders why. The more cynical part of herself (the catty, bitchy lady) implies that her aged appearance is unacceptable. The dreamer appears to be warning herself about overconcern with her aging appearance, that is, it could be destructive of Self.

Oma commented, "Maybe I don't like what I see in the mirror now that I'm aging—wrinkles, hollows, wattles. Yet I have to accept it." Obviously Oma did not enjoy the aspects of physical aging that she observed. However, she had also developed many avenues of self-expression that gave her other pleasures; painting and writing stories, along with recording her dreams, had helped sustain her through the years until her recent death. All of us need to face the image in the mirror, see ourselves as we are, accept it, and still continue to take pleasure and nourishment from the "picnic" of life.

Do You Like Being a Woman?

I asked this question to all the study participants. The overwhelming majority responded with a hearty yes. Less than 10 percent said they only liked parts of being a woman; although a couple of women, as children, wished they had been born boys, none continued to wish she were not a female. Everyone recognized that there are both assets and liabilities to being born a girl. On balance, however, most women had come to value the qualities they associated with femaleness.

In particular, study participants spoke of liking the sensitivity, the intuitiveness, and the gentleness of women; they admired female energy and emotional expression. They felt that women had greater freedom than men. They could develop intellectual skills and yet also take pleasure in dressing up, wearing colorful clothes, and looking pretty. Most of those who were mothers treasured the ability to give birth beyond all other capacities. They valued woman's nurturant qualities. They thought females had more fun.

Being a woman is, to a large extent, what we make of it. Those women who were most developed as individuals were the same women who had the most worldly success and the most loving relationships. They had developed skills and made contributions to society. These women were lovable because they were first of all interesting human beings. Being a person in no way diminished the woman's feminine qualities; it served to enhance them.

As women we tread a different path in life, near enough to touch hands, side by side, but without pacing behind—or before—our men. Our bodies behave differently and are perceived differently; our dreams more abundantly guide us in each round of the spiral of life.

Being Reborn

One day when I was in San Diego, as part of a national publicity tour for one of my books, I had a few spare hours and decided to treat myself to the city's famous zoo. There, amidst the array of exotic creatures, I was most impressed watching a baby chick break out of its shell in an incubation cage. As a suburban-raised woman, the sight of a hatching chick was as foreign to me as a panda munching bamboo.

At first, minute cracks appeared in the upper side of the eggshell. Then the tiny creature's beak poked through a hole, which was gradually pecked wider. What hard work the process was to free itself! What a battle to make the transition from egg to bird. Half in, half out, the chick struggled with enormous effort. But the curious thing was, it did so in spurts.

For several seconds it would wrench and thrust furiously, then fall exhausted into a stupor for an equal length of time. Giving a great lurch, it began again the frantic striving to break free. Stop. Start. Frenzied effort. Total collapse. Alternately stretching and reaching, then resting, then stretching again—for perhaps a half an hour—the damp, tousled being finally emerged to totter away from its clinging shell.

Somehow that tiny chick hatching from its shell made me feel hopeful about the process of death. In a dream from my middle years I saw a little old Chinese man being tied to a chair and submerged into deep water that I thought would surely kill him. I, myself, stood in an underground section that opened onto a lighted area. In the midst of this space stood a great baptismal fountain surrounded by circular steps that spiraled upward. In the waters of the fountain many women were being submerged.

Each woman was at a different stage of life. Some were quite young. One was a girl in a communion gown, another a bride in a wedding dress, still another was naked and beautiful. I knew that at each important event of her life, the woman must come and submerge herself in these waters. I watched in fascination.

Suddenly I heard the men who were watching the old Chinese man under the water shout, "My God, he's completely transformed!" Then I, too, could see him, in a kind of underwater tube. His face and body had totally changed. Instead of dying, which everyone expected, he was transformed. He looked powerful and bristling with life. He was drawn up from the water as though on ropes and emerged strong and alive.

Like the chick breaking out of its shell, like the old man who instead of dying was transformed, our physical death may be the death to a former existence and the birth to a new. As the women of all stages of life climbed the spiral staircase to enter the waters of the circular fountain in my dream, so, too, may we be baptized anew when we reach the last round. When our own lives have come full cycle, we shall see for ourselves.

For years before our death we have prepared ourselves in dreams. We do not know what lies beyond the end. A new beginning? A rebirth? Surely the spark that has dwelt within, though it extinguish for the moment, will in some form and some way flicker into flame elsewhere. We are complete. Expanding, contracting, unbroken, the circle is whole.

The following is a brief description of the study carried out by the author of this book; it served as a basis for the conclusions and as a source of many of the dreams.

The Study

Subjects

Fifty women ranging in age from twenty to ninety-one at the time of the first interview contributed more than 500 dreams to this study. The samples in the groups of women between thirty and fifty years old were larger; the younger and older groups were smaller.

Geographical Origin. The participants in the study were born in a variety of states in the union. Over one third (34%) of the women (n = 17) were born in California, but participants included those born in Pennsylvania, New York, New Jersey, District of Columbia, Florida, Kentucky, Michigan, Minnesota, North Carolina, Ohio, Oklahoma, Rhode Island, Texas, and Virginia.

The majority of the women were born in America, (80%, n = 40). One fifth of the sample (n = 10) were born outside of the United States. Participants in this minority group were born in Canada, China, Romania, Germany, the Middle East, and Ireland.

Current Residence. The women had lived in several different states or Canada during their lives. At the time of the first interview, the majority (n = 38) made their homes in the Bay Area of San Francisco. However, some participants (n = 11) lived at the time we spoke in New York, Florida, Illinois, Iowa, Oregon, or Canada; one lived in Europe.

All subjects but one were currently residing in the United States or Canada, and had been in residence for several years.

Religious Background.   The women in this study followed diverse faiths. Almost half of them (n = 40) were raised as some type of Protestant; more than a quarter of the participants (n = 13) were brought up in the Jewish faith; a minority of the sample (n = 6) were instructed in the Catholic religion; some (n = 6) followed a variety of other types of faith, such as Mormon or Ba Hai; and only one (n = 1) was raised without religion. In their current practice these women varied from devout to inactive.

Educational Background.   The women involved in this study were more highly educated than the average. All were high school graduates. Only 12% (n = 6) had not undertaken extensive further training. Several, (22%, n = 11) had finished specialized training beyond high school, such as business or art school. Almost one-third (32%, n = 16) held bachelor's degrees. More than 20% (n = 10) had earned master's degrees; and 14% (n = 7) had achieved the doctor of philosophy degree.

This sample is therefore underrepresented in women with only grade-school or junior-high-school education. It is, however, a fair distribution of women with college or postgraduate training.

Occupational Class.   Participants were engaged in a multitude of occupations. None of the women in the study could be accurately classified as laborers. Skilled workers (such as body therapist, beautician, photographer) constituted about 10% (n = 6) of the sample. Lower white collar workers, including office clerk, sales clerk, publicist, secretary also made up approximately 10% (n = 7). More than half of the sample, (54%, n = 27) was formed by upper white collar workers or professionals (administrator, director, lawyer, teacher, pharmacist, psychologist, therapist, and social worker). The high level of occupational class is due to the generally high level of education among the women.

Graduate students made up 10% (n = 5) of the group. Housewives also comprised 10% (n = 5) of the sample. Some of these women had advanced degrees; in some cases their husbands were in managerial or professional work.

Marital Status.   The women who partook in the study had considerable marital experience. Less than 20% (n = 9) had never been married, but several of these were currently living with a male. All the remainder had been married at least once.

Over one-quarter of the participants (26%, n = 13) were in their first marriage. Almost another quarter (n = 11) were in their second marriage. A very few (n = 2) were in their third marriage. All together, over half (n = 26) were currently married. Additionally, a couple were separated, awaiting divorce (n = 2). Some were already divorced (n = 8) and some were widowed (n = 5).

Despite this scope of experience, a few participants remained virgins, one in her twenties and one in her eighties. Generally, however, the group were women who had been involved in long-term liaisons. All the women were heterosexual in orientation.

Other factors that characterized the participants, such as age of menarche (first menstruation), age of first intercourse, and so forth were also considered.

Overall, the women were fairly representative of the white upper-middle-class in an urban setting. Thus the conclusions described must be considered as especially applicable to this group and not necessarily true of all women.

Procedure

Each woman was personally interviewed by the author for a minimum of one hour to a maximum of five consecutive hours, the length of the interview determined in part by the age of the woman and the vividness of her dream recall. Older women had broader experience to relate; others had prolific dream recall. Usually one session was sufficient. In a few instances, follow-up contact was made to clarify certain dream passages or to hear new material.

These personal interviews took place between April 1986 and October 1987. Most discussions took place in the author's San Francisco living room, although a few were held in small local restaurants that could provide sufficient quiet and privacy for the personal nature of the questions. Once it emerged that some of the women were moved to tears, I decided it was preferable to conduct the talks in seclusion, in a relaxing atmosphere, whenever possible.

The only material involved was the standard interview form, devised by the author, filled in by her in pen during the interview, along with notecards for recording additional dream content that exceeded the limits of the seven-page form. The questions covered demographic data and information regarding each aspect of the life cycle, in addition to questions about dreams. Tea and a light snack were often provided, enhancing the sense of intimate exchange.

A rare interview was carried out in the home or private office of the participant—this was more likely to be so in the case of elderly participants. Also rare was a public setting, as in an instance when the conversation took place in a quiet corner of the lobby of the Empress Hotel in Victoria, British Columbia. The author's travel schedule sometimes necessitated such arrangements.

Women contributed their dreams in a variety of ways. Some of the participants already kept regular dream diaries. They were kind enough to make copies of the segments relevant to our discussion and gave them to me at the interview or sent them by mail. Some women continued to mail dream reports at regular intervals.

Other women undertook dream diaries especially for the purpose of our talks. One young pregnant woman, for example, who regularly remembers her dreams, was delighted to have a reason to record them. She, and others in this category, provided their records to use. A few telephoned to report dreams they knew the author would be interested to hear without delay. Others, those who were not regular dream recallers, described dreams as best they could from memory.

Occasionally, participants shared artwork, literary or other creative products they had made based on their dreams. A wristwatch was used to keep track of time, to avoid neglecting any portion of the interview when there were time restraints. The time was not strictly limited because "control" of procedures sometimes imposes artificial boundaries that do not allow rapport to develop and significant material to emerge. Most interviews came to a "natural" conclusion. The data collected is more akin to clinically gathered material than to scientific experiment.

The women in this study were largely self-selected. Those who knew about the project told friends who were interested in dreams and they, in turn, volunteered. No payments were involved.

In a few cases, toward the end of the study, additional interviews were requested from women who were in an age category that was insufficiently represented. Only two of these requests were denied. One, a young woman in her twenties who was "not ready to tell secrets," and another in the same age bracket who felt her time was too limited.

In general, women were eager to talk about their lives and to be helpful, especially when given assurance of confidentiality. Although they were offered the option of declining to answer a question, many of them shared secrets never before revealed to anyone. I cherish their openness and their trust.

It is obvious from the above details that the current study was not rigorously controlled in a scientific sense. On the other hand, the interview was standardized so that the questions were asked in the same order and the same procedure was followed throughout by the same person.

The data gathered included demographic information and facts about the participants' life experiences. In addition, each woman contributed at least three dreams: her worst nightmare; her favorite dream; and a recent dream. A few women collected and turned in, or mailed, a large number of dreams, as many as thirty-five apiece. The average participant contributed about six dreams.

Material from the discussion and the collected dreams were analyzed by computer. The Macintosh Apple was used for preliminary computations; more sophisticated calculations were carried out elsewhere, thanks to Dr. Stephen LaBerge of the Sleep Clinic at Stanford University. Also thanks to Philippe Babled of the European University of America for assistance with calculations.

Data was grouped according to age of the participant. Further groupings were made according to life event, for example, those women who were pregnant when interviewed, those about to be married, and so forth.

The Results

Space limitations prohibit any more than a brief presentation of overall results here.

Worst Nightmares

Themes. Among the fifty nightmares contributed by the fifty subjects, the most common category was being chased or attacked. (More than fifty nightmares were described, but only the "worst" one was scored.) Chase or Attack dreams accounted for fifteen (or 30%) of the total nightmares; only two (4%) of these resulted in the death of the dreamer.

Being in the presence of something frightening, without being chased or attacked by it, was the second most common type of nightmare. Sensing Something Scary accounted for twelve (24%) of the total nightmares. Other categories of bad dreams included: Falling (five cases, or 10%); Injury or Death (four cases or 8% with two deaths); Being Frustrated (four cases, 8%); Natural or Man-made Disasters (four cases or 8%); Destruction or Loss of property (three cases, 6%); Being Rejected (two cases, 4%); Being Paralyzed (one case, 2%).

Victim. The dreamer, rather than some other dream character, was almost always the victim. In forty-two cases (84%), the self was victimized; in three cases (6%), the son or son-in-law was the victim; in three cases (6%), the husband or boyfriend was the victim; and in two cases (4%), the mother was the victim. A daughter and "somebody" were each victims once (2%). All fifty dreams contained victims, fifty-two in all.

Villain. Some of the nightmares contained human villains (nineteen cases, 38%). Among these, the villain was a familiar male in nine cases (18%); in seven cases (14%), the villain was a strange male; in two cases (4%), the villain was a strange female; in one case (2%), the villain was a strange person of undifferentiated sex.

Non-human Threats. Other sources of dream danger included: water (five cases, 10%); animals (five cases, 10%); "things" (five cases, 10%); monster-like creatures (two cases, 4%); a nuclear explosion (one case, 2%). Non-human threats appeared in 36% of the nightmares.

Color. Among the fifteen (30%) nightmares that contained color, black, bluish-black, or blackish-gray were mentioned most often (10 cases or 20%). Red was mentioned in a few dreams (three cases, 6%); and white, seldom (two cases or 4%). No other colors than these were spoken of in the nightmares.

Size. Among the twelve (24%) nightmares that mentioned size, all contained references to something big, gigantic, huge, or rapidly growing in size. This was always a source of fear.

Favorite Dreams

Themes. Among the fifty favorite dreams contributed by subjects the largest category involved pleasurable activity with a man. Having fun with a man constituted thirteen (26%) of the fifty dreams; nine (18%) of these were romantic activities such as being in love or dancing; four (8%) were specifically sexual in content.

The second most frequent category of favorite dreams was pleasurable movement or sensation. Sensation dreams accounted for eleven (22%) of the total favorite dreams. These included five (10%) flying dreams; the remainder were assorted swimming, yoga movements, etc. Other categories of favorite dreams included: Being in a Beautiful Place (six cases, 12%); Having a Spiritual Encounter (six cases, 12%); Having Fun with a Child (four cases, 18%); Artistic Activity (four cases, 8%); Fun with a Parent (two cases, 4%); Fun with Friends (two cases, 4%); and Transformation (two cases, 4%).

Contrast to Nightmares. These happy dreams differed from nightmares in several dimensions beyond emotional content. We saw that nightmares were often characterized by a gloomy, gray atmosphere or dark colors. Favorite dreams, in contrast, were often infused with glowing light; nine dreams (18%) contained gleaming radiance. Dreamers often spoke of warm, beautiful colors in their happy dreams. Instead of black, red, or white, happy dreamers mentioned most often blue (six cases, 12%), pinkish-red, green, yellow-gold or lovely colors in general. Those dreams that contained white (five cases, 10%) associated white with glowing light. Although four (8%) women mentioned black or dark in their dreams, it was always a shining, lustrous black or velvety, glowing black, rather than gloomy black. Color was present in twenty-three (46%) of the favorite dreams.

Furthermore, nightmares contained looming, swelling or overwhelming objects or people. Thus, movement in nightmares was mostly increasing size or running in fear; sometimes dreamers were paralyzed. Favorite dreams, in contrast, often mentioned rhythmic movements, such as flying, walking, dancing, sexual intercourse, riding a horse, swimming, gesturing with the hand or body, or feeling the movement of a breeze. Pleasant movement appeared in thirty-five (70%) of the favorite dreams. Beautiful, natural objects often appeared in the favorite dreams; thirty-two cases (64%) included references to nature. The sea, sky, flowers, trees, hills, healing rain, meadows, countryside, space, and friendly animals were mentioned.

For further details on the results of this study on women's dreams, contact the author at Creative Dreaming International, P.O. Box 210452, San Francisco, CA 94118

Preface

1. It is believed that Freud kept an extensive dream diary, which he apparently destroyed in April 1885, at the age of twenty-eight, along with general diaries he had kept for fourteen years; described in Edwin Diamond, *The Science of Dreams* (New York: MacFadden Books, 1963), p. 32. Freud drew heavily on forty-seven of his own dreams, along with some other casual references, for his classic book, *The Interpretation of Dreams*. This is what remains of his dream records.

2. A portion of Jung's original records remain. After his break with Freud, he withdrew from his academic career and spent approximately four years trying to understand his fantasies and dreams. He first recorded them in his "Black Book," which eventually consisted of six small black leather-bound notebooks. Later he transferred them to "The Red Book," a folio volume bound in red in which the dreams were recorded in Gothic calligraphic script and embellished with his drawings. See Carl G. Jung, *Memories, Dreams, Reflections,* ed. Aniela Jaffe (New York: Vintage, 1963). For some beautiful reproductions of Jung's dream drawings, see Aniela Jaffe, ed. *C. G. Jung: Word and Image* (Princeton: Princeton University Press, 1979).

3. Described in Patricia L. Garfield, "Keeping a Longitudinal Dream Record," *Psychotherapy: Theory, Research and Practice* 10, no. 3 (Fall 1973).

4. P. L. Garfield, *Creative Dreaming* (New York: Simon & Schuster, 1974).

5. P. L. Garfield, *Pathway to Ecstasy: The Way of the Dream Mandala* (New York: Holt, Rinehart & Winston, 1979).

6. P. L. Garfield, *Your Child's Dreams* (New York: Ballantine, 1984).

7. Calvin S. Hall and Robert L. Van de Castle, *The Content Analysis of Dreams* (New York: Appleton-Century-Crofts, 1966).

8. P. L. Garfield, Introduction to *Dream Notebook* (San Francisco: San Francisco Book Co., 1976), pp. 7–16.

Chapter One
The Dreaming Woman

1. *Webster's New World Dictionary of the American Language,* college ed. (New York: World Publishing Co., 1957).

2. Erik H. Erikson, Joan M. Erikson, and Helen Q. Kivnick, *Vital Involvement in Old Age* (New York: W. W. Norton & Co., 1986), pt. 1.

3. Howard Staunton, ed. *The Complete Illustrated Shakespeare,* Park Lane ed. (New York: Crown, 1979), p. 144. Jaques tells the Duke,

> *All the world's a stage,*
> *And all the men and women merely players:*
> *They have their exits and their entrances.*
> *And one man in his time plays many parts,*
> *His acts being seven ages.*

He goes on to identify these ages as the infant, the schoolboy, the lover, the soldier, the justice, the old man, and the second childhood, "Sans teeth, sans eyes, sans taste, sans everything."

4. Daniel J. Levinson, et al., *Seasons of a Man's Life* (New York: Ballantine, 1978).

5. Gail Sheehy, *Passages: Predictable Crises of Adult Life* (New York: Bantam, 1977).

6. Else Frenkel-Brunswik, "Adjustments and Reorientation in the Course of the Life Span," in Bernice L. Neugarten, ed. *Middle Age and Aging* (Chicago: The University of Chicago Press, 1968).

7. Sheehy, *Passages,* p. 45.

8. Alfred C. Kinsey, Wardell B. Pomeroy, and Clyde E. Martin. *Sexual Behavior in the Human Male* (Philadelphia: W. B. Saunders, 1948), pp. 186–87.

9. Alfred C. Kinsey et al., *Sexual Behavior in the Human Female* (Philadelphia: W. B. Saunders Co., 1953), p. 125.

10. Ibid., p. 126.

11. Kinsey, Pomeroy, and Martin, *Human Male,* p. 520.

12. Kinsey et al., *Human Female,* p. 215.

13. Stage 1 sleep is identified by the slowing of brain waves from the restful waking pattern of *alpha* (8–12 cycles per second) to mainly *beta* and *theta* activity (1–6 cycles per second). When less than 50 percent of the brain waves are alpha, stage 1 is said to begin, a change measured on the electroencephalograph (EEG) machine. Slow, rolling eye movements are often present.

Stage 2, a few minutes later, is characterized by the appearance of largely *theta* waves, sleep spindles (brief bursts of 12–14 cycles per second), and K-complexes (high-amplitude negative waves followed by positive activity).

Stage 3 is identified by the presence of *delta* (high-amplitude waves of 1–4 cycles per second) in 20–50 percent of the EEG record.

Stage 4 is identified by more than 50 percent delta waves. It is difficult to arouse sleepers from this stage; the longest period of stage 4 usually occurs early in the night during the first cycle. This stage often has only two or three periods a night. Stages 3 and 4 combined are sometimes called "slow-wave sleep." See note 14 for more on sleep stages.

14. Richard M. Coleman, *Wide Awake at 3:00 A.M.: By Choice or by Chance?* (New York: W. H. Freeman & Co., 1986); Michael E. Long, "What Is This Thing Called Sleep? *National Geographic* 172, no. 6 (December 1987); Gene Usdin and David Hawkins, *The Office Guide to Sleep Disorders* (New York: KPR Infor/Media Corp., 1980); Carl F. Wiedemann, "REM and Non-REM Sleep and Its Relation to Nightmares and Night Terrors," in Henry Kellerman, *The Nightmare* (New York: Columbia University Press, 1987), pp. 75–97.

15. In the normal adult the remainder of the sleep time is divided as follows:

5 percent in stage 1 non-REM
50 percent in stage 2
10 percent in stage 3
10 percent in stage 4

(Wiedemann, "REM and Non-REM Sleep," p. 78).

16. Wiedemann, "REM and Non-REM Sleep."

17. See Jerome L. Singer, *Imagery and Daydream Methods in Psychotherapy and Behavior Modification* (New York: Academic Press, 1974), p. 173.

18. Norman MacKenzie, *Dreams and Dreaming* (London: Aldus Books, 1965), pp. 47–49.

19. Sigmund Freud, *The Interpretation of Dreams,* trans. A. A. Brill (New York: Random House, 1950), pp. 34–35.

20. Hervey de Saint-Denys. *Dreams and How to Guide Them,* ed. Morton Schatzman (London: Duckworth, 1982), pp. 105–6. An assumption based on the fact that Saint-Denys described the dream as "supersensual." He said that when he finally kissed the girl, "I was consumed with such a shudder of joy that I felt my reason would not survive." The "intensity of my pleasure" caused him to awake. Elsewhere (pp. 119–21) he cites examples from his fifteen observations of ordinary dreams that led to "sensual episodes." Original appeared in French in 1867, spelled Hervé de Saint Denys.

21. Jean Piaget, *Play, Dreams and Imitation in Childhood* (New York: W. W. Norton & Co, 1962), pp. 179–80. The boy's dream was the following:

In the basin I saw a bean that was so big that it quite filled it. It got bigger and bigger all the time. I was standing by the door. I was frightened. I wanted to scream and run away, but I couldn't. I got more and more frightened, and it went on until I woke up.

22. See notes for chapter 2 of this book, where numerous citations are given that document the female's sexual arousal during dreaming.

23. Calvin S. Hall and Robert L. Van de Castle, *The Content Analysis of Dreams* (New York: Appleton-Century-Crofts, 1966), p. 180.

24. Linda A. Kilner, "Cross-cultural Comparison of Manifest Dream Content: United States and Gusil Females," *Association for the Study of Dreams Newsletter* 4, no. 3 (June 1987).

25. MacKenzie, *Dreams and Dreaming,* pp. 34–35. Ashurbanipal ruled from 669 to 626 B.C.

26. MacKenzie, *Dreams and Dreaming,* pp. 28–29. Called the Chester Beatty papyrus, after its donor, it is currently located in the British Museum, where I examined it.

27. Mandukya Upanishad references are described in David Coxhead and Susan Hiller, *Dreams: Visions of the Night* (New York: Avon, 1975), p. 13.

28. See, for example, the entry for *dream* in the Dictionary-Concordance of *The Holy Bible,* Verse Reference ed. (Philadelphia: A. J. Holman Co., n.d.), p. 56.

29. Artemidorus, *The Interpretation of Dreams: Oneirocritica by Artemidorus* trans. from Greek and commentary by Robert J. White (Park Ridge, N.J.: Noyes Press, 1975).

30. Chapter 9, *"Berochoth."* See Harry A. Savitz, "Dreams in the Talmud: The Prophets of Yore Had the Noblest Dream, *Rhode Island Medical Journal* 64, no. 9 (1981): 427–30.

31. MacKenzie, *Dreams and Dreaming,* pp. 39–40.

32. Personal communications from some Chinese women.

33. See Patricia L. Garfield, *Creative Dreaming,* chap. 2, "Learn From Ancient Dreamers."

Chapter Two
Women's Dreams, Men's Dreams—The Difference

1. Personal communications from some Greek women.

2. Personal communications from some Iranian women.

3. Rosalind D. Cartwright, *A Primer on Sleep and Dreaming* (Menlo Park, Calif.: Addison-Wesley, 1978), p. 44. See also Rosalind D. Cartwright, *Night Life: Explorations in Dreaming* (Englewood Cliffs, N.J.: Prentice-Hall, 1977), p. 39.

4. See, for instance, Ismet Karacan et al., "Characteristics of Sleep Patterns During Late Pregnancy and the Postpartum Periods," *American Journal of Obstetrics and Gynecology* 101, no. 5, pp. 579–86, 1968.

5. Ernest Hartmann, *The Biology of Dreaming* (Springfield, Ill.: Charles C. Thomas, 1967), pp. 60–62. See also Patricia L. Garfield, "Keeping a Longitudinal Dream Record," *Psychotherapy: Theory, Research and Practice* 10, no. 3 (Fall 1973): 223–28.

6. Robert L. Williams, Ismet Karacan and Carolyn J. Hursch, *Electroencephalography (EEG) of Human Sleep: Clinical Applications* (New York: John Wiley & Sons, 1974). This massive undertaking has produced the only full-scale bank of sleep parameters in existence. Since scoring differences exist among laboratories, it was important to obtain data that were gathered with the same procedure and scored in the same way in order to make valid comparisons between age groups. Of the 237 subjects, 115 were female and 122 were male; these were distributed fairly evenly over the entire age span.

7. Ibid., p. 35.

8. Ibid., p. 45.

9. Williams, Karacan, and Hursch, *Electroencephalography*. The figures for percentage of REM time, divided by the amount of sleep time from onset of sleep to final morning awakening, are as follows:

Age Bracket	Females % REM	Males % REM
3–5	31.75	30.26
6–9	29.31	27.33
10–12	27.43	26.39
13–15	25.63	26.70
16–19	22.12	22.02
20–29	25.23	28.00
30–39	26.22	23.47
40–49	26.67	22.85 (significant difference)
50–59	21.77	21.48
60–69	21.43	23.09
70–79	19.46	17.68

10. Ibid., p. 62.

11. René Spiegel, *Sleep and Sleeplessness in Advanced Age* (Jamaica, N.Y.: Spectrum Publications, 1981), p. 130. Spiegel measured 113 subjects of "advanced age," the average age being sixty-four; of these, forty-four were female, sixty-nine male.

12. Ibid., p. 129.

13. Ibid., pp. 129, 167. Spiegel's exact figures differ from Williams's, but the trend of older women exhibiting more deep sleep is the same. In the sixty-to-sixty-nine-year-old group, Williams obtained a percentage of 5 percent stage 4 sleep for women, whereas men of the same age had 1 percent stage 4 sleep. In Spiegel's subjects, with an average age of sixty-four, he obtained 10 percent stage 4 sleep for women and 5 percent stage 4 sleep for men.

14. Ibid., p. 129.

15. Cartwright, *Primer,* p. 22.

16. Hartmann, *Biology of Dreaming,* p. 97. See also Spiegel, *Sleep and Sleeplessness,* pp. 14–22.

17. Hartmann, *Biology of Dreaming,* p. 132. Based on N. Schechter, G. Schmeidler, and M. Staal, "Dream Reports and Creative Tendencies in Students of the Arts, Sciences, and Engineering," *Journal of Consulting Psychology* 29 (1965): 415–21.

18. Ernest Hartmann, *The Nightmare: The Psychology and Biology of Terrifying Dreams* (New York: Basic Books, 1984), pp. 127–28. Hartmann is referring especially to nightmare sufferers.

19. Joseph De Koninck et al. "Dreams During Language Learning: When Is the New Language Integrated?" *Association for the Study of Dreams Newsletter* 4, no. 3 (June 1987): 3. The authors report that they and others have observed "better performance in intensive language learning is associated with increases in REM sleep percentages."

20. Cartwright, *Primer,* pp. 22–23.

21. Robert L. Van de Castle, *The Psychology of Dreaming* (pamphlet) (New York: General Learning Press, 1971), p. 37.

22. Calvin S. Hall and Robert L. Van de Castle, 1966. *The Content Analysis of Dreams* (New York: Appleton-Century-Crofts, 1966), pp. 158–60. Reports under fifty words were also eliminated as well as reports over 300 words.

23. David Foulkes, *Children's Dreams: Longitudinal Studies* (New York: John Wiley & Sons, 1982), pp. 47–48.

24. Ibid., pp. 334, 341.

25. John Nicholson, *Men and Women: How Different Are They?* (Oxford, Eng.: Oxford University Press, 1984), pp. 75–76.

26. Ibid., p. 79.

27. Ibid., pp. 81–84.

28. Ibid., p. 77.

29. Ibid., p. 83.

30. Ibid., p. 84. This study took place at Reading University, England.

31. Described in Thomas Short, 1986 "The Word on Gender" (book review of Dennis Baron, *Grammar and Gender* [New Haven: Yale University Press, 1986]), *Washington Times, Insight,* April 7, 1986.

32. Kenneth M. Colby, *A Skeptical Psychoanalyst* (New York: The Ronald Press Co., 1958). Colby actually counted concepts more than literal words; for instance, he categorized "riding in a canoe" as a "vehicle."

33. Colby used the first dreams quoted in papers appearing in the *Psychoanalytic Quarterly* between 1932 and 1956 and in the *Psychoanalytic Review* between 1932 and 1955.

34. A total of 752 elements were distributed among the following categories: *settings, objects, actions, affects, thoughts, properties.*

35. In yet another study Colby examined a collection of dreams from primitive tribes. Males in this sample were identified by the words or concepts *wife, weapon, coitus, death,* and *animal.* Females in this group were distinguished by use of the words or concepts *husband, mother, clothes,* and *human body.*

36. Charles Berlitz, *Native Tongues* (New York: The Putnam Publishing Group, 1982), pp. 39–40.

37. Ashley Montagu, *The Natural Superiority of Women* (London: Collier Books, 1970), p. 60. The idiot's brain weighed over 2,850 grams compared with the brain of Anatole France, weighing 1,100 grams.

38. Janet L. Hopson, "A Love Affair With the Brain: PT Conversation With Marian Diamond," *Psychology Today* 18, no. 11 (November 1984): 62–73.

39. Keay Davidson, "Sexual Equality May Be All in Your Head," *San Francisco Examiner,* Feb. 22, 1987, p. A-3. See also Doreen Kimura, "Male Brain, Female Brain: The Hidden Difference," *Psychology Today* 19, no. 11 (1985): 50–58.

40. Davidson, "Sexual Equality," p. A-3.

41. Betty Edwards, *Drawing on the Artist Within: A Guide to Innovation, Invention, Imagination, and Creativity* (New York: Simon & Schuster, 1986), pp. 66–95.

42. Calvin S. Hall and Vernon J. Nordby, *The Individual and His Dreams* (New York: New American Library, 1972), p. 38.

43. Hall and Nordby, *The Individual and His Dreams,* p. 38.

44. A similar study conducted by Erikson is described in Colby, *A Skeptical Psychoana-*

lyst, pp. 111–12. Erikson studied the play activity of 468 preadolescents (236 boys and 236 girls) aged twelve to fourteen. He observed that boys built scenes of wild animals, Indians, or auto accidents; they preferred toys that represented motion. Girls, in contrast, built quiet scenes of everyday life at home or school; they preferred enclosures. Erikson compared these play differences to the morphologic differences of the sex organs. For original, see Eric Erikson, "Sex Differences in the Play Configurations of Preadolescents," *American Journal of Orthopsychiatry* 21 (1951); 667–92.

In a study by J. H. Conn, boys four to nine years old were observed to play with toy vehicles or tools more often than girls, who chose dolls and doll furniture. See J. H. Conn, "Children's Awareness of Sex Difference; II: Play Attitudes and Game Preferences," *Journal of Child Psychiatry* (1951) 82–99.

In a study of drawing completion, men were observed to draw objects that move, such as autos and steamships, in comparison with women, who drew containers, houses, vases, fruit, flowers, animals, and people; see K. Franck and E. Rosen, "A Projective Test of Masculinity-Femininity," *Journal of Consulting Psychology* 13 (1949): 247–57.

45. Described in Carolyn Winget and Milton Kramer, *Dimensions of Dreams* (Gainesville, Fla.: University Presses of Florida, 1979). For original, see C. B. Brenneis, *Differences in Male and Female Ego Styles in Manifest Dream Content,* Ann Arbor, Mich., University Microfilms, 1968; or idem, "Male and Female Ego Modalities in Manifest Dream Content," *Journal of Abnormal Psychology* 76 (1970): 434–42.

46. Hall and Van de Castle, *Content Analysis of Dreams,* p. 158.

47. Ibid., p. 159.

48. C. S. Hall et al., "The Dreams of College Men and Women in 1950 and 1980: A Comparison of Dream Contents and Sex Differences," *Sleep* 5, no. 2 (1982): 188–194.

49. Ibid., p. 188.

50. Carol S. Rupprecht, "The Common Language of Women's Dreams: Colloquy of Mind and Body," in E. Lauter and C. S. Rupprecht, eds., *Archetypal Theory: Interdisciplinary Re-Visions of Jungian Thought* (Knoxville, Tenn.: University of Tennessee Press, 1985), p. 203.

51. Monique Lortie-Lussier, Christine Schwab, and Joseph De Koninck, "Working Mothers Versus Homemakers: Do Dreams Reflect the Changing Roles of Women?" *Sex Roles* 12 (1985): 1,009–21.

52. Hall and Van de Castle, *Content Analysis of Dreams,* p. 164. In the group of 1,000 dreams from college students, females had 796 familiar characters out of a total of 1,363 human characters, a proportion of .58; males had 501 familiar characters out of a total of 1,108 human characters, a proportion of .45. Regarding unfamiliar characters, females had 567 out of 1,363 human characters, a proportion of .41; males had 607 out of 1,108, a proportion of .54.

53. In addition to the study referred to in note 51, see Monique Lortie-Lussier et al., "Social Role Impact on the Dreams of Working Mothers and Female Students," *Association for the Study of Dreams Newsletter* 3, no. 2 (June 1986): 7. This material was described in greater detail at a paper presentation by Lortie-Lussier at the Association for the Study of Dreams conference at Ottawa, Canada, in 1986.

54. C. S. Hall and B. Domhoff, "The Difference Between Men and Women Dreamers," in Ralph L. Woods and Herbert B. Greenhouse, eds. *The New World of Dreams* (New York: Macmillan, 1974), pp. 13–16.

55. Lortie-Lussier, Schwab, and De Koninck, "Working Mothers," pp. 1009–21.

56. Hall and Nordby, *The Individual and His Dreams,* p. 42.

57. Van de Castle, *Psychology of Dreaming,* p. 38.

58. Patricia L. Garfield, *Your Child's Dreams* (New York: Ballantine, 1984), pp. 392–93.

59. Foulkes, *Children's Dreams,* pp. 81–82.

60. Quoted in Winget and Kramer, *Dimensions of Dreams,* p. 302. For original, see J. J. Buckley, "The Dreams of Young Adults: A Sociological Analysis of 1,133 Dreams of Black and White Students," in *Dissertation Abstracts International,* vol. 31 [7-A], 3635.

61. Quoted in C. Winget and M. Kramer, *Dimensions of Dreams,* pp. 300, 303. For original, see C. S. Hall and B. Domhoff, "Friends and Enemies in Dreams," Institute of Dream Research, mimeograph, 1962. See also A. F. Paolino, "Dreams: Sex Differences in Aggressive Content," *Journal of Projective Techniques* 28 (1964): 219–26.

62. Quoted in Winget and Kramer, *Dimensions of Dreams,* pp. 300, 303. For original, see Paolino, "Dreams," pp. 219–26. See also Calvin S. Hall and B. Domhoff, "Aggression in Dreams," *International Journal of Social Psychiatry* 9 (1963): 259–67. See also C. Winget, M. Kramer, and R. Whitman, "Dreams and Demography," *Canadian Psychiatry Association Journal* 17 (1972): 203–8.

63. Quoted in Winget and Kramer, *Dimensions of Dreams,* p. 302. For original, see M. J. Feldman and E. Hyman, "Content Analysis of Nightmare Reports," paper presented to the Association for the Psychophysiological Study of Sleep, Denver, Colo., 1968.

64. Hall and Nordby, *The Individual and His Dreams,* p. 51.

65. Winget and Kramer, *Dimensions of Dreams,* pp. 234, 299–300. For original, see Winget, Kramer, and Whitman, "Dreams and Demography." See also J. F. Rychlak, "Recalled Dream Themes and Personality," *Journal of Abnormal Social Psychology* 60 (1960): 140–43: Calvin S. Hall and Bill Domhoff, "Friendliness in Dreams," Institute of Dream research mimeograph, 1962; Hall and Domhoff, "Friends and Enemies in Dreams."

66. Hall and Van de Castle, *Content Analysis of Dreams,* pp. 180–81.

67. Winget and Kramer, *Dimensions of Dreams,* p. 297. For original, see L. Gahagan, "Sex Differences in Recall of Stereotyped Dreams, Sleep-Talking, and Sleep-Walking," *Journal of General Psychology* 48 (1936): 227–36.

68. Ethel M. Swanson and David Foulkes, "Dream Content and the Menstrual Cycle," *Journal of Nervous and Mental Disorders* 145 (1968): 358–63.

69. Winget and Kramer, *Dimensions of Dreams,* p. 189.

70. J. Money, "Phantom Orgasm in Dreams of Paraplegic Men and Women," *Archives of General Psychiatry* 3 (1960): 373–83.

71. Sex occurred in fifty-eight out of five hundred of the men's dreams, yielding 12 percent; sex occurred in eighteen out of five hundred of the women's dreams, yielding 4 percent; see Hall and Van de Castle, *Content Analysis of Dreams,* p. 181.

72. Alfred C. Kinsey et al., *Sexual Behavior in the Human Female* (Philadelphia: W. B. Saunders Co., 1953), p. 215.

73. Alfred C. Kinsey, Wordell B. Pomeroy, and Clyde E. Martin, *Sexual Behavior in the Human Male* (Philadelphia: W. B. Saunders, 1948), pp. 186 and 187. In Kinsey's sample the average age of first orgasm was thirteen years, ten and one-half months; first ejaculation occurred, for 90 percent of the males, between ages eleven and fifteen.

74. Kinsey et al., *Human Female,* pp. 208–12.

75. Ibid., pp. 212 13.

76. Charles A. Padgham, "Colours Experienced in Dreams," *British Journal of Psychology* 66, no. 1 (1975): 25–28.

77. These findings are complicated by the fact that female thresholds vary with phases of the menstrual cycle. In general, sensitivity increases around the time of ovulation. See Mary Anne Baker, *Sex Differences in Human Performance* (New York: John Wiley & Sons, 1987), pp. 11–13.

78. Van de Castle, *Psychology of Dreaming,* p. 37. See also Hall and Van de Castle, *Content Analysis of Dreams,* pp. 160–63. Women mentioned about 9 percent more objects than men.

79. Van de Castle, *Psychology of Dreaming,* p. 37.

80. Patricia Maybruck, *An Exploratory Study of the Dreams of Pregnant Women,* (Ph.D. diss., Saybrook Institute, San Francisco), Ann Arbor, Mich., University Microfilms, 1986.

81. Van de Castle, *Psychology of Dreaming,* p. 37.

82. Personal communication from Chinese man.

Chapter Three
Growing-Up and Menstrual Dreams

1. Readers who would like to refresh their knowledge of the menstrual process may find relevant information in the references that appear below.

2. Quoted in Paula Weideger, *Menstruation and Menopause* (New York: Dell, 1975), pp. 20–21.

3. Weideger, *Menstruation and Menopause,* p. 21.

4. Lynda Madaras with Area Madaras, *What's Happening to My Body? A Growing Up Guide for Mothers and Daughters* (New York: Newmarket Press, 1983), pp. 44–48.

5. Madaras with Madaras, *What's Happening?,* pp. 56–63.

6. H. N. and M. R. Gould, quoted in Paula Weideger, *History's Mistress: A New Interpretation of a 19th-Century Ethnographic Classic* (Harmondsworth, Eng.: Penguin Books, 1986), p. 105.

7. Krieger, a Berlin medical man quoted in ibid., p. 104. Music, too, was once thought to have an influence on early menstruation. In an experiment in Paris in the nineteenth century, an orchestra was brought to the Paris Zoo to play sweet music for the young female elephants. It was later observed that these elephants reached maturity much sooner than wild elephants. At the time the music was believed to have stimulated their hormonal development. Now researchers believe the difference could be attributed to the fact that zoo elephants eat better and exercise less, thus gaining the critical amount of body fat more rapidly. See Weideger. *Menstruation and Menopause,* p. 20.

8. Weideger, *Menstruation and Menopause,* p. 159.

9. Katharina Dalton, *Once a Month* (Pomona, Calif.: Hunter House, Inc., 1979), p. 69.

10. Quoted in Carolyn Winget and Milton Kramer, *Dimensions of Dreams* (Gaines-

ville, Fla.: University Presses of Florida, 1979), p. 274. See also pp. 266–76 for results of various of Calvin S. Hall and Robert L. Van de Castle findings on menstrual dreams.

11. For Japanese concepts regarding menarche, see Kitteridge Cherry. *Womansword: What Japanese Words Say About Women* (New York: Kodansha International, 1987) pp. 17–19, 109–111.

In the Jewish tradition a young woman also celebrates *a Bat Mitzvah*, in which she chants from the Old Testament, leads part of the service, and gives a speech to family and friends. The parents and guests give their blessings as well as bringing gifts. This ritual—traditionally celebrated at thirteen years of age—is meant to mark a joyful entrance into a new phase of life as a woman. See Lyn Reese, Jean Wilkinson, and Phyllis Sheon Koppelman, *I'm on My Way Running: Women Speak on Coming of Age,* 1983. (New York: Avon Books) Several fascinating accounts of puberty rituals are described.

12. A few years ago there was a doll marketed as "Skipper" who was "Barbie's younger sister." The child playing with this doll could turn a knob and the doll's breasts popped out, supposedly simulating the first menstruation. Playthings of this sort, without additional information, could contribute to a girl's confused notions about puberty.

13. For a discussion of the dream changes in his thirteen-to-fifteen-year-old subjects, see David Foulkes, *Children's Dreams: Longitudinal Studies* (New York: John Wiley & Sons, 1982), pp. 229–31.

14. See Dianne Hales, *The Complete Book of Sleep: How Your Nights Affect Your Days* (Menlo Park, Calif.: Addison-Wesley, 1981), pp. 32, 86, 248. Studies at Stanford University indicate that even when adolescents are permitted to sleep as long as they wish at night, they are frequently still sleepy during the daytime. See Lynne Lamberg, *The American Medical Association Guide to Better Sleep* (New York: Random House, 1984), pp. 25–26.

15. Daydreams seem to reach a peak for adolescents between fourteen and seventeen years old. See Jerome L. Singer, *The Inner World of Daydreaming* (New York: Harper & Row, 1975), pp. 150–151.

16. See Dorothy Corkille Briggs, *Your Child's Self-Esteem* (Garden City, N.Y., Doubleday, 1975), pp. 153–76.

17. Anne C. Petersen, "Those Gangly Years," *Psychology Today* 21, no. 9 (September 1987); 28–34. A recent study by Anne Petersen and her colleagues at Pennsylvania State University suggests that the survival of so many adolescent girls unscathed is remarkable. This study of teenagers over their junior high school years suggests that the majority of teenagers weathered adolescence well. Petersen et al found that approximately 15 percent of the sample were traumatized by their adolescence, getting caught in a downward spiral of trouble, turmoil, and depression—still too many wounded in the transition from childhood to adult.

18. Dalton, *Once a Month,* p. 70.

19. Madaras with Madaras, *What's Happening?,* p. 99.

20. Because the corpus luteum is not formed during anovulatory cycles, progesterone is not produced. The typical premenstrual syndrome does not usually occur in anovulatory cycles. See Allen Lein, *The Cycling Female: Her Menstrual Rhythm* (San Francisco: W. H. Freeman & Co., 1979), pp. 70–71.

21. Technically referred to by the German word *Mittelschmerz,* meaning "middle pain." A slight bloody discharge may accompany mittelschmerz.

22. Dalton, *Once a Month,* p. 59. See also Hilary C. Maddux, *Menstruation* (New Canaan, Conn: Tobey Publishing Co., Inc., 1975), p. 56.

23. In general, the whole first half of the cycle preceding ovulation is called the follicular, proliferative, or estrogenic phase; the second half of the cycle following ovulation is known as the luteal, secretory, or progestational phase.

24. Quoted in Winget and Kramer, *Dimensions of Dreams,* p. 275. In a personal communication with the authors, Robert L. Van de Castle reported finding more color in females' menstrual dreams. In general, women report more color than men in their dreams. See pp. 212–13 in the same volume.

25. Robert L. Van de Castle, *The Psychology of Dreaming* (pamphlet) (New York: General Learning Press, 1971), p. 40.

26. Quoted in Winget and Kramer, *Dimensions of Dreams,* p. 235. In a personal communication to the authors, Robert L. Van de Castle reported that the dreamer was more friendly to female characters during the menstrual period, whereas male characters were more friendly to the dreamer during the preovulatory phases.

27. Ethel Swanson and David Foulkes, "Dream Content and the Menstrual Cycle," *Journal of Nervous and Mental Disease* 145 (1968). 358–63. Also see S. A. Lewis & M. Burns, "Manifest Dream Content: Changes with the Menstrual Cycle," *British Journal of Medical Psychology,* vol. 48, 1975, 375–77. Both teams of researchers report greater sexuality in dreams during menses.

28. Paula Jean Smith-Marder, "A Study of Selected Dream Contents in the Dreams of Adolescent and Mature Women During Menstruation," *Dissertation Abstracts International,* vol. 40, no. 10, 5023-B.

29. Therese Benedek and Boris B. Rubenstein, "The Correlations Between Ovarian Activity and Psychodynamic Process: I. The Ovulative Phase," *Psychosomatic Medicine* 1, no. 2 (April 1939): 245–70; idem, "II. The Menstrual Phase," *Psychosomatic Medicine* 1, no. 4 (October 1939): 461–85. See also idem, "The Sexual Cycle in Women," *Psychosomatic Medical Monographs,* vol. 3, nos. 1 and 2 (Washington, D.C.: National Research Council, 1942); or Therese Benedek, "An Investigation of the Sexual Cycle in Women: Methodologic Considerations," *Archives of General Psychiatry* 8 (1963): 311–22.

30. Robert A. Hicks and Ann Cavanaugh, "Oral Contraceptive Use, Menstrual Cycle Phase and the Need for Sleep." *Sleep Research,* Vol. II, 1982, p. 214.

31. Penelope Shuttle and Peter Redgrove, *The Wise Wound: Eve's Curse and Everywoman* (New York: Richard Marek, 1978), p. 99.

32. See n. 25 above.

33. Lein, *The Cycling Female,* p. 117. The thickening of the vaginal mucus around ovulation is sometimes used as a contraceptive method called the Billings ovulation method, sympto-thermal method, fertility awareness method, mucus-temperature method, or natural family planning. It is a more accurate rhythm method. An Australian neurologist, Dr. John Billings, and his wife, pediatrician Dr. Lynn Billings, noticed the connection between observable phenomena and fertility in the 1950s. By observing her body changes, in particular when the cervical mucus becomes more viscous, her basal body temperature, and the position and texture of her cervix, the woman is able to assess when she is fertile. The woman who wishes to conceive may become pregnant with sexual intercourse at the appropriate time; the woman who does not wish to conceive may prevent conception by abstaining from sexual intercourse or by using barrier methods of contraception at this time.

This method of preventing conception is said to be over 90 percent effective with women who are highly motivated.

34. Ernest Hartmann, *The Biology of Dreaming* (Springfield, Ill.: Charles C. Thomas, 1967), pp. 60–61. See also Patricia L. Garfield, "Keeping a Longitudinal Dream Record," *Psychotherapy: Theory, Research and Practice* 10, no. 3 (Fall 1973) pp. 223–28.

35. Not all researchers find baby imagery at the ovulatory and postovulatory phases. Robert L. Van de Castle reported more babies, children, and mother images during menses; see *The Psychology of Dreaming,* p. 40. Benedek and Rubenstein reported more tranquil dreaming postovulatory compared to preovulatory; see n. 28 above.

36. See n. 27 above.

37. See 30 above.

38. "Nail Growth," *University of California, Berkeley, Wellness Letter,* February 1986, p. 7.

39. Robert L. Van de Castle, "Women's Dreams," speech presented at the annual meeting of the Association for the Study of Dreams in Ottawa, Canada, 1986. My own findings confirm the presence of water images in the premenstrual period.

40. Lennart Nilsson, *Behold Man* (Boston: Little, Brown & Co., 1973), p. 48.

41. Weideger, *Menstruation and Menopause,* p. 85.

42. Ibid. See also Dalton, *Once a Month,* pp. 61–63.

43. Madaras with Madaras, *What's Happening?* p. 145.

44. Some researchers say that as many as 70 percent of women notice at least one emotional, physical or behavioral change in the week or so before menstruation. See Janet Hopson and Anne Rosenfeld, "PMS: Puzzling Monthly Symptoms." *Psychology Today* 18, no. 8 (1984): 30–35.

45. Researchers have invented an electronic sensor for dairy cows that is 90 percent accurate in determining a cow's ovulation. Situated in the vaginal opening, the sensor relays a signal to a computer when the genital tissues begin to retain moisture and swell. The dairy farmers know the cow is fertile then and they can artificially inseminate her successfully. See Katie Tyndall, "Mating Time." *Washington Times, Insight*, September 8, 1986, p. 55. A woman must rely on her own sensations of swelling.

46. Dalton, *Once a Month,* p. 64.

47. Emil Gutheil, *The Handbook of Dream Analysis* (New York: Liveright, 1951), p. 152.

48. Dalton, *Once a Month,* pp. 24–26.

49. Dalton, *Once a Month.* See pp. 131–33 for a discussion of the effect of low blood sugar.

50. Dalton, *Once a Month.*

51. Dalton, *Once a Month,* pp. 164–70; Madaras with Madaras, *What's Happening?,* p. 150; Maddux, *Menstruation,* pp. 117–43.

52. Hartmann, *Biology of Dreaming,* pp. 111–13. Women with the most PMT had the highest dream time during the phase of their symptoms.

53. Dalton, *Once a Month,* p. 64.

54. Quoted in Dean Edell, "Dr. Dean Edell's Medical Journal," *San Francisco Chronicle,* March 4, 1987. The original appeared in the *New England Journal of Medicine.* Another prevalent theory concerns the role of endorphins (morphinelike substances that normally exist in the brain). Some researchers find that endorphin levels in some women's brains

fluctuate dramatically during premenstruation, possibly interfering with the transmission of impulses that maintain emotional balance, according to obstetrician-gynecologist Ziyad Hannan at Saint Mary's Hospital and Medical Center in San Francisco; see Ziyad Hannan, "PMS: What It Is and Why," *Saint Mary's Hospital and Medical Center Health Digest*, April 1986.

55. Hartmann, *Biology of Dreaming,* pp. 111–13.

56. Lamberg, *AMA Guide to Better Sleep,* pp. 243–44.

57. Garfield, "Keeping a Dream Record."

58. Katherine Schultz and David Koulack, "Dream Affect and the Menstrual Cycle," *Journal of Nervous and Mental Disease* 168, no. 7 (1980): 436–38. Schultz and Koulack found no evidence of waking mood change or differential dream recall as a function of their menstrual cycles.

However, David Cohen found the greatest percentage of reports of having dreamed without being able to remember the content (contentless dreams) and the smallest percentage of dreamless sleep prior to menses. David B. Cohen, "Failure to Recall Dream Content: Contentless vs. Dreamless Reports," *Perceptual Motor Skills* 34 (1972): 1,000–02.

Judith Baron had eighteen women keep dream and menstrual diaries over two complete cycles, as well as answer a questionnaire on their dreams and their subjective moods. The number of dream reports was greater in the premenstrual than in the preovulatory phase. Maternal dream themes were more likely to occur in the half of the cycle postovulation. Judith E. Baron, "Effects of the Menstrual Cycle on Manifest Content and Affect in Dream Reports," *Dissertation Abstracts International* 36, no. 10 (1974): 5,223-B.

M. A. Ho examined seventeen sleep parameters and found significant changes only in stages 3 and 4. M. A. Ho, "Sex Hormones and the Sleep of Women," *Dissertation Abstracts International* 33 (1972): 1,305-B.

In general, the data on dreams, sleep, and the menstrual cycle are inconsistent.

59. Adele Fekete-Mackintosh, "Dream Content and the Menstrual Cycle in Ovulatory and Anovulatory Cycles." *Dissertation Abstracts International* 40, no. 7 (1979): 3,465-B.

60. Van de Castle, The *Psychology of Dreaming*, p. 40.

61. Working with 135 college women, and making allowances for similar life pattern, stress periods, and commonly eaten foods, McClintock found it took about three to four months for synchrony of menses to become established in women living together. The cause of this synchrony is thought to be based on subtle body odors called pheromones. Martha K. McClintock, "Menstrual Synchrony and Suppression," *Nature* 229 (January 22, 1971): 244–45. See also Shuttle and Redgrove, *The Wise Wound*, pp. 193–94; and Terence Monmaney with Susan Katz, "The Chemistry Between People." *Newsweek,* January 12, 1987. This reference describes the studies of George Preti and Winnifred B. Cutler.

A woman's sense of smell is keenest during ovulation and least keen at menses. Boyd Gibbons, "The Intimate Sense of Smell," *National Geographic* 170, no. 3 (September 1986): 333. Women's olfactory sensitivity is reduced during pregnancy, but, in general, women have a more acute sense of smell than men. See Avery N. Gilbert and Charles J. Wysocki, "The Smell Survey Results," *National Geographic* 172, no. 4 (October 1987) pp. 514–25.

62. Margaret Henderson, "Evidence for Hormonally Related Male Temperature Cycle and Synchrony With the Female Cycle," *Australian and New Zealand Journal of Medicine* 6 (1976): 254.

63. See n. 28 above.

64. Gutheil, *Handbook of Dream Analysis,* p. 71.

65. See n. 39 above. See also K. Cherry, *Womansword,* pp. 26–27.

66. See n. 39 above.

67. See n. 25 above.

68. See n. 27 above.

69. See n. 29 above.

70. Emily Martin, *The Woman in the Body: A Cultural Analysis of Reproduction* (Boston: Beacon Press, 1987), pp. 128–30.

71. Reported by Miriam Van Waters and described in Shuttle and Redgrove, *The Wise Wound,* p. 102. For original, see Miriam Van Waters, "The Adolescent Girl Among Primitive Peoples," *Journal of Religious Psychology* 6, no. 4 (1913): 375–421; and idem, vol. 7, no. 1 (1914): 32–40, 75–120.

72. Reported by Van Waters and described in Shuttle and Redgrove, *The Wise Wound,* p. 98. See n. 67 above.

73. A dissertation by Michelle Dugan at the University of Missouri at Kansas City, described in "Personal Mental Health Affects Menstrual Tension, Missouri Research Shows," *American Psychological Association Monitor,* January 1982. Many athletes are able to perform outstandingly during their periods.

74. Bruno Bettelheim, *The Uses of Enchantment: The Meaning and Importance of Fairy Tales* (New York: Alfred A. Knopf, 1976), pp. 225–36. Bettelheim compares the circular staircase Sleeping Beauty climbs to sexual experience, turning the key in the lock to sexual intercourse, the small locked room to the female sexual organs, and the distaff that pricks her to the phallus.

75. See n. 31 above.

76. See n. 28 above.

77. See n. 27 above.

78. See n. 25 above.

79. See n. 31 above.

Chapter Four
Love and Sex Dreams

1. Described in Mary Jane Moffat & Charlotte Painter, *Revelations: Diaries of Women,* (New York: Vintage, 1974), p. 39.

2. *Incubus* is a word that comes from medieval Latin and refers to a demon that was supposed to cause nightmares. This evil spirit or demon was believed to lie upon sleeping persons, especially women, with whom it sought sexual intercourse. The corresponding figure for men was called a succubus, a female demon thought to have intercourse with sleeping men.

3. For instance, the captain of *The Flying Dutchman,* who lures Senta to her death. See M. Esther Harding, *The Way of All Women: A Psychological Interpretation* (London: Longmans, Green & Co., 1933), pp. 41–77.

4. Harding, *Way of All Women,* pp. 64–72.

5. C. Fisher, J. Gross, and J. Zuch, "Cycle of Penile Erection Synchronous With Dreaming (REM) Sleep," *Archives of General Psychiatry* 12 (1965): 29–45.

6. I. Karacan, A. Rosenbloom, and R. Williams, "The Clitoral Erection Cycle During Sleep," presented at the meeting of Association for the Psychophysiological Study of Sleep, Santa Fe, N.M., 1970.

7. U. Jovanovic. Described in Charles Fisher, H. D. Cohen, R. C. Schiavi, D. Davis, Barbara Furman, K. Ward, A. Edwards & J. Cunningham, 1983. "Patterns of Female Sexual Arousal During Sleep and Waking: Vaginal Thermo-Conductance Studies, *Archives of Sexual Behavior,* 12, no. 2 (1983): 98.

8. *Photo* derives from the Greek word for "light"; *plethys* derives from a Greek word meaning "a condition of being full of blood"; *graph* is from the Greek word meaning "to write." Thus the word *photoplethysmograph* represents a recording (writing), made by means of light, measuring fullness of blood. This instrument was first developed and used to measure differences in female arousal state during erotic versus nonerotic films. Subjective ratings did not always correlate with physiological measures. See James H. Geer, Patricia Morokoff, and Pamela Greenwood, "Sexual Arousal in Women: The Development of a Measurement Device for Vaginal Blood Volume," *Archives of Sexual Behavior* 3, no. 6 (1974): 559–64.

9. Lorna Tener and Carlyle Smith, "Vaginal Blood Volume Changes During Sleep," *Sleep Research* 6 (1977): 57. The team is from Trent University, Peterborough, Ontario.

10. Fisher, et al., "Patterns of Female Sexual Arousal," pp. 97–122. See reference note 6.

11. Recent work suggests that arousability is not at peak during this phase; arousability during ovulation is less than during postmenstrual and midluteal phases. Fisher et al., "Patterns of Female Sexual Arousal," p. 117.

12. In the non-REM periods there was a mean of 4.2 vaginal blood-flow rises, or 16 percent of the total non-REM time of 307 minutes. Individual vaginal blood-flow increases lasted an average of 13.7 in non-REM. The combined value of the total time of vaginal blood-flow rises in REM (31 minutes) with the total time of vaginal blood-flow rises in non-REM (51 minutes) equals 82 minutes. This comes close to being equivalent to the total time for nocturnal penile tumescence and REM (87 minutes, in Karacan, Rosenbloom, and Williams). Thus duration of VBF rises is roughly equal to the duration of REM erections, but there is a different distribution. See Fisher et al., "Patterns of Female Sexual Arousal," pp. 106–107.

13. Fisher et al., "Patterns of Female Sexual Arousal," pp. 106, 110, 115. In 51 percent of the REM cases, the VBF rise was between 10 and 19 mm; 37 percent were between 20 and 29 mm; 7 percent between 30 and 39 mm; and 4 percent between 40 and 45 mm.

14. Results showed that women were more aroused during an erotic film and in a private fantasy period than when they were simply resting. During sleep, the University of Virginia Medical Center researchers found higher vaginal-pressure pulse during REM than in other sleep stages. See Gary S. Rogers, Robert L. Van de Castle, and William S. Evans, "Assessment of Vaginal Responses During Waking and Sleeping Conditions," *Sleep Research* 11 (1982): 38.

15. About 50 percent of the awakenings after vaginal blood-flow rises were associated with overtly sexual dreams; more than 80 percent were associated with symbolic sexual content. Awakenings from REM that do not follow vaginal blood-flow rises yield only 15 percent of dreams that are manifestly sexual. The researchers conclude that there is a

reciprocal interaction between psychic content and the REM sexual excitation in both men and women. See Fisher, "Patterns of Female Sexual Arousal," p. 116.

16. Suggested by June M. Reinisch, "Kinsey Report," *San Francisco Chronicle,* September 30, 1986.

17. Stephen LaBerge, Walter Greenleaf, and Beverly Kedzierski, "Physiological Responses to Dreamed Sexual Activity During Lucid Dream Sleep," *Psychophysiology* 20 (1983): 454–55. See also Stephen LaBerge, *Lucid Dreaming* (Los Angeles: Jeremy P. Tarcher, Inc., 1985), pp. 82–87.

18. Ernest Hartmann, *The Biology of Dreaming* (Springfield, Ill.: Charles C. Thomas, 1967), p. 130.

19. Dianne Hales, *The Complete Book of Sleep: How Your Nights Affect Your Days.* (Menlo Park, Calif.: Addison-Wesley, 1981), pp. 88–89.

20. For a clear description of sexual dream symbols, see Emil Gutheil, *The Handbook of Dream Analysis* (New York: Liveright, 1951), pp. 136–56.

21. Act 2, scene 3, Agrippa to Enobarbus. Howard Staunton, ed. *The Complete Illustrated Shakespeare* (New York: Park Lane, 1979), p. 543. There may be an additional word play on Caesar's "sword," meaning the penis, being "put to bed," that is, into Cleopatra.

22. In the Greek culture, "to dream of a dog is to dream of a friend," according to a Greek woman who described her culture's views about dream symbols. Dogs were believed, in ancient Greece, to help heal an injured person, so their appearance in dreams was regarded as highly favorable. Jung espoused this same notion.

23. Patricia L. Garfield, "Nightmares in the Sexually Abused Female Teenager," *Psychiatric Journal of the University of Ottawa* 12, no. 2 (1987): 93–97.

24. Bubba Nicholson, a graduate student at the State University of New York at Syracuse, reported this in the *British Journal of Dermatology.* Described in *Omni,* April 1987, p. 36.

25. F. Barnard Hollinger, ed., *Outside the Magic Circle: The Autobiography of Virginia Foster Durr* (Tuscaloosa, Ala.: University of Alabama Press, 1987).

26. Robert Burns, "A Red, Red Rose."

27. Some 9 percent of Kinsey's sample had lived into their late forties without reaching orgasm. Alfred C. Kinsey et al., *Sexual Behavior in the Human Female* (Philadelphia: W. B. Saunders Co., 1953), p. 542.

28. Abraham Maslow, "Self-esteem (Dominance-Feeling) and Sexuality in Women," in M. F. DeMartino, ed., *Sexual Behavior and Personality Characteristics* (New York: Grove Press, 1963). Maslow says that open sexual dreams are characteristic of women who are self-assured, poised, independent, and generally capable. Women with low self-esteem usually have romantic, symbolic, anxious, or distorted sexual dreams.

29. Joseph Adelson, "Creativity and the Dream," *Merrill Palmer Quarterly* 6 (1960): 92–97.

Chapter Five
Wedding Dreams

1. In some cultures in olden times, the bride was literally "displayed" in a special showcase.

2. Divorce figures vary for different age brackets. A study released by U.S. Census Bureau experts Arthur Norton and Jeanne Moorman found that the national divorce rate for all women ages twenty to fifty-four who had married is 26.8 percent. Described in the *San Francisco Chronicle,* April 23, 1986.

3. According to the Department of Health and Human Services, National Center for Health Statistics, the divorce rate in 1984 was about 4.9 per 1,000 population, whereas the marriage rate was 10.5 per 1,000. Quoted in Otto T. Johnson, ed. *The 1986 Information Please Almanac* (Boston: Houghton Mifflin Co., 1985), p. 743. A total of 273,000 couples divorced during the first quarter of 1986. The divorce rate was 4.6 per 1,000. During the twelve months ending with March 1986, an estimated 1,183,000 couples divorced. The divorce rate was 5.0 per 1,000. From the same source, quoted in Mark S. Hoffman, ed., *The World Almanac and Book of Facts: 1987* (New York: World Almanac, 1986), p. 769. Currently 5–6 percent of all people over sixty-five have never married, says the Census Bureau. Quoted in *Washington Times, Insight* magazine, October 5, 1987.

4. Emil A. Gutheil, *The Handbook of Dream Analysis* (New York: Liveright, 1951), p. 306.

5. William Shakespeare, *The Taming of the Shrew,* in Howard Staunton, ed., *The Complete Illustrated Shakespeare* (New York: Park Lane, 1979), p. 250. In act 3, scene 2, the wedding day, the servant Biondello says to Baptista, the father of Katharina,

Why, Petruchio is coming, in a new hat and an old jerkin; a pair of old breeches, thrice turned; a pair of boots that have been candle-cases, one buckled, another laced; an old rusty sword ta'en out of the town armoury, with a broken hilt, and chapeless; with two broken points [laces that fasten the outer dress] . . .

6. Michael Robertson, "Love Is a Family Affair," *San Francisco Chronicle,* August 19, 1987.

7. Carl G. Jung, *Psychology and Alchemy* (Princeton: Princeton University Press, 1953), pp. 37, 323, 402, 413, 436, 463. This is called the *nuptiae chymicae,* the "chymical wedding," or the *coniunctio* of alchemy. See also C. G. Jung, *Symbols of Transformation* (Princeton: Princeton University Press, 1956), p. 223.

Chapter Six
Pregnancy and Childbirth Dreams

1. Ernest Hartmann, *The Biology of Dreaming* (Springfield, Ill.: Charles C. Thomas, 1967), p. 61.

2. Julius Segal and Gay Gaer Luce, *Sleep* (New York: Arena Books, 1972), p. 177–79. When researchers Gunnar Heuser and George Ling at the Brain Research Institute at UCLA injected cats with progesterone, the cats had unusually plentiful episodes of REM.

3. E. Hartmann, *The Functions of Sleep* (New Haven: Yale University Press, 1973), p. 75.

4. Ismet Karacan et al., "Some Implications of the Sleep Patterns of Pregnancy for Postpartum Emotional Disturbances," *British Journal of Psychiatry* 115 (1969): 929–35. A total of thirteen subjects were studied for eighty-five nights at the University of Florida;

ten were followed through their late pregnancy and postpartum; three were studied during their entire pregnancy and postpartum. Comparing these subjects with a group of nonpregnant women, it was found that the pregnant women had a greater number of awakenings. The frequency of awakenings began to increase at the end of the second trimester.

The three subjects who were studied from early conception changed the amount they sleep during their pregnancy: they had their greatest total sleep time in the first trimester, it decreased in the second trimester, and fell below normal in the third trimester. Their amount of deep sleep (stage 4) also decreased in the third trimester, but it increased during postpartum to the point where it was more even than what nonpregnant women had.

Amount of REM also changed during pregnancy. This research team found a slight increase in the number of REM periods in the second trimester; at the end of the second trimester REM decreased and continued decreasing during the third trimester. Overall, these three subjects had less REM than nonpregnant women.

However, the investigators mention their study of a young woman whose ovaries had been removed; her REM was increased when estrogen was administered and her stage 4 (deep sleep) was suppressed with progesterone.

5. Hartmann, *Functions of Sleep,* p. 147. In fact, extra dreaming may help consolidate the new learning.

6. Described in Segal and Luce, *Sleep,* p. 177.

7. The number of tusks and details of the dream vary according to the narrator of the account. For a version by Sir Edwin Arnold, see Carl G. Jung, *Symbols of Transformation* (Princeton: Princeton University Press, 1956), p. 320. For an illustration of Maya's dream, see David Coxhead and Susan Hiller, *Dreams: Visions of the Night* (New York: Avon, 1975), plate 37. Jung tells us that, according to a medieval tradition, Mary's conception of Jesus took place through her ear.

8. Adam Bittleston, "Introduction" to Alexander Carmichael, *The Sun Dances: Prayers and Blessings From the Gaelic* (Edinburgh: Floris Books, 1960), p. xviii.

9. J. Kevin Thompson, "Larger Than Life," *Psychology Today* 20, no. 4 (April 1986): 38–44.

10. Thomas F. Cash, Barbara A. Winstead, and Louis H. Janda, "The Great American Shape-up," *Psychology Today* 20, no. 4 (April 1986): 30–37.

11. Patricia Maybruck, "An Exploratory Study of the Dreams of Pregnant Women," Ph.D. diss., Saybrook University, San Francisco, 1986. For architectural symbols, see pp. 68–72.

12. Maybruck, "Dreams of Pregnant Women," p. 68.

13. Ibid., p. 70.

14. Patricia Monaghan, *The Book of Goddesses and Heroines* (New York: E. P. Dutton, 1981), p. 60.

15. Maybruck, personal communication, 1987.

16. Robert Van de Castle, "Phases of Women's Dreams," paper presented to the Association for the Study of Dreams. Ottawa, Canada, June 1986.

17. Maybruck, "Dreams of Pregnant Women," p. 102.

18. Kendall Bradley Wood, "The Weird Dreams of Mothers-to-be: Psychologists Explain the Hidden Meanings," *Working Mother,* March 1987, p. 56. Wood describes the work of Alan Siegel on the dreams to expectant fathers.

19. Robert L. Van de Castle, *The Psychology of Dreaming* (pamphlet) (New York: General Learning Corp., 1971), p. 38.

20. Maybruck, "Dreams of Pregnant Women," p. 67. Although Maybruck reports a figure of 18 percent in her dissertation, this percentage includes small children. With the children excluded, Maybruck (personal communication) tells me that 17 percent of her subjects dreamed of animals.

21. Bruno Bettelheim, *The Uses of Enchantment: The Meaning and Importance of Fairy Tales* (New York: Alfred A. Knopf, 1976), pp. 75–76.

22. Maybruck, "Dreams of Pregnant Women," pp. 67–68, 136.

23. Kitteridge Cherry, *Womansword: What Japanese Words Say About Women,* (New York: Kodansha International, 1987), pp. 82–83.

24. Apparently Ephron was seven months pregnant with her second child when she discovered that like her heroine, Rachel, her husband was having an affair. Ephron's book was made into a movie, also called *Heartburn,* starring Meryl Streep and Jack Nicholson. See Ruthe Stein and Sylvia Rubin, "The Heartburn Syndrome," *San Francisco Chronicle,* July 25, 1986, p. 31.

25. Maybruck, "Dreams of Pregnant Women," p. 59. The presence of the pregnant woman's husband in 24 percent of her dreams exceeds that of the appearance of her mother, with a rate of 14 percent. The pregnant woman's father appeared in only 7 percent of her dreams.

26. According to Eileen Stukane, *The Dream Worlds of Pregnancy* (New York: Quill, 1985), p. 81. Among Maybruck's pregnant subjects, mothers appeared in dreams at twice the rate (14 percent) fathers did (7 percent).

27. Maybruck, "Dreams of Pregnant Women," p. 59.

28. Described in K. B. Wood, "Weird Dreams of Mothers-to-be," p. 56. See also Stukane, *Dream Worlds of Pregnancy,* pp. 32–37, 100–102.

29. Robert D. Gillman, "The Dreams of Pregnant Women and Material Adaptation," *American Journal of Orthopsychiatry* 36 (July 1968): 688–92.

30. Maybruck, "Dreams of Pregnant Women," p. 119.

31. Ibid., p. 96. Babies appeared in 15.5 percent of the total dreams of Maybruck's subjects.

32. R. Gillman, "The Dreams of Pregnant Women."

33. Maybruck, "Dreams of Pregnant Women," p. 113.

34. Ibid., pp. 96–98.

35. Arthur Colman and Libby Colman, *Earth Father/Sky Father: The Changing Concept of Fathering* (Englewood Cliffs, N.J.: Prentice-Hall, 1981), p. 5.

36. Monaghan, *Book of Goddesses,* p. 95. The festival of rebirth, Easter, and the word *estrus,* meaning to be in sexual heat, both reflect the same origin. Eostre's associated symbols were the hare and the egg. According to Brewer, the Teutonic goddess of dawn, called Eostre (or Eastre) had a festival held at the vernal equinox. From ancient times the egg has been a symbol of fertility and renewal of life. See Ivor H. Evans, *Brewer's Dictionary of Phrase and Fable* (New York: Harper & Row, 1981), p. 375–76.

37. The Boston Women's Health Book Collective, Inc., *Our Bodies, Ourselves: A book by and for Women* (New York: Simon & Schuster, 1976), p. 265.

38. Karacan et al., "Uterine Activity During Sleep," *Sleep* 9, no. 3 (1986): 393–97. The ten subjects, aged twenty-two to thirty-one, had continuous all-night measurements

(polysomnograms), including EEG, eye movements, muscle tension, heart rate, breathing, bulbocavernosus muscle activity, clitoral and vaginal photoplethysmograph and uterine activity. The latter was measured using a MicroTip pressure transducer; each uterine contraction was counted. Measurements were all taken on two nights within the first four nights following cessation of menstrual bleeding (start of follicular phase).

The uterus exhibited periodic and rhythmic contractions occurring one to three times each minute. Number of contractions per hour were greater during REM (average 136.75) than during any other sleep stage and greater than in the waking state (average 127.36). There were fewest contractions per hour during slow-wave sleep (average 117.97).

There is a clear relationship between sleep stages and uterine contractility. Previous studies have shown a biological rhythm of uterine resting pressures and contractions over a twenty-four-hour period. These are generally least frequent during dark. However, this study shows that the uterus is active during sleep, especially during REM. The number of contractions change during the menstrual cycle.

39. Maybruck, personal communication. See also n. 18 above.

40. Maybruck, "Dreams of Pregnant Women," p. 113. The effect of self-assertiveness is discussed on pp. 106–115.

41. Carolyn Winget and Frederic T. Kapp, "The Relationship of the Manifest Content of Dreams to Duration of Childbirth in Primiparae," *Psychosomatic Medicine* 34 (1972): 313–20.

42. Pierre Étévenon, personal communication. Paul Tholey's work suggests that the preferred mode of interaction with threatening dream figures may be dialogue. He urges the dreamer to ask, "Who am I?" to hostile characters. Quoted by Jayne Gackenbach-Snyder in a talk at Dreamhouse in San Francisco, on December 8, 1987.

43. Described in Thomas Verny with John Kelly, *The Secret Life of the Unborn Child*, (New York: Delta, 1981), pp. 41–42.

44. Described in Mary Jane Moffat & Charlotte Painter, editors, *Revelations: Diaries of Women*, (New York: Vintage, 1974), p. 239. Kollwitz recorded this dream in April, 1910.

45. C. G. Jung, *Psychology and Alchemy* (Princeton, N.J.: Princeton University Press, 1968), p. 166.

46. M. Esther Harding, *Psychic Energy* (New York: Bollingen Foundation, 1963), p. 448.

Chapter Seven
Career Dreams

1. Described in Michael Robertson, "Shhhhh! No Tension, Please: Are Librarians Really the Least Stressed-Out?" *San Francisco Chronicle*, July 10, 1986, p. 23. Beauticians ranked 3.5, astronomers 3.4, and museum workers 2.8.

2. Diane Wolkstein, Introduction to Diane Wolkstein and Samuel N. Kramer, *Inanna, Queen of Heaven and Earth: Her Stories and Hymns From Sumer* (New York: Harper & Row, 1983), p. xviii.

3. Sorting grains (similar to Wolkstein's cleaning blades of grass) is a characteristic task females must accomplish in mythology and fairy tales. It is said to represent the

woman's need to become clear about her positive and negative reactions, in order to become conscious. See Marie-Louise von Franz, *Problems of the Feminine in Fairytales* (Zurich: Spring Publications, 1974), p. 156–57.

4. D. Wolkstein & S.N. Kramer, *Inanna, Queen of Heaven and Earth: Her Stories and Hymns from Sumer*, (New York: Harper & Row, 1983).

5. Kitteridge Cherry, *Womansword: What Japanese Words Say About Women* (New York: Kodansha International, 1987), pp. 105–106.

6. Betty Allen-Trembly, San Francisco, personal communication, 1987.

7. Sally O'Neil, "Choosing Children Over Careers: More Professional Women Take Time Out," *San Francisco Chronicle,* July 19, 1987, p. D-1. In 1976 only 28 percent of mothers over thirty years who had had a child within the previous twelve months were in the labor force; in 1984 the figure was 52 percent. See Mark S. Hoffman, ed., *The World Almanac and Book of Facts: 1987* (New York: Pharos Books, 1987), p. 217. For predictive figures, see John Wall, "New Roles for Women," *Washington Times, Insight,* February 3, 1986.

8. Monique Lortie-Lussier, Christine Schwab, and Joseph De Koninck, "Working Mothers Versus Homemakers: Do Dreams Reflect the Changing Roles of Women?" *Sex Roles* 12 (1985): 1,009–21.

9. Monique Lortie-Lussier, Natalie Rinfret, Christine Schwab, and Joseph De Koninck, "Social Role Impact on the Dreams of Working Mothers and Female Students," *Association for the Study of Dreams Newsletter* 3, no. 2 (June 1986): 7.

10. Calvin S. Hall and Vernon J. Nordby, *The Individual and His Dreams* (New York: New American Library, 1972), p. 45.

11. Calvin S. Hall and Bill Domhoff, "The Difference Between Men and Women Dreamers," in Ralph L. Woods and Herbert B. Greenhouse, eds., *The New World of Dreams* (New York: Macmillan, 1974), pp. 13–16. On average, women have more dream characters than men do.

12. Robert Louis Stevenson, *Memories and Portraits, Random Memories, Memories of Himself* (New York: Scribner, 1925). At first Stevenson describes his experience in the third person, not revealing until later in the chapter on dreams that he is the dreamer.

13. George Eliot, "How I Came to Write Fiction," appendix to *Scenes of Clerical Life* (Harmondsworth, Eng.: Penguin, 1985), pp. 428–31. Her description from her diary was dated December 6, 1857.

14. Mary Wollstonecraft Shelley, Introduction to *Frankenstein: Or the Modern Prometheus* (New York: New American Library, 1965). Her description was written in 1817.

Chapter Eight
Divorce Dreams

1. L. M. Boyd, "The Grab Bag," *San Francisco Chronicle,* September 29, 1985. Two out of five homicides in the United States involve wives killing their husbands or husbands killing their wives.

2. Described in Mary Jane Moffat & Charlotte Painter, editors, *Revelations: Diaries of Women* (New York: Vintage, 1974) p. 83. Sand's entry was recorded in November, 1834.

3. Jeanette Lauer and Robert Lauer, "Marriages Made to Last," *Psychology Today* 19, no. 6 (1985): 22–26. Viewing the marriage as a long-term commitment or sacred is next most important.

4. Women who have an obstruction in their breathing apparatus or a lung condition may have such dreams. With sexually abused women, these dreams may replay a sensation experienced during the molestation. See Patricia L. Garfield, "Nightmares in the Sexually Abused Female Teenager," *Psychiatric Journal of the University of Ottawa* 12, no. 2 (1987) 93–97.

5. Thomas Holmes and Richard Rahe, The Life Change Scale, also called the Social Readjustment Rating Scale. This scale appears in several publications. See, for instance, Patricia L. Garfield, *Your Child's Dreams* (New York: Ballantine, 1984), p. 415.

Holmes and Rahe rate "death of a spouse" as 100 points, out of a maximum of 100. They rate "divorce" as 73, and marital separation from mate as 65. Holmes says that the more change you have, the more likely you are to fall sick. Of people with a score of 300 or more in the previous year, almost 80 percent got sick soon after. The higher your score, the harder you must work to stay well.

6. Dianne Hales, *The Complete Book of Sleep: How Your Nights Affect Your Days* (Menlo Park, Calif.: Addison-Wesley, 1981), p. 84.

7. Ibid., p. 85.

8. Ibid., p. 84.

9. Rosalind Cartwright, "Affect and Dream Work From an Information Processing Point of View," *The Journal of Mind and Behavior* 7, nos. 2 and 3 (Spring and Summer 1986): 411–27.

10. See Katie Tyndall, "Divorce and Illness," *Washington Times, Insight*, June 30, 1986, p. 53. Tyndall describes the work of Ohio University researchers Janice Kiecoft-Glaser & Ronald Glaser.

11. A total of 273,000 couples divorced during the first quarter of 1986. This was a divorce rate of 4.6 per 1,000 people. During the twelve months ending March 1986, an estimated 1,183,000 couples divorced. This divorce rate was 5.0 per 1,000 people. Mark S. Hoffman, ed., *The World Almanac and Book of Facts: 1987* (New York: World Almanac, 1986), p. 769.

The Department of Health and Human Services, National Center for Health Statistics reports that the divorce rate in 1984 was 4.9 per 1,000 compared with a marriage rate of 10.5 per 1,000. Otto T. Johnson, ed., *The 1986 Information Please Almanac* (Boston: Houghton Mifflin Co., 1985), p. 743.

The average duration of a marriage in the United States is said to be 9.4 years. Lauer and Lauer, "Marriages Made to Last," p. 22.

12. Mel Krantzler, *Creative Divorce: A New Opportunity for Personal Growth* (New York: M. Evans & Co., 1974); idem, *Learning to Love Again* (New York: Bantam Books, 1977); Marilyn Jensen, *Formerly Married: Learning to Live With Yourself* (New York: Jove, 1984).

Chapter Nine
Parenting Dreams

1. Calvin S. Hall, *The Meaning of Dreams* (New York: Harper & Brothers, 1953), pp. 28–29.

2. Delia Ephron, *Funny Sauce: Us, the Ex, the Ex's New Mate, the New Mate's Ex and the Kids* (New York: Viking, 1986), p. 28.

3. Hall, *The Meaning of Dreams,* pp. 61–62. Men in general are more likely to use physical rather than verbal aggression in their dreams. Overall, men have more aggression in their dreams.

4. D. Ephron, *Funny Sauce,* preface.

5. Ibid., p. 31.

6. This incident was described originally in Patricia L. Garfield, *Your Child's Dreams* (New York: Ballantine, 1984), pp. 22–23.

7. C. G. Jung, *Psychology and Alchemy* (Princeton, N.J.: Princeton University Press, 1977), pp. 157, 190. Jung associates dreams of children with the Cabiri, creative dwarf-gods who are kinsmen of the unconscious, giving protection in the journey into darkness and uncertainty.

Chapter Ten
Menopausal Dreams

1. As women live longer in China, the years seventy-three and eighty-two receive similar attention. Each of these numbers is considered to be a year that, if reached, ensures the person longevity for several years to come. They mark hurdles overcome successfully.

In China, people are proud of their age. If you do not ask them, they will volunteer it. Daughters and sons who harm or neglect their elderly parents are severely criticized, sometimes even legally punished. The elders are thought to deserve help and care; they are respected for having earned their experience. This is not to say that women are especially honored in China. The birth of a girl is considered a "small happiness" in comparison with the birth of a boy, which is a "big happiness." (Personal communications from Chinese women.)

2. In the Faery tradition of Witchcraft, too, postmenopausal women are said to have a special title and function. They are identified with the Great Goddess in her aspect as waning moon. Called the Crone (as distinct from the Maiden and the Mother), such a woman is thought to represent the power of fulfilling beginnings, of ending, of losing, of completing a project, of letting go, of destroying what is stagnant, of dying. She embodies wisdom and the ability to see into the future. She is an essential part of the cycle; without her, life—or any undertaking—is incomplete. Because of these beliefs, the older woman is valued and respected. See Starhawk (Miriam Simos), *The Spiral Dance: A Rebirth of the Ancient Religion of the Great Goddess* (San Francisco: Harper & Row, 1979), pp. 78–80.

3. Life-expectancy figures vary, according to authority. The 1988 Almanac lists life expectancy for white females in 1900–1902 as 51.08 years; for all other females, the comparable figure was 35.04; for white males the life expectancy was 48.23; for all other males, 32.54. Otto Johnson, ed., *The 1988 Information Please Almanac* (Boston: Houghton Mifflin Co., 1987), p. 796.

4. Ibid., p. 797. The original source for these figures is the Department of Health and Human Services, National Center for Health Statistics. The comparable figure for white males is 71.8 years; for all other females, it is 75.0; for all other males, it is 67.4.

5. Ibid.

6. Patricia L. Garfield, *Your Child's Dreams* (New York: Ballantine, 1984), pp. 243–45.

7. Age of menopause varies from country to country, as well as between individuals. According to physician Katharina Dalton, the average age of menopause in the United States is fifty-two years, whereas in Britain it is forty-eight. Katharina Dalton, *Once a Month* (Pomona, Calif.: Hunter House, 1979), p. 154.

A cross-cultural comparison of the reported ages of menopause, published in 1935, varied from thirty years for Turkish women to fifty or even sixty for some American Indian women. Described in Paula Weideger, *History's Mistress: A New Interpretation of a 19th-Century Ethnographic Classic* (Harmondsworth, Eng.: Penguin, 1986), pp. 249–50. The most frequently cited average age of menopause in the United States is fifty years.

8. Winnifred B. Cutler, Celso-Ramon Garcia, and David A. Edwards, *Menopause: A Guide for Women and the Men Who Love Them* (New York: Norton, 1983), pp. 51–52.

9. The length of time from a young woman's first menstrual period until she is fully fertile is also approximately seven years. Cutler, Garcia, and Edwards, *Menopause,* pp. 47, 55.

10. Ibid., p. 47.

11. Lynne Lamberg, *The American Medical Association Guide to Better Sleep* (New York: Random House, 1984), p. 246.

12. In addition to hot flashes, night sweats, and vaginal dryness, other menopausal symptoms that have been reported include: tiredness, nervousness, excessive sweating, headaches, sleeplessness, depression, irritability, joint pains, dizziness, palpitations, lassitude, pins and needles, muscle pains, breathlessness, impatience. See Louisa Rose, "What Is Menopause?" in Louisa Rose, ed., *The Menopause Book* (New York: Hawthorn Books, 1977), p. 13.

13. G. W. Molnar, "Body Temperatures During Menopausal Hot Flashes," *Journal of Applied Physiology* 38 (1975): 499–503. Some authorities cite up to an eight-degree temperature rise on the skin, while the internal temperature actually falls. Feminists prefer to call menopausal symptoms "signs," feeling that the word *symptom* suggests disease, whereas menopause is a natural process. Some 47–87 percent of women of menopausal age report hot flashes, surveys say. See Paula B. Doress, and Diana L. Siegal, and the Midlife and Older Women Book Project, *Ourselves, Growing Older* (New York: Simon & Schuster, 1987.) pp. 121–23.

14. Described in Cutler, Garcia, and Edwards, *Menopause,* p. 59.

15. Ibid.

Strangely enough, most Japanese women are thought not to experience hot flashes; there is no word for this phenomenon in the language. Has this gone unidentified or is there some ingredient in the Japanese diet that contains natural estrogen? See Kitteridge Cherry, *Womansword: What Japanese Words Say About Women* (New York: Kodansha International, 1987) p. 126.

16. Quoted in Rose, "What Is Menopause?" p. 6.

17. Aldo Carotenuto, *The Spiral Way: A Woman's Healing Journey* (Toronto: Inner City Books, 1979), p. 11. Carotenuto gives an interesting account of his treatment, in the Jungian tradition, of a woman who was fifty years old at the outset of her treatment. He describes thirty-six of her dreams over a five-year treatment, but tells little of her menopausal process, other than mentioning a deep depression.

18. Lamberg, *AMA Guide to Better Sleep,* p. 246.

19. Joan Thomson and Ian Oswald, "Effect of Oestrogen on the Sleep, Mood and Anxiety of Menopausal Women," *British Medical Journal* 2 (1977): 317–19.

20. Joan Thomson et al., "Relationship Between Nocturnal Plasma Oestrogen Concentration and Free Plasma Tryptophan in Postmenopausal Women," *Journal of Endocrinology* 72 (1977): 395–96. Also see n. 19 above.

21. Ann Mankowitz, *Change of Life: A Psychological Study of Dreams and the Menopause* (Toronto: Inner City Books, 1984).

22. Ibid., p. 34.

23. Marie-Louise von Franz, "The Process of Individuation," in C. G. Jung, ed., and after his death, M.-L. von Franz, ed., *Man and His Symbols* (London: Aldus Books, 1964), p. 215.

24. C. G. Jung, *Modern Man in Search of a Soul* (New York: Harcourt, Brace & Co., 1933), pp. 120–25. Jung says that for a woman there is a significant change in the human psyche that appears sometime between thirty-five and forty years old; for men, he thinks this change appears later, about age forty.

25. Von Franz, "Process of Individuation," p. 196.

26. Patricia L. Garfield, "Dreamstones," *Dreamworks* 3, no. 2 (1983), p. 120.

27. Patricia L. Garfield, *Pathway to Ecstasy: The Way of the Dream Mandala* (New York: Holt, Rinehart & Winston, 1979).

28. C. G. Jung, *Symbols of Transformation* (Princeton: Princeton University Press, 1956), p. 125.

29. Von Franz, "Process of Individuation," pp. 208–10.

30. Sheila Moon, *Dreams of a Woman: An Analyst's Inner Journey* (Boston: Sigo Press, 1983), p. 107.

31. William A. Jenks, "Auschwitz," *World Book* vol. 1 (Chicago: Field Enterprises, 1968), p. 868.

32. Bernice L. Neugarten et al., "Women's Attitude Toward the Menopause," in Bernice L. Neugarten, ed., *Middle Age and Aging* (Chicago: The University of Chicago Press, 1968), pp. 195–200.

33. Robert Peck, "Psychological Developments in the Second Half of Life," in Bernice L. Neugarten, ed., *Middle Age and Aging,* (Chicago: University of Chicago Press, 1968), pp. 88–90.

Chapter Eleven
Dreams of Elder Years

1. *American Association of Retired Persons News Bulletin* 27, no. 5 (May 1986), 2. This publication shows a photograph of Lucille Thompson, age eighty-nine, of Danville, Illinois, demonstrating the technique to disarm an attacker who has a knife. Ages given for some of the other outstanding older women are approximate, based on birthdates given in various sources. Some of these have died recently.

2. Lynne Lamberg, *AMA Guide to Better Sleep* (New York: Random House, 1984), p. 98; see also pp. 97–109. See also Dianne Hales, *The Complete Book of Sleep: How Your Nights Affect Your Days* (Menlo Park, Calif.: Addison-Wesley, 1981), pp. 275–82; and

Wilse B. Webb, *Sleep: The Gentle Tyrant* (Englewood Cliffs, N.J.: Prentice-Hall, 1975), pp. 35–38. Webb points out that there are large individual variations in the pace and timing of sleep changes, especially among older persons. In one study of sixty-year-olds, length of sleep varied from five to eleven hours.

3. See Lamberg, *AMA Guide to Better Sleep,* p. 98.

4. Robert L. Williams, Ismet Karacan, and Carolyn J. Hursch, *Electroencephalography (EEG) of Human Sleep: Clinical Applications* (New York: John Wiley & Sons, 1974), pp. 60–62.

5. René Spiegel, *Sleep and Sleeplessness in Advanced Age* (New York: Spectrum Publications Medical & Scientific Books, 1981), pp. 128–29. Spiegel's twenty younger subjects spent 87.3 minutes in slow-wave sleep; the twenty-three elderly women spent 104.0 minutes in slow-wave sleep; the thirty-four elderly men spent 61.1 minutes in slow-wave sleep.

6. Rosalind D. Cartwright, *A Primer on Sleep and Dreaming* (Menlo Park, Calif.: Addison-Wesley, 1978), pp. 22–24. For original, see n. 4 above.

7. Spiegel, *Sleep and Sleeplessness,* p. 130. Regarding his study of twenty-three older women and thirty-four older men, with an average age of sixty-four, Spiegel says, "There were several women with polygraphic sleep patterns that did not differ significantly in any parameter from those of a younger individual."

8. Ernest Hartmann, *The Biology of Dreaming* (Springfield, Ill.: Charles C. Thomas, 1967), p. 19.

9. Williams, Karacan, and Hursch, *Electroencephalography,* pp. 84–85.

10. Spiegel, *Sleep and Sleeplessness,* pp. 128–29, 166–67. The twenty younger subjects in Spiegel's study had an average of 95.9 minutes in REM; the twenty-three elderly women averaged 82.8 minutes in REM; the thirty-four elderly men averaged 77.5 minutes in REM. Elderly women also exhibited longer cycles between REM periods than the elderly men. Subjectively good sleep was associated with long REM for women only.

11. Spiegel, *Sleep and Sleeplessness,* pp. 125–26. Spiegel says, "It is apparent that habituation to the laboratory differed in men and women: While wake time decreased from the second night in both sexes, REM duration and SWS showed a particular increase in women, whereas it was stage-2 duration which increased in men."

12. Irwin Feinberg's work is described in Hales, *Complete Book of Sleep,* p. 277. For original, see Irwin Feinberg, R. Koresko, and N. Heller, "EEG Sleep Patterns as a Function of Normal and Pathological Aging in Man," *Journal of Psychiatric Research.* 5 (1967): 107–144.

13. Prinz's work is described in Hales, *Complete Book of Sleep,* p. 34. For original, see Patricia N. Prinz, "Sleep Patterns in the Healthy Aged: Relationship With Intellectual Function," *Journal of Gerontology* 32 (1977): 179–86.

14. For a good discussion of apnea and the effect of sleeping pills, see Hales, *Complete Book of Sleep,* pp. 192–94, 280–82.

15. Lamberg, *AMA Guide to Better Sleep,* p. 102.

16. Ibid.

17. Ibid., p. 103.

18. "Restless Leg Syndrome," *Health & Nutrition Newsletter* (Columbia University School of Public Health and Institute of Human Nutrition) 2, no. 10 (October 1986): 8.

19. Ibid. Carbamazepine (Tegretol) or clonazepam (Clonopin), both anticonvulsant medications, helped a majority of patients in small, controlled studies.

20. A survey in New Haven, for example, reported that 2 percent of men and 5.8 percent of women ages eighteen to forty-four had suffered a major episode of depression in the previous six months. Happily married individuals had the lowest incidence of depression; single people the next lowest; separated and divorced people next; and, unhappily married people reported the highest incidence of depression. See "Depression: A Growing Problem," *Health & Nutrition Newsletter* (Columbia University School of Public Health and Institute of Human Nutrition) 2, no. 40 (October 1986): 1.

21. Ibid., pp. 1–3.

22. Robert N. Butler and Myrna I. Lewis, *Aging and Mental Health* (New York: Mosby, 1983), pp. 72–74. This excellent reference book should be in the library of every person interested in the well-being of the elderly. Butler and Lewis point out that the highest rate of suicide occurs for white men in their eighties, perhaps because of depression over loss of status and good health. In comparison, the peak rate of suicide for white women is middle age, rates for nonwhite men and women are much lower, peaking between the ages of twenty-five and twenty-nine. Suicide is three times more common than homicide and is one of the ten leading causes of death in the United States. Although older people account for 11 percent of the population, they make up 25 percent of the suicides. Hence, treatment of depression is especially important.

23. Risk in estrogen replacement therapy is reduced when dosage level is minimal.

24. "Depression: A Growing Problem," *Health & Nutrition Newsletter* (Columbia University School of Public Health and Institute of Human Nutrition) 2, no. 10 (October 1986): 3.

25. Patricia L. Garfield, "Using the Dream State as a Clinical Tool for Assertion Training," in Michael H. Chase, Warren C. Stern, and Pat L. Walter, eds., *Sleep Research,* Los Angeles: Brain Information Service, 1975, vol. 4, p. 184.

26. "Mental Illness Linked to Genetic Defects," *San Francisco Chronicle,* March 20, 1987. See also "Genetic Link to Depression Reported," *Mental Health Association of San Francisco Update* (Winter/Spring, 1987): 5. Chromosome #11 in one study and the X chromosome in another. The X chromosome is the one that carries the gene for female sex: males have 1 X and 1 Y; females have XX (2X's).

27. C. F. Reynolds et al., "Slow Wave Sleep in Elderly Depressed, Demented, and Healthy Subjects," *Sleep Research,* 14 (1985): 277. Elderly depressives spent less time asleep than healthy or demented subjects. They showed a higher delta intensity in the second non-REM period; controls and demented subjects had peak delta in the first non-REM period. See also Hales, *Complete Book of Sleep,* p. 214. Depressed persons tend to enter REM sleep earlier in the night than healthy subjects.

28. Other symptoms may include loss of appetite, weight loss, or excessive eating and weight gain, loss of libido, low energy, decreased effectiveness; decreased attention; social withdrawal; loss of interest; irritability; loss of responsiveness; loss of talkativeness; tearfulness; excessive sleepiness; pessimism about the future. See n. 21 above.

29. Richard M. Coleman, *Wide Awake at 3:00 A.M.: By Choice or by Chance?* (New York: W. H. Freeman, 1986), p. 162.

30. Lamberg, *AMA Guide to Better Sleep,* p. 105.

31. Quoted in Robert L. Van de Castle, "Dreams and the Aging Process," *Dream*

Network Bulletin 4, no. 4 (September/October 1985): 1–4. For original, see D. Kripke et al., "Short and Long Sleep and Sleeping Pills," *Archives of General Psychiatry* 36 (1979): 103.

32. Butler and Lewis, *Aging and Mental Health,* p. 299.

33. Janet L. Hopson, "Marian Diamond: A Love Affair With the Brain," *Psychology Today* 18, no. 11 (November 1984): 62–73.

34. Ibid., p. 73.

35. For instance, at the University of San Francisco, the Fromm Institute offers fascinating courses at nominal fees to people over fifty years of age.

36. See chapter 2 for a discussion of the natural sexual response that accompanies dreaming.

37. Quoted in Butler and Lewis, *Aging and Mental Health,* p. 114.

38. Ibid., p. 113.

39. Ibid., pp. 115–17.

40. The exact current figures for life expectancy are 78.7 for white women; 71.8 for white men; 75.0 for all other females; 67.4 for all other males. Otto Johnson, *The 1988 Information Please Almanac* (New York: Houghton Mifflin, 1987), p. 796.

41. The honor of "oldest living person" changes rapidly. The *Guinness Book of World Records* (1987 edition) reported 113-year-old Mrs. Mamie Eva Keith, nee Walter, born on March 22, 1873, in Anna, Illinois, as the oldest person. Shigechiyo Izumi of Asan, Japan, is listed as the person with the greatest authenticated age; he died at 120 years, 237 days. (David A. Boehm, ed., *1987 Guinness Book of World Records* (New York: Bantam, 1987), p. 15.) The *San Francisco Chronicle* reported that Florence Knapp, born on October 10, 1873, in the Philadelphia area, died in January 1988 at 114. Her predecessor was Anna Eliza Williams of Swansea, Wales, who died on December 27, 1987, at 114. Her successor is Maren Torp, 111, of Norway, according to the editors of the *Guinness Book of World Records.* See "Oldest Person in the World Dies at 114," *San Francisco Chronicle,* January 13, 1987.

42. Butler and Lewis, *Aging and Mental Health,* p. 96.

43. Joseph Adelson, "Creativity and the Dream," *Merrill Palmer Quarterly* 6 (1960): 92–97.

44. Quoted in Van de Castle, "Dreams and the Aging Process," p. 3. For original, see Martin Barad et al., "A Survey of Dreams in Aged Persons," *Archives of General Psychiatry* 4 (1961): 419–24.

45. For original, see Kenneth Altshuler et al., "A Survey of Dreams in the Aged," *Archives of General Psychiatry* 8 (1963): 33–77.

46. Robert N. Butler, "The Life Review: An Interpretation of Reminiscence in the Aged." in Bernice L. Neugarten, ed., *Middle Age and Aging* (Chicago: The University of Chicago Press, 1968), pp. 486–96.

47. Robert Peck, "Psychological Developments in the Second Half of Life," in Bernice L. Neugarten, ed., *Middle Age and Aging,* (Chicago, The University of Chicago Press, 1968), pp. 90–92.

48. Described in Mary Jane Moffat & Charlotte Painter, *Revelations: Diaries of Women* (New York: Vintage, 1974) p. 250.

49. C. G. Jung, *Memories, Dreams, Reflections,* ed. Aniela Jaffé (New York: Random House, 1963), p. 296.

50. Ibid., p. 293.

51. Robert C. Smith, 1987. "Do Dreams Reflect a Biological State?" *Journal of Nervous and Mental Disease* 175, no. 4 (1987); 201–7.

52. Marie-Louise von Franz, *On Dreams and Death* (Boston: Shambala, 1986).

53. See Peck, "Psychological Developments."

Chapter Twelve
A Woman's Life Cycle of Dreams

1. The work of Charlotte Buhler is described by Else Frenkel-Brunswik, "Adjustments and Reorientation in the Course of the Life Span," in Bernice L. Neugarten, ed., *Middle Age and Aging* (Chicago: The University of Chicago Press, 1968), pp. 77–84.

2. Erik H. Erikson, Joan M. Erikson, and Helen Q. Kivnick, *Vital Involvement in Old Age* (New York: W. W. Norton & Co., 1986).

3. Bernice L. Neugarten, "Adult Personality: Toward a Psychology of the Life Cycle." in Bernice L. Neugarten, ed., *Middle Age and Aging* (Chicago: The University of Chicago Press, 1968), pp. 137–47.

4. Daniel J. Levinson et al., *The Seasons of a Man's Life* (New York: Ballantine Books, 1978).

5. This is a paraphrase of Horney's presentation. See Karen Horney, *Feminine Psychology* (New York: W. W. Norton, 1967), pp. 234–35.

6. For a fascinating discussion of the role of dominance and submission in women's lives, see Jean Baker Miller, *Toward a New Psychology of Women* (Boston: Beacon Press, 1976).

7. Marie-Louise von Franz described this dream of hers in part 1, "Descent Into Dreamland," in a film series entitled *The Way of the Dream*, shown in San Francisco, October 18–19, 1986.

8. Nigel Nicholson & Joanne Trautmann, *The Letters of Virginia Woolf*, vol. 6, p. 60. Woolf's letter to Ethel Smyth was dated July 25, 1936.

9. Quoted in Leon Edel, *Bloomsbury: A House of Lions* (Philadelphia: J. B. Lippincott, 1979), p. 85. The original appeared in Virginia Woolf's "A Sketch of the Past."

10. Elisabeth Kubler-Ross, *Death: The Final Stage of Growth* (New York: Simon & Schuster, 1975).

BIBLIOGRAPHY

Adelson, J. "Creativity and the Dream." *Merrill Palmer Quarterly,* vol. 6 (1960) pp. 92–97.

Altshuler, K., et al. "A Survey of Dreams in the Aged." *Archives of General Psychiatry,* vol. 8 (1963), pp. 33–77.

American Association of Retired Persons News Bulletin 1986. vol. 27, no. 5, May, p. 2, photograph of Lucille Thompson, 89, during her test for a black belt in Korean karate.

Artemidorus. *The Interpretation of Dreams.* Park Ridge, New Jersey: Noyes Press, 1975. (Translation and commentary by R. J. White, on Greek treatise on dreams by Artemidorus of Daldis written in the second century.)

Associated Press article. "Oldest Person in the World Dies at 114." *San Francisco Chronicle,* 13 January 1987.

Baker, M. A. ed. *Sex Differences in Human Performance.* New York: John Wiley & Sons, 1987.

Barad, M., et al. "A Survey of Dreams in Aged Persons." *Archives of General Psychiatry,* vol. 4 (1961), pp. 419–23.

Baron, J. E. "Effects of the Menstrual Cycle on Manifest Content and Affect in Dream Reports." *Dissertation Abstracts International,* vol. 36, no. 10 (1974), p. 5223-B.

Benedek, T. & Rubenstein, B. B. "The Correlations Between Ovarian Activity and Psychodynamic Processes: I. The Ovulative Phase." *Psychosomatic Medicine,* vol. 1, no. 2 (April 1939), pp. 245–270.

Benedek, T. & Rubenstein, B. B. "II. The Menstrual Phase." *Psychosomatic Medicine,* vol. 1, no. 4 (Oct. 1939), pp. 461–485.

Benedek, T. & Rubenstein, B. B. "The Sexual Cycle in Women." *Psychosomatic Medical Monographs,* vol. 3, nos. 1 and 2 (1942). Washington, D. C., National Research Council.

Benedek, T. "An Investigation of the Sexual Cycle in Women: Methodologic Considerations." *Archives of General Psychiatry,* no. 8 (1963), pp. 311–322.

Berlitz, C. *Native Tongues.* New York: The Putnam Publishing Group, 1982.

Bettelheim, B. *The Uses of Enchantment: The Meaning and Importance of Fairy Tales.* New York: Alfred A. Knopf, 1976.

Boehm, D. A., ed.-in-chief. *1987 Guinness Book of World Records.* New York: Bantam, 1987.

Boston Women's Health Book Collective, Inc. *Our Bodies, Ourselves: A Book by and for Women.* New York: Simon & Schuster, 1976.

Boyd, L. M. "The Grab Bag." *San Francisco Chronicle,* 29 September 1985.

Brenneis, C. B., "Differences in Male and Female Ego Styles in Manifest Dream Content." Ph.D. dissertation, University of Michigan, University Microfilms 67-17, 734. *Dissertation Abstracts International,* vol. 28 (1968) [7-B], 3056.

Brenneis, C. B. "Male and Female Ego Modalities in Manifest Dream Content." *Journal of Abnormal Psychology,* vol. 76 (1970), pp. 434–42.

Briggs, D. C. *Your Child's Self-Esteem.* Garden City, N.Y.: Doubleday, 1975.

Buckley, J. J. "The Dreams of Young Adults" Ph.D. dissertation, Wayne State University. *Dissertation Abstracts International,* vol. 31 (1970) [7-A], 3635. (A sociological analysis of 1,133 dreams of black and white students).

Burns, R. *"A Red, Red Rose."* In Fuller, E. ed. *Thesaurus of Quotations.* New York: Crown, 1941 p. 560.

Butler, K. "Women Not Surprised by Boom in Divorces." *San Francisco Chronicle,* 23 April 1986, p. 17.

Butler, R. N. "The Life Review: An Interpretation of Reminiscence in the Aged." *Middle Age and Aging: A Reader in Social Psychology.* Edited by B. Neugarten. Chicago: University of Chicago Press, 1968, pp. 486–96.

Butler, R. N., and Lewis, M. I. *Aging and Mental Health.* New York: Mosby, 1983.

Carmichael, A. *The Sun Dances: Prayers and Blessings from the Gaelic,* Introduction by A. Bittleston. Edinburgh: Floris Books, 1960.

Carotenuto, A. *The Spiral Way: A Woman's Healing Journey.* Toronto, Canada: Inner City Books, 1986.

Cartwright, R. D. *Night Life: Explorations in Dreaming.* Englewood Cliffs, New Jersey: Prentice-Hall, 1977.

Cartwright, R. D. *A Primer on Sleep and Dreaming.* Menlo Park, Ca.: Addison-Wesley, 1978.

Cartwright, R. "Affect and Dream Work from an Information Processing Point of View." *The Journal of Mind and Behavior,* vol. 7, nos. 2 and 3 (1986), spring and summer, pp. 411–27.

Cash, T. F., Winstead, B. A. and Janda, L. H. "The Great American Shape-Up." *Psychology Today,* vol. 20, no. 4 (April 1986), pp. 30–37.

Cherry, K. *Womansword: What Japanese Words Say About Women.* New York: Kodansha International, 1987.

Cohen, D. B. "Failure to Recall Dream Content: Contentless vs. Dreamless Reports." *Perceptual Motor Skills,* vol. 34 (1972), pp. 1000–1002.

Colby, K. M. *A Skeptical Psychoanalyst.* New York: The Ronald Press Co., 1958.

Coleman, R. M. *Wide Awake at 3:00 A.M.: By Choice or by Chance?* New York: W. H. Freeman & Co., 1986.

Colman, A. and Colman, L. *Earth Father/Sky Father: The Changing Concept of Fathering.* Englewood Cliffs, New Jersey: Prentice-Hall, 1981.

Conn, J. H. "Children's awareness of sex difference, II: Play attitudes and game preferences." *Journal of Child Psychiatry,* vol. 2 (1951), pp. 82–99.

Coxhead, D. and Hiller, S. *Dreams: Visions of the Night.* New York: Avon, 1975.

Cutler, W. B., Garcia, C.-R., and Edwards, D. A. *Menopause: A Guide for Women and the Men Who Love Them.* New York: Norton, 1983.

Dalton, K. *Once a Month.* Pomona, Ca.: Hunter House, Inc., 1979.

Davidson, K. "Sexual Equality May Be All in Your Head." *San Francisco Examiner,* 22 Feb. 1987, p. A-3.

De Koninck, J.; Christ, G.; Rinfret, N.; and Proulx, G. "Dreams During Language Learning: When Is the New Language Integrated?" *Association for the Study of Dreams Newsletter,* vol. 4, no. 3 (June 1987), p. 3.

Diamond, E. *The Science of Dreams.* New York: MacFadden Books, 1963.

Doress, P. B.; Siegal, D. L.; and the Midlife and Older Women Book Project. *Ourselves, Growing Older.* New York: Simon & Schuster, 1987.

Dugan, M. "Personal Mental Health Affects Menstrual Tension Missouri Research Shows." *American Psychological Association Monitor,* January, 1982. (Describes a dissertation, from the University of Missouri at Kansas City.)

Edel, L. *Bloomsbury: A House of Lions.* Philadelphia: J. B. Lippincott, 1979.

Edell, D. "PMS Clue." Dr. Dean Edell's Medical Journal, *San Francisco Chronicle,* 4 March 1987. (Describes work of N. Brayshaw that originally appeared in *The New England Journal of Medicine* regarding the role of the thyroid function and PMS).

Edwards, B. *Drawing on the Artist Within: A Guide to Innovation, Invention, Imagination & Creativity.* New York: Simon & Schuster, 1986.

Eliot, G. "How I Came to Write Fiction." Appendix to *Scenes of Clerical Life.* Harmondsworth, England: Penguin, 1985, pp. 128–31. (Originally in diary dated Dec. 6, 1857.)

Ephron, D. *Funny Sauce: Us, the Ex, the Ex's New Mate, the New Mate's Ex and the Kids.* New York: Viking, 1986.

Erlik, Yohanan et al. "Association of Waking Episodes with Menopausal Hot Flashes." *Journal of the American Medical Association,* vol 245, no. 17 (1981), pp. 1741–1744.

Erikson, E. "Sex Differences in the Play Configurations of Preadolescents." *American Journal of Orthopsychiatry,* vol. 21 (1951), pp. 667–692.

Erikson, E. H.; Erikson, J. M.; and Kivnick, H. Q. *Vital Involvement in Old Age.* New York: W. W. Norton & Co., 1986.

Evans, I. H. *Brewer's Dictionary of Phrase and Fable.* New York: Harper & Row, 1981.

Fekete-Mackintosh, A. "Dream Content and the Menstrual Cycle in Ovulatory and Anovulatory Cycles." *Dissertation Abstracts International,* vol. 40, no. 7 (1979), p. 3465-B.

Feldman, M. J., and Hyman, E. "Content Analysis of Nightmare Reports." Paper presented to the Association for the Psychophysiological Study of Sleep, Denver, Colorado, 1968.

Feinberg, I.; Koresko, R.; and Heller, N. "EEG Sleep Patterns as a Function of Normal and Pathological Aging in Man." *Journal of Psychiatric Research,* vol. 5 (1967), pp. 107–144.

Fisher, C.; Cohen, H. D.; Schiavi, R. C.; Davis, D.; Furman, B.; Ward, K.; Edwards, A.; and Cunningham, J. "Patterns of Female Sexual Arousal During Sleep and Waking: Vaginal Thermo-Conductance Studies." *Archives of Sexual Behavior,* vol. 12, no. 2 (1983), pp. 97–122.

Fisher, C.; Gross, J.; and Zuch, J. "Cycle of Penile Erection Synchronous with Dreaming (REM) Sleep." *Archives of General Psychiatry,* vol. 12 (1965), pp. 29–45.

Foulkes, D. *Children's Dreams: Longitudinal Studies.* New York: John Wiley & Sons, 1982.

Franck, K., and Rosen, E. "A Projective Test of Masculinity-Femininity." *Journal of Consulting Psychology,* vol. 13 (1949), pp. 247–257.

Frenkel-Brunswik, E. "Adjustments and Reorientation in the Course of the Life Span." *Middle Age and Aging.* Edited by B. L. Neugarten. Chicago: The University of Chicago Press, 1968.

Freud, S. *The Interpretation of Dreams.* Translated by A. A. Brill. New York: Random House, 1950.

Furman, B.; Cunningham, J.; and Fisher, C. "REM and NREM Mental Content in Relation to VBF (vaginal blood flow) Fluctuations." *Sleep Research.* Edited by M.H. Chase, D.F. Kribpe and P.L. Walters, vol. 10 (1981), p. 54.

Gackenbach-Snyder, J. Presentation on P. Tholey, at Dreamhouse, San Francisco, December 8, 1987.

Gahagan, L. "Sex Differences in Recall of Stereotyped Dreams, Sleep-Talking, and Sleep-Walking." *Journal of General Psychology,* vol. 48 (1936), pp. 227–36.

Garfield, P. L. "Keeping a Longitudinal Dream Record." *Psychotherapy: Theory, Research and Practice,* vol. 10, no. 3, (Fall 1973) pp. 223-28.

Garfield, P. L. *Creative Dreaming.* New York: Simon & Schuster, 1974.

Garfield, P. L. "Using the Dream State as a Clinical Tool for Assertion Training." *Sleep Research.* Edited by M. H. Chase, W. C. Stern, and P. L. Walter, vol. 4 (1975), p. 184.

Garfield, P. L. Introduction to *Dream Notebook.* San Francisco: San Francisco Book Co., 1976.

Garfield, P. L. *Pathway to Ecstasy: The Way of the Dream Mandala.* New York: Holt, Rinehart & Winston, 1979.

Garfield, P. L. "Dreamstones." *Dreamworks,* vol. 3, no. 2 (1983), p. 120–26.

Garfield, P. L. *Your Child's Dreams.* New York: Ballantine, 1984.

Garfield, P. L. "Nightmares in the Sexually Abused Female Teenager." *Psychiatric Journal of the University of Ottawa,* vol. 12, no. 2 (1987), pp. 93–97.

Geer, J. H.; Morokoff, P.; and Greenwood, P. "Sexual Arousal in Women: The Development of a Measurement Device for Vaginal Blood Volume." *Archives of Sexual Behavior,* vol. 3., no. 6 (1974), pp. 559–64.

Gibbons, B. "The Intimate Sense of Smell." *National Geographic,* vol. 170, no. 3 (September 1986), p. 333.

Gilbert, A. N. and Wysocki, C. J. "The Smell Survey Results." *National Geographic,* vol. 172, no. 4, (October 1987), pp. 514–25.

Gillman, R. D. "The Dreams of Pregnant Women and Maternal Adaptation." *American Journal of Orthopsychiatry,* vol. 36 (July 1968), pp. 688–692.

Gutheil, E. *The Handbook of Dream Analysis.* New York: Liveright, 1951.

Hales, D. *The Complete Book of Sleep: How Your Nights Affect Your Days.* Menlo Park, Ca.: Addison-Wesley, 1981.

Hall, C. S. *The Meaning of Dreams.* New York: Harper & Brothers, 1953.

Hall, C. S., and Domhoff, B. "Friendliness in Dreams." Institute of Dream research mimeograph, 1962.

Hall, C. S., and Domhoff, B. "Friends and Enemies in Dreams." Institute of Dream Research, mimeograph, 1962.

Hall, C. S., and Domhoff, B. "Aggression in Dreams." *International Journal of Social Psychiatry,* vol. 9 (1963), pp. 259–67.

Hall, C. S., and Domhoff, B. "The Difference Between Men and Women Dreamers." *The New World of Dreams.* Edited by R. L. Woods and H. B. Greenhouse. New York: Macmillan, 1974, pp. 13–16.

Hall, C. S., and Nordby, V. J. *The Individual and His Dreams.* New York: The New American Library, Inc., 1972.

Hall, C. S., and Van de Castle, R. L. *The Content Analysis of Dreams.* New York: Appleton-Century-Crofts, 1966.

Hall, C. S.; Domhoff, G. W.; Blick, K. A.; and Weesner, K. E. "The Dreams of College Men and Women in 1950 and 1980: A Comparison of Dream Contents and Sex Differences." *Sleep,* vol. 5, no. 2 (1982), pp. 188–194.

Hannan, Z. "PMS: What It Is and Why." *St. Mary's Hospital and Medical Center Health Digest,* April 1986.

Harding, M. E. *The Way of All Women.* London: Longmans, Green & Co., Inc., 1933.

Harding, M. E. *Psychic Energy.* New York: Bollingen Foundation, 1963.

Hartmann, E. *The Biology of Dreaming.* Springfield, Illinois: Charles C. Thomas, 1967.

Hartmann, E. *The Functions of Sleep.* New Haven: Yale University Press, 1973.

Hartmann, E. *The Nightmare: The Psychology and Biology of Terrifying Dreams.* New York: Basic Books, 1984.

Health & Nutrition Newsletter. "Depression, a Growing Problem." Edited by R. J. Weiss. Publ'n. of Columbia Univ. School of Public Health & Institute of Human Nutrition., vol. II, no. 10 (October 1986), pp. 1–3.

Health & Nutrition Newsletter. "Restless Leg Syndrome. Edited by R. J. Weiss. Publ'n. of Columbia Univ. School of Public Health and Institute of Human Nutrition, vol 11, no. 10 (October 1986), p. 8.

Henderson, M. "Evidence for Hormonally Related Male Temperature Cycle and Synchrony with the Female Cycle." *Australian and New Zealand Journal of Medicine,* vol. 6 (1976), p. 254.

Hicks, R. A. & Cavanaugh, A. "Oral Contraceptive Use, Menstrual Cycle Phase, and the Need for Sleep." *Sleep Research.* Vol. 11, 1982, p. 214.

Ho, M. A. "Sex Hormones and the Sleep of Women." Doctoral dissertation, Yeshiva University. *Dissertation Abstracts International,* vol. 33 (1972), pp. 1305-B.

Hoffman, M. S., ed. *The World Almanac and Book of Facts: 1987.* New York: World Almanac, 1986.

Hollinger, F. B., ed. *Outside the Magic Circle: The Autobiography of Virginia Foster Durr.* Tuscaloosa, Alabama: Univ. of Alabama Press, 1987.

Holmes, T., and Rahe, R. The "Life Change Scale," also called "The Social Readjustment Rating Scale." (This scale appears in several publications. See, for instance P. L. Garfield, *Your Child's Dreams.* New York: Ballantine, 1982, p. 415.)

Holy Bible. Verse Reference Edition. Undated. Philadelphia: A. J. Holman Co.

Hopson, J. L. "A Love Affair with the Brain: PT Conversation with Marian Diamond." *Psychology Today,* vol. 18, no. 11 (Nov. 1984), pp. 62–73.

Hopson, J. L., and Rosenfeld, A. "PMS: Puzzling Monthly Symptoms." *Psychology Today,* vol. 18, no. 8 (1984), pp. 30–35.

Horney, K. *Feminine Psychology,* New York: W. W. Norton, 1967.

Jaffé, A., ed. *C. G. Jung: Word and Image.* Princeton: Princeton University Press, 1979.

Jenks, W. A. "Auschwitz." *World Book.* Chicago: Field Enterprises, vol. 1 (1968), p. 868.

Jensen, M. *Learning to Live with Yourself: Formerly Married.* New York: Jove, 1984.

Johnson, O. T., ed. *The 1988 Information Please Almanac.* Boston: Houghton Mifflin Co., 1987.

Jovanovic, U. "Sexuelle Reaktionen und Schlafperiodik Bei Menschen." *Beitrage Zur Sexualforschung.* Edited by H. Burger-Prinz, G. Schmidt, E. Schorsch, and V. Siqusch. Vol. 51 (1972). Stuttgart: Ferdinand Enke Verlag.

Jung, C. G. Undated (translator's preface dated 1933). *Modern Man in Search of a Soul.* New York: Harcourt, Brace & Co.

Jung, C. G. *Psychology and Alchemy.* Princeton: Princeton University Press, 1968.

Jung, C. G. *Symbols of Transformation.* Princeton: Princeton University Press, 1956.

Jung, C. G. *Memories, Dreams, Reflections.* Edited by A. Jaffé. New York: Vintage, 1963.

Karacan, I.; Heine, W.; Agnew, H. W.; Williams, R. L.; Webb, W. B.; and Ross, J. J. "Characteristics of Sleep Patterns During Late Pregnancy and the Postpartum Periods. *American Journal of Obstetrics and Gynecology,* vol. 101, no. 5, pp. 579–586.

Karacan, I.; Moore, C. A.; Hirshkowitz, M.; Sahmay, S.; Narter, E. N.; Tokat, Y.; and Tuncel, L. "Uterine Activity During Sleep." *Sleep.,* vol. 9, no. 3 (1986), pp. 393–97.

Karacan, I.; Rosenbloom, A.; and Williams, R. "The Clitoral Erection Cycle During Sleep (Abstract)." Presented at the meeting of the Association for the Psychophysiological Study of Sleep. Santa Fe, New Mexico, 1970.

Karacan, I.; Williams, R.; Hursch, C.; McCaulley, M; and Heine, W. "Some Implications of the Sleep Patterns of Pregnancy for Postpartum Emotional Disturbances." *British Journal of Psychiatry,* vol. 115 (1969), pp. 929–35.

Kilner, L. A. "Cross-Cultural Comparison of Manifest Dream Content: United States and Gusil Females." *Association for the Study of Dreams Newsletter,* vol. 4, no. 3 (June 1987).

Kimura, D. "Male Brain, Female Brain: The Hidden Difference." *Psychology Today,* vol. 19, no. 11 (1985), pp. 50–58.

Kinsey, A. C.; Pomeroy, W. B.; and Martin, C. E. *Sexual Behavior in the Human Male.* Philadelphia: W. B. Saunders Co., 1948.

Kinsey, A. C.; Pomeroy, W. B.; Martin, C. E.; Gebherd, P. H., et al. *Sexual Behavior in the Human Female.* Philadelphia: W. B. Saunders Co., 1953.

Krantzler, M. *Creative Divorce: A New Opportunity for Personal Growth.* New York: M. Evans & Co., 1974.

Krantzler, M. *Learning to Love Again.* New York: Bantam Books, 1979.

Kripke, D., et al. "Short and Long Sleep and Sleeping Pills." *Archives of General Psychiatry,* vol. 36 (1979), p. 103.

Kübler-Ross, E. *Death: The Final Stage of Growth.* New York: Simon & Schuster, 1975.

LaBerge, S. *Lucid Dreaming.* Los Angeles: Jeremy P. Tarcher, Inc., 1985.

LaBerge, S.; Greenleaf, W.; and Kedzierski, B. "Physiological Responses to Dreamed Sexual Activity During Lucid REM Sleep." *Psychophysiology,* vol. 20 (1983), pp. 454–55.

Lamberg, L. *The American Medical Association Guide to Better Sleep.* New York: Random House, 1984.

Lauer, J., and Lauer, R. "Marriages Made to Last." *Psychology Today,* vol. 19, no. 6 (1985), pp. 22–26.

Lein, A. *The Cycling Female: Her Menstrual Rhythm.* San Francisco: W. H. Freeman & Co., 1979.

Levinson, D. J. with Darrow, C. N.; Klein, E. B.; Levinson, M. H.; and McKee, B. *Seasons of a Man's Life.* New York: Ballantine, 1978.

Lewis, S. A. & Burns, M. "Manifest Dream Content: Changes with the Menstrual Cycle." *British Journal of Medical Psychology,* vol. 48, 1975, pp. 375–377.

Liversidge, A. "Sealed with a Kiss." *Omni,* April, 1987, p. 36 (Describes work of B. Nicholson that originally appeared in the *British Journal of Dermatology*).

Long, M. E. "What Is This Thing Called Sleep? *National Geographic,* vol. 172, no. 6 (December 1987).

Lortie-Lussier, M.; Rinfret, N.; Schwab, C.; and De Koninck, J. "Social Role Impact on the Dreams of Working Mothers and Female Students." *Association for the Study of Dreams Newsletter,* vol. 3, no. 2, (June 1986), p. 7. (Described more fully in a paper read by Lortie-Lussier at the Association for the Study of Dreams conference at Ottawa, Canada, June 1986.)

Lortie-Lussier, M.; Schwab, C.; and De Koninck, J. "Working Mothers Versus Homemakers: Do Dreams Reflect the Changing Roles of Women?" *Sex Roles.,* vol. 12 (1985), pp. 1009–1021.

MacKenzie, N. *Dreams and Dreaming.* London: Aldus Books., 1965.

Madaras, L. with Madaras, A. *What's Happening to My Body? A Growing Up Guide for Mothers and Daughters.* New York: Newmarket Press, 1983.

Maddux, H. C. *Menstruation.* New Canaan, Conn.: Tobey Publishing Co., Inc., 1975.

Mankowitz, A. *Change of Life: A Psychological Study of Dreams and the Menopause.* Toronto, Canada: Inner City Books, 1984.

Martin, E. *The Woman in the Body: A Cultural Analysis of Reproduction.* Boston: Beacon Press, 1987.

Maslow, A. "Self-Esteem (Dominance-Feeling) and Sexuality in Women." *Sexual Behavior and Personality Characteristics.* Edited by M. F. Demartino. New York: Grove Press, 1963.

Maybruck, P. *An Exploratory Study of the Dreams of Pregnant Women.* Ph.D. dissertation, Saybrook Institute, San Francisco, California, 1986.

McClintock, M. K. "Menstrual Synchrony and Suppression." *Nature.,* vol. 229, 22 January 1971, pp. 244–45.

Mental Health Association of San Francisco Update. "Genetic Link to Depression Reported." Edited by M. Weiss. (Winter/Spring 1987), p. 5.

Miller, J. B. *Toward a New Psychology of Women.* Boston: Beacon Press, 1976.

Moffat, M. J. & Painter, C. eds. *Revelations: Diaries of Women.* New York: Vintage, 1974.

Molnar, G. W. "Body Temperatures During Menopausal Hot Flashes." *Journal of Applied Physiology,* vol. 38 (1975), pp. 499–503.

Monaghan, P. *The Book of Goddesses and Heroines.* New York: E. P. Dutton, 1981.

Money, J. "Phantom Orgasm in Dreams of Paraplegic Men and Women. *Archives of General Psychiatry,* vol. 3 (1960), pp. 373–83.

Monmaney, T. with Katz, S. "The Chemistry Between People." *Newsweek*. January 12, 1987, pp. 54–55.

Montagu, A. *The Natural Superiority of Women*. London: Collier Books, 1970.

Moon, S. *Dreams of a Woman: An Analyst's Inner Journey*. Boston: Sigo Press, 1983.

Neugarten, B. "Adult Personality: Toward a Psychology of the Life Cycle." *Middle Age and Aging: A Reader in Social Psychology*. Edited by B. L. Neugarten. Chicago: University of Chicago Press, 1968, pp. 137–147.

Neugarten, B. L.; Wood, V.; Kraines, R. J.; and Loomis, B. "Women's Attitude Toward the Menopause." *Middle Age and Aging*. Edited by B. Neugarten. Chicago: The University of Chicago Press, 1968, pp. 195–200.

New York Times syndicated article. (no author given.) "Mental Illness Linked to Genetic Defects." *San Francisco Chronicle*. 20 March 1987.

Nicholson, J. *Men and Women: How Different Are They?* Oxford: Oxford University Press, 1984.

Nilsson, L. *Behold Man*. Boston: Little, Brown & Co., 1973.

O'Neil, S. "Choosing Children over Careers: More Professional Women Take Time Out." *San Francisco Chronicle*, 19 July 1987, p. D-1.

Padgham, C. A. "Colours Experienced in Dreams." *British Journal of Psychology*, vol. 66, no. 1 (1975), pp. 25–28.

Paolino, A. F. "Dreams: Sex Differences in Aggressive Content." *Journal of Projective Techniques*, vol. 28 (1964), pp. 219–26.

Peck, R. "Psychological Developments in the Second Half of Life." *Middle Age and Aging*. Edited by B. Neugarten. pp. 88–90, 1986.

Petersen, A. C. "Those Gangly Years." *Psychology Today*, vol. 21, no. 9 (September 1987), pp. 28–34.

Piaget, J. *Play, Dreams and Imitation in Childhood*. New York: W. W. Norton & Co., 1962.

Prinz, P. N. "Sleep Patterns in the Healthy Aged: Relationship with Intellectual Function." *Journal of Gerontology*, vol. 32 (1977), pp. 179–186.

Reese, L.; Wilkinson, J.; and Koppelman, P. S., eds. *I'm on My Way Running: Women Speak on Coming of Age*. New York: Avon., 1983.

Reinisch, J. M. "Kinsey Report." *San Francisco Chronicle*. 30 Sept. 1986.

Reynolds, C. F.; Kupfer, D. J.; Taska, L. S.; Hoch, C. C.; Sewitch, D. E.; and Grochocinski, V. J. "Slow Wave Sleep in Elderly Depressed, Demented, and Healthy Subjects." *Sleep Research*, vol. 14 (1985), p. 277.

Robertson, M. "Shhhhh! No Tension, Please: Are Librarians Really the Least Stressed-Out?" *San Francisco Chronicle*, 10 July 1986, p. 23.

Robertson, M. "Love is a Family Affair." *San Francisco Chronicle*. 19 August 1987.

Rogers, G. S.; Van de Castle, R.; and Evans, W. S. "Assessment of Vaginal Responses During Waking and Sleeping Conditions." *Sleep Research*, vol. 11 (1982), p. 38.

Rose, L. "What is menopause?" *The Menopause Book*. Edited by L. Rose. New York: Hawthorn Books, 1977.

Rupprecht, C. S. "The Common Language of Women's Dreams: Colloquy of Mind and Body." *Archetypal Theory: Interdisciplinary Re-Visions of Jungian Thought*. Edited by E. Lauter and C. S. Rupprecht. Knoxville: University of Tennessee Press, 1985, pp. 187–219.

Rychlak, J. F. "Recalled Dream Themes and Personality." *Journal of Abnormal Social Psychology*, vol. 60 (1960), 140–43.

Saint-Denys, H. de. *Dreams and How to Guide Them.* Edited by M. Schatzman. Translated by N. Fry. London: Duckworth. 1982.

Savitz, H. A. "Dreams in the Talmud: The Prophets of Yore Had the Noblest Dream." *Rhode Island Medical Journal*, vol. 64, no. 9 (1981 pp. 427-30).

Schechter, N.; Schmeidler, G.; and Staal, M. "Dream Reports and Creative Tendencies in Students of the Arts, Sciences, and Engineering." *Journal of Consulting Psychology.*, vol. 29 (1965), pp. 415–421.

Schultz, K., and Koulack, D. "Dream Affect and the Menstrual Cycle." *The Journal of Nervous and Mental Disease.*, vol. 168, no. 7 (1980), pp. 436–38.

Segal, J., and Luce, G. G. *Sleep.* New York: Arena Books, 1972.

Shakespeare, W. *The Taming of the Shrew* and *Antony & Cleopatra, The Complete Illustrated Shakespeare.* Edited by H. Staunton. New York: Park Lane, 1979.

Sheehy, G. *Passages: Predictable Crises of Adult Life.* New York: Bantam, 1977.

Shelley, M. *Introduction to Frankenstein: Or the Modern Prometheus.* New York: New American Library, 1965. (Originally published in 1817.)

Short, T. "The Word on Gender." *Washington Times, Insight,* 7 April 1986. (Book review of D. Baron, 1986. *Grammar and Gender.* New Haven, Conn.: Yale University.)

Shuttle, P., and Redgrove, P. *The Wise Wound: Eve's Curse and Everywoman.* New York: Richard Marek, 1978.

Singer, J. L. *Imagery and Daydream Methods in Psychotherapy and Behavior Modification.* New York: Academic Press, 1974.

Singer, J. L. *The Inner World of Daydreaming.* New York: Harper & Row, 1975.

Smith, R. C. "Do Dreams Reflect a Biological State?" *Journal of Nervous and Mental Disease,* vol. 175, no. 4 (1987), pp. 201–7.

Smith-Marder, P. J. "A Study of Selected Dream Contents in the Dreams of Adolescent and Mature Women." *Dissertation Abstracts International,* vol. 40, no. 10, 5023-B.

Spiegel, R. *Sleep and Sleeplessness in Advanced Age.* Jamaica, New York: Spectrum Publications, 1981.

Starhawk (Miriam Simos). *The Spiral Dance: A Rebirth of the Ancient Religion of the Great Goddess.* San Francisco: Harper & Row, 1979.

Stein, R., and Rubin, S. "The Heartburn Syndrome." *San Francisco Chronicle.* 25 July 1986, p. 31.

Stevenson, R. L. "A Chapter on Dreams." *Memories and Portraits, Random Memories, Memories of Himself.* New York: Scribner, 1925.

Stukane, E. *The Dream Worlds of Pregnancy.* New York: Quill, 1985.

Swanson, E. M., and Foulkes, D. "Dream Content and the Menstrual Cycle." *Journal of Nervous and Mental Disease,* vol. 145 (1968), pp. 358–63.

Tener, L., and Smith, C. "Vaginal Blood Volume Changes During Sleep." *Sleep Research,* vol. 6 (1977), p. 57.

Thompson, J. K. "Larger than Life." *Psychology Today,* vol. 20, no. 4 (April 1986), pp. 38–44.

Thomson, J.; Maddock, J.; Aylward, M.; and Oswald, I. "Relationship between Nocturnal Plasma Oestrogen Concentration and Free Plasma Tryptophan in Post-Menopausal Women." *Journal of Endocrinology.*, vol. 72 (1977), pp. 395–96.

Thomson, J., and Oswald, I. "Effect of Oestrogen on the Sleep, Mood and Anxiety of Menopausal Women." *British Medical Journal,* vol. 2 (1977), pp. 317–19.

Tyndall, K. "Mating Time." *Washington Times, Insight* 8 September 1986, p. 55 (on ovulation of cows).

University of California, Berkeley, Wellness Letter. "Nail Growth." Edited by R. M. Friedman. February 1986, p. 7.

Usdin, G., and Hawkins, D. *The Office Guide to Sleep Disorders.* New York: KPR Information/Media Corp., 1980.

Van de Castle, R. L. *The Psychology of Dreaming* (pamphlet). New York: General Learning Press, 1971.

Van de Castle, R. L. "Dreams and the Aging Process." *Dream Network Bulletin,* vol. 4, no. 4, (Sept./Oct. 1985), pp. 1–4.

Van de Castle, R. L. "Phases of Women's Dreams." Paper presented to the Association for the Study of Dreams. Ottawa, Canada. June, 1986.

Van Waters, M. "The Adolescent Girl Among Primitive Peoples." *Journal of Religious Psychology,* vol. 6, no. 4 (1913), pp. 375–421.

Van Waters, M. "The Adolescent Girl Among Primitive Peoples." *Journal of Religious Psychology,* vol. 7, no. 1 (1914), pp. 32–40, 75–120.

Verny, T. with Kelly, J. *The Secret Life of the Unborn Child.* New York: Delta, 1981.

Von Franz, M.-L. "The Process of Individuation." *Man and His Symbols.* Edited by C. G. Jung, and after his death by M. L. Von Franz, London: Aldus Books, 1964.

Von Franz, M.L. *Problems of the Feminine in Fairytales.* Zürich: Spring Publications, 1974, p. 156–57.

Von Franz, M.-L. Von Franz's own dream described in part 1, "Descent into Dreamland," in a film series entitled *The Way of the Dream,* shown in San Francisco, October 18–19, 1986.

Von Franz, M.-L. *On Dreams and Death.* Boston: Shambala, 1986.

Wall, J. "New Roles for Women." *Washington Times, Insight,* 3 February 1986.

Webb, W. B. *Sleep: The Gentle Tyrant.* Englewood Cliffs, New Jersey: Prentice-Hall, 1975.

Webster's New World Dictionary of the American Language. College edition. New York: World Publishing Co., 1957.

Weideger, P. *Menstruation and Menopause.* New York: Dell, 1975.

Weideger, P. *History's Mistress: A New Interpretation of a 19th-Century Ethnographic Classic.* Harmonds Worth, England: Penguin Books, 1986.

Wiedemann, C. F. "REM and Non-REM Sleep and Its Relation to Nightmares and Night Terrors." *The Nightmare.* Edited by H. Kellerman. New York: Columbia University Press, 1987.

Williams, R. L.; Karacan, I.; and Hursch, C. J. *Electroencephalography (EEG) of Human Sleep: Clinical Applications.* New York: John Wiley & Sons, 1974.

Winget, C., and Kramer, M. *Dimensions of Dreams.* Gainesville, Florida: University Presses of Florida, 1979.

Winget, C.; Kramer, M.; and Whitman, R. "Dreams and Demography." *Canadian Psychiatric Association Journal,* vol. 17 (1972), pp. 203–208.

Wolkstein, D., and Kramer, S. N. *Inanna, Queen of Heaven and Earth: Her Stories and Hymns from Sumer.* New York: Harper & Row, 1983.

Wood, K. B. "The Weird Dreams of Mothers-To-Be: Psychologists Explain the Hidden Meanings." *Working Mother,* March 1987, pp. 54–58.

About the Author

Dr. Patricia Garfield is an international authority on dreams. A clinical psychologist who graduated *summa cum laude* from Temple University in Philadelphia, she has been studying dreams professionally for twenty years.

Dr. Garfield's *Creative Dreaming* is considered a classic in the field. First published in 1974 (Ballantine paperback, 1976), this bestseller has appeared in nine foreign languages.

Dr. Garfield is also the author and illustrator of *Pathway to Ecstasy: The Way of the Dream Mandala* (Holt, Rinehart & Winston, 1979) and *Your Child's Dreams* (Ballantine, 1984). She is a frequent contributor to magazines and professional journals and has recorded a tape on dreams (Audio Rennaissance, 1988).

From her home base in San Francisco, Dr. Garfield travels widely, collecting materials for her work. She lectures and teaches special seminars on dreaming for universities and other organizations around the world. Frequently appearing on radio and national television—including three features on ABC's "20/20" news magazine show—her work has also been described in such prominent magazines as *People, Harper's, Woman's Day, Bride's, Family Circle, Parents, Parenting,* and *American Baby,* as well as several foreign magazines.

Dr. Garfield somehow finds the time to record her dreams, in a diary of over thirty-nine years, containing more than 20,000 dreams—perhaps the most extensive dream journal in the world.